Toward the Century of Words

Johann Friedrich Cotta, Baron von Cottendorf, 1764–1832. Oil painting by Karl
Leybold, 1824. Schiller-Nationalmuseum, Marbach am Neckar. Photograph
courtesy of the Schiller-Nationalmuseum, Deutsches Literaturarchiv, Marbach
am Neckar.

Toward the Century of Words

of Words

Johann Cotta and the Politics
of the Public Realm in Germany,
1795–1832

Daniel Moran

UNIVERSITY OF CALIFORNIA PRESS

Berkeley   Los Angeles   Oxford

University of California Press
Berkeley and Los Angeles, California

University of California Press, Ltd.
Oxford, England

Printed in the United States of America
1   2   3   4   5   6   7   8   9

Library of Congress Cataloging-in-Publication Data

Moran, Daniel.
  Toward the century of words : Johann Cotta and the politics of the
public realm in Germany, 1795–1832 / Daniel Moran.
    p.   cm.
  Bibliography: p.
  Includes index.
  ISBN 0-520-06640-5 (alk. paper)
  1. Cotta, Johann Friedrich, Freiherr von, 1764–1832.
2. Journalists—Germany—Biography.   3. Politicians—Germany—
Biography.   4. Germany—Politics and government—1789–1900.
5. Press and politics—Germany.   I. Title.
PN5213.C67M6   1990
070.5'092—dc20
[B]   89-4952
                                   CIP

The paper used in this publication meets the minimum requirements of American
National Standard for Information Sciences—Permanence of Paper for Printed
Library Materials, ANSI Z39.48-1984. ⊚

Contents

Acknowledgments

To learn to read and understand a German newspaper is a thing which must always remain an impossibility to a foreigner.

Mark Twain

Mark Twain's observation has occurred to me more than once in the course of writing this book. To the extent that it has finally proven untrue there are a number of people and institutions to thank for it. Despite the passage of more than a few years, it is still a pleasure to recall the friendliness and professionalism of the archivists and staffs of the Bayerische Hauptstaatsarchiv in Munich; the Haus, Hof, und Staatsarchiv in Vienna; and most especially the Deutsche Literaturarchiv in Marbach, who went out of their way to make this particular foreigner feel right at home. The faculty and members of the Institute for Advanced Study in Princeton provided indispensable stimulation and encouragement, and tolerated a certain amount of reclusive, antisocial behavior in return. I would like to thank *Central European History* for permission to reproduce, in Chapter 4, some material that appeared in somewhat different form in that journal. And, to acknowledge a form of support too easily overlooked, I would also like to thank the University of California Press, which, despite the usual fears that it won't make a dime off this book, has decided to publish it anyway.

Thanks are also due to T.C.W. Blanning, Gordon Craig, Carl Degler, Felix Gilbert, Carolyn Lougee, Monika Neugebauer-Wölk, and Jeremy Popkin, all of whom provided expert advice at various stages, always with due regard for that all-important factor, author morale. To Peter Paret, finally, I owe a special debt of gratitude, since without his unfailing friendship and support this book would not exist.

Introduction: Life and Times

One great mistake that all governments, and ours especially, have made since the beginning of the Revolution is to believe it is unimportant, or beneath the dignity of their cause, or even dangerous to address the public. . . . To despise public opinion is as perilous as despising moral principles. Posterity will scarcely believe it, that we should have regarded silence as an effective weapon in this, the Century of Words.

Klemens von Metternich to Philipp Stadion, June 23, 1808

In recent decades the history of publishing has come into its own as an aspect of European cultural history. It is a field whose works resist categorization. Some are truly "history from below," focusing on the social genesis of ideas and the means by which they percolate upward into print. Others are just as clearly "history from above," analyzing the mechanism by which elite culture is disseminated and the changes it undergoes as a result. The majority, however, might be described most aptly as "history from the middle." Books and periodicals are "media" in the simplest sense: they stand in the middle of things, subject equally to the pressures of the marketplace and the power of ideas. The middle ground they occupy is the subject of this book.

These mediating institutions have been less thoroughly explored in Germany than elsewhere, for reasons that are neither surprising nor discreditable. If historians have tended to step gingerly over the middle ground east of the Rhine, they have generally done so out of an appreciation of how treacherous that ground can be. For most of its history, German society lacked a firm political frame of reference and a cultural center of gravity. The middle ground was thus not merely uncharted; it displayed an unnatural tendency to move about, from one perspective seeming to lie between the masses and the elite, from another between state and society, and from another still between art and politics.

Historiographically the political press in particular has remained a poor relation of literature, whose intellectual excellence it could never match, and a stepchild of the state, to which it was usually obliged to submit. Although no professional today would adopt such a dismissive tone, few have bothered to dispute the conclusion of one nineteenth-century English observer that "the preparation, manufacture, and sale of political intelligence are as much a royal monopoly in Germany as those of tobacco in France." Little wonder that the German press should have seemed "without interest, without influence, without character, without sympathy."[1]

Comparisons of this kind have too often plagued writing about the German past, by requiring historians to explain what German institutions were not. Better to focus on what they were. In studying the German press we are bound to go wrong if we begin by assuming that German writers and publishers were deficient in will or imagination as compared to their colleagues in the west, and that such interest as they retain derives from their suffering at the hands of their enemies. The only sensible approach to such broad impressions is to try to make them, not less broad, but more substantial. The history of the Cotta press is a good place to start. Johann Cotta has long been a famous figure in the history of German literature, known above all as the publisher of the great figures of the *Goethezeit*. He was also the archetypal middleman of his generation: the first German to convert cultural prestige into political power by means of the press, and the first German publisher whose career can be seen to express a clear vision of what politics is supposed to be. Neither a statesman nor an intellectual in his own right, Cotta stood as a fixture at the crossroads of his nation's public life. It is a vantage from which a great deal can be learned about a society casting off the reticence of the Old Regime as it enters the Century of Words.

THE BONAPARTE OF PUBLISHERS

In 1852, twenty years after Johann Cotta's death, Heinrich Heine wrote a letter to Cotta's son, Georg, which began as follows:

Most esteemed Baron!

Since I am troubling you today with a request, which I am certain you will be glad to fulfill, I shall also take the opportunity to refresh your memories with one of my own. This is indeed a pleasure for me, since you are the son of my old and dear friend Cotta. Because my physical infirmity cuts me off from life outside, I find a substitute in the dreamlike world of reminiscence, so that my life becomes merely a meditation on the past. There the image of your dear departed father often appears before my eyes—that valiant, worthy man, who combined the most multifaceted culture with a practical sense seldom found in Germany: fine and honorable, courteous, even courtly, unprejudiced, far-sighted. And a man who, for all his great services to the spiritual and material interests of the Fatherland, nevertheless possessed the kind of touching modesty one expects to

---

1. *Foreign Quarterly Review* 33 (1844): 372; in Lenore O'Boyle, "The Image of the Journalist in France, Germany, and England, 1815–1848," *Comparative Studies in Society and History* 10 (1967–68): 302–4.

find only among gallant old soldiers. He was a man who had his hand over the entire world!—so, I think, says the tailor about Charles V in Goethe's *Egmont*.[2]

This letter has probably influenced Cotta's posthumous reputation more than any other document. All subsequent accounts of his life refer to it, and all have taken their cue from it: diversity and practicality are invariably identified as the hallmarks of Cotta's career. It is easy to see why. Even by the standards of a naturally heterogeneous industry, the list of the Cotta Verlag in Johann Cotta's time was uncommonly broad, dominating the world of letters and including important works in a variety of scholarly and scientific fields, as well as over forty periodicals devoted to everything from horse breeding to astronomy.[3] Publishing aside, Cotta at one time or another owned two factories and a hotel, a good deal of land, and part interest in two steamships. That this same man should have been the advisor of monarchs, the confidant of Goethe and Schiller, and the chief financial support of so many of the best writers of his time would seem more than sufficient to justify the terms of Heine's recollection.

But the breadth of Cotta's career has also created the impression that it lacked the depth of commitment that characterized the lives of so many of his clients. This, too, is understandable. Cotta, after all, was a *Verleger* in the original sense of the word—a merchant, in this case a merchant in ideas, but without productive facilities of his own. He is thus remembered mainly as a friend and servant of the great, to whom the "touching modesty" to which Heine refers was entirely becoming. And here, perhaps, the Olympian tone of Heine's tribute may have led posterity astray. Heine met Cotta late in life, when he had indeed become a venerable figure. To those who knew him earlier and longer, however, Cotta resembled not an old soldier but a young one—Bonaparte[4]—and his personality was distinguished not so much by multifaceted culture or touching modesty as by driving ambition, and not a little cunning.

This study addresses the aspect of Cotta's career in which cunning and ambition found their fullest development—politics, particularly political journalism. As a window on the age in which he lived, Cotta's political career opens onto less familiar vistas than those afforded by his service to Germany's intellectual elite. The view, however, is no less clear,

---

2. Heinrich Heine to Georg von Cotta, 26 March 1852, in *Heinrich Heine Säkularausgabe* (East Berlin and Paris, 1970–), 23 : 193.

3. Liselotte Lohrer, *Cotta: Geschichte eines Verlags, 1659–1959* (Stuttgart, 1959), pp. 47–95 passim.

4. Georg Joachim Göschen to Karl August Böttiger, 8 Oct. 1805, in Luise Gerhardt, ed., *Schriftsteller und Buchhändler vor hundert Jahren* (Leipzig, 1911), p. 184; Böttiger to Cotta, 23 Jan., 30 April 1807, Cotta Archiv, Deutsches Literaturarchiv, Marbach am Neckar (hereafter cited as CA); Friedrich Buchholz to Cotta, 5 Jan. 1807, CA.

and at least equally compelling. Cotta's success as a cultural entrepreneur was remarkable, but not exceptional in itself, being proportionate to the talent of the artists and intellectuals with whom he worked. His political enterprises, in contrast, were not at all proportionate to the public life of Germany as he found it, and his desire to transform his political surroundings, to give them the same sophistication and significance as the literary culture to which he was also drawn, demanded a degree of personal effort and an acceptance of personal risk quite different in kind from those required by any of his other ventures.

Does such an approach distort Cotta's sense of himself? He put great stock in the good opinion of his literary clientele, and his pronounced sense of personal dignity was certainly connected to the respect he commanded among them. To his family and friends, however, it was no surprise that he should always have considered the *Allgemeine Zeitung* his "favorite child" and that, when he came to have his portrait painted in middle age, he presented himself not as a man of letters but in the uniform of the Württemberg Chamber of Deputies, the only political office he ever held.[5] If we can judge an individual's commitments by his persistence in the face of adversity, there can be no question that politics and public service were at the center of Cotta's existence.

Politics and public service. Today these expressions flow together so nicely they seem almost synonymous. Not so in Cotta's Germany. There the forces of absolutism and Enlightenment had combined to establish a clear connection between "politics" and "service"; but the object of political service was the state, not the public. This is how Cotta looks to us in his uniform, and no doubt how he meant to look: like a servant of the state, a document of some kind at his right hand, his left hand resting on a sword. "Public" remained a difficult word and a troublesome idea, resistant to theoretical clarification and bureaucratic control and entirely beyond the ken of conventional portraiture. In his portrait Cotta stands before a landscape idyllic in its emptiness. Yet no one knew better than he that, politically speaking, the landscape was filling up.

THE PRESS, THE PUBLIC, AND THE CENTURY OF WORDS

It has been estimated that when Cotta was born, in 1764, roughly 15 percent of the inhabitants of the German-speaking lands could read. By the turn of the century this figure was approaching 25 percent; at Cotta's death thirty years later it had reached about 40 percent, somewhat higher in the south and west.[6] Although these estimates, based on di-

---

5. Frontispiece.

6. Rolf Schenda, *Volk ohne Buch: Studien zur Sozialgeschichte der populären Lesestoffe, 1770–1910* (Frankfurt, 1970), p. 444; see also Rolf Engelsing, *Analphabetentum und Lektüre: Zur Sozialgeschichte des Lesens in Deutschland zwischen feudaler und industrieller Gesellschaft* (Stuttgart, 1973), pp. 53–100.

verse and fragmentary sources, are certain to be revised as our knowledge increases, the tendency and scale of the change they describe are clear. This general development is compounded by equally clear, if still incomplete, evidence that those who could read were reading more, and more widely. By the end of the eighteenth century the "intensive" reading habits of the early Enlightenment, characterized by repeated study of a small number of devotional works, had given way to "extensive" reading of works of literature, practical advice, and popular philosophy.[7] The effect is evident in the expansion of the market for German books (the last half of the eighteenth century saw twice as many books published as the first half)[8] and, even more strikingly, German periodicals, whose number more than doubled between 1770 and 1800.[9]

The social and intellectual transformation reflected in these figures constitutes the essential underpinning of Cotta's professional existence and the central challenge of his political life. And there is no mistaking

7. On the distinction between "intensive" and "extensive" reading see Rolf Engelsing, "Die Perioden der Lesergeschichte in der Neuzeit: Das statistische Ausmaß und die soziokulturelle Bedeutung der Lektüre," *Archiv für Geschichte des Buchwesens* 10 (1970), cols. 945–1002; and idem, *Der Bürger als Leser: Lesergeschichte in Deutschland, 1500–1800* (Stuttgart, 1974), pp. 182–277. Although there is little dispute about the character of the change Engelsing describes, there is less agreement about when it occurred. Martin Welke, "Gemeinsame Lektüre und frühe Formen von Gruppenbildung im 17. und 18. Jahrhundert: Zeitungslesen in Deutschland," in *Lesegesellschaften und bürgerliche Emanzipation: Ein europäischer Vergleich*, ed. Otto Dann (Munich, 1981), pp. 29–53, argues that "extensive" reading was well established by midcentury, particularly among readers of newspapers—a suggestive conclusion in the present context, but not one that overturns the prevailing impression that the last decades of the eighteenth century were a period of rapid growth and change. The best overall study, focusing on the literary market, is Albert Ward, *Book Production, Fiction, and the German Reading Public, 1740–1800* (London, 1974).

8. Engelsing, *Analphabetentum und Lektüre*, p. 53; cf. the statistical summaries in Helmuth Kiesel and Paul Münch, *Gesellschaft und Literatur im 18. Jahrhundert: Voraussetzungen und Entstehung des literarischen Markts in Deutschland* (Munich, 1977), pp. 181–203. The expansion of the market for German books was even more rapid than these estimates suggest, since it began in earnest only after the close of the Seven Years' War (see Paul Raabe, "Buchproduction und Lesepublikum, 1770–1780," in *Bücherlust und Lesefreuden: Beiträge zur Geschichte des Buchwesens im 18. und frühen 19. Jahrhundert* [Stuttgart, 1984], pp. 51–65), and it occurred simultaneously with the collapse of the market for books published in Latin, which accounted for 28 percent of all books published in Germany in 1740 and only 4 percent in 1800 (Rudolf Jentzsch, *Der deutsch-lateinische Büchermarkt nach den Leipziger Ostermeß-Katalogen von 1740, 1770, und 1800 in seiner Gliederung und Wandlung* [Leipzig, 1912], p. 333).

9. See the statistical appendix to Joachim Kirchner, *Die Grundlagen des deutschen Zeitschriftenwesens* (Leipzig, 1928–31), 2:323–47. Kirchner's figures have been criticized as incomplete, not least because they exclude newspapers (Martin Welke, "Zeitung und Öffentlichkeit im 18. Jahrhundert: Betrachtungen zur Reichweite und Funktion der periodischen deutschen Tagespublizistik," in *Presse und Geschichte: Beiträge zur historischen Kommunikationsforschung*, ed. Elger Blühm [Munich, 1977], pp. 72–75), but they have not been improved upon by more recent scholarship, nor is there any reason to assume that more exact knowledge would alter the general picture he presents.

that it was a challenging transformation, even to those who stood to profit from it. Freedom from the restraints of aristocratic patronage and a market dominated by the needs of scholars and clergymen came at the price of dependence on a public whose social character and cultural aspirations seemed increasingly diverse and uncertain. The "reading revolution," like all revolutions, was an event full of cross-purposes, which engendered new feelings of self-confidence and social significance among those carried along by it and, as one scholar has pertinently remarked, equally strong feelings of "astonishment, disaffection, anxiety, and even fear." [10]

Until relatively recently those who investigated the emergence of what Frederick Hertz called "the German public mind" [11] were primarily concerned to characterize its contents, with a view to linking the public mind with more concrete historical developments to which it was presumed to have contributed. For most historians that development was German nationalism, toward which the public mind was seen to tend, shedding in the process its original cosmopolitan and particularist character. The "national movement" became a kind of analytic lodestone that could be applied to an almost limitless mass of documentary material, separating what was essential and enduring in the collective consciousness of Germany from what was transient, local, backward-looking, or otherwise mistaken. There is no question that such work made a significant contribution to historical understanding, if only by insisting on the importance of ideas and sources that more conventional histories were inclined to overlook. [12] But even setting political preconceptions aside, the limitations of a purely empirical approach, which seeks to persuade through the sheer accumulation of disparate bits of evidence, are obvious. It is hardly surprising that these same veins have recently been shown to yield ore of an entirely different type, testifying to the continuing vitality of the Holy Roman Empire. [13]

---

10. Wolfgang von Ungern-Sternberg, "Schriftsteller und literarischer Markt," in *Hansers Sozialgeschichte der deutschen Literatur vom 16. Jahrhundert bis zur Gegenwart*, vol. 3: *Deutsche Aufklärung bis zur Französischen Revolution, 1680–1789*, ed. Rolf Grimminger (Munich and Vienna, 1980), p. 134.

11. Frederick Hertz, *The Development of the German Public Mind: A Social History of German Political Sentiments, Aspirations, and Ideas*, 2 vols.; and vol. 3 (posthumous), *The German Public Mind in the Nineteenth Century*, ed. Frank Eyck (London, 1957–75).

12. Among older works that retain their usefulness see Ludwig Salomon, *Geschichte des deutschen Zeitungswesens von den ersten Anfängen bis zur Wiederaufrichtung des Deutschen Reiches* (Oldenburg and Leipzig, 1906–7; reprint Aalen, 1973); and Otto Tschirch, *Geschichte der öffentlichen Meinung in Preussen vom Baseler Frieden bis zum Zusammenbruch des Staates (1795–1806)*, 2 vols. (Weimar, 1933–34).

13. See, for instance, John G. Gagliardo, *Reich and Nation: The Holy Roman Empire as Idea and Reality, 1763–1806* (Bloomington, 1980); and Christoph Prignitz, *Vaterlandsliebe und Freiheit: Deutscher Patriotismus von 1750 bis 1850* (Wiesbaden, 1981). A work that could

The difficulty with work of this kind is not its selectivity, but rather the naïveté of its underlying assumption that the public mind can be grasped by summarizing or somehow taking the average of the ideas contained in the "private" minds that compose it. This objection was first raised in a long-overlooked dissertation by Hans Gerth,[14] and with more telling effect thirty years later by Jürgen Habermas.[15] Habermas has argued in broad terms for the existence not of a "public mind," but of a "public realm," a metaphoric political space situated between state and society, with a distinctive social and institutional structure that is itself subject to change. What counts most about the public realm for Habermas is not the shared ideas or feelings it contains, or even the extent of its social reach (though this is important), but rather the fact that its contents are actively communicated. The public realm does not think. It simply houses what might be called the means of communication, by which ideas are transmitted and through which the natural isolation of private minds is made to yield to the demands of civil society. It is the effort of communication that creates the "public" and gives it qualities of cohesion and authority quite different from those possessed by any mere congeries of individuals, however large.

Habermas's *Strukturwandel der Öffentlichkeit* is a work of social theory rather than historical scholarship. Its ideological and political purposes are obvious, since it was not the author's intention to conceal them, and they have been sufficiently commented on elsewhere.[16] Its empirical basis, however, is not obvious, and a quarter-century of research, stimulated in good part by Habermas's theories, has done little to strengthen it. Habermas's analysis suffers from some of the same defects as the nationalist historiography it was intended to displace: a certain teleological neatness and rigidity, which the very idea of "structural" change tends to enforce; a distinct insensitivity to regional and local conditions, whose significance is one of the most prominent impressions to be derived from recent scholarship on eighteenth- and early-nineteenth-century Ger-

be said to bridge the gap between these interpretive strains is Wolfgang Zorn, "Reichs- und Freiheitsgedanken in der Publizistik des ausgehenden 18. Jahrhunderts (1763–1792): Ein Beitrag zur Vorgeschichte der deutschen Nationalbewegung," in *Darstellung und Quellen zur Geschichte der deutschen Einheitsbewegung im neunzehnten und zwanzigsten Jahrhundert*, ed. Paul Wentzcke (Heidelberg, 1959), pp. 11–66.

14. Hans Gerth, "Die sozialgeschichtliche Lage der bürgerlichen Intelligenz um die Wende des 18. Jahrhunderts," Ph.D. diss., Frankfurt, 1935; published as *Bürgerliche Intelligenz um 1800: Zur Soziologie des deutschen Frühliberalismus* (Göttingen, 1976).

15. Jürgen Habermas, *Strukturwandel der Öffentlichkeit: Untersuchungen zu einer Kategorie der bürgerlichen Gesellschaft* (Neuwied am Rhein und Berlin, 1962).

16. For a sympathetic discussion, oriented more toward literary scholarship, see Peter Uwe Hohendahl, "Kritische Theorie, Öffentlichkeit, und Kultur: Anmerkungen zu Jürgen Habermas und seinen Kritikern," *Basis: Jahrbuch für deutsche Gegenwartsliteratur* 8 (1978): 60–91.

many;[17] and what Franz Schneider has called "an underemphasis on the problem of freedom,"[18] with respect both to the way the public realm operates internally and to its relations with the state. By replacing the rhetoric of national consciousness with that of class and critical theory, Habermas has given new life to an old vision of German, and indeed European cultural history. The public realm, emerging by a process akin to pure rationacination from the literary culture of the Old Regime, passes (relatively painlessly) into the hands of a politically self-conscious bourgeoisie, seeking to free itself from the chains of absolutism, and then (somewhat more painfully) into the hands of the democratic mass, where its mechanisms, ostensibly designed for the dissemination of Enlightenment, are found to possess unexpected capacities for manipulation and self-deception. This view is no less inspiring than it ever was, and no more.

All this having been said, it remains true that, by shifting the focus of scholarly attention from the ideational content of the public mind to the institutional structure of the public realm, Habermas has at least delivered a sharp reminder that ideas change when they are used. In relation to Cotta's generation, moreover, his work has the additional merit (though perhaps not one he would claim himself) of corresponding to some extent with contemporary intimations of what the reading revolution was all about. After all, something like a "structural change" seems to be involved in the difference between the Age of Enlightenment and what Metternich called, rather more ominously to his way of thinking, the Century of Words.

Some small part of that difference involves the difference between books and periodicals, particularly newspapers. It has recently been proposed that, for much of the eighteenth century, reading was regarded as a private act, motivated by personal piety or a yen for secular learning and hedged about by the constraints of family and community.[19] Far more persistently than books, periodicals seemed to undermine the pri-

17. Notwithstanding some outstanding works of synthesis, notably Thomas Nipperdey's *Deutsche Geschichte, 1800–1866: Bürgerwelt und starker Staat* (Munich, 1980), the growing interest in the smaller German lands and the institutions of the Holy Roman Empire has only confirmed the continuing strength of German particularism, and the corresponding diversity of German political experience, in the early decades of the nineteenth century. Although the literature is immense, the trend is evident, for instance, in two recent collections of essays: Helmut Berding and Hans-Peter Ullmann, eds., *Deutschland zwischen Revolution und Restauration* (Düsseldorf, 1981); and Eberhard Weis, ed., *Reformen im rheinbündischen Deutschland* (Munich, 1984).

18. Franz Schneider, *Pressefreiheit und politische Öffentlichkeit: Studien zur politischen Geschichte Deutschlands bis 1848* (Neuwied am Rhein and Berlin, 1966), p. 13.

19. This very interesting observation by Roger Chartier and Daniel Roche ("Les pratiques urbaines de l'imprimé, XVIIe–XVIIIe siècles," in *Histoire de l'édition française*, ed. Henri-Jean Martin and Roger Chartier [Paris, 1982–], 2:402–29) is based on a study of the

vate sphere to which reading was confined, and conferred upon it some of the overtones of public participation. In their contents periodicals proved adaptable to the needs of almost every class and avocation. In their form they symbolized a desire, beyond personal culture, for a more rational and integrated society. In so doing they created the essential lineaments of the public realm, binding readers, writers, and publishers together in enduring, reciprocal, and increasingly extended communities of interest: to Ludwig Börne periodicals were like roads and canals, whose number and quality bore witness to the good governance of the state;[20] Heine, less optimistically, would see them as the fortresses in the war of ideas.[21]

Either way it is durability that counts. Although there is some evidence that magazines and newspapers were more likely than books to be read aloud in public places,[22] there was nothing about the economics of publishing in Cotta's day that would have brought periodicals a larger or more diverse audience than books. All German periodicals, including newspapers, were sold by subscription, and the initial cost to the customer, whether an individual, a reading circle, or a public establishment like a coffeehouse, was no different than it would have been for a book of the same aggregate size and quality. The formal continuity that distinguished periodicals from books also distinguished them from broadsides and pamphlets—which explains the pronounced preference of German governments for the latter forms on those occasions when they were called on to address the public directly. In matters of public communication Germany's princes were reluctant to create expectations about the future. It was one of the more disconcerting features of the reading revolution, fostered above all by the periodical press, that such expectations should have begun to emerge by themselves.

Among German periodicals a special place had always been reserved,

way reading is represented in the French art and literature of the period. Keith Baker ("Politics and Public Opinion Under the Old Regime: Some Reflections," in *Press and Politics in Pre-revolutionary France*, ed. Jack R. Censer and Jeremy D. Popkin [Berkeley and Los Angeles, 1987], pp. 205–6) has noted some exceptions, which multiply after 1789, all of which involve newspapers.

20. Advertisement for the *Wage*, 26 May 1818.

21. Heine to Gustav Kolb [assistant editor of the *Allgemeine Zeitung*], 11 Nov. 1828, in Heine, *Säkularausgabe* 20:350.

22. Welke, "Zeitung und Öffentlichkeit," passim. A considerable share of the resources of reading societies also seems to have gone into subscriptions to periodicals. The issue has not been looked at systematically, but see Otto Dann, "Die Lesegesellschaften des 18. Jahrhunderts und der gesellschaftliche Aufbruch des deutschen Bürgertums," in *Buch und Leser*, ed. Herbert Göpfert (Hamburg, 1977), pp. 160–193; and Irene Jentsch, "Zur Geschichte des Zeitungslesens in Deutschland am Ende des 18. Jahrhunderts, mit besonderer Berücksichtigung der gesellschaftlichen Formen des Zeitungslesens," Ph.D. diss., Leipzig, 1937.

by law and custom, for newspapers. Unlike more specialized journals, rooted in the communicative needs of the academically educated elite, newspapers did not originate in the cultural aspirations of the Enlightenment. They are an older form with more diverse origins: in the mercantile economy of the early seventeenth century, in the political culture of the Free Cities and "home towns" of the Holy Roman Empire,[23] and in the emerging bureaucracies of the absolutist state.[24] In conceptual terms newspapers were distinguished from other periodicals by their relatively frequent appearance (every week or so at the start of the eighteenth century, several times a week at the end); an exclusive focus on recent, primarily political events; and a superficially objective point of view that tended to obscure the individuality of their authors. Periodicals of this kind were numerous in Germany at the end of the Old Regime—far more so than in France[25]—a fact that reveals less about the vitality of German public life than about the fragmentation of German political experience. German press laws typically said little about newspapers, preferring simply to lump them together with wall posters and advertising flyers rather than with other periodicals.[26] For the most part Germany's princes had learned to view them with indifference instead of alarm.

23. The term is of course Mack Walker's (*German Home Towns: Community, State, and General Estate, 1648–1871* [Ithaca, N.Y., 1971]); his famous study, although vigorously affirming the political qualities of hometown culture, tells us almost nothing about the reading habits of the inhabitants. But see Martin Welke, "Die Legende vom 'unpolitischen Deutschen': Zeitungslesen im 18. Jahrhundert als Spiegel des politischen Interesses," *Jahrbuch der Wittheit zu Bremen* 25 (1981): 160–83.

24. The best general history of the early German newspaper press, particularly in its relation to mercantilism, is Kurt Koszyk, *Vorläufer der Massenpresse: Oekonomie und Publizistik zwischen Reformation und Französischer Revolution* (Munich, 1972). See also two older works by Johannes Kleinpaul, *Die Fuggerzeitungen, 1568–1605* (Leipzig, 1921), and *Das Nachrichtenwesen der deutschen Fürsten im 16. und 17. Jahrhundert: Ein Beitrag zur Geschichte der geschrieben Zeitungen* (Leipzig, 1930); and Julius Otto Opel, "Die Anfänge der deutschen Zeitungspresse, 1609–1650," *Archiv für Geschichte des deutschen Buchhandels* 3 (1879): 1–268.

25. Welke ("Gemeinsame Lektüre," p. 30) estimates that two hundred newspapers were published in Germany in 1789, with a combined circulation of about three hundred thousand copies per week; on the French side see Jack Censer and Jeremy Popkin, "Historians and the Press," in *Press and Politics in Pre-revolutionary France*, ed. Censer and Popkin, pp. 18–19.

26. This was equally true of the relatively mild Censor Patent of Austria's Joseph II (1781) and the notoriously repressive Edicts on Religion and Censorship of Prussia's Frederick William II (1788). Neglect, particularly when based on contempt, is obviously not the same as tolerance. Wherever newspapers began to test the limits assigned them by habit and precedent they began to attract more legal attention. In 1783 Bavaria banned book advertisements that contained anything other than a summary of the book's contents; the Prussian *Censorreskript* of 1784 took the trouble explicitly to deny that private individuals had any right to be informed of the actions of the state. Only in the 1790s, however,

As the pace of political events in Europe began to change this indifference would become insupportable. Under the pressure of war and revolution, whose reality and weight the censors were powerless to conceal, newspapers were transformed from banal, parochial chronicles of commerce and court life into the essential organs of political opinion in the nineteenth century, focusing public attention on immediate events and the conduct of the state with an insistency that no other form of publicity could match. This was a transformation in which Cotta would play a central part, and its complexities are a recurring theme of this book. But its general character can be expressed very concisely: the newspapers Cotta read as a young man were remotely and inconsequentially about politics; those he published in his maturity would be most decidedly in politics—a development whose consequences, even for him, were difficult to judge.

These are large ideas, and they provide a useful frame of reference in which Cotta's career can be understood. But they are not themselves a description of that career, or of the times in which Cotta lived and worked. To a historian description is more important than metaphor; even fruitful and instructive metaphors—the "public realm" or, for that matter, "the Century of Words"—can never be objects of historical investigation in themselves. If we conceive of the transition from the Enlightenment to the Century of Words simply as a "structural change," however complex, we are almost certain to misunderstand the dynamics and ambiguities of Cotta's situation. In the final analysis, the history of the Cotta press tells us less about the structure of the public realm in Germany than about the concrete political struggle necessary to secure its existence in the first place—a struggle whose character has generally been reduced to a straightforward contest between freedom and repression but whose real object, the use to which the ideas expressed in the Cotta press were to be put, was reform.

THE COTTA PRESS AND THE PROBLEM OF REFORM

The impulse to reform is a component of modernity, resting on assumptions about the rationality and responsibility of human institutions that are by no means universal. In Germany, the homeland of religious reformation, its application to politics comes relatively late. It is entirely possible, after all, to govern effectively with no thought of curbing

---

do newspapers become a real focus of legal concern. See Otto Groth, *Die Geschichte der deutschen Zeitungswissenschaft: Probleme und Methoden* (Munich, 1948), p. 95; Ernst Consentius, "Die Berliner Zeitungen während der Französischen Revolution," *Preussische Jahrbücher* 117 (1904): 454–56; and, more generally, Ulrich Eisenhardt, *Die kaiserliche Aufsicht über Buchdruck, Buchhandel, und Presse im Heiligen Römischen Reich Deutscher Nation (1496–1806): Ein Beitrag zur Geschichte der Bücher- und Pressezensur* (Karlsruhe, 1970).

abuses of power or redressing social inequity. But such disregards may become vulnerable as a society's material and cultural aspirations increase, as they were throughout much of western and central Europe in the last decades of the eighteenth century. By the end of the Old Regime, reform, chiefly in the guise of administrative and legal centralization, had become an incidental aspect of government in most of the larger German lands, and an incidental concern of some segments of the academic community, for whom rational and responsible government was essential to the realization of mankind's perfectibility. In the face of external forces whose power and persuasiveness cannot be matched by traditional means, however, reform ceases to be an incidental concern, and becomes a matter of political survival.

This was true everywhere in Germany during the French Revolution and the wars that accompanied and succeeded it. The reforms these events inspired have always been difficult to summarize. Many were barely distinguishable in form or purpose from the time-honored expedients of enlightened absolutism. In an atmosphere of ideological tension and political danger, however, even modest endeavors can achieve a heightened effect. In the case of the reform generation, the collective weight of its efforts altered for good the narrowly fiscal relations that had bound the ruler and the ruled in Germany since the Thirty Years' War. The state henceforth became the object of popular political expectations to which it had long been apathetic.

The social and administrative reforms for which the Reform Era was named represented, in aggregate, a significant acceleration and expansion of the rationalizing initiatives characteristic of late absolutism, combined with a variety of more dramatic measures for which no precedents existed, dictated by the military emergency of the Napoleonic Wars and the manifold territorial changes that flowed from them. Without exception they were intended to provide the surviving German states with new means of self-aggrandizement and self-defense. Their contribution to the political education of the German public was unimportant in theory and modest in practice. One recent student of the "social-political motivation and background" of the reform movement in Bavaria has concluded that, however broad the effects of some of the reforms, their genesis and implementation were the work of "perhaps thirty men" with relatively similar social backgrounds and intellectual dispositions.[27] In Prussia, where the stakes riding on reform were highest, the political and social energies mobilized in defense of the state proved to be of

---

27. Walter Demel, *Der bayerische Staatsabsolutismus 1806/08–1817: Staats- und gesell-schaftspolitische Motivationen und Hintergründe der Reformära in der ersten Phase des Königreichs Bayern* (Munich, 1983), pp. 555–56.

limited range and dissipated rapidly once the crises of war and revolution had passed. One of the more pessimistic interpreters of the Prussian case has even argued that, in the land where "reform" would be most closely associated with the idea of "liberation," public opinion did not exist.[28]

Strictly speaking this could hardly have been so. Reform certainly impressed many Germans with the capacity of government to act decisively in ways that directly affected their lives and futures. And in Prussia at least, the experience of war and occupation aroused widespread feelings of anger, anxiety, and despair. But to the extent that these feelings bore on the state's interests, their influence was vitiated by the fragmentary, localized character of public life. The ordinary citizen's political horizons were circumscribed by the characteristics of his own class and community. If he was not, as is sometimes supposed, "apolitical," neither was he inclined to compromise parochial interests in behalf of the common good, and still less to feel any moral connection to the actions of the government.[29] With the possible exception of the Prussian army in the extremity of the War of Liberation, Germany had never fostered any means of mediating between state and society at such a general level. It remained to be seen whether, under new conditions, it could.

Certainly the ascendancy of public opinion to new prominence in the wake of reform is unmistakable. In the early 1790s Georg Forster still complained that even the expression *öffentliche Meinung* scarcely existed in German.[30] By 1808, however, Metternich would warn his colleagues that public opinion had become a force comparable to religion in its power to penetrate the hidden recesses of politics.[31] In 1813 the allies could plausibly threaten the princes of the Rheinbund with the wrath of

28. Walter M. Simon, *The Failure of the Prussian Reform Movement, 1807–1819* (Ithaca, N.Y., 1955), p. 13.

29. Rudolf Ibbeken's characterization of political opinion in Prussia after the Peace of Tilsit may stand as a useful comment on Simon's more lapidary judgement. "A desire for cohesiveness and clarity, for consciousness and a new order," Ibbeken writes, "is unmistakable. But as soon as we look in any particular direction we encounter an image of such bewildering diversity, an intellectual separatism with so many variations, that it is simply impossible to imagine how anything like a relatively unified public opinion could have arisen. . . . Strictly in political terms," he concludes, "the rich intellectual life of Germany's years of deep distress was like an enormous display of fireworks, which set a thousand lights to blinking throughout the heavens, but which could scarcely have achieved a specific orientation" (*Preußen, 1807–1813: Staat und Volk als Idee und in der Wirklichkeit* [Cologne and Berlin, 1970], pp. 223–24).

30. Undated letter fragment, in Georg Forster, *Sämtliche Schriften* (Leipzig, 1843), 5:248–49.

31. Metternich to Philipp Stadion, 23 June 1808, in Klemens von Metternich, *Aus Metternich's nachgelassenen Papieren,* ed. Alfons von Klinkowström and Prince Richard Metternich-Winneburg (Vienna, 1880–84), 2:192.

their own people if they did not abandon the French.[32] By 1820 the regulation of public life had become the principal concern of the German Federation.[33] And a decade later most educated Germans would have agreed with Ludwig Uhland that, one way or another, the continuing struggle over the rights of the press was "destined to represent, and incorporate into itself, all other questions pertaining to the free development of national life."[34]

The overall dynamic, however, is perplexing. Public opinion advances steadily but gains no ground. It emerges as an object and instrument of policy, but without winning any discernible influence over the conduct of government. In the end it achieves significant recognition as a component of political life—recognition that can best be measured by the rigor with which it was controlled by the authorities. Uhland, a friend of the press, compared it to the ghost of a warrior that could find no rest, haunting the halls of government.[35]

To anyone searching the Reform Era for evidence of a nascent democratic tradition it is a disturbing and paradoxical process, the more so because the limitations of reformism are difficult to explain solely with reference to the forces that opposed it. As far as the press was concerned there were great obstacles in the way of those trying to supply public opinion with an institutional base. But it is also true that the obstacles were not so great that the task seemed impossible. In Cotta's case his disappointments were matched by his successes, and despite all setbacks there were times when he had reason to feel that progress was possible. One may argue that this feeling was unjustified. But it did not seem so at the time. Cotta knew his opportunities were limited, but he also believed they were real. The way in which he and his contemporaries exploited the chances they had did much to define the prospects for political journalism in Germany for the rest of the century.

Cotta's political career has never been studied comprehensively. Neither has it been entirely neglected: Cotta's proprietorship of the *Allgemeine Zeitung* and his connections with Goethe and Schiller have insured that his name should turn up regularly even in general histories of the period. There is, moreover, no dispute about his political sympathies. Cotta is always identified as a liberal, for good reason. He was one of the first landlords in Württemberg to free his tenants from entailed servitude. He was a champion of Jewish emancipation. As a legislator he

32. Declaration of Kalisch, 25 March 1813, in Philipp Guido von Meyer, ed., *Corpus Juris Confoederationis Germanica* (Frankfurt am Main, 1822), 1:146–47.

33. Federal Press Law of 20 Sept. 1819, in *Protokolle der Deutschen Bundesversammlung* (Frankfurt am Main, 1817–28), vol. 4, pt. 8, pp. 667–69.

34. Speech given in the Württemberg Chamber of Deputies, 3 Nov. 1833, in Walther Reinöhl, *Uhland als Politiker* (Tübingen, 1911), p. 115.

35. Ibid., p. 113.

stood for modernity and progress when passivity and reaction were the norm. He invested heavily, even imprudently, in steam engines. These are all sound liberal credentials. But even so, as applied to Cotta's generation the term *liberal* takes a good deal for granted. The same, of course, could be said of "reformer," a simplifying label in its own right and one that, like "liberal," lends Cotta's politics a programmatic quality they did not possess. Yet he was recognizably a figure of the Reform Era: a practical idealist, at once challenged, inspired, and threatened by the onset of the French Revolution; a man whose life was dominated by the need to find a concrete expression for his enlightened values. However one may characterize Cotta's politics, it is clear that they were shaped first of all by the conflict between traditional values and revolutionary change, which threatened to overwhelm the society in which he was raised. It was to interpret and communicate the significance of that conflict that the Cotta press was established.

"Cotta press" is not an expression Cotta used. Here it is a term of convenience, intended to refer not to the entire production of Cotta's firm, but to the newspapers and political journals he financed and directed over the years. Strictly speaking this usage is anachronistic: in German the word *press* acquired a special association with political journalism only in the 1840s.[36] But the legal and political distinctions on which it depends were already familiar during Cotta's lifetime. It is less certain that Cotta would have acknowledged the Cotta press as a personal enterprise. Cotta's publications defy ideological categorization. To a greater or lesser extent they were all public forums, committed to the impartial presentation of news and opinion. Cotta wrote little himself, and he found the (quite common) suggestion that the Cotta press was his personal instrument deeply insulting. At the same time, it would be naïve to suppose that the unity of the Cotta press was merely commercial. Cotta always maintained control over the political style and contents of his publications. However free his editors may have been in the day-to-day conduct of their business, in the end they worked for Cotta, and knew it. In this regard it would be hard to improve on another of Heine's observations, apropos of the *Allgemeine Zeitung*, that "the mouth may be in Augsburg, but the nose is definitely in Stuttgart."[37] This was true of

36. The meaning of this word, which began as the name for a machine and ended as a symbol of public life in general, is thoroughly examined in Franz Schneider, "Presse, Pressefreiheit, Zensur," in *Geschichtliche Grundbegriffe: Historisches Lexikon zur politisch-sozialen Sprache in Deutschland*, ed. Otto Brunner, Werner Conze, and Reinhard Koselleck (Stuttgart, 1972–), 4:899–927.

37. Heine to Hermann von Pückler-Muskau, 17 Oct. 1854, in Heine, *Säkularausgabe* 23:384.

In considering the evolution of journalists from "private individuals" into "public servants of the mass media," Habermas argues that Cotta's decision to employ an editor for

all Cotta's political publications. Collectively they constituted the only "biblio-political Great Power" in the otherwise Balkanized world of German journalism.[38] They reveal a continuity of inspiration and a coherence of values that could only have come from Cotta himself.

They also reveal a coherence of another kind, deriving not from their owner's character but from their political context. The deepest questions confronting the reform generation were constitutional: What is the body politic, and how does it concentrate and legitimize its power? Does the democratization of knowledge imply a parallel democratization of authority, or is the dissemination of Enlightenment merely an expedient of government? Can political controversy be made useful to public order, or must it be suppressed as a threat to the unity of the state? The history of the Cotta press derives much of its interest from the persistent efforts of its proprietor to formulate an institutional response to this complex of problems, one that was both intellectually convincing and serviceable in practice. Conviction and serviceability were not, however, easily reconciled. In an age when "legitimate opposition" would have seemed a contradiction in terms, to become isolated from the state was to court, not necessarily extinction, but certainly irrelevance. Yet to accept the state's embrace too readily was to sacrifice the credibility on which the press's constitutional role—its relation to the body politic, however defined—depended.

As a cross-section of "reform" journalism the Cotta press is not typical. It was created and nurtured in a style that other publishers could

his newspaper was indicative of an important structural change: a new division of labor between "publicistic and economic functions" that echoed larger developments in the surrounding society. He then goes on to observe that the "editorial autonomy" Cotta afforded was linked to another important development—the increasing prevalence of editorials in German newspapers—and, furthermore, that the editor's freedom was of the same kind "as characterized the communication of private individuals [construed] as the general public" during "the phase when the political function of the public realm was establishing itself" (*Strukturwandel der Öffentlichkeit*, p. 202). If nothing else, this illustrates how easily a preoccupation with structure can lead one away from the facts. Cotta's contemporaries had no doubt whatever that he personally was the political heart of the *Allgemeine Zeitung* (hereafter referred to as *AZ*), and there is nothing in the historical record with which to dispute them. Nor did anything resembling an editorial ever appear in the *AZ* during Cotta's lifetime—a development that would have contradicted the spirit of the whole enterprise and undermined the paper's intellectual authority as well. As to whether the public realm of the early nineteenth century was "characterized" by freedom, that, finally, is a matter of interpretation. My reading of the evidence suggests that, among those whose lives were spent trying to supply the public realm with an institutional base, freedom was for most a fervent hope, for some a dangerous threat, and a characteristic experience for hardly any.

In relation to Habermas's larger argument, these are matters of detail. But it is at least worth noting that, although Cotta was incontestably the most prominent publisher in Germany before 1848, Habermas does not mention him except in the passage discussed here.

38. Rolf Engelsing, "Zeitung und Zeitschrift in Nordwestdeutschland 1800–1850: Leser und Journalisten," *Archiv für Geschichte des Buchwesens* 5 (1964): col. 859.

not match, and its successes and failures were in some respects unique. Nevertheless, it is exemplary, in the sense that its successes and failures illuminate the conditions under which all journalists and publishers had to operate. During Cotta's lifetime the German press was subject to conflicting pressures, which gave rise to diverging ambitions among its members. On the one hand, the revolutions in France and America afforded an unmistakable demonstration of the power of the printed word. On the other hand, the response of German society to these events left the princes' control of political information unchallenged. The imposing example of revolutionary journalism—an exfoliating popular press, a king pilloried in newspapers that sold on the street for a few pennies—was of little use to Germans trying to draw inspiration from changing conditions, but without straining the patience of their own governments. A vigorous, independent press was not yet the hallmark of political liberty, and its dependence on a specifically democratic constitution was neither clear nor particularly agreeable. No one doubted that the press could do the work of revolution. But how the press might contribute to the work of reform, which sought to pacify antagonistic social forces and reconcile them to the state, was not obvious.

The reformers of Cotta's generation differed from their liberal successors less in the character of their political sympathies, or even in the social range over which those sympathies extended—that part of the population with an economic and cultural stake in the country—than in the manner in which they were held. The politics of reform tended to be instrumental rather than ideological, aimed at rationalizing rather than challenging or even limiting the power of the state. For this reason it is a serious oversimplification to assume that a steadily adversarial tone dominated relations between government and the press during the years of reform, or even during the years of reaction that followed. However troublesome his role, the censor was not an alien presence in the world of German journalism. With few exceptions neither the press nor the state was willing to concede political legitimacy to open opponents of the existing regime. Censorship, capricious and cynical in practice, was in principle an expression of this rejection of adversary politics on the part of the state, a rejection that found its echo in the pervasive rhetoric of impartiality that characterized the political press of Cotta's generation. These protestations of disinterested loyalty may have been self-serving, but they were not hypocritical. On the contrary, impartiality and universality were part of the very idea of "public,"[39] the only part that gave the

39. This was true both politically and etymologically. Cf. Mona Ozouf, "L'Opinion publique," in *The French Revolution and the Creation of Modern Political Culture*, vol. 1: *The Political Culture of the Old Regime*, ed. Keith Michael Baker (Oxford, 1987), pp. 419–34; and Lucian Hölscher, "Öffentlichkeit," in *Geschichtliche Grundbegriffe*, ed. Brunner, Conze, and Koselleck, 4:413–67.

public any claim to moral authority in relation to the state. When Cotta decided to call his great newspaper the *"Allgemeine"* *Zeitung*, he was not just thumbing his nose at the provincialism of the past; he was making a statement about the character of the public realm as he envisioned it, a statement whose elaboration and defense would occupy the rest of his political career.

For Cotta and his contemporaries freedom of the press was not an absolute value but a means to a variety of ends, all of which involved the further integration of state power and the public interest. A free press, it was argued, would educate the people about their responsibilities as citizens, foster patriotism, stimulate the arts, promote trade, and improve the efficiency of government. But there were other ways to do all these things, and to that extent press freedom, like any other instrumental policy, had to be judged in terms of the risks it posed as well as of the benefits it promised. No one who survived the revolutionary era supposed that the risks were negligible. Cotta believed the restraints on his profession were irrational and excessive, a burden to be avoided if possible. But his efforts to limit the effects of official manipulation were always accompanied by parallel efforts to insure cooperation between himself and the authorities. His aim was to define, and institutionalize, a realm of thought and action beyond the control of the state, but short of opposition to it—a "public" realm in which intellectual independence and political loyalty would be equally well served. For such a project it was not the freedom of the press but the power of the press that counted. And in the maintenance of productive relations with the manifold centers of power in Central Europe, Cotta was second to none.

ONE

Origins

I am standing in the midst of a lovely garden, decked all 'round by a chaos of splendid flowers from many lands. I inhale the sweet perfume, and marvel at the bright colors. When suddenly, a hideous monster springs out from among the blossoms. It seems swollen with poison, its translucent skin shining in every color, its entrails winding like worms. It is large enough to inspire fear, with pincers reaching out on all sides. It hops off like a frog, and creeps back again, with sickening suppleness, on a multitude of tiny feet. Terrified, I turn to flee, but it tries to follow, so, summoning my courage, I strike it a great blow on the back. And at once it appears to be nothing more than a common toad. I am astounded, and still more, when a faraway voice behind me says: "That is public opinion. And the joke's on you: your false friends, the flowers, are all wilted now."

Friedrich Schlegel, *Lucinde*, 1799

This chapter and the two that follow are concerned with Cotta's political education and, more or less simultaneously, with the early history of the Cotta press. It may be admitted in advance that this simultaneity makes its demands on the reader, who will occasionally be obliged to retrace the same ground from different directions. But it is simply true that, in its educational dimension, the early stages of Cotta's career present the appearance not of an apprenticeship but of a sink-or-swim encounter with the great world of power and ideas, in which a wide range of intellectual, institutional, and personal elements converge. Since our aim in any case is not to recapture the full complexity of Cotta's experience but rather to use his experience to illuminate his age, it has seemed reasonable to consider these elements one at a time.

The way one thing turns into another, as Schlegel's dream in *Lucinde* suggests, is never easy to describe. This is particularly true when the transition is only partially recognized and reluctantly acknowledged by those involved. The emergence of a serious newspaper press in Germany where none had been before occurs in an intellectual setting quite remote from the concerns of modern journalism but closely bound up with the academic and literary culture of the late Enlightenment. The significance of this culture to the moral education of the reform generation has rarely been questioned. It was, as James Sheehan has observed, "the first truly German phenomenon, the first set of values and institutions to move between the localism of the populace and the internationalism of the elites."[1]

---

1. James J. Sheehan, "What Is German History? Reflections on the Role of the Nation in German History and Historiography," *Journal of Modern History* 53 (1981): 19.

The genesis of the Cotta press offers one example of how these cultural influences could make themselves felt in ways that contemporaries found unexpected and even disconcerting. When Cotta founded his first political periodicals he did not see himself starting down a wholly uncharted path. On the contrary, the Cotta press was intended to stimulate the growth of a political culture parallel to, and based upon, the intellectual achievements of the last thirty years—a political culture that would "move between" a politically inexperienced public and the ruling elite, and so bind the nation to the state.

It was difficult to foresee what consequences might flow from such a project. But for there to be any consequences at all it would be necessary in the first place to rescue journalism from the contempt of the educated. Much of the time and toil required to bring the Cotta press into existence was devoted to this problem. Cotta brought to politics the same standards of intellectual and moral refinement he admired and promoted in the world of letters. For him politics was a complicated matter, in which the pursuit of excellence outweighed the desire for progress. His sense of complexity would permeate the Cotta press.

Cotta's connection to the world of letters was of course different from that of the public at large. Literature was Cotta's business in a way that politics was not. This fact, too, forms part of the context out of which the Cotta press emerged. Publishing was a demanding trade, informed by a distinctive social vision and beset by commercial pressures that threatened to sap the vitality and profitability from the new literature that Cotta so admired. The only possible allies in this struggle were Germany's princes, whose reluctance to take their cultural responsibilities seriously did not prevent them from becoming the main focus of the book trade's hopes for the future. By the time Cotta came of age, publishing had become an ethically charged, deeply conflicted profession, in which impulses toward intellectual independence and political deference were equally apparent. It promised only modest financial rewards, supplemented by feelings that one served the nation and the cause of Enlightenment. These were real satisfactions; but they were not impervious to the corrosive effects of the marketplace, the mastery of which was an indispensable prerequisite to Cotta's political career.

THE BOOK TRADE AT THE END OF THE OLD REGIME

Cotta decided to go into publishing when he was twenty-three years old, having considered and rejected careers in the church, the army, and finally the law, in which he had just received his doctorate from Tübingen University. He had at his disposal, as he later recalled, about twenty gulden of his own,[2] plus another fifteen hundred that had been

---

2. Cotta to Karl Böttiger, 28 Nov. 1803, in Ernst Friedrich Sondermann, *Karl August Böttiger: Literarischer Journalist der Goethezeit in Weimar* (Bonn, 1983), p. 143.

given to him by a Polish nobleman after a position as *Hofmeister* to the nobleman's family failed to materialize—enough altogether to support a comfortable existence for about six months. Cotta used it all as a down payment on an establishment that had been in his family for more than a century, ever since his great-great-grandfather, Johann Georg Cotta, had been appointed by Tübingen University to look after the interests of the widow of the local book dealer.[3] How Johann Georg had come to be in Tübingen is an elaborate story, for the Cotta family was an old one, extending back at least to the nobility of tenth-century Lombardy, and perhaps a good deal further than that.[4] The French invasion of Italy at the end of the fifteenth century forced the Cottas to move north, finally settling in Saxony and Thuringia. There they made ends meet through a variety of expedients, of which the most successful were the pulpit and the printing press. By the time Johann Georg Cotta received his call to Tübingen in 1659, his patent of nobility had ceased to count; the family crest—a griffin *passant*, emblematic of magnanimity and resolution—would survive as the trademark of the Cotta Verlag.

In 1692 the shop passed into the hands of Johann Georg's son, and in 1712 into those of his grandson, J. G. Cotta III, the first Cotta to recognize that changes in the political climate might allow him to improve his position. Twenty years before, Württemberg's duke, Eberhard Ludwig, had begun to reshape his land's economic institutions by dismantling feudal barriers to competition and replacing them with a centralized system of privileges. The effect of these changes on the book trade, in Württemberg as elsewhere, was twofold: they favored a new form of monopoly, based on state guarantees rather than corporate custom; and they released new entrepreneurial energies, which did not disappear once the new legal apparatus was in place. As a result, the eighteenth century saw the blossoming of literary piracy among those who had lost out in the contest for privileges. As a basis for copyright the new system was only marginally effective, since the means of evasion far outstripped those of enforcement. But it was well suited to its higher purpose, which was to increase the dependency of publishers on the state.

Johann Georg III, who had already seen his family's position in Tübingen undermined by the duke (who refused to acknowledge the firm's

---

3. On the early history of the Cotta Verlag, see Lohrer, *Cotta*, pp. 11–46; and Hans Widmann, ed., *Der deutsche Buchhandel in Urkunden und Quellen* (Hamburg, 1965), 1: 281–86, 2:49–51.

4. Cotta is a name of great antiquity. It appears in the histories of Suetonius and Tacitus and can be seen inscribed on Roman ruins in northern Italy. The earliest Cottas were the brothers Gaius Aurelius and Marcus Aurelius Cotta, who lived ca. 124–70 B.C. The former was a friend of Cicero, the latter a Roman general and consul, whose daughter Aurelia was Julius Caesar's mother. There are many gaps in the genealogical record, but Johann Cotta believed himself to be descended from this ancient line, as do his heirs. See Regina von Cotta, *Werden, Sein, und Vergehen des Verleger-Geschlechts: Cotta* (Zurich, 1969).

monopoly right to work produced by the Tübingen faculty), recognized that loyalty to the university could no longer insure his prosperity. He therefore began to strengthen his connections at court. His technique, exemplified by his acquisition of a calendar privilege once reserved for printers and binders, was to offer an unusually large sum (in this instance, two thousand gulden, five times the going rate) and wait for the duke's insatiable hunger for ready money to do its work.[5] More often than not he was successful, since his competitors were mainly artisans, unable to command the capital that two generations of prudent management had left at Johann Georg's disposal.

When he died in 1770, Johann Georg III had presses of his own in three cities, and he had become official printer to the court in Stuttgart. This impressive growth had been achieved by appealing to the interests of the crown and by gaining a reputation for producing a top-notch product. For all his campaigning after calendar privileges, Johann Georg did nothing to alter his firm's original commitment to a traditional audience of scholars, clerics, and bureaucrats. The reading revolution of the eighteenth century made no great impression on him, or on his son Christoph. The burgeoning demand for vernacular literature and popular culture, which was among the most visible features of eighteenth-century life, was scarcely detectable in the Cotta inventory when young Johann Cotta took over the Tübingen plant in 1787.

By then the house of Cotta had fallen on hard times. Expansion had been expensive, and it had strained Johann Georg's organizational talents to their limit. The decline worsened under Johann's father, Christoph Friedrich Cotta, who was content to be printer to the crown and neglected his family's ancestral holdings in Tübingen.[6] At the same time, changes in the publishing industry as a whole worked to undermine the firm's position. Over the course of the eighteenth century the intellectual center of gravity in Germany shifted to the north, where the literature of Enlightenment had prospered—a development symbolized and hastened by the migration of the major book fairs from Frankfurt to Leipzig.[7] Southern publishers, no longer able to attract the best authors, gained a reputation for illicit practices and shoddy merchandise that only deepened their professional isolation.

This last consideration was much on Johann Cotta's mind, judging by

5. Lohrer, *Cotta*, p. 27.

6. Lohrer, *Cotta*, pp. 30–34.

7. Felix von Schröder, *Die Verlegung der Büchermesse von Frankfurt a. M. nach Leipzig* (Leipzig, 1904); Walter Fischer, "Die Abwanderung des Buchhandels von der Frankfurter Messe nach Leipzig," Ph.D. diss., Leipzig, 1934. By the end of the eighteenth century the cultural backwardness of Cotta's native region was proverbial; see Günter Erning, *Das Lesen und die Lesewut: Beiträge zu Fragen der Lesergeschichte, dargestellt am Beispiel der schwäbischen Provinz* (Bad Heilbrunn, 1974), pp. 11–23.

a letter he wrote to Philipp Reich, the influential proprietor of the Wied-mann'sche Verlag in Leipzig:

> As you doubtless know, my father, the court publisher Cotta, is the owner of the J. G. Cotta bookshop in Tübingen. I wish to purchase it, and would like to hear your thoughts on the matter. . . . I would particularly like to know how I ought to determine the value of the business. Mr. Deichmann, the present manager, has inventoried the books in bales. How, then, would I know how to gauge the approximate value of the bales, in which good and bad wares are mixed? Naturally a distinction must also be made be-tween retail merchandise and our own publications. You know the work of the Cotta Verlag. The best products are Tafinger's *Jus camerale*, Lauter-bach's *Collegium pandectarum*, Gerhard's *Loci theologici*, and Stewart's *Staats-wissenschaft*, along with several less well known works of local interest. The retail department, however, mixes these in with other, inferior books. . . . Good and bad products naturally demand different appraisals. If you would be kind enough to advise me, I would be better able to determine a fair price for the firm.
>
> Perhaps you will also allow me to tell you how I intend to begin my new business. Since the credit of the Cotta Verlag has fallen considerably of late, I must in the first place seek to restore it. I would therefore immedi-ately send all other dealers whatever is still owed them from the last fair. I would take enough money to the next fair to discharge these accounts, and also to pay cash on the spot for the most outstanding new books. [Sev-eral associates] have assured me that dealers offer the lowest prices for cash. Can you tell me if this is true? And furthermore, whether the other dealers would welcome and support an industrious newcomer, whether they would try to make his apprenticeship easier? I would accept only good books for publication, and always use only fine type and paper. My busi-ness principles would be those of Garve.
>
> I have often been shaken in my resolve to take over the firm by doubts whether, in the end, I will emerge free of debt. . . . When I consider most of the publishers in this area, however, I must tell you frankly that these doubts diminish. They would disappear completely if I might flatter my-self that you would allow me to turn to you in this matter.[8]

Leipzig was a long way to go for this sort of advice. It is safe to assume, however, that Cotta was less interested in bookkeeping than in winning acceptance by his peers. His letter was a summary of his credentials to join a trade that had been groping toward modernity and working hard to consolidate its moral position. And for this purpose Reich's goodwill would be invaluable, since he was the leader of the northern publishers in their struggle against the pirates in the south.

This struggle was aggravated by the structure of the book trade itself,

---

8. Cotta to Philipp Reich, 11 July 1787, in Karl Buchner, ed., *Aus den Papieren der Wiedmannschen Buchhandlung* (Berlin, 1871), pp. 3–4. Reich's reply has not survived; but see Cotta to Reich, 18 Dec. 1787, ibid., pp. 4–5.

which, even in the 1780s, transacted most of its wholesale business by barter: dealers simply exchanged their books among themselves on a sheet-for-sheet basis—a practice that worked well enough as long as the goods being exchanged were of comparable quality and marketability. As the attractiveness of southern goods declined, however, northern publishers became less willing to swap for them. The southerners retaliated by reprinting popular books and selling them at bargain prices. The defenders of this practice were numerous, since it promoted competition, lowered prices, and expanded the distribution of books, particularly in Austria, where there was scarcely any legitimate book trade at all.[9] Mercantilist doctrine also favored the pirates, since they reduced the flow of money from one state to another. At the same time, of course, piracy depressed the fees paid to authors and prejudiced the acceptance of works of high quality but limited appeal, which might otherwise have been subsidized by the revenues from a best-seller.

Legitimate publishers, led by Reich and Friedrich Nicolai in Berlin, sought safety in organization. In 1764 they founded the German Book Dealers' Association, which was supposed to protect the financial interests of its members by limiting access to trade fairs. It also encouraged honest publishers to think of themselves not as ordinary businessmen, but as servants of German culture. According to the association, publishers ought to be men of taste and learning, with goals beyond profit. Whereas a common tradesman, indifferent to the character of his goods, responded solely to market forces, a publisher was distinguished by the spiritual nature of his wares. He should therefore feel honor-bound to produce only books of real merit, and to deal only with those who did likewise.[10]

9. Ursula Giese, "Johann Thomas Edler von Trattner: Seine Bedeutung als Buchdrucker, Buchhändler und Herausgeber," *Archiv für Geschichte des Buchwesens* 3 (1961): cols. 1172–73.

10. The best discussion of the *Nachdruckszeitalter* is still Friedrich Kapp and Johann Goldfriedrich, *Geschichte des deutschen Buchhandels* (Leipzig, 1886–1913), 3: 1–246. See also Otto Bettmann, "Die Entstehung buchhändlerischer Berufsideale im Deutschland des XVIII. Jahrhunderts," Ph.D. diss., Leipzig, 1927; and the case study by Bernd Breitenbruch, "Der Karlsruher Buchhändler Christian Gottlieb Schmieder und der Nachdruck in Südwestdeutschland im letzten Viertel des 18. Jahrhunderts," *Archiv für Geschichte des Buchwesens* 9 (1968): cols. 643–732. There is as yet no reliable estimate of the size of the pirate press in Germany. Recent work by Robert Darnton on the publishing industry in the French-speaking parts of Europe (*The Business of Enlightenment: A Publishing History of the "Encyclopédie," 1775–1800* [Cambridge, Mass., 1979] and *The Literary Underground of the Old Regime* [Cambridge, Mass., 1982]) demonstrates the general importance of illicit publishing to the dissemination of ideas. It seems certain that similar conditions prevailed in Germany. A preliminary study by Hans-Joachim Koppitz, "Zur Bibliographie der deutschen Buchproduktion des 18. Jahrhunderts," *Zeitschrift für Bibliothekswesen und Bibliographie* 9 (1962): 21–22, concludes that "virtually all figures attached to German book production in the 18th century, insofar as they are based on trade fair catalogues, are more or less false."

As a commercial lobby, the Book Dealers' Association was partially effective. In 1769 Reich and his colleagues convinced the duke of Saxony to exclude pirated works from his lands, and they subsequently beat back efforts by the so-called *Reichbuchhändler*—those book dealers expelled from, or unable or unwilling to attend, the Leipzig fairs—to set up competing fairs of their own. The association also reorganized the Leipzig fairs on a cash basis.[11] This change eliminated some of the uncertainty attached to barter transactions, making more exact calculations of costs and profits possible. Failing decisive political assistance, however, the struggle remained a difficult one. The association prevented the pirates from organizing on a national scale, but it did not drive them out of business. At the same time, the group's moralizing, and the equally moralistic rejoinders it inspired,[12] further polarized the publishing industry, widening the gap between those who served the life of the mind and those who served the public appetite. In the final analysis, Cotta's letter to Reich was a declaration of allegiance to the first group, which would in fact dominate German publishing during his lifetime.

This decision cannot be said to have come naturally. Tübingen was only an outpost of the legitimate book trade, but it was a capital of the pirate press. The taint extended even to Cotta's family: Christian Gottlieb Cotta, brother of Johann Georg III, had operated a well-known reprinting operation there for years, using the same facilities Johann Cotta had just bought.[13] Continuing in the pirate trade, however, would certainly have condemned Cotta to a provincial existence. Except for textiles, books were the only products manufactured in Germany for which a national market existed. The reformed book fairs offered a means of tapping that market and of lifting oneself over the city wall and into a setting where talent might find some scope. In this respect Cotta's reference to the philosopher Christian Garve in his letter to Reich is suggestive, and not just in relation to Garve's "business principles," which favored the kind of cash marketplace Reich was trying to create in Leipzig. Garve was also one of the first to proclaim the existence of a "new estate" in Germany, composed of scholars, public servants, and businessmen, on which the nation would rely for its prosperity.[14] It was this com-

---

11. Hans Widmann, *Geschichte des Buchhandels vom Altertum bis zur Gegenwart*, 2d rev. ed. (Wiesbaden, 1975), pt. 1, pp. 106–13.

12. Typical of the antipiracy literature are Reich's pamphlet *Der Bücher-Verlag in allen Absichten genauer bestimmt* (Leipzig, 1773), and the more academic analysis by the Göttingen professor Johann Stephan Pütter, *Der Büchernachdruck nach ächten Grundsätzen des Rechts geprüft* (Göttingen, 1774). The most famous defense of piracy was *Der gerechtfertigte Nachdrucker* (1774) by Johann Thomas von Trattner of Vienna; like many similar works, it bore the fictitious imprint "Leipzig: Wiedmanns Erben und Reich."

13. Lohrer, *Cotta*, pp. 37–39. On piracy in Tübingen see Hans Widmann, *Tübingen als Verlagsstadt* (Tübingen, 1971), pp. 144–45; also Werner Siebeck, "Der Tübinger Buchhandel um 1800," *Tübinger Blätter* 19 (1927–28): 4–15.

14. Walker, *German Home Towns*, pp. 119–33.

pany, and not just the company of reputable bookmen, that Cotta was determined to join.

It is hard to know what sort of political predispositions Cotta might have brought to his new profession. Cotta's father had spent his youth as an officer in the Austrian cavalry, so it seems likely that Cotta's earliest loyalties were directed toward the Empire. At the university he must have been exposed to a broader range of ideas, if not by the faculty, then by his fellow students. The 1780s were years of subdued unrest at Tübingen, where, as one writer has put it, "the fair breeze of Enlightenment had begun to play across the fortress of Lutheran orthodoxy." Within Cotta's circle there was much admiration for Rousseau, for the writings of Georg Forster, and for the educational reformers at the University of Göttingen, one of whom, August Schlözer, was also among the most prominent journalists in Europe.[15] Yet it is probably true that Cotta's life acquired a clear political direction only following the outbreak of the French Revolution in 1789. By then his professional course was set, in a way that would color his response to that event.

Respectable publishers of the sort Cotta hoped to become were liable to have broader horizons than other businessmen. They thought of their trade as socially significant, and they prided themselves on their readiness to satisfy the public's craving for knowledge of every kind. At the same time, organized resistance to piracy almost demanded that one should cultivate a certain disdain for the unaffluent, intellectually underprivileged audience the pirates were supposed to serve. One enduring consequence of the struggle against piracy was that, psychologically and morally, German publishers learned to identify with their clients rather than their customers,[16] a habit that limited the book trade's recep-

---

15. Wilhelm Lang, "Die Jugendjahre des Grafen Reinhard," *Württembergische Vierteljahrshefte für Landesgeschichte*, n.s., 2 (1893): 79–90; quote p. 79. Cotta's association with the free-thinking students described by Lang is clear. See Karl Reinhard to Karl Philipp Conz, 12 Dec. 1884, in Wilhelm Lang, "Analekten zur Biographie des Grafen Reinhard," *Württembergische Vierteljahrshefte für Landesgeschichte*, n.s., 17 (1908): 45.

16. The tendency of piracy to undermine this personal bond was resented almost as much as its economic depredations. To some authors, the unending plague of pirates raised the question of whether publishers were really of any use at all. In 1774 Friedrich Klopstock, then at the height of his fame, suggested in a widely read book, *Die deutsche Gelehrtenrepublik* (Hamburg, 1774), that writers and readers constituted a natural "republic of letters" with its own structure, laws, and values, which (by implication) might best protect its interests by means of subscription series and other forms of self-publication, and dispense with publishers altogether. Reich reacted bitterly to Klopstock's proposal, insisting that the defeat of piracy demanded absolute solidarity between authors and publishers (*Zufällige Gedanken eines Buchhändlers über Herrn Klopstocks Anzeige einer gelehrten Republik* [Leipzig, 1774]). He went on to observe that any *Gelehrtenrepublik* would be at the mercy of a parallel *Buchhändlerrepublik*, which could print and sell any book more economically than writers could themselves. Although this last ominous argument would seem unassailable, self-publishing schemes remained a threat to the industry until the end of the century; see Kapp and Goldfriedrich, *Geschichte des Deutschen Buchhandels* 3:116–84.

tivity to the broadening of popular political aspirations. The mission of the publishing community in its own eyes was to promote and defend the national culture, a task that would be made no easier by the deregulation of intellectual life routinely demanded by reformers in other areas. The corporate interest of the book trade ran in the opposite direction: toward persuading Germany's princes to take more seriously their responsibility to protect the nation's intellectual resources. Cultural vitality seemed to depend not on the disappearance of state intervention, but on an improvement in its precision and consistency.[17]

Cotta should not be identified too closely with the mainstream of the book trade. As a Württemberger, he had grown up in a land where political power was less concentrated than elsewhere, with strong traditions of municipal self-government and a living constitution that limited the prince's power to dictate the terms of public life. Nor were Cotta's politics defined primarily by his problems as a businessman. In one respect, however, Cotta's politics bore the stamp of his industry's troubled history: he took it for granted that the nation's political vitality, like its cultural vitality, depended on the husbandry of the state.

The defensive social assumptions of Cotta's profession did not keep him from sympathizing with the French revolutionary program. But those assumptions did influence his sense of how politics was connected to other areas of life. Cotta expected his business to be a unified enterprise, whose scholarly, literary, and political components would complement one another. All the products of the Cotta Verlag were aimed at the same well-educated, well-to-do audience, for whom politics was but one element of personal culture, and not the most important. The French Revolution persuaded Cotta that politics was central to an individual's existence, but it did not shake his faith in the cosmopolitan traditions of the Old Regime.

SCHILLER

Cotta was not a rich man when he decided to try his hand at politics, but he evidently had visions of becoming one. While his ambition would have flabbergasted Philipp Reich, it seems to have come as no surprise to one of Cotta's old schoolmates, a fellow lawyer named Christian Zahn, whom Cotta enlisted as an investor in the fall of 1788.[18] Six months before, Cotta had been so hard up that he had been forced to attend his first Leipzig fair on foot—a difficult trek, but well worth it. Publishing,

---

17. Cf. Franz von Spaun, *Politisches Testament: Ein Beitrag zur Geschichte der Preßfreiheit im allgemeinen und in besonderer Hinsicht auf Bayern* (Erlangen, 1831), pp. 209–51; and Otto Groth, *Die Geschichte der deutschen Zeitungswissenschaft*, pp. 118–20, 131–33.

18. Ernst Rheinwald, "Christian Jacob Zahn, 1765–1830," *Schwäbische Lebensbilder* (Stuttgart, 1941), 2:522–36; and idem, "Johann Friedrich Cotta in seiner Tübinger Verlagsanfängen," *Tübinger Blätter* 44 (1957): 7–9.

he discovered, was "pure speculation," but of an attractive kind, because the risk of loss was limited by the structure of the fairs. As long as he had a decent product to sell, he told Zahn, he could be assured of disposing of a certain number of copies of almost any book. At the same time, because the fairs in effect fixed the prices of books throughout Germany, there was hardly any competition among dealers at the retail level. By planning each edition so that costs did not exceed what was to Cotta's way of thinking a guaranteed return, he figured to do no worse than break even on everything he published. It seemed inherent in the nature of things that, in the long run, his firm could expand "as far as its capital would reach." [19]

Cotta's impressions were not all so rosy. He believed that the arrival of what a later generation would call the cash nexus would make the book trade more profitable; but he also feared its tendency to shift profit toward the retail book trade, to which he seems to have accorded no independent social significance whatever. Immediately following his return, Cotta played the leading role in circulating an open letter to this effect, signed by nineteen southern publishers, asserting that the social and cultural mission of publishing per se should not be sacrificed to financial modernization. [20]

These reservations were not confided to Zahn. But even so, and despite the fact that Cotta's startling indifference to piracy would soon prove to be misplaced, [21] Zahn never had cause to complain about his partner's management of their money. Cotta was as prudent as he seemed, and the results were as expected: slow, steady growth, paced by works of predictable marketability within the scholarly community. Whatever impulses Cotta might have felt to break out of his firm's traditional mold were limited to the publication of some innovative works in law and mathematics, fields in which Cotta felt sure of his expertise.

19. Cotta to Zahn, 28 Nov. 1788, in Lohrer, *Cotta*, pp. 50–51.

20. F. Herm. Meyer, "Der deutsche Buchhandel gegen Ende des 18. und zu Anfang des 19. Jahrhunderts," *Archiv für Geschichte des deutschen Buchhandels* 7 (1882): 199–200. The effect of this letter seems to have been to lend support to those who opposed reform altogether, which was hardly Cotta's intention. But the fears it expressed were characteristic, and well founded. See chapter 5, below.

21. As early as March 1790 Cotta found it necessary to ask the duke of Württemberg for a "general privilege against piracy" (Widmann, *Tübingen als Verlagsstadt*, p. 147). It was the first of many such requests, which became more urgent as Cotta's list became more attractive. This first one, and most of the others, were turned down (Rudolf Krauss, "Zur Geschichte des Nachdrucks und Schutzes der Schillerschen Werke," *Württembergische Vierteljahrshefte für Landesgeschichte*, n.s., 13 [1904]: 187–201; and Joseph Prys, "Das württembergische Nachdruckprivileg für Goethe," *Württembergische Vierteljahrshefte für Landesgeschichte*, n.s., 39 [1933]: 136–60). It was not until 1826 that Cotta achieved any effective protection from pirates, in the form of a federal copyright for Goethe's *Collected Works* (Heinz Frobe, "Die Privilegierung der Ausgabe 'letzter Hand' Goethes sämtlicher Werke," *Archiv für Geschichte des Buchwesens* 2 [1960]: cols. 186–229). The question of piracy is taken up again in chapter 5.

"Industrious, clever, and exceptionally thrifty" were the adjectives that came to the mind of Zahn's wife when she recalled Cotta's conduct during these early years.[22] It must have come as some surprise, then, when Cotta, recently married and still in debt,[23] decided to spend some of his hard-earned profits on a trip to Paris.

Cotta had gone to Paris once before, in 1785, as a way of rounding off his university education. Now it was the summer of 1792, and although his reason for returning to the French capital is unknown, it can be guessed: like a good many other Germans, including his older brother, Friedrich, and his old friend from the university Karl Reinhard, Cotta must have wanted to see the Revolution for himself.[24] The impression it made on him can also be imagined. Gustav Kolb, writing in the *Allgemeine Zeitung* shortly after Cotta's death, claimed that it was during "frequent trips to Paris, before and especially after the outbreak of the Revolution," that Cotta

> grasped what a powerful lever a well-planned and competently edited national newspaper could be in such stormy times. Outside of the Hamburg *Correspondent* and a few Frankfurt papers, Germany had only provincial gazettes, all of which wore court livery or catered to the philistines. [Count Gustav von] Schlabrendorff spoke to Cotta about this in Paris. Georg Forster, [Konrad] Oelsner, and other Germans living there revealed to him what had to be done back home.[25]

Kolb's remarks, which can only have been based on secondhand knowledge, have been generally accepted as fact. They go beyond the surviving evidence—a single letter from Cotta to Reinhard, with whom Cotta stayed during the visit in 1792[26]—but much in them is plausible. Cotta knew the men Kolb mentions and almost certainly shared their political sympathies.[27] Furthermore, the condition of the Parisian press during

---

22. Undated notebook, in Lohrer, *Cotta*, p. 53.

23. Cotta married Wilhelmine Haas, the daughter of a local pastor, on 11 Jan. 1791. It would be another six years, however, before he finished paying his father for the purchase of the firm.

24. See Karl Hammer, "Deutsche Revolutionsreisende in Paris," in *Deutschland und die französische Revolution*, ed. Jürgen Voss, 26–42. *Beiheft* to *Francia* 12 (1983).

25. *AZ*, 16 Jan. 1833 (außerordentliche Beilage).

26. Cotta to Reinhard, 30 Oct. 1792, CA.

27. Schlabrendorff and Reinhard wrote for the *AZ*, as did Oelsner some years later. Cotta's relations with Georg Forster are less clear. No letters between them survive. Forster kept a record of letters sent and received in 1791–92 in which the name *Cotta* appears twice ("Postbuch," in *Werke: Sämtliche Schriften, Tagebücher, Briefe* [East Berlin, 1968–], 16:597–611), a reference, the editors believe, to Johann Cotta. But these entries more likely refer to Johann's brother Friedrich, an important publicist himself (see note 30 below) and, like Forster, a member of the Jacobin Club in Mainz. Forster was not in Paris when Cotta visited there in 1792. On the intellectual atmosphere of this circle of émigrés, see Klaus Deinet, *Konrad Engelbert Oelsner und die Französische Revolution* (Munich and Vienna, 1981); and Hammer, "Deutsche Revolutionsreisende."

the third summer of the Revolution was so changed from what it had been during his first visit seven years before that it is hard to believe the contrast did not inspire some reflections on the "leverage" exerted by public opinion.[28] It is unlikely, however, that Cotta returned home with any definite plan in mind.[29] Almost two years passed, during which the German public's admiration for the Revolution would wane considerably, before Cotta acted on whatever advice his friends may have given—an occasion in which political, literary, and commercial considerations are equally prominent.

The Cotta press and the Cotta literary empire share a common moment of origin: a conversation between Cotta and Friedrich Schiller in the spring of 1794. In judging Cotta's political commitments it is an important coincidence. Whatever inspiration Cotta may have derived from his experience in France, he was not persuaded of the feasibility of simply importing the new French journalism into Germany. Others, men not so different in background from Cotta, were so persuaded. Although the futility of their efforts has led most historians to discount their importance, it is still true that, throughout the 1790s, sporadic attempts were made to create a revolutionary press in Swabia and the Rhineland.[30] Cotta's attitude toward these efforts is not known, but he presumably considered them premature at best. His own plans were more respectable.

Cotta believed that politics, as a practical matter, should not be indulged in by those unfamiliar with its theoretical basis. The first task of

28. In 1785 four political newspapers were published in Paris, counting the *Gazette de France*, an official organ of the foreign ministry. The number appearing in 1792 is uncounted but very large. Between the fall of the Bastille and the imprisonment of the king three years later the Parisian press enjoyed virtually absolute freedom. The fall of the monarchy brought new restrictions on counterrevolutionary and royalist publications, but it was only under the Terror that comprehensive repression reappeared, and only under the Consulate that it became fully effective. See J. Gilchrist and W. J. Murray, eds., *The Press in the French Revolution* (New York, 1971), pp. 1–43; and, more generally, Jeremy D. Popkin, *The Right-Wing Press in France, 1792–1800* (Chapel Hill, 1980).

29. In his letter to Reinhard, Cotta does not mention a newspaper; but he does solicit Reinhard's contributions for a new "Monatsschrift für [das] weibliche Geschlecht," which appeared in 1793, entitled *Flora: Teutschlands Töchtern geweiht* and edited by Zahn.

30. The literature on the German Jacobins is large and growing. Most studies have been aimed at revising the prevailing impression of their insignificance. T.C.W. Blanning, "German Jacobins and the French Revolution," *Historical Journal* 23 (1980): 985-1002, provides a highly skeptical summary, as does Elisabeth Fehrenbach, "Deutschland und die französische Revolution," in *200 Jahre Amerikanische Revolution und moderne Revolutionsforschung,* ed. Hans-Ulrich Wehler, *Geschichte und Gesellschaft,* Sonderheft 2 (Göttingen, 1976), pp. 238–42; see also the symposium volume edited by Otto Büsch and Walter Grab, *Die demokratische Bewegung in Mitteleuropa im ausgehenden 18. und frühen 19. Jahrhundert: Ein Tagungsbericht* (Berlin, 1980). Not by any stretch of the imagination could Johann Cotta be considered a Jacobin; nonetheless, they were part of his political world. See especially Heinrich Scheel, *Süddeutsche Jakobiner: Klassenkämpfe und republikanische Bestrebungen im*

the press, therefore, had to be educational. And political education was, if not strictly an academic undertaking, certainly one in which intellectuals had a great role to play. Cotta's objective was to create the means by which Germany's intellectuals, who were almost as politically isolated as the public they were supposed to instruct, could fulfill their educational responsibility.[31] Schiller seemed the perfect man for the job: a poet and historian of acknowledged brilliance, and a hero of the Revolution too—an honorary citizen of France, whose work had been blessed by the French Assembly. Cotta believed that Schiller shared his desire to unite Germany's best minds in a great public enterprise, and Schiller did. But Schiller did not interpret the educational task facing Germany in political terms. Nor was the great enterprise he had in mind a newspaper.

Cotta and Schiller first met toward the end of 1793, when Schiller was on an extended visit to his native Württemberg. The acquaintance was sought by Cotta, who hoped to obtain the rights to one of the poet's works. Schiller was already bound by honor and friendship to G. J. Göschen of Leipzig, and he had nothing for Cotta at the moment,

---

deutschen Süden Ende des 18. Jahrhunderts (East Berlin, 1962), and the volume of source material edited by Scheel, *Jakobinische Flugschriften aus dem deutschen Süden Ende des 18. Jahrhunderts* (East Berlin, 1965).

One of the most prominent revolutionary journalists was Cotta's older brother Friedrich. From 1788 to 1791 Friedrich Cotta, a lawyer by training, taught at the Höhere Karlsschule in Stuttgart, where he became the only member of the faculty openly to support the French Revolution (Robert Uhland, *Geschichte der Hohen Karlsschule in Stuttgart* [Stuttgart, 1953], pp. 230–31, 250). In the summer of 1791 he gave up his post, accepted French citizenship, and moved to Strasbourg, the center of the French effort to mobilize opinion in the German southwest (see Roland Marx, "Strasbourg, centre de la propagande revolutionnaire vers l'Allemagne," in *Deutschland und die Französische Revolution*, ed. Voss, pp. 16–25). There he produced journals and pamphlets promoting the revolutionary cause as a natural extension of traditional Swabian liberties. Although Friedrich almost lost his life in the Terror, he remained a loyal servant of France until 1810. Thereafter he served briefly as an assistant editor of the *Allgemeine Zeitung* but was forced to leave following a falling out with the editor-in-chief (see note 43, chapter 4), an episode that seems to have ended his career in journalism. A brief account of Friedrich's life is contained in Wilhelm Vollmer, ed., *Briefwechsel zwischen Schiller und Cotta* (Stuttgart, 1876), pp. 187–93; see also Guido Sautter, "Friedrich Cotta, General-Postdirektor der Französischen Republik in Deutschland, 1796," *Historisches Jahrbuch der Görres-Gesellschaft* 37 (1916): 98–121. A bibliography of Friedrich's early work is in Johann Jacob Gradmann, *Das gelehrte Schwaben, oder Lexicon der jetzt lebenden schwäbischen Schriftsteller* (Ravensburg, 1802; reprint Hildesheim, 1979), pp. 88–90.

The Cotta brothers have sometimes been confused, most egregiously by Kolb (*AZ*, 17 Jan. 1833 [außerordentliche Beilage]), who attributed pronounced Bonapartist sympathies to Johann Cotta on the basis of a book by Friedrich (*Das Haus Bonaparte* [Karlsruhe, 1814]). Not much is known about their relationship; they seem to have been cordial to each other, but not especially close.

31. Cotta initially saw his newspaper chiefly in terms of "German scholars" addressing the "great public." See Cotta to Böttiger, 1 Dec. 1797, in Sondermann, *Böttiger*, p. 113.

though he suggested to a friend that, for thirty carolins, he might let Cotta publish his next play.[32] Cotta made it plain, however, that he was ready to pay a good deal more than that to attract an author of Schiller's stature, and that their relationship might go well beyond the publication of a play. When the day came for Cotta to deliver two hundred gulden as a kind of general retainer, he took the opportunity to bring up his newspaper project as well. Schiller, it turned out, had an idea for a special project of his own, at which Göschen had already balked. On May 4 the two men took a walk together along the Neckar River. Of what was said we know nothing, except the outcome: two contracts, one (in Cotta's hand) for a newspaper called the *Allgemeine europäische Staatenzeitung*, the other (in Schiller's hand) for a literary monthly called the *Horen*.[33]

Apart from a natural desire to solidify a promising business relationship, it is hard to say why Schiller agreed to Cotta's half of their bargain. As a young man Schiller had identified social progress with the triumph of freedom over tyranny. In recent years, however, his views had become more pessimistic and more personal. The brutality of the French revolutionaries surprised many Germans who had applauded the ideas of 1789, only to be brought up short by the execution of Louis XVI four years later. It was at just this time, moreover, that Schiller had begun to think more deeply about politics, mainly under the influence of Immanuel Kant, in whose work he had been absorbed since the appearance of the *Critique of Judgment* in 1790.

Kant's theories illuminated the drift of events in France in a way that allowed Schiller's instinctive revulsion at political violence to harden into permanent disillusionment. By the time Schiller met Cotta he had left the ardent radicalism of his early plays behind and was moving toward a more rigorous ethical individualism, which held that the establishment of a just state depended on the moral improvement of its citizens. His enthusiasm for the Revolution had come to depend on how far it served to liberate men from what Kant had called their "self-imposed minority." During his visit to Württemberg Schiller repeatedly voiced private doubts that the institutions thrown up by the Revolution could contribute anything to humanity's moral education—doubts that extended specifically to the revolutionary press, whose complicity in the death of the king repelled him.[34] In May 1794, however, he was still

32. Schiller to J.C.F. Haug, 30 Oct. 1793, in Vollmer, *Briefwechsel*, p. ix.

33. Ibid., pp. 9ff.

34. See Schiller to C. G. Körner, 14 Dec. 1792, 8 Feb. 1793, in *Briefwechsel zwischen Schiller und Körner von 1784 bis zum Tode Schillers* (Stuttgart, 1895), 2:352, 3:23; Karoline von Wolzogen, *Schillers Leben: Verfasst aus Erinnerungen der Familie, seinen eigenen Briefen, und den Nachrichten seines Freundes Körner*, 2d ed. (Stuttgart, 1851), p. 218; also Friedrich Wilhelm von Hoven, *Biographie des Doctor Friedrich Wilhelm von Hoven ... von ihm selbst geschrieben* (Nuremberg, 1840), p. 113.

poised between the enthusiasms of his youth and a new, equally idealistic concern with the perfection of human character. If Cotta's proposal had been cast just a little differently—if it had been for anything but a newspaper—it might have offered a way around this impasse. Instead, it forced Schiller to face his dilemma and make his choice.

Schiller broke his contract for the *Staatenzeitung* for reasons that he would later describe as "very weighty."[35] The reasons he gave at the time—ill health, inexperience, and a disinclination "to associate his name with anything that was not well done"—were not so weighty.[36] But the last reason, at least, is not without interest. Despite his liking for Cotta, Schiller had good reason to suppose that any newspaper would fall into the category of things done badly. As indicated earlier, German newspapers under the Old Regime were a distinctive form of journalism, characterized by a specific focus on contemporary events and a corresponding avoidance of commentary and *raisonnements*. Such a fine distinction between fact and interpretation was only imperfectly maintained in practice. As the eighteenth century neared its close, many newspapers tried to introduce *raisonnements* into their pages by aping more sophisticated periodicals. Yet it is broadly true that political argument was excluded from German newspapers under the Old Regime, because of direct pressure from the authorities and because journalists, governments, and the reading public all agreed that "newspapers report, journals reflect."[37]

The special concern of newspapers, in short, was not political ideas, but political information, which remained the exclusive preserve of the state. A few writers hoped that newspapers might be adapted to aid the downward spreading of useful knowledge; but the ideal newspaper reader was still supposed to be a thinking person, to whom newspapers presented the raw material on which to exercise an already cultivated judgment. This assumption, however, did not prevent newspapers from being regarded (somewhat inconsistently) as vulgar and potentially dangerous: for all their dull factuality, they still seemed to find their way into the hands of the lower classes, who had no need for private political judgments and, as the Revolution had apparently demonstrated to Schiller's satisfaction, were ill equipped to form them.

Schiller had no wish to encourage such tendencies, even within the more congenial format of a quarterly review, which he held out at first as a kind of compromise.[38] Cotta was prepared to negotiate: the

35. Schiller to Cotta, 2 Oct. 1794, in Vollmer, *Briefwechsel*, pp. 23–25.
36. Schiller to Cotta, 19 May 1794, ibid., pp. 7–8.
37. Cf. Groth, *Zeitungswissenschaft*, pp. 29–92; and F. Schneider, *Pressefreiheit und politische Öffentlichkeit*, pp. 55–100.
38. Schiller to Cotta, 19 May and 4 June 1794, in Vollmer, *Briefwechsel*, pp. 7–8, 13–14; cf. Günter Schulz, *Schillers Horen: Politik und Erziehung* (Heidelberg, 1960), p. 9.

contract he offered Schiller said nothing whatever about the format of the *Staatenzeitung*, confining itself to the question of how much Schiller would be paid. At bottom, however, the issue was not the preservation of intellectual appearances, or even class loyalty. Cotta's periodical, whatever its structure, whatever its audience, was manifestly intended to democratize political information, stimulate political debate, and broaden public participation in the life of the state. Its pretensions to excellence notwithstanding, it would remain bound to the constitutional reformism that Schiller now rejected, for himself and, he hoped, for Cotta; Schiller therefore urged Cotta to give up his plan in order to devote himself whole-heartedly to the *Horen*.[39]

The *Horen*, which appeared to much acclaim in January 1795, was no part of the Cotta political press. It was, indeed, antipolitical in its objectives, and hence relevant here mainly as an index of cultural attitudes that Cotta's newspaper would have to overcome. Potential contributors to the *Horen* were warned that the editors were determined "to exclude without exception everything having to do with established religion or political-constitutional issues." To the public Schiller announced that politics, having been corrupted by "an impure, partisan spirit," had become unworthy of consideration by anyone interested in truth and beauty.[40] Cotta was in no position to dispute these views, and he made no attempt to soften the *Horen*'s resolute indifference to the public world. It is hard to say whether such an effort would have improved the journal's chances. At least one editor, Christian Körner, was moved to wonder whether readers so preoccupied with "public and private war" would take an interest in anything that was not political.[41] Schiller, however, preferred to wait and see whether "we move the public, or the public moves us."[42] In the end neither side gave an inch. After three years of steadily declining sales, the *Horen* collapsed under the weight of its own erudition.[43] It has remained ever since a monument to German literary culture and a symbol of the political complacency with which Germany's finest writers faced the end of the Old Regime.

A full appreciation of the *Horen*'s achievements falls outside the scope of this study. Even a summary of its contents strains the limits of acceptable digression: the first three issues alone included most of Schiller's *Letters on the Aesthetic Education of Man*, essays by Goethe, Fichte, Herder,

39. Schiller to Cotta, 14 June 1794, in Vollmer, *Briefwechsel*, pp. 13–15.

40. Schulz, *Schillers Horen*, pp. 10–12.

41. Körner to Schiller, 12 Dec. 1794, ibid., p. 16.

42. Schiller to Göschen, 2 March 1795, ibid.

43. The first issue of the *Horen* was as close to a literary sensation as contemporary conditions allowed, and had to be reprinted twice. About two thousand subscribers had signed up by the end of 1795, but only half were left in 1797. Most issues of the last volume were late. The final number appeared in March 1798, only because Cotta insisted that obligations to subscribers had to be met for financial reasons. See Lohrer, *Cotta*, pp. 55–56.

and Wilhelm von Humboldt, and the first installment of a new translation of Dante's *Inferno* by August Schlegel. In all, forty-seven individuals are known to have contributed to the *Horen* during its brief existence.[44] This, as much as the high quality of its contents, accounts for its monumental aspect: the *Horen* was intended not just to promote serious writing, but to monopolize it, an impulse detectable in Cotta's political ventures as well. Schiller and Cotta both believed that cultural progress demanded concentration of effort, if necessary at the expense of existing journals, particularly C. M. Wieland's *Teutscher Merkur*, which they hoped to drive out of business.[45] Cotta was also hopeful that the *Horen's* contributors should publish only with him—not just their essays and poetry, but their book-length works, too.[46]

For this they were to be well treated, a fact that warrants some examination. Fees for the *Horen's* writers ranged from three to eight louis d'or per sheet—unprecedented sums, calculated to bring an end to what Goethe would call the "literary sansculottism" of German life. "Nowhere in Germany," Goethe wrote in the *Horen's* fifth number,

> is there a center of society, life, and culture, where writers could come together and develop their talents, each in his own field, with a certain unity of manner and aim. Born at scattered points, educated very differently, left for the most part to their own devices and to the impressions made on them by quite different circumstances; . . . repeatedly led astray by a large public without taste, ready to swallow the bad with just as much pleasure as the good; . . . [then] stimulated again by contemporaries working and doing their best alongside them—it is in this way that German writers finally reach manhood, when they are compelled, by concern for their own maintenance and for their families, to look about them in the world outside, where, sick at heart, they must often earn, by means of works that they despise, the income that enables them to produce those things with which their mature minds would like to occupy themselves exclusively.[47]

That the *Horen* should have failed under such circumstances is not surprising. As it was, the effort proved rewarding enough, at least to Cotta. When the time came, he was more than happy to get the *Horen* off his books; but by then it was already becoming clear that Schiller's journal would be the making of his firm. Cotta was the first German publisher to pay his writers at a rate we would consider equitable today,

44. See Vollmer, *Briefwechsel*, pp. 670–81.

45. Cf. Cotta to Schiller, 24 June 1794, and Schiller to Cotta, 10 July 1794, ibid., pp. 15–16.

46. Cotta to Schiller, 15 Sept. 1794, ibid., p. 20.

47. "Litterarischer Sanskullotismus," *Horen* 1, no. 5 (1795): 50; translation based on that of W. H. Bruford, *Culture and Society in Classical Weimar, 1775–1806* (New York, 1962), pp. 317–18.

a practice that endeared him to all those laboring under the difficult conditions Goethe described. Cotta was almost reluctant to profit too conspicuously from their devotion. Particularly in relation to Goethe himself, a towering figure even then, Cotta worried that his solicitude would be interpreted as a craven desire for profit.[48] His fears were misplaced. The *Horen* was, if nothing else, a demonstration of Cotta's willingness to pay a fair price for intellectual excellence. Almost overnight it lifted the Cotta Verlag from complete obscurity into the first rank of European literary houses, creating a fund of goodwill on which Cotta would draw for years to come.

When Schiller first suggested that Cotta might have his next play for thirty carolins, he obviously considered that a handsome sum.[49] Yet by conventional reckoning, thirty carolins would have kept a university student alive for about six months; it represented a third of what Schiller needed to live for a year when he was single, which he no longer was.[50] In light of Schiller's expectations, the sum Cotta actually paid for his next play—2,596 gulden for *Wallenstein*—seems almost philanthropic. In fact it was simply realistic, in that it bore some relation to the time and effort needed to produce what was being sold. Over the course of ten years Cotta paid Schiller about 3,200 gulden annually,[51] a comfortable living, but no better than that of the headmaster of the grammar school in Weimar, and less than Fichte would receive as a professor at the University of Berlin.[52] The same prudent but rational principle determined the fees that Cotta paid the contributors to all his periodicals. Honoraria for the *Horen* were several times higher than was customary,

48. Cotta to Schiller, 3 Oct. 1797, in Vollmer, *Briefwechsel*, pp. 261–62; cf. Dorothea Kuhn, "Schiller und Goethe in ihrer Beziehung zu Johann Friedrich Cotta," in *Goethes und Schillers Literaturpolitik*, ed. Wilfried Barner, et al. (Stuttgart, 1984), pp. 169–85.

49. A full discussion of the value of money in Cotta's day is beyond the competence of the author, and possibly of anyone. There is a useful summary in Widmann, *Der deutsche Buchhandel* 2:423–26. Cotta kept his books in Rhenish gulden, a silver coin whose value was fixed at twenty-four to the Cologne mark—a solid silver bar weighing some 284 grams, against which the weight of precious metal in German coins was reckoned. The Cologne mark had stood between Germany and financial chaos since the days of the Hohenstaufen, and it should have allowed Cotta to turn his silver gulden into the gold carolins that Schiller wanted relatively painlessly. In practice, however, calculations based on the Cologne mark are spuriously precise. Currency exchanges, then as now, were subject to negotiation, as well as to the actual availability of the currency in question. In this case, for instance, Cotta paid Schiller not in carolins but in Saxon thaler, thus saving about fifteen gulden (Cotta to Schiller, 20 March 1794, in Vollmer, *Briefwechsel*, p. 1). Cotta did business all over Germany, in a dozen different currencies. It is no wonder that, on the roster of contributors to Cotta periodicals, bankers are well represented.

50. Kapp and Goldfriedrich, *Geschichte des deutschen Buchhandels* 3:95.

51. Lohrer, *Cotta*, p. 90; cf. Vollmer, *Briefwechsel*, pp. 682–90.

52. Bruford, *Culture and Society*, p. 428; and Peter Paret, *Clausewitz and the State* (New York, 1976), p. 211n.

but still within the confines of profitability. Schiller calculated that, at an average fee of five louis d'or (about 45 gulden) per printer's sheet (eight quarto pages), the *Horen* would break even if it attracted thirteen hundred subscribers. Although he was wrong to consider such an achievement "trivial," it did occur during the journal's first year, and part of the second.[53]

I have said that Cotta went into business intending to get rich. One reason for believing this is that he did in fact get rich: at his death his assets exceeded his liabilities by about one and a half million gulden. Exactly how he did so remains something of a mystery. Many of Cotta's contemporaries assumed that he made his money outside the book trade, having failed to notice that most of his nonpublishing investments came in the last ten years of his life, after his fortune was secure. And many of those ventures, which encompassed real estate, manufacturing, and shipping, seem to have been losers financially.[54] Despite the absence of decisive evidence among the firm's surviving papers, it seems that Cotta's wealth must have been built on books. Schiller's calculations support this conclusion. It is easy to see why some of Cotta's colleagues, especially those like Göschen who lost valuable clients to him, would insist that he must have been buying the services of his authors with money made elsewhere. But he was not. What he was doing was treating his authors not as labor but as what a latter-day captain of industry would call (for want of a better word) "plant." As his early letter to Zahn shows, Cotta grasped at once that the reform of the Leipzig fairs would make publishing a more capital-intensive industry. At the same time, he seems to have guessed that, although pirates would not vanish from the scene, the substitution of cash transactions for barter, together with the continuing expansion of the reading public itself, would reduce the level of uncertainty in the system to a manageable level. The exceptional fees that Cotta paid his best authors were not wages but investments, from which he realized a remarkable long-term return.[55]

Cotta's success as a literary publisher was achieved primarily because

53. Schiller to Cotta, 1 Sept. 1794, in Vollmer, *Briefwechsel*, pp. 18–19.

54. Cf. the correspondence of two unfriendly witnesses, Ludwig Börne to Jeanette Wohl, 21 Jan. and 15 Feb. 1831, in Börne, *Sämtliche Schriften*, ed. Inge Rippmann and Peter Rippmann (Düsseldorf and Darmstadt, 1964–68), 4:1281–83; and Joseph Hormayr to Eduard von Schenk, 17 Dec. 1831, Bayerische Staatsbibliothek, Schenkiana II 7.

55. For further discussion of Cotta's financial practices, see Dorothea Kuhn, ed., *Goethe und Cotta: Briefwechsel, 1797–1832* (Stuttgart, 1979–83), vol. 3, pt. 1, pp. 16–19. One gets some sense of the sheer energy Cotta poured into his business in its early years from his estimate, on the sixteenth anniversary of his entry into the book trade, that he had so far ushered two million sheets (sixteen million quarto pages) of printed matter into the world—this by a firm with but a handful of permanent employees and a physical plant that fit easily into a Tübingen townhouse (Cotta to Böttiger, 28 Nov. 1803, in Sondermann, *Böttiger*, p. 143).

of the combination of psychological, intellectual, and financial acumen demonstrated in the founding of the *Horen*. That success in turn made his political career possible, in two respects. Financially, it allowed him to be patient: only at the end of the 1820s is there any evidence that even the *Allgemeine Zeitung* could turn a profit. Socially, it brought Cotta a kind of prestige to which he was not entitled by birth, and which money could not yet buy. The cultural values of the Cotta Verlag were deemed quite correctly to be his. And these somehow seemed to certify and sanitize the political aspirations of the Cotta press, a more dubious assumption that does credit to the personal sophistication of Germany's rulers, but not to their shrewdness.

Institutionally, however, the Cotta press remained a thing unto itself. Few of Cotta's literary friends shared his sense of political engagement. This was in part an accident of history. The Peace of Basel in 1795 brought a decade of neutrality to northern Germany, where most of Cotta's best authors lived, and created conditions under which, as Leopold von Ranke wrote, "the peaceful development of the German spirit" could proceed apace.[56] In the south, in contrast, the distractions of war and upheaval only became more insistent, a development Cotta could not have escaped. Despite the difference in their circumstances, Cotta continued to hope that if only he could make his political publications sophisticated enough his new friends in Jena and Weimar would come around. The reluctance of Schiller and the others to support him politically remained puzzling, the more so since, as will be seen, Cotta shared some of Schiller's reservations about the moral consequences of political struggle.

What he did not share was Schiller's fear that, in a revolutionary setting, politics was inevitably corrupting. Cotta's desire to exert political influence made Schiller wary, in good part because it was so obviously inspired by the success of the French press. But Cotta believed he could achieve significant results without giving in to the "impure partisan spirit" that Schiller despised or forgoing the appeal to personal culture that would bring him such striking success in the rest of his business. Whatever else the *Staatenzeitung* might have become, as a companion to the *Horen* it would have been devoted not to the mobilization of public opinion but to the consolidation of authoritative political judgments. And, like the *Horen*, the *Staatenzeitung* would have derived its authority not from the public, or even from the state, but from the stature of its contributors and the intelligence of its arguments. Schiller believed the Revolution had torn authority and intelligence apart, leaving the first in the hands of the princes or the mob and the second in the care of a few

56. Leopold von Ranke, *Hardenberg und die Geschichte des preussischen Staates von 1793–1813*, 2d ed. (Leipzig, 1879–81), 1:286.

men like himself. Cotta believed the times demanded that intelligence and authority be brought together, and that it was the responsibility of the press to do so. Schiller's resignation was a setback, but it was not the end.

POSSELT

Schiller was certainly Cotta's first choice to head up his newspaper, but he was not the first with whom he discussed the idea. By strict reckoning, the project is first mentioned in Cotta's correspondence with a very different sort of man named Ernst Posselt, a well-known political writer in the neighboring principality of Baden.[57] Posselt's politics were those of the "German Girondins" whose circle Cotta frequented in Paris in 1792, and, like them, he was concerned about the banality of political journalism in his homeland. Early in 1794 he and Cotta began corresponding about producing a history of the war between France and the Empire. In describing his plans it occurred to Posselt that, while waiting for the war to end, Cotta might also be interested in publishing a new kind of newspaper, the uncommon seriousness of which would be expressed by printing it in Latin, "in which one can say so much that cannot be said to the *profanum vulgus* in German." It was apparently this chilling suggestion, altogether characteristic of a troubled time, that inspired Cotta to take up the matter with Schiller.[58] But he also wrote back to Posselt, asking him to elaborate his ideas, which turned out to be similar to Cotta's. "I think," Posselt replied,

> that there has never been a time richer in news, or hungrier for it, than our own; that we are entirely lacking in serious [*raisonierte*] newspapers ... ; and that, for these and other reasons, a properly produced newspaper would be an exceptionally interesting and rewarding undertaking. This is so obvious that I have already been approached about it by the owners of some existing newspapers. ...
>
> I would not undertake such a project, however, unless it could be done on a scale commensurate with its importance. It would have to be, in effect, the main business of both the editor and the publisher. In this case, under this condition, I would be glad to hear the details of your proposal.

The main detail, that Schiller would lead the venture, left Posselt "surprised," and not pleasantly. He had pictured himself as editor-in-chief,

---

57. See Emil Vierneisel, "Ernst Ludwig Posselt, 1763–1804," *Zeitschrift für die Geschichte des Oberrheins*, n.s., 49 (1936): 243–71; 51 (1938): 89–126; 52 (1939): 444–99.

58. Posselt wrote Cotta on 9 April 1794 (Maria Fehling and Herbert Schiller, eds., *Briefe an Cotta* [Stuttgart and Berlin, 1925–34], 1:400). Cotta wrote Schiller on the eleventh, the day Posselt's letter arrived (the date of receipt is on the back of Posselt's letter, CA). Posselt had recently written a pamphlet entitled *Bellum populi Galici adversus hungaricae Borusciaeque eorumque socios* (Göttingen, 1793), which may account for his interest in publishing in Latin. This pamphlet was republished in German the following year.

and felt he had to insist that his collaboration with Schiller be on absolutely equal terms.[59] By the time he had composed this response, however, Schiller had already withdrawn, sparing Cotta the embarrassment of sending Posselt a copy of the *Staatenzeitung* contract, which called for one editor and two assistants, and leaving Posselt in charge.

Cotta's parallel negotiations with Schiller and Posselt strengthen the impression that he came to the newspaper business hoping to integrate cultural and political values. It also reflects his confidence in his ability to reconcile contrasting personalities. As compared to Schiller's austere and reflective nature, Posselt was given to grandiloquence in expression and to pathos in his personal life. A friend recalled him as short and stout, with a flushed face and fiery eyes, who favored attire that combined court dress with elements of the famous costume in which young Werther died. His hair was done in what he believed to be the French style—curled, powdered, and worn in a pigtail—and topped by a three-cornered hat tied under his chin with a ribbon.[60] He possessed a natural if disconcerting warmth and adopted the familiar form of address even with those he knew only slightly.[61]

Posselt was an enthusiast, for causes and individuals alike. Since 1792 he had been living with a woman everyone regarded as his social and intellectual inferior and whom he declined to marry until years later, a decision that set him outside the polite society his position as secretary to the margrave of Baden entitled him to enter. In 1796 he became infatuated, even more disastrously, with the French general Jean Victor Moreau, whom Posselt met during one of the general's campaigns in Germany. Moreau would become a great figure to other Germans who had hailed the Revolution in arms, only to discover that the dashing General Bonaparte was less sympathetic as emperor than he had been as a soldier of the republic. But few of Moreau's admirers responded to his arrest for sedition in 1804 as Posselt did, by throwing himself from a third-floor window, leaving a wife and three children to mourn him.[62]

Despite the extravagance of his character, Posselt was an acute and accomplished writer. As a young man he had attended the University of Göttingen, the main center for professional historical studies in Germany. The Göttingen historians were pioneers in the critical use of documents and in the development of an individualizing view of the

59. Posselt to Cotta, 18 June 1794, ibid., pp. 402–4.

60. Eduard Heyck, *Die Allgemeine Zeitung, 1798–1898: Beiträge zur Geschichte der deutschen Presse* (Munich, 1898), p. 10.

61. See Posselt to Cotta, 4 Sept. 1799, CA.

62. Cf. Eleonore Posselt to Cotta, 21 June 1804, in Fehling and Schiller, *Briefe an Cotta* 1:434; and Cotta to Schiller, 19 June 1804, in Vollmer, *Briefwechsel*, pp. 516–17. Friedrich Buchholz to Cotta, 15 Dec. 1805, CA, implies that Cotta also found Moreau an attractive figure.

past.[63] They were programmatic empiricists, who taught their students to understand other societies in their own terms, as products of complex historical processes rather than as examples of an eternal typology. They also recognized that the same process of accretion and change that operated elsewhere and in the past continued to operate in Germany in the present. They thus became the leading practitioners of a field that as yet had no name. "Contemporary history" is linguistically an invention of the revolutionary era, but it already existed at Göttingen a decade before. Courses like Gottfried Achenwall's *Statistik* (then a branch of political economy) and August Schlözer's *Zeitungscollege* attracted students from all over, who came to Göttingen looking for a usable past. Posselt came in 1780. By the time he left three years later he had learned, conventionally enough, to practice law and love the ancients. He had also learned to think about contemporary events according to a historical method he believed was scientifically accurate and politically relevant, and to write about them in a compelling way.

Posselt's teachers were vigorous in pursuing their educational objectives beyond the confines of the university, through handbooks and reference works aimed at the average reader and by means of periodicals devoted to historical and political themes. The collectively edited Göttingen *Gelehrte Anzeiger* (1753–70), Johann Gatterer's *Historisches Journal* (1772–81), and Schlözer's *Briefwechsel* (1774–82) and *Stats-Anzeigen* (1782–93) helped define a new style of journalism, characterized by a concern for recent political, military, and diplomatic events, which were analyzed by means of historical analogies and examples. Periodicals of this kind, so-called historico-political *Zeitschriften*, multiplied rapidly during the last decade of the eighteenth century, when they became one of the chief means by which the German public sought to understand the French Revolution.[64]

One might imagine that the term *historico-political* had no mean-

63. The Göttingen historians are discussed in detail in Peter Hans Reill, *The German Enlightenment and the Rise of Historicism* (Berkeley and Los Angeles, 1975). On Schlözer, the dominant figure in the group, see Friederike Fürst, *August Ludwig Schlözer: Ein deutscher Aufklärer im 18. Jahrhundert* (Heidelberg, 1928), esp. pp. 71–91.

64. Over eighty historico-political *Zeitschriften* were founded between 1791 and 1800, as compared to nineteen during the previous decade (Joachim Kirchner, *Das deutsche Zeitschriftenwesen: Seine Geschichte und seine Probleme* (Wiesbaden, 1958–62), 1:213–22; cf. idem, *Die Grundlagen des deutschen Zeitschriftenwesens* 2:332–33). The fullest discussion is Ingeborg Salzbrunn, "Studien zum deutschen historischen Zeitschriftenwesen von der Göttinger Aufklärung bis zur Herausgabe der 'Historischen Zeitschrift' (1859)," Ph.D. diss., Münster, 1968. This growth was not shared by books on historical subjects, whose market share remained flat through the last half of the eighteenth century (Kiesel and Münch, *Gesellschaft und Literatur im 18. Jahrhundert*, pp. 201–2). Clearly the "political" dimension of the "historico-political" genre, expressed in part by the periodicity of its institutions, was crucial to attract and hold the public's interest.

ing, except as a way of dressing up an otherwise suspect interest in politics. In practice, however, the historicization of political discussion decisively favored the defense of local institutions against encroachment by the centralized state. Historico-political *Zeitschriften* almost always displayed an underlying sympathy for constitutional government, and a corresponding confidence in the reforming capacity of the *Ständestaat*, whose historically conditioned character recommended it to those who found absolutism, and the natural-law tradition to which its proponents looked for justification, dangerously rationalistic and abstract. Historico-political *Zeitschriften* presented themselves as history's minions, preparing the ground for future progress by exposing the roots of existing institutions so the public and the authorities could decide which were dead-wood—serfdom, censorship, and the excesses of court life were often mentioned—and which were healthy plants. The genre as a whole was thus intrinsically reformist in spirit, reform being the only rational response to the reality of historical change.

All these values were evident in Posselt's early works, which were numerous. By the time he met Cotta he had acquired a well-deserved reputation as a journalist and historian.[65] Posselt saw the Holy Roman Empire as a kind of limited monarchy, in which the Treaty of Westphalia held a place analogous to that of the English Magna Carta. This was the crux of an early book on the League of Princes, which he defended as an attempt to modernize the imperial constitution. Although the league today appears to be a transparent Prussian scheme to isolate Austria, Posselt's was an unexceptional view at the time.[66] It was less unexceptional, however, that Posselt's admiration for the league and its instigator, Frederick the Great, should have led him, two years later, to embrace the French Revolution. Here he parted company with most other writers of the historico-political sort, who tended to oppose the Revolution, despite its liberalizing aspects, as an ill-advised breach with the past.[67] To Posselt, however, the rising of the French was a fulfillment of their national his-

---

65. Posselt had edited (and written most of) two quarterly reviews, the *Wissenschaftliche Magazin für Aufklärung* (1785–88) and the *Archiv für ältere und neuere, vorzüglich Teutsche Geschichte, Staatsklugheit, und Erdkunde* (1790–92), and begun a series of *Taschenbücher für die neueste Geschichte* that would continue to appear until 1800. He had also written three books: an essay, *Ueber die Reden der grossen Römer in den Werken ihrer Geschichtsschreiber* (1786); *Die Geschichte der deutschen Fürstenvereine* (1787); and the two-volume *Geschichte der deutschen Stände* (1789–90).

66. Gagliardo, *Reich and Nation*, pp. 80–82.

67. Salzbrunn, "Studien zum deutschen historischen Zeitschriftenwesen," p. 481; cf. Jörn Garber, "Geschichtsphilosophie und Revolution: Spätaufklärerische Geschichtstheorien im Einflussfeld der Französischen Revolution," in *Deutschland und die Französische Revolution*, ed. Voss, pp. 168–93. On the impact of the Revolution on Göttingen and Hanover generally, see Carl Haase, "Obrigkeit und öffentliche Meinung in Kurhannover, 1789–1803," *Niedersächsisches Jahrbuch für Landesgeschichte* 39 (1967): 192–294.

tory, which had previously been characterized by an unnatural devotion to the person of the monarch. For a century or more France had been, proverbially, an absolute monarchy tempered by songs. Posselt believed the spell had now been broken. Louis XVI had learned the lesson Frederick the Great had tried to teach Germany and accepted a constitution and a free citizenry as the basis for his rule. Posselt therefore urged his readers to turn their eyes to "the land of freedom across the Rhine," there to glimpse a new dawn.[68]

Posselt never suffered Schiller's disillusionment, but as his discussions with Cotta became more detailed it emerged that he did share Schiller's doubts about whether the moment was just right to publish a newspaper. Although the prospect of placing his work before a larger audience excited him, his fear that ordinary readers would misunderstand him, and that the attempt might invite persecution, continued to nag.[69] In August he and Cotta compromised: they would publish a newspaper called the *Europäische Zeitung*, to appear three times a week, and, in addition, a supplementary monthly journal that would raise the tone of the whole venture by providing "an overview of the political situation in Europe."[70] The ink was hardly dry on their agreement, however, before the newspaper part of it was in logistical trouble. Posselt, who lived in Gernsbach, Baden, felt financially unable to give up his government job, which meant the paper would have to be printed in Rastatt, the nearest town with appropriate facilities.[71] Badenese law required that the manuscripts for every issue be sent to Karlsruhe for censorship—a five-hour journey on a dry day, and a major impediment to frequent publication. Posselt's plea for an exemption was blocked by protests from a local publisher,[72] leaving him to conclude that "there is nothing left but [to find] another place to publish the newspaper, or the journal. I must say," he added,

I'm very much for the latter idea. I think a really good start can be made that way. The newspaper will come along later, of course, since everyone can see all too clearly how close we are to the day when we Germans will also be free to publish all types of literary matter, if only by way of reaction [to the French]. You will recall what a predilection the people in Jena had for the idea of a journal. Think about it once more![73]

68. Ernst Posselt, "An die Nation," *Archiv für ältere . . . Geschichte* 1 (1790): 1–13.

69. Posselt to Cotta, 2 August 1794, in Fehling and Schiller, *Briefe an Cotta* 1:404.

70. Contract dated 28 August 1794, CA; cf. Vollmer, *Briefwechsel*, pp. 606–7.

71. Cotta's arrangements with Posselt were less generous than those he offered to Schiller. Under his original contract Schiller would have received two thousand gulden annually, plus another fifteen hundred gulden if subscriptions exceeded six thousand. Posselt was to be paid for what he wrote, at the standard rate of twelve gulden per sheet, plus half the profits from sales beyond one thousand subscriptions. In the end Posselt made more than he would have under Schiller's contract, but the money was not guaranteed.

72. Posselt to Cotta, 19 Sept. 1794, CA.

73. Posselt to Cotta, 12 Oct. 1794, in Fehling and Schiller, *Briefe an Cotta* 1:405.

A month before, Cotta had been ready to give up the whole project.[74] Now he settled for what he could get. Schiller's cautious view triumphed despite his withdrawal, and Posselt's supplement became a monthly journal in its own right, appearing in Tübingen in January 1795 under the title *Europäische Annalen*.

The *Annalen* was Cotta's first political publication, and it was in most respects typical of the historico-political tradition from which it emerged. Its appearance helped fill the gap created by the suppression two years before of August Schlözer's famous *Stats-Anzeigen*—a sinister development that probably contributed to Posselt's nervousness about the censors. Like Schlözer, Posselt was animated by a desire to make history "the textbook of life."[75] Like the *Stats-Anzeigen*, the *Annalen* would discuss "whatever occurred in Europe of historical importance," always adhering to "the armed neutrality of the truth." Posselt, however, did not possess his old teacher's resources, or his circumspection. Schlözer had relied heavily on outside contributors to fill his pages, a feature that had distinguished his journal from others like it.[76] Posselt had to work mainly from other periodicals, whose contents he synthesized himself. In the beginning virtually everything in the *Annalen* was Posselt's work.[77] This was almost inevitable. To Schlözer the historian was a schoolmaster; to Posselt he was an artist, a dramatist, whose job was not just to instruct, but "to inspire, to sparkle, to move the reader to wonder and horror." Moreover, Posselt had not the slightest doubt about the nature of the drama unfolding in Europe: a struggle between republicanism and despotism, which would be remembered alongside Noah's flood and the fall of Rome as a turning point in history, and about which "only a child was entitled to remain ignorant."

Cotta had imagined that his journal would have a more conventional, encyclopedic format, and he wrote Posselt after the first issue warning him not to become preoccupied with France and urging that the affairs of the major states be regularly reviewed. Posselt offered to include something along this line in the second number but complained, tellingly enough, that it seemed to him "a bit like a peep show to parade the doings of all the realms of Europe one after another in such a small space."[78] Despite their disagreements, however, Cotta had reason to be

74. Posselt to Cotta, 19 Sept. 1794, CA.

75. This and the other quotations in this paragraph are from Posselt's introductory essay, *Europäische Annalen* 1 (1795): 1–14.

76. Renate Zelger, "Der historisch-politischer Briefwechsel und die Staatsanzeigen August Ludwig von Schlözer als Zeitschrift und Zeitbild," Ph.D. diss., Munich, 1953, pp. 76–78.

77. In December 1795 Posselt was paid the entire honorarium for the preceding quarter. See Posselt to Cotta, 31 Dec. 1795, CA.

78. Posselt to Cotta, 2 Feb. 1795, in Fehling and Schiller, *Briefe an Cotta* 1:406–7.

satisfied with Posselt's performance. Like the *Horen*, the *Annalen* found about two thousand subscribers by the end of its first year.[79] Unlike the *Horen*, the *Annalen* was a modest venture financially. A year's subscription cost four gulden, about half the price of Schiller's journal, and its contributors, whose numbers increased with time, were paid at the rate of twelve gulden per sheet. By 1800 Posselt's journal was reaching three thousand subscribers, fewer than Schlözer's journal in its best years, but better than Wieland's *Merkur*, and far above the 750 sales Cotta needed to break even.[80] Cotta knew where the credit for this success lay, and at the end of the first year he agreed to give his editor a larger share of the profits.[81]

Despite its polemical subtext, the *Annalen* was a journal of ideas, in which factual reporting was not a consideration.[82] "The miserable tone of a newspaper," Posselt was pleased to note, was absent.[83] But so too was the sense of immediacy and involvement that newspapers, in theory, could convey to their readers. Although this theory was as yet untested in Germany, it was at least in the air: even Posselt had admitted, before his attack of cold feet, that several publishers besides Cotta were interested in producing a "raisonierte Zeitung." At the end of 1795 this concept received its first clear articulation, in the form of a book called *Ueber Zeitungen* by the Hanoverian diplomat Joachim von Schwarzkopf.

Like Posselt, Schwarzkopf was a product of the *Staatswissenschaftliche Fakultät* at Göttingen, and his book was essentially an attempt to extend the educational values of the historico-political tradition to newspapers. The originators of that tradition had dismissed newspapers as superficial and corrupting, and, in their traditional form, Schwarzkopf did too. But Schwarzkopf believed their ascendancy was inevitable, thanks to the growth of the literate public, which Schwarzkopf was among the first to visualize not as a hypothetical "educated reader" but as a collectivity. This collective opinion required careful cultivation if it was to rise above the mob spirit into which it always threatened to subside. For this purpose previous practices were irrelevant: it was no longer enough to paste together a miscellany of extracts with no attention to their reliability or significance. In the past, newspapers had been defined by their contents—political news of a trivial sort. In the future they would be defined

---

79. Cotta to Posselt, 13 Jan. 1796, CA.

80. The subscription figure for the *Annalen* is from Salzbrunn, "Studien zum deutschen historischen Zeitschriftenwesen," p. 494. The *Stats-Anzeigen* had forty-four hundred subscribers at its peak. The *Merkur* never sold more than twenty-five hundred copies (Reill, *German Enlightenment*, p. 255).

81. Posselt to Cotta, 31 Dec. 1795, and Cotta to Posselt, 13 Jan. 1796, CA.

82. Posselt to Cotta, 1 March 1795, CA.

83. Posselt to Cotta, 25 Jan. 1795, CA.

by the universality of their audience and by the "currency" and "periodicity" of their format.[84]

Schwarzkopf believed a newspaper press could flourish without jeopardizing established legal and intellectual hierarchies. *Zeitungen*, like *Zeitschriften*, could become socially specialized as their audience grew. There could be newspapers for peasants, for women, for young people, and so on, which could instill feelings of political involvement in their readers and insure that those feelings were directed toward the government.[85] At the apex of his system stood so-called *Gelehrtezeitungen* ("scholarly" newspapers). By virtue of their intellectual sophistication, *Gelehrtezeitungen* could be left unmolested by the censors; by virtue of their price, which Schwarzkopf thought should be artificially elevated, they could be kept out of the hands of common folk.[86] They could therefore function freely as vehicles of political communication among the educated and as bridges between the rulers and the ruled.

Although it is inconceivable that Cotta did not know Schwarzkopf's work—Schwarzkopf wrote for the *Annalen*, and he mentions Posselt in his book[87]—his reaction to it is unrecorded. But it is probably safe to assume that whatever pleasure Cotta may have taken in seeing some of his own efforts mirrored in print must have been accompanied by an uneasy feeling that such innovations were more easily described than accomplished. "The newspaper idea," Posselt wrote in June 1795, "stands like a colossus before my soul."[88] Yet despite the personal freedom afforded by a state pension a few months later, he continued to fight shy of Cotta's plans. It would be almost two years before Cotta got Posselt's signature on a contract to edit a newspaper, to begin in April 1797.[89] Even then Posselt remained uncertain that the times were truly auspicious. "Everything," he feared, depended on "whether our German public has sufficient intelligence. If so, then we don't intend to disappoint them. If not, then I would rather not begin at all." In any case, he did not want to proceed unless he could be "assured of a brilliant success."[90]

The April deadline therefore passed unnoticed, to the relief of Cotta's

---

84. Joachim von Schwarzkopf, *Ueber Zeitungen: Ein Beytrag zur Staatswissenschaft* (Frankfurt am Main, 1795), pp. 68–100. This book inaugurated the academic study of journalism in Germany; it is thoroughly discussed in Groth, *Zeitungswissenschaft*, pp. 60–81.

85. Schwarzkopf, *Ueber Zeitungen*, pp. 122–23.

86. Ibid., pp. 116–21.

87. See Posselt to Cotta, 21 July, 1 Oct. 1795, CA. Schwarzkopf mentions Posselt in the final chapter, "Prospects for Improvement," (pp. 125ff.), as one of several writers capable of editing the new kind of newspaper Schwarzkopf called for.

88. Posselt to Cotta, 10 Jan. 1795, in Fehling and Schiller, *Briefe an Cotta* 1:409.

89. Contract dated 13 Jan. 1797, summarized in Vollmer, *Briefwechsel*, p. 607.

90. Posselt to Cotta, 11 March 1797, CA.

partner, Zahn, who had lost whatever stomach he once possessed for Cotta's project. Although Zahn had supported the expansion of the Cotta Verlag into literary publishing three years before, his political inclinations were traditional and unadventurous. Cotta, however, was now free of debt and no longer needed the financial backing of his old friend. At the beginning of October Zahn left the firm—"a great victory," Cotta wrote to Schiller.[91] Another victory followed a few weeks later, when an advertisement was distributed offering subscriptions to a newspaper called *Neueste Weltkunde*. Its composition had been, for Posselt, "most disagreeable work,"[92] but it had at last been done, and on January 1, 1798, the *Weltkunde*'s reluctant editor addressed the public for the first time, in language so urgent as to belie his private apprehensions.

Introduction

Suppose, suddenly, the first scene of creation is renewed. The Alps from Mont Blanc to Istria fall into the abyss. England is flung from the sea. The headwaters of the Rhine and Danube become choked with earth. Africa is again joined to Spain by an eruption of land. Such a revolution in the physical world would yield no greater or more decisive transformation in the face of Europe than the revolution we have witnessed since 1789 has wrought in Europe's politics.

The Asiatic colossus has advanced to the Vistula. Warsaw is the seat of a Prussian government. Austria is a sea power through the acquisition of Venice. The Dutch *Stadtholder* is bound to the Utrecht Union. There is a new republic on the Po, which figures to be among the powers of Europe. There is no more aristocracy in Genoa; no Savoy, no Nice for the king of Sardinia; no Belgium, no Milan, no Mantua for Austria. And, most menacing—no left bank of the Rhine for Germany. Thus the state on whose ancient constitution the equilibrium of Europe seemed to rest is threatened with complete destruction.

The cause of this unparalleled upheaval was in itself insignificant. The people of France, having surpassed all others in their loyalty to their king, "suddenly decided, as if in a frenzy, to become the freest people on God's earth." In doing so, however, they unleashed a new and dangerous power—the power of principle—"against which all the kings of Europe bring arms in vain."

"Principles will not be destroyed by bayonets," say their philosophers. "The more enemies, the more triumphs," cry their brave young citizens, as they rush from their plows to the colors. And so it has been! The whole world would force them to return all power to their king, whom they left with such authority as seemed compatible with their freedom. Instead, with an-

91. Cotta to Schiller, 3 Oct. 1797, in Vollmer, *Briefwechsel*, pp. 261–62.
92. Posselt to Cotta, 17 Oct. 1797, CA.

gered pride, they proclaim a republic. France a republic! How the worldly-wise diplomats laughed at this paradox! It seemed to them a soap bubble, a hallucination. And yet this new republic suits the old Europe so little that one of two things must follow: the republic must be destroyed, or Europe must be transformed.

It would seem to be, on its face, a situation in which no compromise was possible. Two systems, "as antagonistic as fire and water," had constituted themselves, one in the north, the other in the south.

The first has been demonstrated in Poland, the other in France. One is dangerous to peoples, the other, in a much higher degree, to monarchs. The first is fixed in the minds of a few men. The second has captured the imaginations of millions, whose numbers can be swelled so easily with new millions. For, just as one can work infinitely more upon the mind than upon the body, so a contagion (in the good as in the evil sense) is spread incomparably more rapidly in the moral world than in the physical. One can draw up a cordon against the latter, impose quarantines, etc. But no wall of bayonets will be strong enough to bar the way to opinions.

The outcome of such an uneven struggle would appear to be preordained. And Posselt, despite his all-too-visible effort to be fair, goes on to suggest that, so far at least, it had been.

The French fought for principles. They fought as a whole people, against mere armies. The result was as it must be in such cases. No attack, even by a host of enemies, simultaneously, on all borders; no want of skill by their own troops; no incompetence on the part of their generals; no conspiracy; no civil war could prevail against the enthusiasm of a nation that believed itself to be fighting for a great and noble cause.

The Revolution in arms was thus utterly unlike "the sinister schemes of a Philip, a Ferdinand, or a Louis," against whom the cabinets of Europe had enjoyed the support of "all mankind." On the contrary, the heart of the new system was its "seductive popularity." The allies now faced forty million men, in a dozen states from the Rhineland to the Levant, who had been united as if under a single flag by "the magic formula: Freedom and Equality." The future would be fearful.

The French fought for principles. The allies, by inference, fought to preserve their power. The *Weltkunde*, however, would fight in the most unlikely cause of all: tolerance. The fate of Europe, Posselt concluded, was "no longer a matter of cabinet diplomacy."

Each of us is directly and essentially involved. Each of us, if he is a friend of humanity, must work within the sphere in which fate has set him, not in futile and impotent opposition to the spirit of the age, but to give it a direction that does not culminate in revolution—the ultimate embodiment of every type of misfortune. Everyone must try to bring himself and others to realize that the happiness or misery of the individual is determined by the excellent administration of a state; that it is better to live under the most unrestrained autocracy, if it is well governed, than under a republic fashioned by a committee of Platos and Montesquieus, if it is ruled by passion and vice; . . . that nothing is perfect for all times and in all places; that the Good that is certain though flawed is preferable to the New that is lustrous but untested; that a world of quarreling republics would be no better than a world of quarreling philosophers; and, finally, that mankind will only be happy when all constitutions exist side by side, and when each government will have the wise and noble ambition to govern its own people best.

The *Neueste Weltkunde* will be written in this spirit.

There will be occasion in the next chapter to consider the political objectives of Cotta's newspaper more fully. Having gotten to the end of the first issue, however, any reader would have to be forgiven for wondering whether, in a world full of what Posselt himself called "extremes, paradoxes, and singularities," the *Weltkunde*'s spirit could protect it for long.

TWO

The Politics of Impartiality

The events of the last decade of the eighteenth century are no less challenging and significant for the philosopher than for the man of the world. . . . A law of Solon the Wise condemned the citizen who did not choose a party in an uprising. If there has ever been a time when such a law could be applied, it is the present, when the whole fate of mankind lies in the balance and when, so it seems, no one can remain neutral without displaying culpable indifference toward those things that men hold most sacred.
Friedrich Schiller to Friedrich von Augustenberg, July 13, 1793

Cotta decided to go into political publishing when he was thirty years old, after seven years of determined effort to put his firm on a sound financial footing and at least one thought-provoking trip to Paris, the most politically exciting place in the world. Because he was a publisher, rather than a writer or even an editor, our understanding of his intentions must be inferred largely from the arrangements he made to produce and market his publications and to defend them from public criticism and official abuse. This chapter will consider those arrangements as they pertain to the appearance and almost immediate disappearance of the *Neueste Weltkunde*, the first political venture in which Cotta's personal values and objectives can be seen to predominate and, as precursor to the *Allgemeine Zeitung*, among the most important he would ever undertake. Its brief history exposed Cotta to organizational and philosophical dilemmas he would face again and again over the next forty years, and to a kind of personal risk he had not yet encountered.

Throughout the history of the Cotta press the question of risk is never far from the surface. Cotta's business, as I have said, was not politics; but inevitably the two were closely linked. Cotta was not born into the ruling class. The only way he could satisfy his political ambition was to pursue it in the course of making a living. His public conduct was always influenced by commercial considerations, at least to the extent that his political periodicals could not be allowed to place the rest of his livelihood in jeopardy. The Revolution had lent politics a new urgency and had elevated political writing to the margins of respectability, but it also made journalism a more perilous enterprise, in which even the most detached observer could be overtaken by events. To some writers of the next generation, for whom the revolutionary era was at most a childhood memory, the Cotta Verlag was self-evidently a hostage to fortune, and the very fact of Cotta's political survival was a sign of servility. There is no need to prejudge this question. It is enough to note that, in the early stages of Cotta's career at least, the personal stakes were high. For him the price of failure would not be a dignified retreat to some country estate, but penury and humiliation. It did not take long for this lesson to be brought home in the clearest possible way.

TECHNICALITIES

Like the *Europäische Annalen* before it, Cotta's *Weltkunde* attracted a respectable following: fourteen hundred subscriptions were sold before the first issue appeared, and an extra six hundred copies were printed for sale as sets by book dealers.[1] Who these fourteen hundred subscribers were is a mystery. Certainly the *Weltkunde*'s readership extended beyond the circle of "historians and statesmen" to whom its prospectus was addressed.[2] Some customers were presumably readers of the *Annalen*, to which the *Weltkunde* was linked in its advertising. Many were probably groups or institutions—government offices, libraries, reading societies, coffeehouses, and so on—where a single issue would pass through many hands.[3] Only one thing is certain: whoever may have read the *Weltkunde*, those who bought it were well off. A year's subscription cost eighteen gulden, a staggering figure, equivalent to the annual rent on two acres of land.

Cotta had hoped for something cheaper. His original contract with Schiller had anticipated sales on the order of six thousand subscriptions per year, and his first agreement with Posselt specified a selling price of four gulden, comparable to local papers of inferior quality. Posselt had taken it for granted that a publication aimed at a national audience would attract a large following.[4] In this respect, however, the synthetic character of the *Weltkunde* worked to its disadvantage. It was supposed to combine the best features of sophisticated and popular publications; but it combined the worst features too: high editorial costs and high distribution costs, which together made the *Weltkunde* the most expensive newspaper in Germany.[5]

1. Cotta to Schiller, 20 Jan. 1798, in Vollmer, *Briefwechsel*, p. 284.
2. The prospectus is reprinted ibid., pp. 608–13.
3. Conventional wisdom suggests that every issue of a newspaper in this period found about ten readers (Welke, "Gemeinsame Lektüre," pp. 30–31). This is speculation, but not unreasonable. If anything it is on the low side, since, as Welke shows in detail, newspapers were commonly read aloud in groups.
4. Posselt to Cotta, 2 Aug. 1794, in Fehling and Schiller, *Briefe an Cotta* 1:404.
5. H. F. Meyer, "Zeitungspreise in Deutschland im 19. Jahrhundert und ihre gesellschaftliche Bedeutung," Ph.D. diss., Münster, 1967, pp. 118–20.

Schiller believed the *Weltkunde* would make Cotta a fortune.[6] Cotta hoped it would make a profit.[7] Neither would have imagined that, page for page, a newspaper could end up costing 15 percent more than the *Horen*, which had just set a new standard for financial profligacy among German periodicals.[8] Newspapers, because they appeared so often, were by nature more labor-intensive than other publications. In the case of *Gelehrtezeitungen*, however, the labor did not come cheap. The editorial board of the *Horen* had been paid about five hundred fifty gulden per year for its time, which amounted to a couple of days a month. The editors of the *Weltkunde*—Posselt and two full-time assistants—received salaries totaling six thousand gulden.[9] Another fifty-five hundred gulden went to pay correspondents, without whom the editors would have had to rely too heavily on secondhand material.[10] As it was, five hundred gulden was spent on subscriptions to periodicals.[11] Paper cost thirty-six gulden per bale; a year's run consumed twenty-eight bales.[12] Printers' wages came to four gulden per day.[13] Cotta also agreed to pay for Posselt's lodgings in Tübingen and to contribute thirty louis d'or to defray his travel expenses back and forth to Baden, where his family still lived.[14] In all, expenses during the *Weltkunde*'s first year came to just under fifteen thousand gulden—roughly the sum Cotta had paid for the whole firm ten years before.

By the time Cotta signed his second contract with Posselt in 1797 he had given up the idea of trying to compete directly with local papers. But he still believed he could sell a decent newspaper for a reasonable price—ten gulden per year—and break even after a thousand subscriptions. The figures in the previous paragraph suggest that this goal was optimistic. He might have come close, however, if he had not decided, in the teeth of custom and common sense, to publish every day.[15] Once

6. Schiller to Cotta, 8 Jan. 1798, and Schiller to Goethe, 19 Jan. 1798, in Vollmer, *Briefwechsel*, pp. 283, 280n.

7. Cotta to Schiller, 20 Jan. 1798, ibid., p. 284.

8. According to Schiller's calculations (Schiller to Cotta, 1 Sept. 1794, ibid., p. 18), honoraria and editors' fees for the *Horen* came to about fifty-six gulden per sheet. For the *Weltkunde*, in aggregate almost twice as large, the comparable figure was sixty-five gulden, thirty kreuzer.

9. Cotta to Duke Frederick of Württemberg, 20 Aug. 1798, ibid., p. 646.

10. Cotta to Frederick, 28 Aug. 1798, ibid.

11. Contract between Posselt and Cotta, 28 Aug. 1794, CA.

12. *Druckauftragsbuch*, CA; cf. Lore Sporhan-Krempel, "Die Papierrechnungen von Johann Fr. Cotta, 1788–1806," *Archiv für Geschichte des Buchwesens* 5 (1964): cols. 1369–1471.

13. Cotta to Frederick, 28 Aug. 1798, in Vollmer, *Briefwechsel*, p. 646.

14. Contract between Posselt and Cotta, 16 Jan. 1798, CA.

15. If Cotta had gone ahead with the paper he planned in 1794—i.e., one that appeared three times a week (with supplements)—the total outlay for fourteen hundred subscriptions, based on the costs actually incurred by the *Weltkunde*, would have been 14,660 gulden.

this choice was made it was inevitable that Cotta would end up paying his postman even more than he was paying his editors. Transportation expenses accounted for 40 percent of the *Weltkunde*'s purchase price, the fees being divided between the imperial post office and a private courier, whose assistance was necessary because Tübingen was a small town, from which mail could be sent only three times a week. On the other four days Cotta had to have the paper carried to Stuttgart and Cannstatt, where it could be turned over to the regular postal service.[16]

Cotta's problem, it need hardly be said, was shared by every newspaper publisher in Germany, almost all of whom settled for publishing three, or at most five, times per week—whatever the mail wagon allowed. To an experienced journalist like Johann von Archenholz, editor of the Hamburg *Minerva*, Cotta's attempt to defeat the system seemed especially quixotic, since, as he was careful to point out, in the end it accomplished nothing. "In Paris and London," Archenholz wrote, "a daily publication schedule is worth something, because in such cities there is a guaranteed audience for that kind of paper. Every morning a thousand people want to know what went on around them the day before. In Germany everything is different. Except for a few cities, all the rest only *receive* mail twice a week—so daily publication is really quite superfluous."[17]

Superfluous as a practical matter, certainly. The *Weltkunde*'s daily schedule was not even a selling point in its advertising, which urged customers to compare its cost not to other newspapers but to a collection of books of similar aggregate size—an illustration, like Posselt's odd remark early on about publishing in Latin, of how imperfectly the formal properties of newspapers were understood during these years, or at any rate of how reluctant Cotta was to trade on them directly. The *Weltkunde* was printed on high-quality book paper (which retains its pliability to this day) and was meant to be saved and bound in volumes; all pages were numbered consecutively throughout the year, a practice the *Allgemeine Zeitung* would continue. Beginning in the 1820s annual indexes would be produced as a service to subscribers. In its physical form, in other words, Cotta's newspaper would express not the transience of the events it reported, but rather the permanence of the historical memory to which it was supposed to contribute.

Even so, daily publication had a symbolic importance of its own. In some circles the intention to publish every day could raise embarrassing questions; it suggested a craving for popularity and the attention of the

16. Postal Contract of 24/25 Oct. 1797, CA; Cotta to Frederick, 28 Aug. 1798, in Vollmer, *Briefwechsel*, p. 646.

17. Johann von Archenholz to Cotta, 7 Nov. 1798, in Heyck, *Allgemeine Zeitung*, pp. 67–68.

crowd, and mimicked the Parisian press too closely for comfort. In 1792 the Prussian government rejected a plan by a secretary of the Academy of Science to publish a daily called the *Erzähler, ein tägliches Volksblatt,* on the grounds that the very idea of a daily newspaper would cause unrest.[18] In Cotta's case such fears would have been absurd. At eighteen gulden the *Weltkunde* would never be a *Volksblatt.* As a symbol of popularity, daily publication was just too expensive to be credible. As a symbol of political engagement, however, it may have been worth the price Cotta paid. It is safe to assume that the *Weltkunde* appeared every day, even though Germans did not wake up wondering what had happened the day before, because Cotta thought they ought to wonder. For all his sensitivity to the traditional values of the German press, he was on this point unwilling to compromise with the backwardness of German institutions. Politics happened every day; therefore he would publish every day, if only as a gesture of defiance against the provincialism of his situation.

Surprisingly enough, it was also a gesture for which no price was exacted. On the contrary, the exigencies of daily production worked in Cotta's favor in one unlikely way: they became the basis of an appeal for relief from censorship. Under a law enacted in 1791, newspapers and political journals published in Württemberg were to be censored "precisely."[19] Publishers were cautioned against "serious breaches of propriety" respecting religion, morality, or the constitution of the state, and required to maintain "a restrained and dignified tone . . . appropriate to the importance of their subject." Censors, however, were not to stand in the way of a "healthy spirit of inquiry," nor were they to prevent journalists from contributing to the education of the people. What this was supposed to mean is anyone's guess; one would be hard pressed to decide whether Württemberg's press law reflected political fear or a devotion to Enlightenment. Cotta evidently did not care. As experience would reveal time and again, the statutory language used to regulate the press was almost irrelevant to its real condition. German press laws might or might not provide an accurate index of official attitudes; but all of them, regardless of their apparent liberality or conservatism, were intended to reserve legal initiative in the hands of the state. How that initiative was employed depended on the underlying values of the prince and his officials, the efficiency and intelligence of the censors, and the force of circumstance, all of which were beyond the reach of the law.

In the present instance these factors were disposed to favor Cotta's project. Württemberg was not Prussia. It had been twenty years since

---

18. Consentius, "Berliner Zeitungen," pp. 465–67.

19. Censor Order dated 13 July 1791, in August Ludwig Reyscher, ed., *Vollständige, historisch und kritisch bearbeitete Sammlung der württembergischen Gesetze* (Stuttgart, 1826–51), 14 : 1067–69.

the press had caused a serious problem there. Although that incident, involving the poet Christian Daniel Schubart, remained fresh in the minds of the duke's advisors, the punishment meted out—ten years in Asperg prison—had been sufficient to deter subsequent offenders.[20] In recent months, moreover, the government had tolerated a high level of political publicity, inspired by the convening of the territorial Diet (see chapter 3). Thus, although the court in Stuttgart had plenty to worry about in the fall of 1797, censorship was not high on the list. The government's attention was directed elsewhere: domestically to the state of its finances; diplomatically to preserving its independence in the face of growing pressure from Austria, to whom Württemberg owed historic allegiance, and from France, to whom it owed an indemnity from the last war. Under these conditions Cotta did not need to rely on the duke's devotion to the spirit of inquiry. He supposed instead that the government would forgo its right to censor if it could be persuaded that, by doing so, it would spare itself some inconvenience and serve its own interests.

Three weeks before the *Weltkunde* was scheduled to appear, Cotta appealed to the duke for an exemption from censorship.[21] A daily paper, he argued, operated on such a strict timetable that censors would face the disagreeable task of doing their work in the middle of the night. Even then the delay would compromise the *Weltkunde*'s appeal to the public, which was being asked to pay a great deal for the privilege of being up to date. Not all the duke's councillors found this argument convincing, but a majority conceded that censorship was "a serious liability for a paper that would derive its interest mainly from the timely reporting of current political events." They dismissed the minority's fears of setting an unpleasant precedent, since "the enterprise in question distinguishes itself so conspicuously from other institutions that might appear similar at first glance, and especially from ordinary newspapers, that it would certainly seem difficult for anyone else to build his hopes on what is done in this case." In any event, Cotta's material interest in the paper would promote caution.

> The undertaking is so large, and requires such considerable expense, and promises, if successful, such a handsome profit, that the attention of all

---

20. On the general state of political writing in Württemberg, see Eugene J. Griffity, "Political Writing and Enlightened Monarchy in Württemberg During the Reign of Duke Carl Eugen, 1744–93," Ph.D. diss., University of Illinois, 1979. Gerhard Storz (*Karl Eugen: Der Fürst und das "alte gute Recht"* [Stuttgart, 1981], pp. 186–206) discusses Schubart's case in detail. Schubart's work was highly personal, hence entirely different from the kind of paper Cotta had in mind. But there was a personal connection: Posselt admired Schubart enormously and wrote to him while he was in prison (Vierneisel, "Posselt," 49:270); Schubart for his part considered Posselt his "heart's brother" (Schubart to Posselt, 29 March 1791, in Christian Friedrich Daniel Schubart, *Briefe* [Munich, 1984], pp. 326–27).

21. Vollmer, *Briefwechsel*, p. 613.

concerned must be directed toward securing the widest possible circulation for their paper. They must therefore exercise the greatest care to eliminate whatever might be offensive to anyone. . . . In addition, the price of the paper is so clearly aimed at the lovers of reading among the propertied and educated classes that, if it is to endure, it must recommend itself to them through excellence of exposition and the maintenance of a high tone. It dare not fall into the low road by which so many political authors seek to gain access to a more diverse public.

The council therefore had "every reason to hope that this enterprise would bring the Fatherland not only great honor, but also such pecuniary benefits as a well-organized state economy ought never to forget to take into account."[22]

After promising to accept personal responsibility for everything in the *Weltkunde*, Cotta got the exemption he wanted. Never again would he be able to solve his legal problems so easily. Even in Württemberg such an agreement would soon become unthinkable. For the moment, however, Cotta benefited from the government's inexperience. The fears and frustrations of the next century were as yet only dimly foreseen by the Württemberg Council, whose attitude, like that of the old absolutism generally, was marked not by greater liberality but at least by less anxiety than the future would permit. And in one respect their confidence seems well founded. If, as one scholar has suggested, newspapers achieve their influence by creating a reciprocating echo between themselves and their audience,[23] then it is hard to fault the council's conclusion that overt political activism would find no place in the *Weltkunde*. Everything they knew about the Cotta Verlag suggested that this newspaper would remain loyal to ideas with which they were comfortable and would appeal to social groups they did not fear.

This calculation was reasonable, but it did not go far enough. In Germany press freedom was not just a social question; it had always been a diplomatic question as well. Although the duke's councillors had done their social sums well enough, they had underestimated the *Weltkunde*'s capacity to annoy other governments, which proved to be considerable.

In November 1797, a congress of powers had assembled in Rastatt to ratify what was militarily a fait accompli—the secession of the left bank of the Rhine to France. Almost every issue of the *Weltkunde* included some discussion of the congress, based on official protocols. To Posselt, Austria's conduct was suspect. The Austrian representatives had kept their distance from the rest of the imperial delegation and discouraged resistance to French territorial demands; the government had already given up its Belgian territories in exchange for compensation in Italy,

22. Report of the Council to Frederick, 20 Dec. 1797, ibid., pp. 614–16.
23. Engelsing, "Zeitung und Zeitschrift," col. 849.

and it had abandoned Mainz to French troops. The *Weltkunde's* readers might therefore have concluded that Austria was preparing to renege on its imperial responsibilities in order to further specific dynastic objectives.[24]

This point of view did not conflict with the duke of Württemberg's interests, which focused on retaining his claim to the imperial county of Mompelgard on the left bank. But the Austrian representative in Stuttgart was incensed, both at the *Weltkunde* and at the semiofficial *Schwäbische Chronik*, which routinely echoed the *Weltkunde's* reports. At the end of February he sent a sharp note to Württemberg's foreign minister, alerting him to the "slanders of these short-sighted and malicious scribblers" and demanding that something be done to curb them.[25] A week later a second note arrived, declaring that "the impudence of the *Neueste Weltkunde* reaches new heights with every passing day," and not just with respect to Rastatt.[26] The issue of March 5, for instance, described a religious festival that was disrupted when a young man substituted some pictures of Bonaparte for a packet of holy images and managed to have these blessed by a priest.

Worse, Posselt had begun to air his favorite theme of moral confrontation between the enlightened south and the barbaric north.[27] It was one thing to stand with the imperial estates against Austria; it was another to stand with France against the rest of Europe. Under the circumstances, the Austrian ambassador, Count Fugger, was not going to stand aside while Württemberg chose its own response. He declared that the *Weltkunde's* exemption from censorship violated imperial law and insisted that it be withdrawn immediately, a demand seconded the next day by the Russian ambassador.[28]

The Austro-Russian protest that Cotta encountered two months into his career as a newspaper publisher was the first trickle of what would become a steady stream of official indignation, which threatened on occasion to reduce his working life to one long, tendentious negotiation. As clearly as any that followed, this first complaint exposed the iron logic of censorship on which all successive protests would depend, and from which no exemption could be sought. The views expressed in Cotta's

24. Posselt was not the only one who saw things this way; cf. Gagliardo, *Reich and Nation*, pp. 188–89.

25. Fugger to Zeppelin, 27 Feb. 1798, in Vollmer, *Briefwechsel*, pp. 626–27. Cf. *Neueste Weltkunde*, 19 Feb. 1798; and *Schwäbische Chronik* (a supplement to the *Schwäbische Merkur*), 21 Feb. 1798.

26. Fugger to Zeppelin, 7 March 1798, in Vollmer, *Briefwechsel*, pp. 627–28.

27. Posselt, "Frankreich und der Nord," *Neueste Weltkunde*, 2, 3 March 1798; also Vollmer, *Briefwechsel*, pp. 628–32.

28. Fugger to Zeppelin, 7 March 1798, and de Maltitz to Zeppelin, 8 March 1798, in Vollmer, *Briefwechsel*, p. 633.

newspaper, no matter how factual or innocuous, could never be merely personal, nor entirely impersonal either, not because the *Weltkunde* spoke for the public—something that everyone involved would have denied—but because, despite all disclaimers, it implicitly spoke for the state. A government that could legally suppress ideas or information and did not do so was held responsible by other governments for the promulgation of those ideas. The Duchy of Württemberg might decline to censor its citizens; it might even tolerate criticism of itself; but it could not renege on its obligation to the international community. Austria thus demanded an accounting not from Cotta, whose pledge of personal responsibility had no bearing on the case, but from his prince, whose impolitic tolerance had called his loyalty to the Empire into question.

Frederick's councillors were not inclined to yield. They noted that the *Weltkunde*'s coverage of Rastatt had been tacitly approved by the *Schwäbische Chronik*'s censor and that the protocols of the congress showed the reports to be true. If the facts had been presented from "a false point of view," that was the fault of the censor. The council therefore decided that the *Chronik*, rather than the *Weltkunde*, should publish an apology, and that the responsible official should be scolded. As to the *Weltkunde*'s other delinquencies, the council accepted Cotta's explanation that his newspaper was suffering from the disorganization that was natural to any new venture. Although the articles in question were found to be objectionable, particularly since they were distributed to an audience which the council now described as "most widespread and, intellectually and morally, most diverse," the duke's advisors felt a retraction would only call attention to the original reports. They concluded that, rather than interfere in a project they still regarded as financially promising, they would simply warn Cotta to take better care in the future.[29]

This would not be easy. As far as disorganization went, Cotta could only hope that the arrival of the second of Posselt's assistants, Ludwig Huber, would straighten things out. Huber, like Posselt, was an early supporter of the Revolution, with ties to political clubs in Mainz, Strasbourg, and the Rhineland. When the French occupied Mainz in 1792 he had fled to Switzerland, where he and his wife, Georg Forster's widow, Therese, had since been living on his meager earnings as a writer.[30] Huber was a broad-minded and even-tempered man, an old friend of Schiller's, and, like Schiller, intellectually more attuned to art and phi-

29. Council to Frederick, 24 March 1798, ibid., pp. 634–42; cf. Heyck, *Allgemeine Zeitung*, pp. 53–56.

30. Ludwig Huber, *Sämtliche Werke seit dem Jahre 1802, nebst seiner Biographie* (Tübingen, 1806), 1:62–161 passim; cf. Schiller to Huber, 31 Jan. 1795, in Vollmer, *Briefwechsel*, p. 67n. Sabine Dorothea Jordan, *Ludwig Ferdinand Huber (1764–1804): His Life and Works* (Stuttgart, 1978), includes an excellent bibliography.

losophy than politics. In many ways he offered a nice contrast to Posselt. If broad-mindedness could have helped the *Weltkunde*, his presence might have made a difference.

As it was, the paper's position was more tenuous than Cotta guessed. Freedom from censorship had relieved him of bureaucratic meddling, but it had also made the *Weltkunde* unduly vulnerable to outsiders. Cotta wanted to substitute cooperation for regulation. He had always envisioned his newspaper as in some respects a tool of government—"a German *Moniteur* written by Germans."[31] As a matter of principle the *Weltkunde* was open to everyone, including its critics. But when Cotta offered to publish material supplied by the Austrian and Russian courts as a way of avoiding disagreements, he was ignored.[32] Austria and Russia did not want to address the public by means of a privately held newspaper, and certainly not on equal terms with their adversaries. They wanted to control the means of political discussion, and they resented Frederick (whom they suspected on other grounds of conniving with France) for preempting their right to do so. Having been rebuffed by the Württemberg Council, they turned to the *Reichshofrat* in Vienna, which on August 13 declared Cotta's newspaper a threat to public order and banned it throughout the Empire.[33] With that the *Weltkunde*, four years in the making and not yet nine months old, disappeared.

PRINCIPLES

The most immediate explanation for the *Weltkunde*'s failure is also the simplest: it was slapped down by powerful conservative forces that would have found an uncensored newspaper intolerable no matter what. Once he had conceded this point, it was a fairly simple matter for a man of Cotta's resourcefulness to save himself. He had good reason to try: politics aside, the *Weltkunde*'s suppression confronted him with a potential loss of over seventeen thousand gulden, enough to threaten the existence of the Cotta Verlag itself.[34] Under the circumstances, Cotta was

31. Cotta to Böttiger, 1 Dec. 1797, in Sondermann, *Böttiger*, p. 113. In evaluating this remark it should be remembered that the *Moniteur*, despite its revolutionary origins, was at this time the most respected official organ in Europe, viewed with something like jealousy even by France's opponents. The Napoleonic period would make official journalism synonymous with manipulation; under the Old Regime it had been a symbol of lawful government (Jeremy Popkin, "The Prerevolutionary Origins of Political Journalism," in *The French Revolution and the Creation of Modern Political Culture*, vol. 1: *The Political Culture of the Old Regime*, ed. Keith Michael Baker [Oxford, 1987], p. 205).

32. Cotta and Posselt to Duke Frederick, 21 March 1798, in Vollmer, *Briefwechsel*, p. 634.

33. Resolution of the *Reichshofrat*, 13 Aug. 1798, ibid., p. 645.

34. Cotta to Frederick, 28 Aug., 2 Sept. 1798, in Vollmer, *Briefwechsel*, pp. 646–47, 650.

not about to fall on his sword in defense of freedom of the press, a concept toward which he had so far displayed the same pragmatic attitude as the authorities in Stuttgart. Even before official notice of the imperial ban arrived, Cotta had begun to prepare his defense, and the day after the decree was announced he presented Frederick with a proposal to continue the paper under a different name and with a different editor. The council, acting to preserve a semblance of independence, endorsed this idea, while stipulating that the new journal would be subject to regular censorship.[35] Cotta agreed and moved the paper to Stuttgart, where it could be supervised efficiently. He then went a step further and appealed directly to the *Reichshofrat* for an imperial privilege against piracy—a meaningless piece of paper for which Cotta had not previously felt any need, but emblematic of his new understanding of the complex logic that had brought him down. This privilege was granted without comment.[36] By then the first number of the new paper had already appeared, on September 9, 1798, under the title *Allgemeine Zeitung*, edited by Ludwig Huber.

To say, then, that the *Weltkunde* disappeared does not seem quite right. One might say instead that it shed its skin. On the surface, everything was different, in ways that were perfectly apparent to readers. Yet Cotta and Huber felt no need to offer any public explanations, for the simple reason that, in all essentials of political outlook and editorial practice, the *Allgemeine Zeitung* would be based on the same principles that had guided its predecessor. In this instance, furthermore, Cotta clearly suspected that the *Weltkunde*'s course would have been smoother, and longer, if it had adhered more closely to its own canons of tolerance and impartiality. Having gotten to the end of the *Weltkunde*'s short history, then, it will be worthwhile to return briefly to its beginning, to consider its intellectual and institutional character in more detail.

The prospectus with which Cotta first announced the *Weltkunde*'s existence had two parts.[37] The second part, written by Cotta personally, described the paper as a supplement to the *Europäische Annalen*, with which it would proceed hand in hand, under a single editor. In the *An-*

35. Report of the Württemberg Council to Frederick, 29 Aug. 1798, ibid., pp. 647–49.

36. Reichshofratsagent Borsch to Frederick, 10 Oct. 1798, ibid., p. 651. Cotta knew of the impending ban by the middle of July and believed at first that it would force him to move his newspaper out of Württemberg, perhaps to Hamburg, Leipzig, or Weimar, all of which he imagined to be more tolerant than his homeland. (Cotta to Böttiger, 17 July 1798, in Sondermann, *Böttiger*, p. 120). Cotta's friends disabused him of this idea (Böttiger to Cotta, 1 Aug. 1798, ibid., pp. 120–21; Archenholz to Cotta, 7 Nov. 1798, in Heyck, *Allgemeine Zeitung*, pp. 67–68). In the end Cotta seems to have been surprised and relieved at having managed to save himself. Böttiger, indeed, doubted that he had really succeeded, and was convinced only when Cotta produced his new imperial privilege, rather like a rabbit from a hat (Cotta to Böttiger, 19 Oct. 1798, in Sondermann, *Böttiger*, p. 125).

37. "Die neueste Weltkunde," in Vollmer, *Briefwechsel*, pp. 608–13.

nalen one would find "true contemporary history," in the *Weltkunde* the "data" on which that history was based. There was no more traditional role for a newspaper to fill; and, despite Cotta's pledge that the *Weltkunde* would be "all things to all people," it is not obvious why anyone would pay so much for "sources" when the *Annalen's* "conclusions" could be had for less than half the price.

Posselt, too, considered the *Weltkunde* a companion to the *Annalen*. In his part of the prospectus, however, one sees that the *Weltkunde* would offer something worthwhile in its own right. In the past the German press had suffered from "an incongruity of form and content." The *Weltkunde* would overcome this shortcoming by combining "German diligence and German respect for other lands" with "a somewhat British frankness." Five principles would guide the effort: comprehensiveness; a devotion to truth (as against conjecture, unsubstantiated opinion, or "hot air"); clarity of exposition; eloquence of expression; and nonpartisanship "in the broadest sense of the word." The result would be "a faithful mirror reflecting the true and complete shape of our age."

The divided tone of the *Weltkunde's* advertisement reflected the mixed heritage—quotidian and "historico-political"—to which the paper laid claim. Was the *Weltkunde* a conventional German newspaper? Hardly. If it had been it would not have received such fine treatment from Frederick's advisors. Was it a new departure in German journalism? Not in any of its particulars. All the points made in the prospectus had been made somewhere else before. Complaints about "incongruity of form and content" had been voiced in the first number of the *Journal von und für Deutschland* in 1784, in advertisements for Schirach's *Politisches Journal* in 1789,[38] and in Schwarzkopf's *Ueber Zeitungen*. The *Weltkunde's* five principles would have been familiar to readers of the *Stats-Anzeigen*, not to mention the *Annalen*. British and French parliamentary proceedings, which Cotta's paper took as a staple, were well reported in the Hamburg *Correspondent*. Even the Shakespearean tag that Posselt tacked onto his part of the prospectus had been used before, as the motto for Archenholz's *Minerva*. As a daily the *Weltkunde* tested the limits of contemporary practice: its format implied that ordinary citizens needed to keep abreast of public affairs. But daily newspapers were not unprecedented in Germany, and this feature was so costly and troublesome as to suggest that whatever novelty the *Weltkunde* might possess would work to its detriment.

Nevertheless, two features of the *Weltkunde* were different enough to be important. The first had to do with the aspirations implicit in its title: "Latest News of the World." No German newspaper had ever taken the whole world as its province. Most included their town of origin on the

---

38. *Stats-Anzeigen* 12, no. 48 (1789): 512.

masthead, and even the mighty *Correspondent* of Hamburg, which numbered its readers in the tens of thousands, covered international news in a parochial, business-oriented way. Whether Cotta had the resources to make good on his claim was a question that could not be answered in advance, but anyone familiar enough with politics to subscribe to the *Weltkunde* would have recognized that its publisher's ambitions were without precedent, wholly outside the tradition from which it wished to claim descent.

The second novel feature was of more immediate significance. The *Weltkunde*, like all German newspapers, was anonymous—or, more precisely, the *Weltkunde* was anonymous because it was a newspaper. Other, more sophisticated kinds of periodicals might or might not include unsigned work; the *Horen* did, for reasons of its own, the *Annalen* usually did not.[39] In all cases, however, the contents of such publications were understood to be the work of individual authors, named or not, and were never subsumed under any collective structure. Newspapers were different. They were, as the very word *Zeitung* implies, concretizations of time itself, hence always anonymous, since there was nothing in a purely factual account of the world for which an individual could take credit. But the account of the world in the *Weltkunde*, and in the rest of the Cotta press for that matter, was not purely factual. To Cotta's critics nothing was more galling than his tendency to present his publications as impersonal chronicles of history while publishing material that would have been deemed argumentative or obviously personal anywhere else. For all Cotta's soothing talk about the difference between conclusions and sources, he knew that his contributors would have their own points of view, which custom would allow him to conceal. Nor should the strength of this custom be underestimated: although editing, publishing, and even printing a newspaper would all become hazardous occupations in Germany in the next few years, none of the press laws enacted during Cotta's lifetime challenged the rightful anonymity of a newspaper's correspondents.[40]

Anonymity—or, better, impersonality—was part of the rhetoric of newspapers under the Old Regime, accepted by both the public and the authorities as a sign of objectivity rather than prudence. As in his decision to publish every day, Cotta was here appropriating a symbol while altering the underlying reality. The *Weltkunde* was a newspaper in a formal sense; but it was not a mere chronicle, any more than it was a mere

39. Goethe had proposed that the *Horen* reveal the names of its authors only at the end of the year, to symbolize its collegial spirit (Schulz, *Schillers Horen*, p. 38). Unattributed articles in the *Annalen* were by Posselt, a fact that everyone seems to have known without being told.

40. Such a proposal was still a novelty when it was put forward by Franz Adam Löffler in *Ueber die Gesetzgebung der Presse* (Leipzig, 1837).

Volksblatt. Far from being purely objective, by prevailing standards the *Weltkunde* was not even fair. Within the limits of Cotta's means, its coverage was comprehensive; and within the limits of Posselt's skill, the writing was clear and eloquent (almost too eloquent—Wieland's *Teutscher Merkur,* which otherwise praised the *Weltkunde* warmly, found Posselt's elevated style annoying).[41] But no one considered the *Weltkunde* impartial. Its "modish adulation of the so-called *Weltfranken*" showed through everywhere.[42] Many of those on the other side of the fence politically, Friedrich Gentz for instance, or Herder, or Schiller, were prepared to forgive the paper its "French principles" in return for reporting that offered "some food for the intellect."[43] Although they regretted, as Goethe did, that Posselt's "inability to maintain even the appearance of impartiality" should have brought the *Weltkunde* down so quickly, they never doubted that its claim to nonpartisanship was a sham.[44]

They were not entirely wrong: if the *Weltkunde* had openly identified itself as a "newspaper of opinion," it would have been immediately branded a contradiction in terms. But the aspiration to impartiality in the formulation of opinion was nevertheless real, and closely connected to the nascent historicism of Posselt's teachers. The *Weltkunde*'s pledge of nonpartisanship was not simply a promise to be fair: *Unparteilichkeit,* as Posselt and Cotta understood it, was specifically a function of historical understanding. Leopold von Ranke, writing half a century later, spoke for journalists and historians alike when he argued that nonpartisanship did not mean one had to "approach the great struggles of might and ideas" with no opinion, but only that one must "recognize the positions occupied by the active forces in history, and do justice to the relationships peculiar to each."[45]

At the start of the French Revolution, Germans, particularly those engaged in defending traditional rights against outsiders, were already used to thinking about politics in historical terms. The Revolution, which excited new interest in history everywhere its influence was felt, strengthened this tendency by demonstrating the apparent dangers of

41. *Neuer Teutsche Merkur,* Jan. 1799, pp. 3–27.

42. Ibid.

43. Schiller to Cotta, 8 Jan. 1798, in Vollmer, *Briefwechsel,* p. 283. Cf. J.W.L. Gleim to Johann Gottfried Herder, 2 May 1798; Herder to Gleim, 29 June 1798; Gleim to Caroline Herder, 4 July 1798, in Heinrich Düntzer and Ferdinand Gottfried von Herder, eds., *Von und an Herder: Ungedruckte Briefe aus Herders Nachlass* (Leipzig, 1861–62), 1 : 241–45; Friedrich von Gentz to Böttiger, 1 Feb. 1798, 3 March 1799, in F. C. Wittichen and Ernst Salzer, eds., *Briefe von und an Friedrich von Gentz* (Munich and Berlin, 1909–13), 1 : 248, 254–55.

44. Goethe to Cotta, 14 Sept. 1798, in Fehling and Schiller, *Briefe an Cotta* 1 : 79.

45. Leopold von Ranke, *Die deutschen Mächte und der Fürstenbund,* in *Sämtliche Werke* (Leipzig, 1875–90), 31/32:viii, quoted in George Iggers, *The German Conception of History* (Middletown, Conn., 1968), p. 77.

political rationalism. By the turn of the nineteenth century historicism had ceased to be simply one mode of academic argument and had become the universal substrate of intellectual life. Linguistics, philology, economics, art, law, philosophy, theology—in George Iggers's words, "all the humanistic and cultural sciences"—became historically oriented studies.[46] History became the common language of politics during the Reform Era, and no field was more profoundly affected by its rise than political journalism.

By adopting the viewpoint of the historian, a political writer could comment on policy without challenging the authority of those who formulated it. There was, of course, something disingenuous in this. Someone like Posselt could turn politics into "history" almost by magic: the passage of only a few weeks was supposed to make events seem faintly academic and render an account of them fit for public consumption. Sometimes, as in the case of the *Weltkunde*, the magic did not work, but on the whole it did, because on the whole the historicization of political discussion was backed by an authentic desire, as Ranke put it, to do justice.

By appropriating the methods and the rhetoric of the historian, the *Weltkunde* and the *Allgemeine Zeitung* would help blaze the path by which German journalists would escape the obscurity to which enlightened absolutism had consigned them. At the same time, historicism had political implications of its own, which the expansiveness of its nonpartisan ideal tended to mask. Two of these are of particular importance to the history of the Cotta press, especially in its early years. The first is a virtual indifference to constitutional forms, an attitude that historicism would elevate to the level of political principle. This is not to say that the historicist point of view was inhospitable to constitutionalism; if anything, the opposite was true. But because *Unparteilichkeit* demanded that the political practices of each state be analyzed in terms of their historical genesis, it was impossible to prefer one constitutional formula over another as a matter of right. The final paragraphs of Posselt's introduction to the *Weltkunde*, quoted at the end of the previous chapter, demonstrate how an otherwise unflinching political argument can be softened and diffused by the introduction of historicist principles, which emphasize ends rather than means, with the understanding that the choice of means can safely be left to those already in power.

The second implication is less handily illustrated but of equal consequence. By embracing historicism, German journalists cut themselves off from the intellectual resources of the natural-law tradition, which strengthened the position of the press elsewhere. Within the terms of Cotta's nonpartisan principles, the prerogatives of the press could enjoy no special status: they were subject to the same vagaries of historical

46. Iggers, *German Conception of History*, p. 4.

circumstance as all other elements of political life. Freedom of the press in Germany therefore became a question of public utility rather than public right. The questions that troubled Posselt and Schiller in their early discussions with Cotta continued to be asked for the next fifty years: Is the public ready for a free press? Does the public deserve a free press? Or perhaps only part of the public, and not the rest?

A few journalists, especially those who came to prominence during the War of Liberation, believed that history offered a clear answer to these questions. To them, history was the expression of a people's character, and a record of its deeds. The journalist's subject was nothing less than history in the making, and his work was an expression of the public mind and will. For the most part, however, political writers were unwilling to assert themselves in this way. They were no more prepared to put their cause in the hands of an alien class—"the people"—than they were to argue their case on the basis of an alien, revolutionary ideology. It was in the natural evolution of the modern state toward greater freedom, rather than in the political awakening of the masses, that Cotta and the rest of the reform generation vested their hopes. He must have believed the future would favor him. But he always remained sensitive to the charge that the interpretation of history presented in his publications was faulty, or incomplete, or, most damning of all, partisan.

In characterizing the nonpartisan position that Cotta and Posselt tried to stake out for themselves, it would be hard to improve on Ranke's remark about "doing justice." Ranke, however, was writing from the point of view of one to whom the raw materials necessary for his craft were readily available. For a journalist, access to information was itself a political issue. It was here, as a practical matter, that the analogy between the historian and the publicist was most apt to break down. It was one thing to confine yourself, as Posselt promised, to "historically significant facts" and to proclaim your "equal regard for all constitutions and all lands." But what if all constitutions and all lands did not have equal regard for you? In states with parliaments and a vigorous press—Britain, France, and the "sister republics"—historically significant facts were already in the public domain. In those lands, moreover, public opinion was itself a "fact," and so part of the *Weltkunde*'s chosen ground. States without representative institutions, however, where politics was the secret business of a few, placed many obstacles in the way of the impartial observer. Although Posselt promised to exercise the same care in covering "despotically governed states" and "democratic and monarchical free states," he would accept no blame if the evidence at his disposal tended to favor the latter group. In this he could only bow before the wisdom of Tacitus, to whom "the thoughts of a free man of Athens were worth more than the whole north of Hermann the Cherusker."[47]

47. *Neueste Weltkunde*, 2 Jan. 1798.

One sees here the seeds of the *Weltkunde*'s destruction: Posselt believed in history, but he did not trust it. Cotta, however, was prepared to
be patient. Posselt's departure was in some ways a relief to him, because
it eliminated any lingering uncertainty about who was in charge and
gave him new hope, as he wrote to Goethe, that he would finally be able
"to maintain the true tone of the historian in this newspaper, and raise
it to the highest level of comprehensiveness."[48] Under Huber's steady
hand, made steadier by the duke's censors, the *Allgemeine Zeitung* would
more nearly approximate the nonpartisan ideal the *Weltkunde* had first
articulated.

Even so, the incident that forced the *Weltkunde*'s metamorphosis into
the *Allgemeine Zeitung* left Cotta shaken. He knew that his escape had
been a narrow one, and that even with Frederick's protection his position
could become impossible at any moment. For several months after the
affair was behind him Cotta thought of putting some distance between
himself and his enemies by moving the *AZ* to Hamburg, the most cosmopolitan of German cities and the one with the most sophisticated
press.[49] But the high costs and vigorous competition that prevailed there
dissuaded him, which was just as well. For the time being, Cotta had
nothing more to fear from the barbaric north: the *Neueste Weltkunde*
would be the last newspaper to meet its end at the hands of the Holy
Roman Empire. One could already feel the wind shifting. Three months
after the *Weltkunde*'s suppression, Cotta would write to his friend Karl
Reinhard about a "black storm" threatening Europe, a storm that was
gathering not in the land of the Cheruski, but in France.[50]

48. Cotta to Goethe, 28 Oct. 1798, in Kuhn, *Goethe und Cotta* 1:39. Cotta had been
uneasy about the criticism Posselt's Francophile posture had attracted among the *Weltkunde*'s readers; although he always insisted that his editor was well-intentioned, he did not
deny the truth of the complaints. See Cotta to Böttiger, 10 April 1798, in Sondermann,
Böttiger, p. 117.
49. Archenholz to Cotta, 7 Nov. 1798, in Heyck, *Allgemeine Zeitung*, pp. 67–68.
50. Cotta to Karl Reinhard, 16 Nov. 1798, CA.

THREE

The End of the Good Old Law

There are only two true constitutional governments in Europe: England's, and Württemberg's.

Charles James Fox, 1796

The years during which Cotta conceived his plan for a newspaper were troubled ones everywhere in Germany, as the princes and princelings of the Holy Roman Empire pondered the gestation of the new French imperium with increasing dismay. In Württemberg, the largest principality in the southwest, the dismay was especially pronounced, because the duchy's location made it a likely battlefield and suitable trophy in any conflict between France and Austria, and because its domestic arrangements insured that any external crisis would fuel internal dissension. For over three centuries the dukes of Württemberg had been, with no more than the usual lapses, politically reliable vassals of the Empire. The French invasion of 1796 made these habits obsolete almost overnight and forced the duchy to pursue a policy whose risks and rewards were unknown to living memory. At the same time, as would be true in Prussia ten years later, war and occupation shattered the restraints on new ideas and provided an opportunity to revise or replace those institutions that had failed to preserve the state from disaster.

In Württemberg this opportunity took the form of a reconvening of the territorial Diet, in recess since 1770. Although Cotta had no official part in these proceedings, he was caught up in them as the publicist for a coalition of reformers in the assembly, and as a mediator between Württemberg's estates and the French government. His conduct reveals him to be a loyal supporter of his homeland's constitutional tradition, which he valued because he believed that beneath the obscurity and entrenched privilege there was a kernel of republican virtue worth cultivating, and to which he would hold fast for the rest of his life.

THE OLD LAW AND THE REVOLUTION

Among the larger German states, Württemberg was the only one to preserve an effective clerical-patrician oligarchy into the revolutionary era.

67

Under an arrangement dating back to the peasant wars of the sixteenth century, the dukes of Württemberg had been entitled to initiate legislation, appoint the clergy and civil administration, and represent the state in foreign affairs. Such prerogatives had formed the basis for the growth of absolutism throughout most of Europe. In Württemberg, however, the consolidation of princely authority remained incomplete. The reasons for this are complex, and they have recently been gone into in exemplary detail.[1] As an introduction to the more personal dimensions of Cotta's political life, however, a brief review of Württemberg's unusual constitutional tradition may be helpful.

In general one can point to three features of the Swabian political landscape that obliged the dukes of Württemberg to follow a different course from that taken by the rulers of Brandenburg and Bavaria. First, Württemberg had no indigenous aristocracy. By the beginning of the sixteenth century almost all the large landowners in southwestern Germany had succeeded in making themselves *reichsunmittelbar*, that is, subject directly to the emperor. Although the regional nobility was well disposed toward the House of Württemberg, they owed it no allegiance, they paid it no taxes, and they had no constitutional standing in the state. The duchy's rulers were therefore unable to secure the support of the landed elite by offering them places in the army or at court, institutions for which most of Württemberg's dukes had strong inclinations. These inclinations, however, were not shared by the urban magistracy, or *Ehrbarkeit*, thrifty and sober-minded town dwellers who resisted the crown's pretensions to power and prestige—which, they knew, would have to be paid for with their money.

Second, between 1734 and 1797 all the dukes of Württemberg were Catholics, who, to secure their succession, had agreed to forgo the benefits of the Religious Peace of Augsburg and so were forced to rule over a land of evangelical Lutherans. The crown was thus deprived of the organizing power and symbolic support of the territorial church, which remained in the hands of men with close ties to the secular *Ehrbarkeit* who were inclined to suspect the duke's motives in any cause that found Catholics and Protestants at odds. Württemberg's rulers were therefore unable to "go to the people" as a way of outflanking their opponents. So, for that matter, was the *Ehrbarkeit* itself, which did not enjoy much support beyond the confines of the towns it controlled. Württemberg's constitution was originally formulated to regulate relations between the ruling house and the municipal elite, and to secure the privileges of both at the expense of those who worked the land. Although much had changed since the drafting of the original Tübingen Contract of 1514, Württemberg's peasants and villagers were still substantially excluded from terri-

1. James Alan Vann, *The Making of a State: Württemberg, 1593–1793* (Ithaca, N.Y., 1984).

torial politics at the end of the eighteenth century. Their disenfranchisement had helped preserve what was called "the Good Old Law." It also constituted a significant inequity in the eyes of reform-minded individuals, who believed that if the duke's subjects were to withstand the temptations of revolution, the duchy's political practices would have to be brought up to date.

Finally, Württemberg's constitution was underwritten by the constitution of the Empire as a whole. While this was true in theory for all German states, in Cotta's homeland it was also true in fact. By the time Cotta was born the rulers of most of the larger German lands had found the leverage they needed to free themselves from the more obnoxious forms of imperial interference in their affairs. The dukes of Württemberg had not. They and their estates were repeatedly obliged to seek help and protection from the Empire and, in the case of the estates, from the Empire's most powerful Protestant vassals, Hanover, Prussia, and Denmark. These powers had guaranteed the rights of the *Ehrbarkeit* following the conversion of the ruling house to Catholicism. In 1770 they were called on again to enforce a constitutional compromise, the so-called Hereditary Agreement (*Erbvergleich*), made necessary by the egregious illegality of the duke's conduct during the Seven Years' War.

The Hereditary Agreement was a defeat for the crown, which was forced to acknowledge economic and legal privileges it had been trying for two centuries to take away, but it was not a pure victory for the Old Law. Rather, the new arrangement strengthened the oligarchic character of the government, which had been growing more pronounced in any case, by vesting the full power of the estates in an executive committee drawn from the upper echelons of the *Ehrbarkeit*. The executive committee was technically an organ of the Diet, intended to represent that body between sessions. By elevating this elite group to a status approaching that of co-regent, however, the Hereditary Agreement made diets as such superfluous and, to members of the committee, unwelcome—a circumstance that the estates' senior legal advisor, J. J. Moser, had condemned in advance as unconstitutional.[2] Yet to the leadership of the estates, the compromise of 1770 offered an efficient and personally rewarding way of doing business with the prince, while less prominent members were glad to be spared the trouble and expense of territorial politics.

By the end of the eighteenth century Württemberg was governed not by an absolute monarch but, as James Vann has shown, by a "corporate duumvirate,"[3] which functioned more through nepotism and co-

2. Mack Walker, *Johann Jakob Moser and the Holy Roman Empire of the German Nation* (Chapel Hill, 1981), p. 269.

3. Vann, *The Making of a State*, pp. 294–97; cf. Erwin Hölzle, *Das alte Recht und die Revolution: Eine politische Geschichte Württembergs in der Revolutionszeit, 1789–1805* (Munich and Berlin, 1931), pp. 3–39.

optation than through the orderly application of law. In a small and peaceful land this is not the worst form of government. In a land at war with powerful neighbors, however, it is far from the best, particularly when the two halves of the duumvirate view foreign affairs mainly as a way of securing domestic advantage. That Württemberg's estates should have tried to conduct a quasi-independent foreign policy was not in itself so unusual. Although their counterparts elsewhere did not always possess the Württembergers' undisputed right to represent themselves in other courts, the estates of other German lands usually managed to make themselves heard abroad and regularly cooperated with each other on matters of mutual interest. It was unusual, however, that, following the outbreak of war between France and the Empire in 1792, the policy of Württemberg's estates should have ceased so completely to complement that of Württemberg's duke.

In that war Württemberg lost all its crown lands west of the Rhine, and so acquired a permanent interest in the outcome of the conflict between France and the eastern powers. To Duke Frederick Eugen, that interest demanded unswerving loyalty to the Empire in which his rights were vested. The estates, however, had no stake in the recovery of dynastic lands and hoped to keep Württemberg out of further conflict. Theirs was a policy of peace at any price, which they began to pursue through private mediation in the summer of 1794.

It was an improbable idea. One would not expect the leaders of the centralized, democratized French republic to have much patience for the special pleading of Württemberg's notables, and at first they did not. In time, though, internal changes in the Directory would produce a policy of negotiation with south German governments as a means of securing France's natural borders. The Peace of Basel, which promised to concentrate any future war in the south, had in any case strengthened the estates' hand considerably. For more than a year the duke wavered, pressed on one side by the *Ehrbarkeit* and on the other by an anti-French coterie led by the heir to the throne, Frederick. Austrian military successes allowed a postponement of the decision until the summer of 1796, when Moreau's army drove the imperial forces out of Württemberg. All opportunity for compromise departed with them, and in August a separate peace was signed by which the duke agreed to refrain from assisting the Empire against France and to accept compensation for his lost territories by secularizing church lands on the right bank of the Rhine.[4]

From the beginning, the duke, the crown prince, and the estates all viewed the treaty differently. Prince Frederick believed that his family could exploit a European war to win its long struggle with the estates.

4. Hölzle, *Das alte Recht*, pp. 127–29; and Karl Klüpfel, "Die Friedensunterhandlungen Württembergs mit der Französischen Republik, 1796–1802," *Historische Zeitschrift* 46 (1881): 385–92.

But his hatred of the Revolution kept him from urging a pro-French strategy on his father. The duke accepted the peace as an unpleasant expedient that might be withdrawn if the fortunes of war favored Austria. To the estates, finally, a treaty with France offered the possibility of permanent friendship with a great power that could protect their rights from infringement by the duke. Within the estates, however, the limits of this friendship remained in dispute. Most of the *Ehrbarkeit* regarded the connection with France as unsentimentally as did the duke. Their ancestors had disliked the French for their military adventurism and cultural imperialism, and the Revolution had done nothing to change their minds. They had no sympathy for the French system and did not envision any alteration in Württemberg's internal structure.

Alongside these traditionalists, however, was a nascent party of reform, which believed that a lasting alliance with France would provide a natural basis for modernizing Württemberg's antique constitution. This group drew its strength from two sources: younger and better educated members of the *Ehrbarkeit*, who believed that the French Revolution pointed the way to enlightened government; and village leaders, whose local influence had been enhanced by the Hereditary Agreement of 1770 and who were now looking to play a role in territorial government. Like the rest of the estates, they wanted to prevent any erosion of existing checks on the duke's authority. They also wanted to reform the assembly itself. By expanding the franchise, adopting a regular schedule of plenary sessions, and restricting the power of the executive committee, they hoped to make the Diet the true *corpus repraesentativum* of the nation, as the constitution required. It was to this group that Cotta would be drawn.

Their opportunity to be heard came in the fall of 1796. Part of the price of peace with France had been an indemnity of four million francs, a sum that could be raised only with the consent of a full Diet. The call for elections, the first in a generation, evoked an unprecedented response, in the form of hundreds of pamphlets and articles, addressing candidates and electors on subjects ranging from road repair to the divine right of kings. The resemblance of this outpouring to the *cahiers* of prerevolutionary France was unmistakable, though truly radical sentiments were conspicuous in their absence. Even so, there was no question that the educated public sided with the reformers, and that they expected great things from their representatives.[5]

Cotta was not a member of the parliamentary reform group, he did not stand for election to the Diet, and there is nothing to suggest that he contributed to the formulation of the reformers' program. But he cer-

---

5. Hölzle, *Das alte Recht*, pp. 171–75; and Walter Grube, *Der Stuttgarter Landtag, 1457–1957: Von den Landständen zum demokratischen Parlament* (Stuttgart, 1957), pp. 453–55.

tainly moved in the same circles they did, circles in which visitors from other lands found the political discussion to be exceptionally lively.[6] His sympathies were not in doubt. Neither was his professional skill, which the reformers needed if they were to make use of the ground swell of public opinion that had, for the moment, given them the upper hand in the Diet.

It is at least possible that the proposal to publish a journal in connection with the Diet came from Cotta himself.[7] At the end of 1796 his plans for a European newspaper were no closer to fruition than they had been two years before, and he might well have decided to lower his sights a little as a way of getting started. But no matter whether he approached the reformers or they approached him, it is clear that, philosophically, the journal entitled *Landtag im Herzogthum Wirtemberg*, which appeared shortly after the Diet convened in March of 1797, anticipated the *Weltkunde* in some respects. It was created in the hope that "publicity [will] awaken and restore a true common spirit." The *Landtag* would provide the public with authoritative reports on the Diet, free of "judgmental" commentary but with the "historical" analysis necessary to clarify the proceedings.[8] Cotta was not the author of these remarks—they were written by Elias Steeb, a young law professor at Tübingen who became the journal's editor—but they reflect his point of view. As compared to the *Weltkunde*, of course, the *Landtag* was a work of extremely limited conception and range. Nevertheless, if it had succeeded it might have altered the sorry course of events that followed, and spared Cotta some personal distress as well.

The *Landtag* was the first of several publications that Cotta would create over the years to publicize the work of a parliamentary body. It appeared every week or so, in issues of between twenty and ninety octavo pages, and as an organ of the Diet it was not subject to censorship.[9] Apart from a few essays on the history of the estates, its contents were strictly documentary—the documents being chosen with an eye to the reformers' interest in reorganizing the assembly. Being mainly documentary, the *Landtag* needed no independent rationale: it was simply supposed to extend the representative function of the Diet to a broader public, whose attention would be a spur to action and a deterrent to unconstitutional conduct by the duke.

6. Grube, *Stuttgarter Landtag*, p. 451.

7. Cf. Posselt to Cotta, 22 March 1797, in Fehling and Schiller, *Briefe an Cotta* 1:416–17.

8. *Der Landtag im Herzogthum Wirtemberg* 1, no. 1 (1797): 3–5.

9. Beginning in the fall of 1797, the *Landtag* was identified on its cover as "Eine officielle Zeitschrift," edited by Steeb and published by Cotta and Metzler (who printed it in Stuttgart). Before then it may have been a private venture by Cotta and Steeb—though the official designation does not correspond to any change in the *Landtag*'s contents.

If the Diet had been a representative body, Cotta's journal would have done this work well enough. But the Diet was not representative, at least not in the sense that its members had gathered to represent the views of some constituency. Instead they had assembled to symbolize the rights of a traditional elite, for which purpose they had always met, appropriately enough, in private. Cotta's journal was a concession to the times, an acknowledgment that the Diet's conduct had become a matter of public interest. Its appearance was in itself a victory for the reformers, who hoped to create a public atmosphere that would transform the Diet into a kind of national assembly for Württemberg. Many of them cherished the example of English constitutional history, which seemed to demonstrate that such a transformation could occur without revolution.[10] Most, however, did not appreciate that the passage from Magna Carta to the Bill of Rights had required centuries. Given that the old Europe was collapsing around them, Cotta and his colleagues could count on a couple of years at most.

There is not much in the record to indicate what the *Landtag*'s impact on its readers was. During the early months of the Diet the journal was popular enough to inspire an unofficial competitor, virtually a pirate edition, called *Verhandlungen aus dem Wirtemberg Landtag*, which sold for the rock-bottom price of three kreuzer per sheet.[11] And although Cotta's journal could hardly be said to have made the duke fear for the love of his people, the experience of having the state's business bruited about in public was unfamiliar enough to produce "extreme dissatisfaction and disapproval" on the part of the crown.[12] But the *Landtag* had no discernible effect on the Diet itself. The assembly's rules had evolved through generations of successful resistance to change, and initiative of any sort was difficult to sustain. By the end of 1797, debate was proceeding along lines that would have been familiar to the participants' great-grandfathers: a dispute on military recruitment had led to a dispute over taxation, which could now be expected to lead either to the Diet's acquiescence in some extraconstitutional stratagem of the duke's (if the estates felt weak) or to a compromise mediated by outsiders (if the estates felt strong). In this instance the estates, doubly protected by the Hereditary Agreement and the treaty with France, and led by the reformers in their midst, believed themselves to be strong. Once it became clear that Cotta's journal could not provide the necessary lubricant for the old machinery

10. Admiration for the English Whigs was widespread among Württemberg's reformers, including Cotta (cf. Reinhard to Cotta, 25 Aug. 1798, in Fehling and Schiller, *Briefe an Cotta* 1:457).

11. The *Verhandlungen* was edited by Chancellery Councillor Georg Christian Pur... (except for vol. 1, which was edited by Privy Councillor E. F. Hesler) and published by A. F. Macklot and J. F. Steinkopf.

12. Grube, *Stuttgarter Landtag*, p. 465.

and that public opinion did not offer any weapon against the duke,[13] they did not hesitate to look beyond Württemberg's borders for help.

The stagnation of domestic politics in Stuttgart stood in marked contrast to an extremely fluid diplomatic situation. Württemberg's representative in Paris, Konradin Abel, was a skillful and effective diplomat who had done much over the years to improve his government's relations with France.[14] His efforts were now being hampered, however, by the heir to the throne, Frederick, whose intriguing caused the leaders of the Diet to worry about the future of the French treaty.[15] The Diet therefore decided to send additional representatives of its own into the field. A new executive committee was formed, including key figures from the reform party and other, more traditionally minded delegates who had supported the separate peace. These two factions shared little beyond a distrust of the duke and his son and a belief that constitutional government depended on preserving the power of the estates. The bareness of these principles was reflected in the committee's choice of agents: Ludwigsburg *Bürgermeister* Christian Friedrich Baz, an outspoken republican, who hoped for a settlement modeled on the French Constitution of 1792;[16] and a man of equally developed but wildly diverging views, Eberhard Georgii, "the last of the Old Württembergers," whose affinity for the reform program may be judged by an essay he wrote for Cotta's *Landtag*, in which he argued that the Diet and its committees should be reorganized as they were in the seventeenth century.[17] In November these two set off for Paris and Rastatt respectively, where they were supposed to see to it that the Diet would have the right to approve any settlement affecting Württemberg.[18] Before they could accomplish anything, however, the old duke died unexpectedly, and both men returned home.

Frederick's accession brought no immediate change in Württemberg's policy. The new duke began by announcing his readiness to cooperate with the Diet and abide by the French treaty. Early in 1798 he gave Abel new instructions full of peaceful reassurance, detailing the acquisitions the duke felt were necessary to make his country a worthy ally of

13. The *Landtag* expired in May 1799 for want of readers. The previous summer complaints were already being heard in the Diet about its lack of influence (ibid., p. 458).

14. See George Willem Vreede, ed., *La Souabe après la paix de Bâle: Recueil de documents diplomatiques et parlementaires . . .* (Utrecht, 1879), pp. 15–48.

15. Hölzle, *Das alte Recht*, p. 148; cf. Johann Amadeus von Thugut to Franz von Colloredo, 18 Nov., 17 Dec. 1796, in *Vertrauliche Briefe des Freiherrn von Thugut: Beiträge zur Beurteilung der politischen Verhältnisse Europas in den Jahren 1792–1801*, ed. Alfred von Vivenot (Vienna, 1872), 1:353, 372.

16. Jacques Droz, *L'Allemagne et la Révolution Française* (Paris, 1949), p. 127.

17. *Der Landtag im Herzogthum Wirtemberg* 2, no. 3 (1797): 33–64.

18. Vreede, *La Souabe*, pp. 56–66.

France—a list that included most of the imperial lordships between the Danube and Lake Constance, and all the Free Cities in Swabia. The Austrian ministry, which had already been offered the same list privately, was dumbfounded but without recourse, and for a while it appeared that Frederick would be the beneficiary of the French alliance he had so earnestly opposed.[19] Within a few months, however, rumors of sedition and conspiracy in the Diet had revived Frederick's hostility to the estates and driven him back into the Austrian camp.

Frederick's fears were not groundless. In 1798–99 the deadlock in the Diet inspired a lot of excited talk among its members, some of whom began to meet secretly to make plans for an "Allemanic Republic" in Swabia. Discussions of this kind were encouraged by local representatives of the Revolution like the ambassador from the Batavian Republic, who opened his home in Stuttgart to disaffected members of the reform party, and by clandestine French emissaries, who had arranged Baz's trip to Paris and who continued to insinuate that their government would support dramatic initiatives in Württemberg.[20]

This was untrue. The revolutionary potential of a group like the "Circle of Free Men," which included many of the reformers and which met at the home of a French agent in Ludwigsburg,[21] would have been small in any case, since its deliberations reflected the same cross-purposes that hampered the Diet in other areas. The president of the hypothetical Allemanic Republic, for instance, was to have been Georgii, the assembly's most authentically conservative member. In the absence of strong support from France, moreover, Württemberg's revolutionary potential declined to zero. The reformers did not know that the Directory was resolved to cut itself loose from patriotic groups in Germany and that, when the time came, its generals would not assist indigenous revolutionary movements. Frederick had been told this, but he did not believe it.[22] When war resumed in 1799 he abandoned the separate peace. After removing himself to neutral territory, he placed his troops under Austrian command and instructed his officials to raise the countryside against the French.

The estates, left to face the inevitable French retaliation alone, were

19. Thugut to Colloredo, 31 Dec. 1797, in Thugut, *Vertrauliche Briefe* 2 : 75.

20. Hölzle, *Das alte Recht*, pp. 212–39; and Theodor Bitterauf, *Geschichte des Rheinbundes*, vol. 1: *Die Gründung des Rheinbundes und der Untergang des alten Reiches* (Munich, 1905), pp. 48–63.

21. Hölzle (*Das alte Recht*, pp. 234–35) mentions Steeb and Ludwig Huber in connection with this group, but not Cotta.

22. Klüpfel, "Friedensunterhandlungen," pp. 406–10; Raymond Guyot, *Le Directoire et la paix de l'Europe: Des Traités de Bâle à la deuxième coalition (1795–1799)* (Paris, 1911), pp. 865–67; and Thugut to Colloredo, 23 Jan. 1799, in Thugut, *Vertrauliche Briefe* 2 : 143.

in despair, but repeated pleas for Frederick to return and set things right brought no response. On the advice of Prussia, who promised diplomatic support as one of the original guarantors of the Hereditary Agreement,[23] the Diet again decided to send its own man to Paris, even though in this instance they had been forbidden to do so by the duke.[24] This time they chose Cotta. Apart from his sympathy for the reformers, Cotta was uniquely qualified for the mission by virtue of his long-standing friendship with Karl Reinhard, whose skill and tenacity in the face of ever-shifting political winds had just brought him appointment as foreign minister of France.[25] Reinhard's ascendancy suggested a way out for the estates, because as a native Württemberger it was assumed that he would instinctively side with the Diet and because his correspondence with Cotta had kept him abreast of developments in Stuttgart.

Time was short. When Cotta started for Paris, French troops were within hours of Stuttgart and Ludwigsburg. He had hardly reached the frontier, however, before the French commander, having vowed to take revenge for Württemberg's treachery, received orders to spare the cities. By the time Cotta arrived, Reinhard's hold on his office had been loosened by the coup d'état of 18 Brumaire; although his sympathies were all with Cotta, there was nothing he could do for his old friend.[26] But Cotta remained in town and eventually delivered his message to Reinhard's successor, Talleyrand, who despite his undoubted indifference to Württemberg's special problems was known to be susceptible to bribery, a contingency for which Cotta had prepared, just in case.[27] He returned home confident of success, only to find himself completely undone: the French in retreat, the Diet suspended, and Frederick secure on his throne, with an Austrian army at his back.

In the course of its long struggle with the ruling house a fair number of the Diet's schemes had miscarried, but none had ever unraveled as badly as this. The failure of Cotta's *Landtag* to mobilize public opinion behind the reformers had forced them to fall back on the time-honored expedient of foreign intrigue to maintain their position. Now that strategy had betrayed them, too. Although Cotta and his associates did not know it, his trip to Paris marked the beginning of the end for Württemberg's reformers, and for the Good Old Law as well.

23. Ludwig Hofacker to Cotta, 10 April 1800, in Vollmer, *Briefwechsel*, p. 384.

24. Klüpfel, "Friedensunterhandlungen," p. 416.

25. Wilhelm Lang, "K. Fr. Reinhard im auswärtigen Ministerium zu Paris," *Preussische Jahrbücher* 56 (1885): 362–88. Reinhard is the only German ever to hold this office.

26. Ibid. Before leaving office on November 21, Reinhard wrote to the executive committee to express his concern for their plight (Wilhelm Lang, *Graf Reinhard: Ein deutsch-französisches Lebensbild, 1761–1837* [Bamberg, 1896], p. 234).

27. Hölzle, *Das alte Recht*, p. 258.

TRUE REPUBLICANS

Cotta's mission was the climax of the Reform Diet's efforts to enlist a great power in its conflict with the crown. It was the assembly's most genuinely conspiratorial action, and it eventually provided the ammunition Frederick needed to defeat his enemies. At first the Diet suffered only for the least of its sins. It was dissolved not because of its secret diplomacy, but because it had thwarted the duke's efforts to raise the territorial militia. Cotta's trip remained a secret for more than a month, only to be revealed in the collapse of yet another attempt by the assembly to save itself.

Ever since the spring of 1799 Frederick had been looking for a pretext to step in and free his land from the grip of the estates.[28] He thought he had found one in the failure of the assembly to support the war with France, and when he returned to Stuttgart he filed a complaint with the *Reichshofrat*, asking its endorsement of his technically illegal decree of prorogation. This was granted.[29] Shortly thereafter the Austrian commander-in-chief, Archduke Charles, sent Frederick a note alleging a republican plot within the estates.[30] On the night of January 10 a dozen of the Diet's leaders were arrested and taken to prison, where a tribunal headed by Frederick's most trusted minister, Count Zeppelin, was convened to interrogate them. Those on the executive committee who were still free protested in vain, then decided, remarkably, to appeal to the Empire for help. Their chosen agent, even more remarkably, was the arch-Francophile C. F. Baz, who was immediately arrested by the Viennese police at Frederick's request. All the documents in his home and office were confiscated, including evidence of extensive contacts between the estates and French secret agents, a copy of Cotta's confidential instructions, and his canceled passports.

Cotta was arrested in Tübingen in the middle of the night on February 28 and hauled before Zeppelin's commission, where he testified for several hours.[31] Then he was let go. His defense, summarized in a memorandum a few weeks later, was unapologetic. There had been, he argued, no reason to doubt the Diet's power to name its own diplomatic representatives, since the crown had acquiesced in the earlier missions by Baz and Georgii. The military danger at the time was indisputable—witness Frederick's hasty departure to Franconia. A personal appeal to Reinhard offered the only hope of preserving the country from destruction at the hands of a state with which Württemberg was legally

---

28. Ibid., p. 253.
29. Imperial Decree of 17 Dec. 1799, in Klüpfel, "Friedensunterhandlungen," p. 415.
30. Archduke Charles to Frederick, 6 Jan. 1800, ibid., p. 417.
31. Report of State Secretary Vellnagel, 20 March 1800, ibid.

at peace. Whatever decisions the duke might have made countermand-
ing the existing treaty had been unknown to Cotta and everyone else,
since, although Frederick's adherence to the separate peace had been
widely publicized a year before, his order to transfer Württemberg's
troops to Austrian command had been kept out of the newspapers by
the censors—a nice point in view of the recent unpleasantness about the
Weltkunde. As far as Cotta could see, the Diet had merely been doing its
duty, in which he had gladly cooperated.[32]

This testimony, of course, was all nonsense. Cotta had known perfectly well that his mission to Paris was illegal in the eyes of the duke,[33]
and it is in any case hard to believe such a disingenuous defense could
have kept him out of prison by itself. The rump executive committee
presented its case in similar terms a few weeks later and aroused a good
deal of public sympathy, but without securing the release of its colleagues.[34] Cotta was probably saved less by his wits than by his friendship
with the Archduke Charles, to whom, in the words of an Austrian police
report, he had "rendered essential and dangerous service" by "communicating the results of his connections with France."[35] This was presumably less sinister than it sounds.[36] Cotta was, by virtue of his position as
publisher of the *Allgemeine Zeitung,* exceptionally well informed, and he
did not hesitate to use the information that came his way to ingratiate
himself with powerful men like the archduke, whose confidence flattered Cotta as much as did the friendship of a great artist like Schiller.

32. Cotta, Memorandum to the Württemberg Council [March/April 1800], in Vollmer,
Briefwechsel, pp. 382–84.

33. Cotta to Reinhard, 10 Jan. 1799, CA.

34. Vollmer, *Briefwechsel*, pp. 593–605. The estates' defense was sympathetically reported in the press, particularly in Carl Häberlin's *Staats-Archiv*, published by the firm of
Vierweg in Brunswick. Cotta purchased this journal sometime in 1800, and thereafter its
already favorable treatment of Württemberg's estates became even more pronounced.
Frederick tried to reply by paying for the printing of an essay by one of his councillors
called "Bemerkungen über den Wirtembergischen Landtag von 1797–99," but the distribution of this document was hindered, according to Hölzle (*Das alte Recht*, p. 254), by
"publishers friendly to the Estates."

35. Karl Glossy, "Ein Kapitel aus der Zeitungsgeschichte Alt-Österreichs," *Jahrbuch der
Grillparzer-Gesellschaft* 33 (1935): 136. Herbert Schiller ("Johann Friedrich Cotta," *Schwä-
bische Lebensbilder* [Stuttgart, 1943], 3 : 90) claims that Charles stepped in on Cotta's behalf.
A few letters between the two, which do not mention this episode, survive: Charles to
Cotta, [summer] 1799, 4 March 1801, and 19 Dec. 1803, CA.

36. Or maybe not. Cotta would one day set the value of his reports very high. In 1828
he told Austria's police minister Sedlnitzky that "the results in 1805 [at Austerlitz] would
certainly have been different if my accurate reports on the location and direction of the
French army had been believed" (Cotta to Count Joseph Sedlnitzky, 26 June 1828, in
Ursula Giese, "Studie zur Geschichte der Pressegesetzgebung, der Zensur, und des Zeitungswesens im frühen Vormärz," *Archiv für Geschichte des Buchwesens* 6 [1966]: cols.
496–97).

Some months before, Charles had rescued Posselt from arrest by one of his subordinates,[37] and there is no reason to suppose he would not have done the same for Cotta. But neither the archduke nor his brother the emperor had any reason to discourage Frederick from proceeding further against the estates.

Frederick believed that Cotta's mission was evidence of widespread disloyalty of a kind never contemplated by the Old Law. The emperor agreed and empowered Frederick to "restore trust between the ruler and the estates" by unilaterally dissolving the executive committee and holding new elections, from which all reformist elements would be excluded.[38] But complete victory continued to elude him. He had underestimated the resilience of the estates: new elections under Frederick's personal control yielded an assembly dominated by the *Ehrbarkeit*'s old leadership, but this body proved as intractable as the Reform Diet it displaced. Worse, Frederick had chosen the wrong side in the war. By the beginning of summer he was once again in flight before a French army under Moreau. It would be more than a year before he could return home, by which time French domination of southern Germany had become a certainty.

When the members of the executive committee testified before Zeppelin's commission, they insisted that the duke's interests had not been harmed by Cotta's mission, which Reinhard's fall from office had rendered fruitless. Cotta, in contrast, believed that he had been entirely successful and only regretted that the results of his trip had not been fully exploited.[39] During the first year or so following Moreau's advance across Swabia, Cotta's assessment seems closer to the truth. He had indeed reminded France of the friendly sentiments of Württemberg's estates. The indemnity levied in 1801 was heavily weighted against the duke, who also bore more than his share of the expense of quartering the French army of occupation. For a while there was talk of doing away with the Duchy of Württemberg altogether, a satisfactory solution to many of the reformers, and even to Frederick's Habsburg protectors. The duke, however, had friends of his own, including his nephew the czar, who was unwilling to see a member of his family cast adrift.[40] Even so, such loose talk about the future soon persuaded Frederick that he could expect nothing further from Austria. Whatever approximations of principle may once have guided his policy—loyalty to the Empire, hatred of the Revolution—had by now lost their meaning. By the middle of 1802 the duke had rehabilitated his relations with France to the point

37. Heyck, *Allgemeine Zeitung*, p. 238.
38. Imperial Rescript of 18 March 1800, in Vollmer, *Briefwechsel*, p. 382.
39. Cotta to Schiller, 18 April 1800, ibid., p. 378.
40. Klüpfel, "Friedensunterhandlungen," p. 424; Vreede, *La Souabe*, pp. 213–15.

where an agreement on compensation for his properties on the left bank could finally be signed. This settlement was confirmed the following year in the Final Decree of the Imperial Deputation, which also awarded Frederick the electoral title his family had coveted for so long.

During the years leading up to the founding of the Confederation of the Rhine, Cotta remained a firm friend of the old, now visibly enfeebled, imperial estates. So did others who had sympathized with the Revolution, only to be let down when the French abandoned constitutional government in their pursuit of national power. Throughout this period, those who stood for liberty in politics often found themselves standing alongside those whose privileges, however pernicious in practice, acted as a check on the authority of the state. Even after the reform movement in Württemberg had collapsed, Cotta did what he could. In 1801 he returned to Paris to plead for the preservation of Hohenzollern-Hechingen, a tiny enclave of Württemberg whose recent history had been marked by reformism and political compromise similar to that attempted in Württemberg, and which under the logic then prevailing might have been ceded to Frederick.[41] He also maintained his ties to disaffected groups in the *Ehrbarkeit*, which closed ranks around Frederick's son, William. When a personal grievance against his father drove William into exile in France, Cotta provided him with money and news of developments at home, thus aiding the prince's efforts, in concert with the estates, to overthrow the duke.[42] Such behavior only confirmed Frederick's distrust, at a time when the range of action open to the enemies of the crown was contracting steadily. The migration of French support toward the southern princes, combined with temporarily friendly Franco-Russian relations, gradually gave the crown an overwhelming advantage. The final reckoning came in December 1805, when the executive committee was summoned to the palace one last time, to learn that Frederick, now king, was setting aside the old constitution.

The alliance of convenience between revolutionary France and the Württemberg estates that shaped Cotta's politics as a young man could never have survived the ascendancy of Napoleon and the collapse of the Holy Roman Empire. This is true whatever one may think of the intricate web of argument linking the old freedoms of the German lands with the new freedoms of the French citizen, which provided the alliance with

41. Cotta to Goethe, 3 March 1801, in Kuhn, *Goethe und Cotta* 1:83; and Gustav Ströhmfeld, "Johann Friedrich Cotta: Der Volksfreund," *Balinger Tagblatt*, no. 304 (28 Dec. 1932). On the reform movement in Hohenzollern-Hechingen, see Volker Press, "Von den Bauernrevolten des 16. zur konstitutionellen Verfassung des 19. Jahrhunderts: Die Untertanenkonflikte in Hohenzollern-Hechingen," in *Politische Ordnungen und soziale Kräfte im alten Reich*, ed. Hermann Weber (Wiesbaden, 1980), pp. 85–112.

42. William to Cotta, 10 May, 21 July 1804, [June 1805,] and 18 July 1805, CA; cf. Erwin Hölzle, *Württemberg im Zeitalter Napoleons und der deutschen Erhebung* (Stuttgart and Berlin, 1937), pp. 137–39.

its intellectual basis. For the most part posterity has judged these arguments harshly, because the intellectual dexterity that marked them was
rarely matched by a willingness to face hard social questions. The widespread belief that German society already harbored the seeds of those
same liberties for which so many Frenchmen were dying was often sustained only by wishful thinking and willful ignorance. Yet the failure of
Württemberg's reformers to transform the Diet into a modern parliament does not mean they were incompetent or deluded. Their attempts
to create a constituency for themselves, to mobilize and take account of
public opinion, may have been inadequate, but they were not misguided.
Certainly it would be hard to argue that the political acumen of the reform generation in Germany was inferior to that of the early French
revolutionaries, whose interest in political liberalization did not include
delivering the state into the hands of anyone other than themselves.

The Revolution shattered the Württemberg *Ständestaat* not through
the force of its political ideas or its social vision, but through its repeated
recourse to violence,[43] which forced the estates to exceed their constitutional authority in order to protect themselves. If one sets aside the historical particulars of Württemberg's constitutional debate, it is clear that
the strategy of the reformers—with its emphasis on publicity and coalition building—was just what might be expected of parliamentary leaders
in a constitutional monarchy. Diplomatically, however, the Reform Diet
suffered from ever-worsening disorientation. When the estates appeal
to Austria to underwrite the separate peace with France; when the executive committee sends Baz to Vienna to complain about Frederick's
conduct; when Cotta demands, as he did following his arrest, that the
Zeppelin commission submit his case to the *Reichshofrat* for arbitration[44]—at these moments any student of the revolutionary era is likely
to feel a little giddy. Württemberg's reformers assimilated the major elements of the revolutionary agenda—expanded suffrage, land and tax
reform, separation of powers, and so on—to their own satisfaction, but
they were unable to grasp, at least to grasp quickly enough, that the
international system that had supported the estates in the past was ceas-
ing to exist. To the collapse of the Empire, and of the principle of legality that it represented for them, the only response they could formulate—arguably the correct one—was despair.

43. The Swabian experience thus seems to mirror that of the Rhineland, as described
by T.C.W. Blanning, *Reform and Revolution in Mainz, 1743–1797* (Cambridge, 1974); and,
more generally, idem, *The French Revolution in Germany: Occupation and Resistance in the
Rhineland, 1792–1802* (Oxford, 1983). Certainly the French army proved an unreliable
agent of liberation in southwest Germany. Although it might be too much to say of Württemberg, as Blanning says of the Rhenish lands, that the 1790s were "the age of counterrevolution" (*French Revolution in Germany*, p. 336), the decade certainly proved less conducive to reform at the end than the beginning seemed to promise.

44. Cotta to Zeppelin, 5 April 1800, in Vollmer, *Briefwechsel*, pp. 384–85.

When Cotta went to Paris at the end of 1799, he believed it was still possible to win useful concessions from the French. He also believed the larger cause of constitutional government was already lost, in Württemberg and in France too. Throughout the previous year Cotta had maintained a lively correspondence with Karl Reinhard, who was then serving as French ambassador to Florence.[45] In the beginning Cotta's letters held out some hope that piecemeal administrative reform would gradually produce significant improvement.[46] Within six months of Frederick's accession, however, he had come to believe that the Diet was overmatched and that in the end "it will probably be the estates that give way."[47] The international situation offered no comfort. Rastatt was a victory for the princes, a disaster for everyone else.[48] Prussia in particular was playing an "unworthy" role, by clinging to neutrality and failing to act as an honest broker between France and the Empire. This, Cotta believed, was to some extent forgivable, "when you consider that the king fears revolution in his own lands and does not trust his councillors." Still, "who in Germany can play a decisive role now, if Prussia cannot?"[49] Prussian support, after all, had been essential to the survival of Württemberg's constitution in 1770. In its absence, Cotta thought, "the future looks grim for us; the moment approaches when we will be thrown into the abyss."[50]

By the summer of 1798 the prospect of renewed fighting between France and the Empire had produced complete paralysis in Stuttgart, both because it made the future so uncertain and because it exacerbated what had long been a key issue dividing the duke and the estates: control of the army. "Our affairs," Cotta reported to Reinhard in August,

> continue as always along their old course—that is, hardly ever a step forward. What the duke seems to concede one day, when the horizon is warlike, he takes back the next, when the news points to peace. Except by force of open rebellion I cannot imagine the estates getting the duke to agree that, militarily, all we need is a territorial militia. Although the duke is on the one hand a good man and a good prince, he is on the other hand too vain to recognize his true interest here, and there are those around him who hold him back still more. In the estates themselves there are two parties. One group wants to secure and further develop our constitution; the other wants to overthrow everything and establish a republic. If war breaks

45. Reinhard visited Cotta in Tübingen at the end of 1797 while on his way to Italy (Heyck, *Allgemeine Zeitung*, p. 171). For the next eighteen months Cotta wrote to him regularly about events in Württemberg and the rest of Germany.
46. Cotta to Reinhard, 19 March 1798, CA.
47. Cotta to Reinhard, 20 June 1798, CA.
48. Cotta to Reinhard, 31 Dec. 1798, CA.
49. Cotta to Reinhard, 21 Aug. 1798, CA.
50. Cotta to Reinhard, 6 Feb. 1799, CA.

out, as seems inevitable at the moment, then the latter will be the fate of Swabia and a great part of Germany.[51]

It was not a fate Cotta could bring himself to wish for. He carried no brief for Germany's "gothic edifice," riven by self-destructive illusions and internal competition.[52] But the failure of the republican insurgency that had begun in France a decade before seemed equally clear, and more dangerous. Republicanism had promised to bring a "pure spirit of truth" to public life, as against the "spirit of dissimulation" that had prevailed in the past,[53] but it also demanded an unprecedented and perhaps unrealistic degree of discipline and self-sacrifice from its adherents. Could any political system so responsive to personal ambition overcome "the longing, which necessarily develops in men of common stamp, to extract the greatest use from their place?" "For great men," Cotta continued, "for true republicans, this is of no consequence. But we must take men as they are. And are not most bound to become greedy, rapacious, and inordinately eager to turn their office to their personal profit?" This was not an abstract question. Cotta believed himself to be a "true republican," and he feared he would suffer for it:

> When I think what would happen if, by some chance, those who admire and trust me should call on me to become finance minister: I would have to accept the office and leave my business behind. After a few years someone else would take over, and I would become superfluous. I would then return to the household gods, to find a ruined business, with my powers exhausted or diverted in such a way that they could not easily be turned to new commercial ventures. In short, I would be without bread. . . . Not everyone believes that it is man's duty to develop himself into a citizen of the world through physical and spiritual exertion, both for the present and for the sake of what awaits us after death. For the most part men seek calm, a carefree life, comfort in external wealth.[54]

Given the state of affairs in Württemberg at the time, the chances that Cotta would be called to the finance ministry (a recurring rumor for much of his life) were so slim as to make his diffidence quite unconvincing. Surely Cotta would have welcomed the chance to rise above the venality he despised, just as he welcomed the chance offered by his trip to Paris to step forward and do his part in a crisis. Cotta's fear that politics might not be good for his business was well founded: the *Neueste Weltkunde* had been suppressed just two weeks before, and he was writing to Reinhard in part to express his relief that he had managed to

51. Cotta to Reinhard, 21 Aug. 1798, CA.
52. Ibid.
53. Cotta to Reinhard, 3 Aug. 1798, CA.
54. Cotta to Reinhard, 27 Aug. 1798, CA.

patch things up with the duke and would not be going bankrupt after all. It seemed to him perversely unjust that, in good times and bad, in war as in peace, the demands of his profession remained unchanging and unforgiving of mistakes. Even years later, when his personal fortune had been rendered impervious to such setbacks, Cotta would routinely complain whenever public affairs took him away from his business for too long.[55] Although there is no reason to doubt the sincerity of these feelings, they were always outweighed by Cotta's sense of responsibility as a "citizen of the world" and by his desire, which he seems to have reconciled easily enough with the demands of true republicanism, to distinguish himself from other men. In the course of his long career, Cotta never refused an opportunity to make himself useful to any government.

For the most part, Reinhard sympathized with his friend. The suppression of the *Weltkunde* seemed to him a "sign of the times" and fresh evidence of Russian meddling in Germany.[56] The future of republicanism in Europe, however, meant nothing to him except as it related to the future of the French republic. As to that, he could only insist that "the republic is in the hands of republicans":

> Certainly the longing to make good the errors of the past becomes stronger every day. We live in a time when no clear choice exists except between the French system, with all its shortcomings, and the system of [Czar] Paul I, with all its privileges. If you want to see Pitt's system as a middle way, so be it. But it is too artificial to be applicable to Europe as a whole, and Russian brutality and stupidity are at least more natural than the cold, treacherous cruelty of the English.[57]

There is unfortunately nothing in Cotta's letters with which to flesh out Reinhard's remark about "Pitt's system," though, as I have said, admiration for England was widespread among Württemberg's reformers. More fundamentally, however, Reinhard had missed Cotta's point. The competition between "systems" that dominated the political horizon was itself inimical to the growth of the republican spirit, in Cotta's eyes, because it neglected the question of how free public institutions could be harmonized with man's moral nature. "It is increasingly my conviction," Cotta wrote a few months later,

> that a constitution such as ours [in Württemberg], improved and purified, is the most salutary for men as they are right now. A higher level of freedom requires a higher spirit and a higher ethical culture. This, i.e. ethical

55. Cf. Cotta to Reinhard, 21 Jan. 1799, CA; and Cotta to Goethe, 26 Sept. 1816, in Kuhn, *Goethe und Cotta* 2:26–27.

56. Reinhard to Cotta, 15 Sept. 1798, in Fehling and Schiller, *Briefe an Cotta* 1:459.

57. Reinhard to Cotta, 25 Aug. 1798, ibid., p. 457; cf. Lang, *Graf Reinhard*, pp. 195–96.

culture, seems to be declining rather than increasing. Thus, although you have so splendidly removed some of my earlier doubts, some still remain. I fear that republicanism in its present form inflames human passion too much. Avarice and ambition, the two most powerful human motives, are given the greatest scope. Where must this lead men who do not possess the highest level of moral cultivation? Indeed, if men like you were able to found and govern a republic fashioned in a nonrepublican spiritual climate, then certainly, by and by, the masses would be improved. And finally a true republic would exist, free of the play of passion, as the still higher fulfillment of all our powers.[58]

Cotta was not a political philosopher, and his thoughts on republicanism will not bear the kind of analysis one might apply to the ideas of someone like Schiller, with whom Cotta obviously shared a good deal. At the time of his correspondence with Reinhard, however, Cotta was clearly preoccupied, as Schiller had been a few years before, with the morality rather than the mechanism of politics. In his letters, "republicanism" refers to the proper disposition of the gifted individual toward society, a disposition that was unrelated to any political program, democratic or otherwise. For Cotta the "true republican" was admirable not because he personified the will of the people, but because his selflessness made him fit to lead.

By the time he met Cotta, Schiller had decided that such individuals were too rare to be counted on to solve the desperate problems of the modern world, which he understood mainly in moral terms.[59] Cotta was inclined to agree. If he failed to follow Schiller into a dignified political quietism, it was because he believed that the ordinary, unedifying processes of growth and compromise exemplified by Württemberg's constitution retained their usefulness. That he should have felt this way despite his contempt for the pettiness and corruption around him may seem peculiar. But it is at least understandable that a prudent man, faced with the choice between revolution and tyranny offered by Reinhard, would look for a way to choose neither.

To repeat, then, an earlier observation: ideas change when they are used. Ideas like "republicanism" and "nonpartisanship" run like red threads through the history of the Cotta press. They were intended to be taken seriously, not as slogans concealing resignation or empty tolerance, but as positive values, to be cherished for their own sakes and for the sake of other, more universal values—intelligence, legality, individualism—to which they were linked. They thus represent Cotta's best attempt to appropriate the cultural and political experience of the Old Regime and apply these to a changing world. When Cotta founded the *Allgemeine Zeitung*, his republicanism, shorn of its emotional and patri-

58. Cotta to Reinhard, 16 Nov. 1798, CA.
59. See Körner to Schiller, 7 Nov. 1794, in Schiller and Körner, *Briefwechsel* 2: 122–24.

otic content, amounted to scarcely more than an honorable conviction that no man should rule alone. *Unparteilichkeit* was to him what "Enlightenment" was to his friend Schiller: the best means of maintaining one's integrity in a revolutionary situation. In the Europe of Napoleon, it would become a political position in its own right, to be defended against those who would compel everyone to choose a side.

To a successful pragmatist like Reinhard, Cotta's concern for "ethical culture" seemed more than a little remote. Such reply as he could offer he offered in person. When Cotta arrived in Paris to plead for Württemberg's estates, Reinhard informed him that, whatever the merits of his cause, politics had nothing to do with love for mankind.[60] We do not know the tone—rueful? angry? impatient?—in which Reinhard delivered this remark, but it cannot have been all that shocking. Cotta may not have been a natural-born *Realpolitiker*, but neither was he inclined to self-deception. Paris, which had made such a seminal impression only a few years before, now seemed to him "a city of childishness, folly, and frivolity." He was convinced, moreover, that "the majority of Germans are deceiving themselves about these people."[61] When he returned two years later his views had become harder still. The French capital, he wrote to Goethe, had once again become "a royal city, more dreadful and muddled than ever. It would have been hard to find more ostentation and despotism under Louis XIV than under the present First Consul." It was in all "a sorry spectacle," whose end was "nowhere in sight."[62]

60. Hölzle, *Das alte Recht*, p. 258.
61. Cotta to Goethe, 10 Dec. 1799, in Kuhn, *Goethe und Cotta* 1 : 62.
62. Cotta to Goethe, 7 April 1801, ibid., p. 84.

FOUR

French Hegemony

Introduction:
  Journalism overall is the frank and simple art of informing people about what is happening in the world. It is an entirely private matter, and all the ends of government, however one may describe them, are foreign to it.
Amplification:
  French journalism is the art of making the people believe what suits the government. It is an entirely official matter, and all meddling by private individuals, including the distribution of private letters on current affairs, is forbidden.
Two Fundamental Principles:
  What the people don't know won't hurt them.
  Whatever you tell the people three times, they believe.
                      Heinrich von Kleist, "Textbook of French Journalism," 1809

Historians have not found much to argue about as far as the French treatment of the German press is concerned, in contrast to most other aspects of Napoleonic statecraft. For good reason: on the one occasion when Napoleon had a German publisher entirely in his hands, he had him shot, an act whose simplicity, indeed finality, does not leave much room for quibbling over details. Selective execution was not Napoleon's entire policy; but it may serve as a reminder that, among the ruling personalities of Europe, it was the emperor of the French who set the greatest store in the power of the press. Napoleon had seen an aroused nation at first hand, and as the leader of Europe's first postrevolutionary society he brought to the regulation of public opinion a degree of determination unknown to the Old Regime. One of his earliest acts as first consul had been to suppress most of the newspapers published in France, and he soon domesticated those that remained. His aim was not to expel public opinion from the political arena, but to remove it from the hands of the public and make it serve him. The same purpose guided his policy in Germany.

The *Allgemeine Zeitung* (*AZ*) was one of the first German newspapers to attract Napoleon's attention. Despite its recent appearance it had quickly become one of the most influential periodicals in central Europe. Although it sold fewer copies than some of its competitors, it was aimed at the people who counted, and its reach extended wherever those people were found—"from England to Sicily and from Paris to Moscow . . . and even Turkey," as Cotta would later recall.[1] While two thou-

---

1. Cotta to Gabriel de Bray [Bavarian ambassador in Vienna], 24 Dec. 1828, in Heyck, *Allgemeine Zeitung*, p. 254. The reference to Turkey was not an idle boast; cf. Miljan Mo-

sand copies would obviously spread awfully thin in such a space, those who could get their hands on one were provided a quality of coverage they could get nowhere else.

Unlike all but a handful of German newspapers, the *AZ* gathered and published its own news. In this respect it outstripped even its great rival, the Hamburg *Correspondent*, whose editors declined to violate the traditional prohibition on *raisonnements* in newspapers—a custom that Cotta preferred to honor in the breach. As a *raisonierte Zeitung* with European range, in short, the *AZ* was unique.[2] Like its less prosperous cousins, Cotta's newspaper included a lot of secondhand material; but private correspondence was the *AZ*'s hallmark, the concrete realization of the impartial universality to which Cotta aspired. The appearance of private reports alongside the public documents and official explanations that constituted what Posselt had called "the facts" symbolized the individual's right to draw his own conclusions about the meaning of events. If, as Napoleon intended, the press was to be reduced to an instrument of state power, such a newspaper would have to be brought to heel. This proved to be a complicated problem.

THE FRENCH PURSUIT OF THE *ALLGEMEINE ZEITUNG*

Shortly after his dismissal as editor of the *Neueste Weltkunde*, Ernst Posselt wrote to Cotta to express his pleasure that their paper would be continuing under another name. At the same time he confessed to doubts that the *Weltkunde*'s successor had much of a future. As editor of the *Europäische Annalen*, Posselt had played a leading role in the public defense of the Peace of Basel in southern Germany and had repeatedly advocated peace with the Revolution on almost any terms.[3] Now, however, his skepticism about the kind of peace one might achieve had begun to deepen. If the *Allgemeine Zeitung*'s more factual emphasis made it unsuited to the turmoil of wartime, it seemed to Posselt even more likely that the newspaper would be suppressed as a challenge to the status quo

jasevic, "Die Augsburger *Allgemeine Zeitung* in der fürstlich-serbischen Kanzlei, 1821–1834," *Archiv für Kulturgeschichte* 47 (1965): 338–50.

2. Karl Glossy, "Ein Kapitel aus der Zeitungsgeschichte Alt-Österreichs," *Jahrbuch der Grillparzer-Gesellschaft* 33 (1935): 134–35. The quality of the *AZ*'s reporting and the influential character of its audience were mutually reinforcing. Contributions to the *AZ*, as Heinrich Laube later remarked, came from "the most important people in the Fatherland. Every minister took care that his news appeared in this paper, that it was well presented, well supported. Every publicist strove to have his views expounded there, because he knew that all the powerful read it" (Max von Boehn, *Biedermeier: Deutschland von 1815–1847* [Berlin, 1932], p. 373).

3. Kari Hokkanen, *Krieg und Frieden in der politischen Tagesliteratur Deutschlands zwischen Baseler und Lunéviller Frieden (1795–1801)*, Studia Historica Jyväskyläensia, no. 11 (Jyväskylä, Fin., 1975), pp. 46–50, provides copious references.

once peace was achieved.[4] To Cotta, who dreaded war, this must have seemed a strange comment. It proved to be remarkably astute.

The *AZ* survived during its first few difficult years partly on the strength of Cotta's connection with Archduke Charles, whose civilian aide, Matthias von Fassbender, kept the paper informed about the war with France. As Cotta recalled later on, the *AZ* thus became "in effect a German or Austrian *Arméezeitung*, directed against the enemies of the Empire."[5] Alongside these reports, however, were others of different import, articles by political activists in the Rhineland, Alsace, Baden, and Switzerland, who continued to portray the French advance into Germany as an opportunity for political progress.[6] Württemberg's Duke Frederick found the paper's editorial mix less than ideal but tolerable, since the *AZ* stayed clear of the duchy's domestic problems.

With the promulgation of the Final Decree of the Imperial Deputation in February 1803, however, the struggle between the Empire and its enemies seemed to have reached its end. The necessary innovations had been made, and the time for consolidation had come. Such a moment should presumably have favored a paper with aspirations to impartiality, but it did not. Frederick's toleration of the *AZ* had reflected the uncertainty of his own diplomatic position, which made it convenient to shelter a paper that managed, after a fashion, to serve the interests of both his potential patrons. Having received an electoral title from the hands of the French, however, such forbearance was no longer necessary, and in October 1803 Frederick ordered the *AZ* to cease publication.[7]

4. Posselt to Cotta, 2 Oct. 1798, CA.

5. Cotta to Bray, 28 Dec. 1828, in Heyck, *Allgemeine Zeitung*, p. 254.

6. A number of the *AZ*'s early correspondents have been identified by Heyck (*Allgemeine Zeitung*, pp. 130–43, 168–71, 238) on the basis of letters in the Cotta Archive. Beginning in 1807 it is sometimes possible to discover the source of an article by referring to the marginal notations in a surviving editorial exemplar (CA). The editor marked each number of the paper to indicate who sent in a given story, and then forwarded the marked copy to Cotta, who handled the necessary payments. The source identified in this way was not necessarily the author of the piece. Many of the *AZ*'s regular contributors acted as clearinghouses for material sent by third parties. Articles from a single source could thus carry many different datelines. Cotta himself is by far the most frequent source mentioned, a designation that usually indicates nothing more than that the editors had received a manuscript indirectly, via Cotta, and that only Cotta knew whom to pay.

Early in its history the *AZ* developed organizational principles to which it adhered thereafter. Correspondence and related official or secondhand material would be grouped together by country, and correspondence was almost always identified as such in the text. Over the years typographical insignia—asterisks, daggers, etc.—were devised to identify (and occasionally obscure) the work of regular contributors. In references to *AZ* articles after 1807, the names of contributors identified in the editorial exemplar will hereafter be enclosed in brackets.

7. "Decree Respecting the Suppression of the *Allgemeine Zeitung*," 12 Oct. 1803, in Vollmer, *Briefwechsel*, p. 660.

It is a measure of the strength of Frederick's position that he felt no
obligation to explain his decision, one that has since been attributed either to his displeasure at an article on the French Legion of Honor,
which he might have taken as disparaging of his new status as elector,[8]
or to his anger at Cotta's support of his disaffected son William.[9] Frederick had twice before taken offense at the AZ's oblique criticism of his
policies. In December 1799 he suspended the paper for eight days because of a few lines in an article on the English theater that seemed to
call his devotion to peace into question.[10] Three months later he ordered
the senate of Tübingen University to investigate some advertisements
promoting books of which he disapproved.[11] That these incidents should
have occurred in the wake of Cotta's clandestine trip to Paris made them
especially alarming, but the connection was more apparent than real.
Cotta's mission was still a secret when the AZ was suspended, and although Cotta's obstructive attitude toward Zeppelin's commission probably contributed to the duke's decision to have the paper's advertisements investigated, the small fine that the law prescribed in such cases
was hardly the stuff of a prince's revenge. Even so, it was only reasonable
to suppose that Cotta would have to pay a price for his involvement with
the duke's opponents.[12] Cotta believed his support of Crown Prince William had made the duke his "personal enemy";[13] but he also knew that
the duke's motives were more than personal. Frederick might have put
down the AZ at any time. He finally did so in the fall of 1803 because
he was asked to, as part of a French-inspired campaign to pacify public opinion in Switzerland—a cause less remote from its effect than it
may seem.

From the beginning, the AZ had paid more attention to the new Hel-
vetic Republic than to any state but France, partly because events there
were of intrinsic interest to the Swabian reformers but also because Switzerland was close by, which made swift reporting easy and cheap. The
first and most important of Cotta's correspondents there was the Zurich
physician Paul Usteri. As a member of the Swiss Constitutional Commission, Usteri had voted with the federalist majority in favor of a strong,
unified state capable of enforcing domestic peace. When the commission
failed to accomplish this, however, the French began to favor compromise with the patriciate of the individual Swiss cantons, which, like the

8. Ibid., p. 661; cf. AZ, 13 Oct. 1804.
9. Erwin Hölzle, "Cotta, der Verleger und die Politik," Historische Vierteljahrsschrift 29
(1934): 580.
10. Vollmer, Briefwechsel, p. 653; cf. AZ, 10 Dec. 1799.
11. Vollmer, Briefwechsel, pp. 656–57.
12. Cf. J. C. Mellish to Schiller, 9 April 1800, ibid., p. 377.
13. Cotta to Schiller, 11 Nov. 1803, ibid., p. 501.

conservative elements of Württemberg's estates, refused to stand aside while its traditional rights were disposed of.

It was Karl Reinhard who was given the job of dishing the Swiss federalists, having been named ambassador to Bern following his brief stint as foreign minister. Cotta was dismayed by his friend's support of the Swiss conservatives, and when he was back in Paris in 1801 he put it about that Reinhard, whom he had visited in Switzerland the year before, was letting himself be used by the nobility.[14] The rift between the two men never healed, in part because Reinhard's tenure provided Usteri with material for a series of articles exposing what he judged to be France's duplicity.[15] By then the *AZ* had already become a de facto organ of the Swiss opposition.[16] It was only following Napoleon's Act of Mediation two years later that a concerted effort was made to subdue the Swiss press, and particularly to subdue Usteri, who had become one of the most impressive and outspoken of Swiss journalists.[17] As Usteri's main foreign venue, the *AZ* was a principal target of this campaign, which was conducted by Napoleon's personal choice as chief magistrate of the Swiss Confederation, Louis d'Affry, and orchestrated, Cotta supposed, by Talleyrand himself.[18]

If there was a bright side to all this it was, as Cotta wrote to Reinhard, that now "everyone can see that we have never stood in the pay of France."[19] True enough. Although Cotta and his editor had not hesitated to publish material favorable to Usteri's opponents, they received very little. Cotta had been aware early on that his paper's treatment of Swiss affairs was attracting unfavorable comment, and at one stage he tried to recruit the Swiss counterrevolutionary journalist Karl Ludwig von Haller as spokesman for the other side.[20] It seems unlikely, however,

14. Else R. Gross, ed., *Karl Friedrich Reinhard, 1761–1837: Ein Leben für Frankreich und Deutschland. Gedenkschrift zum 200. Geburtstag* (Stuttgart, 1961), p. 153; and Lang, *Graf Reinhard*, pp. 259–60.

15. These articles appeared regularly under the rubric "Schweiz" throughout the first half of 1801.

16. Verger [Bavarian envoy in Bern] to Maximilian von Montgelas, 10 April 1804, Bayerisches Hauptstaatsarchiv, Abteilung I: Geheimes Staatsarchiv, Archiv des Innenministeriums (hereafter cited as M Inn) 25097/I.

17. Gottfried Guggenbühl, *Geschichte der Schweizerischen Eidgenossenschaft* (Erlenbach and Zurich, 1947–48), 2:283–84.

18. Cotta to Reinhard, 15 Oct. 1803, CA.

19. Ibid.

20. In 1798 Karl Böttiger wrote to Cotta that the *Weltkunde*'s treatment of Swiss affairs "can only outrage the most fervent supporters of representative republicanism" and that he knew many right-thinking men in the north, "*not aristocrats*," who had given up their subscriptions. Cotta replied that he took the point, but that the *Weltkunde* had also been subject to "bitter complaints about its democratic attitude." The best he could do, in the absence of contributors with an objective point of view, was to print material from both

that a better reportorial balance could have saved the *AZ*: a paper that was equally admired by Archduke Charles and General Moreau must, after all, have been doing pretty well in this respect. In the end the *AZ* was undone not because of any specific offense, but because it stood in the way of a political reconciliation that Napoleon believed could best be accomplished with a minimum of publicity.

Like so many of Napoleon's seemingly effortless victories, however, this one had depended on the skillful exploitation of local conditions—on the mutual hostility of Cotta and his prince, and on Frederick's need for French support against the estates. Similar pressure applied to the Hamburg *Correspondent* at about this same time yielded less satisfactory results because of the obstinacy of the city fathers.[21] Even with the *AZ*, the French success was short-lived. The particularism of the German states had always presented obstacles to the ambitions of outsiders, and that was still the case. It was not all that surprising, then, that, three weeks after Frederick's ban, Cotta's newspaper should have resurfaced unscathed just across the Bavarian border, in Ulm.

If Cotta had needed any reassurance about the *AZ*'s standing in Germany, he surely found it in the offers of sanctuary he received from a half-dozen of Württemberg's neighbors.[22] One of the most attractive proposals had come from Baden, a state with a reputation for liberality toward the press. In the end, however, Cotta preferred to cast his lot with Bavaria. Although Ulm could not match the intellectual resources of Heidelberg, it offered numerous commercial advantages, including excellent transportation by land and water and ideal postal service—the mail coach arrived every morning and did not leave until late afternoon. Bavaria also agreed to supplement Ludwig Huber's salary as editor by giving him a nominal position in the district school administration, to bear part of the cost of incoming mail, and to let Cotta operate his own printing presses—all valuable concessions, in relation to which legal considerations shrank to insignificance.[23]

Before the arrival of the *AZ*, Bavaria had possessed only the most rudimentary press[24] and a correspondingly rudimentary press law. In

sides, as he also tried to do with respect to France itself (Böttiger to Cotta, 30 March 1798, and Cotta's reply, 10 April 1798, in Sondermann, *Böttiger*, pp. 115–17). On Cotta's approach to Haller, see Heyck, *Allgemeine Zeitung*, p. 140; and Christoph Pfister, *Die Publizistik Karl Ludwig von Hallers in der Frühzeit, 1791–1815* (Bern, 1975), p. 64.

21. Ernst Baasch, *Geschichte des hamburgischen Zeitungswesens von den Anfängen bis 1914* (Hamburg, 1930), p. 7.

22. Cotta to Schiller, 11 Nov. 1803, in Vollmer, *Briefwechsel*, p. 501.

23. Cotta to Max Joseph, 7 Nov. 1803, M Inn 25097/I.

24. An exception, albeit only of regional significance, must be made for the press of the Pfalz; see Christel Hess, *Presse und Publizistik in der Kurpfalz in der zweiten Hälfte des 18. Jahrhunderts* (Frankfurt, 1987).

comparison to the situation in Baden, where the much-admired Press Edict of 1797 provided the margrave's officials with a detailed set of regulatory procedures, in Bavaria censors were directed in their work by ad hoc cabinet memoranda[25]—a less consistent system, but one whose flexibility appealed to the man who devised it, Maximilian von Montgelas. Furthermore, ever since Montgelas's arrival in 1799 political censorship had been in the hands of the foreign ministry; Bavaria had thus become one of the first German states to acknowledge officially what Cotta had already learned at some cost: that the management of the press was a matter for diplomats, not sheriffs.

This shift of emphasis and authority was not in itself a liberalizing reform, but it did incorporate a more instrumental approach to press regulation than had prevailed in the past. Whereas the old Office of Spiritual Affairs had dedicated itself unreservedly to checking the spread of new ideas, Montgelas was prepared to consider a more constructive policy, one that could exploit the press to enhance Bavaria's influence and prestige. Montgelas was therefore happy to have attracted a famous newspaper to his newly enlarged state, just as Cotta was thankful for Bavaria's evident goodwill.[26] It did not take long, however, for the legal basis of their relationship to be put to the test.

In March 1804 the *AZ* once again found itself in trouble with the Swiss, who lodged a series of protests against its "scandalous efforts to compromise the amicable relations and close alliance that the Swiss Confederation enjoys with the government of France."[27] In place of the swift satisfaction provided by Württemberg's Duke Frederick, however, the Swiss now found themselves entangled in an elaborately pointless correspondence involving the Bavarian embassy in Bern, the foreign ministry in Munich, the district government in Ulm, and the Cotta Verlag in Tübingen. Baron Verger, Bavaria's ambassador, thought the Swiss complaints were reasonable, since in his view the *AZ*'s influence there had become "extremely dangerous."[28] Montgelas, hearing this, de-

25. On Baden's press law, see F. Schneider, *Pressefreiheit und politische Öffentlichkeit*, p. 140; the Bavarian ordinance is discussed in Theodor Bitterauf, "Die Zensur der politischen Zeitungen in Bayern, 1799–1825," *Riezler-Festschrift*, ed. Karl Alexander von Müller (Gotha, 1913), pp. 306–8.

26. The Bavarian authorities had hoped that Cotta would move his entire firm to their territory, a plan that seems to have been encouraged by Cotta's friend and client Friedrich Schelling, then a professor at Würzburg. Although these hopes were disappointed (as they would be again twenty years later), Cotta was decidedly impressed by the efficiency and straightforward manner of the ministry in Munich. While efficiency would not prove to be the hallmark of Bavaria's administration, the good personal chemistry that Cotta sensed at the outset would count for a great deal. See Cotta to Böttiger, 28 Nov. 1803, in Sondermann, *Böttiger*, pp. 141–43.

27. Chief Magistrate Wattenwyl to Verger, 3 April 1804, M Inn 25097/I.

28. Verger to Montgelas, 4 April 1804, ibid.

manded an explanation from Huber, who replied, as Cotta had to the Austrians six years before, that all the articles in dispute were based on official sources and that he would gladly publish whatever comparable material the Swiss might supply.[29] But since the bone of contention was precisely the unauthorized publication of official documents, this simply begged the question, and led to further correspondence. Under the circumstances, the Swiss would have been justified in feeling that Montgelas was not playing by the rules. After months of wrangling, though, Bavaria's foreign minister remained unmoved by the notion that the *AZ*'s existence might not be in the Swiss interest. He considered it imprudent to suppress factual material in a paper that his own censors had pronounced "the envy of all enlightened governments,"[30] and he would insist only that the editor publish appropriate corrections, as Huber had already offered.[31]

In Württemberg, Swiss success had depended on direct French support. This was not forthcoming in Bavaria until October, when an article entitled "Views of the Imperial City of Paris, in the First Days of the 13th Year of the Republic" caught the eye of the head of the French legation in Munich, Ludwig von Otto.[32] The piece was by any standard arresting, focusing as it did on the reemergence of royalist etiquette in anticipation of Napoleon's coronation, with ancillary discussions of such matters as the execution of the duc d'Enghien, the humiliation of the church under the recent concordat, the difficulty war veterans had pronouncing the words *Most Serene Highness,* and the mixed feelings of the prostitutes around the Palais Royal, who looked forward to the upcoming festivities for reasons of their own but worried that their relatives might come to town and find them out. That such a report should have appeared under the protection of a government friendly to his own was to Otto beyond belief. But Bavaria's elector, Max Joseph, had remained cool toward Napoleon's imperial pretensions, and his cabinet offered only a perfunctory response to the ambassador's protest. Five days later Otto's government banned the importation of the *AZ* into France.[33]

Politically and financially, this was a severe blow: apart from the prospect that other states would follow the French lead, France itself now governed a large German-speaking population in the Rhineland, to which the *AZ* was effectively denied access. It need hardly be said that the article in question was not typical of the *AZ*'s coverage, which had

29. Ludwig Huber, "Pro Memoria," 8 April 1804, ibid.

30. District President Hartling to Montgelas, 10 April 1804, ibid.

31. Montgelas to Verger, 25 June 1804, ibid.

32. Otto to Montgelas, 24 Oct. 1804, ibid. The article appeared on October 22 and attracted considerable comment (cf. Friedrich Gentz to Böttiger, 19 March 1803, 6 Nov. 1804, in Wittichen and Salzer, *Briefe* 1 : 268, 277).

33. Huber to the Ulm Commissariat, 6 Nov. 1804, M Inn 25097/I.

always been respectful, even when it was not sympathetic. Some of what it had to say about the new royalism was true, as Cotta had seen for himself three years before. But that he would have deliberately let such an article appear in print is unimaginable; it is indeed unlikely that he even read it, since he was at this time once more on the verge of flight to avoid imprisonment by Frederick, whose assault on his domestic opponents was entering its final stage.[34] Huber certainly had not seen it—he was away on vacation when it arrived. In all probability only Karl Stegmann, a protégé of Usteri's hired to assist Huber, had reviewed the article; and he readily admitted that it should never have been published.[35]

None of this would have mattered if the *AZ's* editorial laxity had not mirrored that of the authorities. What, after all, were censors for, if not to prevent this sort of thing from happening? Fifteen months earlier, Max Joseph had ordered an end to censorship of books and nonpolitical periodicals. Although this measure did not apply to newspapers, its language was (characteristically) vague. Thus, when the Imperial Deputation assigned part of Franconia to Bavaria, the ministry sent a clarifying memorandum to the district governor there to insure that the *Bamberger Zeitung*, which would now appear under his authority, would be properly supervised.[36] When the *AZ* moved to Ulm five months later, however, no similar explanation was provided, and so local officials believed that the *AZ* was protected by a "guarantee of freedom of the press."[37] Stegmann had understandably regarded the district government as a kind of political safety net and assumed that even incompetent censorship conveyed some sort of political protection. But this assumption was not shared in Munich, where his appeals for help in getting the ban lifted went unanswered. Since the end of the war Montgelas had tried to maintain a neutral posture toward all the great powers. The French, facing a new war with Austria, now served notice that this would no longer do,[38] and the *AZ* was left to strike its own bargain.

Negotiations to end the ban took months, during which time the price of French cooperation rose steadily. It was demanded first that the *AZ* should publish official French bulletins on request, then that the paper

34. Cotta to Schiller, 11, 17 Sept. 1804, in Vollmer, *Briefwechsel*, pp. 528–30.

35. Protocol of an interview between Karl Stegmann and District President von Arco, 3 Nov. 1804; cf. Huber to the Ulm Commissariat, 6 Nov. 1804, M Inn 25097/I.

36. Bitterauf, "Zensur der politischen Zeitungen," p. 313.

37. Montgelas to Arco, 27 Oct. 1804; cf. Hartling to Montgelas, 10 April 1804, M Inn 25097/I. This misunderstanding was shared by the magistrates of Nuremberg. When that city was incorporated into Bavaria in 1806, its leaders eliminated municipal censorship of newspapers in order to comply with what they believed was Bavarian law (Ernst Meier, *Zeitungsstadt Nürnberg* [Berlin, 1963], p. 40).

38. Wolfgang Quint, *Souveränitätsbegriff und Souveränitätspolitik in Bayern: Von der Mitte des 17. bis zur ersten Hälfte des 19. Jahrhunderts* (Berlin, 1971), p. 148n.

should also accept commentary prepared by French officials, and finally that the editor himself should write articles supporting French policy. Stegmann, who became editor-in-chief of the *AZ* following Huber's unexpected death in December, had no reservations about the first two of these stipulations; he would have accepted such material from any European government. But he could not accept the final condition, for it was contrary to the very nature of the *AZ*, which "as a rule confines itself strictly to true, factual reports, and to historical expositions based on sources from both sides."[39] If this standard were to be abandoned, he argued, the *AZ*'s support would not be worth having.

The French therefore relented a little. Stegmann agreed to treat war news in a way that did not prejudice French interests, and to report English domestic affairs along the same lines as Whig opposition papers like the *Morning Chronicle*—more or less as he had all along. He also promised to publish occasional pieces of his own, disguised as the work of foreign correspondents and "written," he told Cotta, "in a spirit that should please the people in Paris, if anyone there can read German." In return the French promised to lift their ban and to keep the *AZ* supplied with authoritative reports on French affairs.[40]

Thus, by sacrificing a measure of its independence, the *AZ* regained entry into France. The deal also included some sweeteners for both sides. Cotta had achieved a modest commercial foothold in the French capital the year before, through the publication of a literary quarterly called *Archives littéraires de l'Europe*. Now, he believed, he enjoyed "relations of a sort that put me in a position to publish anything at all there"—a belief that proved to be mistaken.[41] The French, for their part, had acquired a respected German voice that could "present the positive results of the great operations of the emperor with the calmness and moderation of the foreigner."[42]

They also acquired a new source of information on German affairs. In addition to everything else, Stegmann agreed to keep the French police ministry informed of any news that might later turn up in the French papers. To the French this was the best part of their bargain with the *AZ*. One might indeed argue that the *AZ*'s editor was virtually a French spy, who, in complicity with Germany's most powerful publisher,

39. Stegmann to Cotta, [July 1805], excerpt in Heyck, *Allgemeine Zeitung*, pp. 173–75; in its entirety, CA.

40. Ibid.

41. Cotta to August Schlegel, 29 July 1805, in Josef Körner, ed., *Krisenjahre der Frühromantik: Briefe aus dem Schlegelkreis* (Brünn, 1936–58), 1:221–22; cf. Roland Mortier, "Une Revue germanisante sous l'Empire: *Les Archives littéraires de l'Europe* (1804–08)," *Revue de la littérature comparée* 25 (1951): 43–64.

42. Stegmann to Cotta, [July 1805], CA.

maintained a secret correspondence with the sinister Fouché himself. In all likelihood Stegmann did nothing illegal to obtain the material he sent to Paris, any more than Cotta had a few years before, when he enjoyed an equally confidential relationship with Archduke Charles. Still, one naturally thinks of Stegmann's unfortunate contemporary, August von Kotzebue, who would be murdered a few years later for providing a similar service to the czar. Certainly the Bavarian police took an uncharitable view of the whole affair once they got wind of it—but that was not until 1813, and by then Montgelas preferred to let the matter drop.[43]

No government ever bent Cotta's newspaper to its will as thoroughly as did Napoleonic France. Yet it is an open question how far the French would have had to go to suppress the AZ if they had had a mind to. Although the execution of J. P. Palm in August 1806 leaves no doubt about Napoleon's seriousness in such matters, seriousness does not always bring success. Napoleon chose to bargain with the AZ rather than to crush it because he was eager to promote acceptance of his regime in central Europe. That a year later he should have been reduced to the expedient of judicial murder is testimony not so much to the forcefulness of his policy as to the limitations of his power. Palm was chosen for his grizzly fate not because his conduct was so outrageous, but precisely because he was respectable enough that his death could be expected to strike fear into the hearts of those, like Cotta, who might otherwise have considered themselves beyond the reach of physical retribution. He was also vulnerable because, as a citizen of the Free City of Nuremberg, there was no one with any political weight to speak for him. On September 8, with Palm two weeks in his grave, Nuremberg would be incorporated into the kingdom of Bavaria. His two codefendants, both Bavarians, would subsequently be spared as a courtesy to Max Joseph and his chief minister.[44]

To someone in Cotta's position the affair was in every way instructive. Montgelas had done his best for Palm and his associates, and in the years to come he would continue to be more adamant, and more successful,

43. See Stegmann to Cotta, 4 June 1813, CA, and the exchange of letters between Police Director Wirschinger and Montgelas, 20, 30 July 1814, M Inn 25097/I. Stegmann's letter reveals that the police found out about his correspondence from Cotta's brother, Friedrich, who came to work for the AZ sometime after 1810. Perhaps because he was jealous of Stegmann's authority or his close relationship with Cotta, Friedrich began to read Stegmann's mail, and so discovered the suspicious connection with the French police. It is not obvious how Stegmann managed to write to the French police regularly for so many years without being discovered. Possibly he enclosed his reports in routine letters to Cotta, who passed them on to the French envoy in Stuttgart in return for material destined for the AZ.

44. Marcel Dunan, Napoléon et l'Allemagne: Le Système continental et les débuts du royaume de Bavière, 1806–1810 (Paris, 1942), pp. 45–47.

than his colleagues elsewhere in Germany in deflecting outside interference in his country's press.[45] Between 1805 and 1813 more than a dozen complaints were lodged against Cotta's paper by France or its clients. Although retractions were always forthcoming, preliminary correspondence always took so long that restitution was made weeks after the original delinquency had been forgotten. In every case but one—and in that one Cotta was happy to oblige, since it involved a correspondent from Napoleon's own entourage—the government brushed off demands for an author's identity, accepting Stegmann's claims that he usually did not know where articles came from and that manuscripts were burned after they were printed. No attempt was made to restrain this evasive practice or to resolve the question of ultimate accountability posed by Cotta's continued residence in Württemberg, outside Bavarian jurisdiction.[46]

In the end the French gained control over the *AZ*'s coverage of news from within France itself and of military affairs everywhere, in which areas Cotta was forced to rely on extracts from the *Moniteur*, supplemented by official material from the French embassy in Stuttgart.[47] Beyond this, however, Napoleon's influence was limited by the shallowness of his policy. His desire to keep all the threads of power in his own hands deterred him from imposing a comprehensive constitutional settlement on his German clients. The Rheinbund, which under different circumstances might have produced such a settlement, remained nothing more than a regional protectorate administered in France's interest, with no pretense to political coherence and no claim on public loyalty. As it was, Napoleon left the *Bund* states without any mutual cohesion or frame of reference, increasingly ignorant of his purposes, and resentful of his methods.

Cotta's decision to accommodate Napoleon's demand for special access to the *AZ* came at a moment when Franco-Bavarian relations were growing more intimate. Six months later, following the emperor's victory at Austerlitz, where Bavarian troops fought alongside the French, these relations reached the height of amity, where they remained for

45. F. Schneider, *Pressefreiheit und politische Öffentlichkeit*, pp. 175–77; and Bitterauf, "Zensur der politischen Zeitungen," p. 319.

46. The relevant documents are in M Inn 25097/I.

47. Jorma Tiainen (*Napoleon und das napoleonische Frankreich in der öffentliche Diskussion der "Dritten Deutschland," 1797–1806*, Studia Historica Jyväskyläensia, no. 8 [Jyväskylä, Fin., 1971], pp. 26–27) claims, on the basis of some earlier studies, that about 35 percent of the material in the *AZ* was taken from the *Moniteur*. There is no indication of how this figure was originally arrived at, but there is no reason to dispute it. The same cannot be said for Tiainen's more fundamental contention that, owing to such dependencies, newspapers played no role in the formation of German public opinion before 1848, a conclusion no government of that era would have shared.

perhaps six months more, buoyed by public elation at the coronation of
Max Joseph as king and official satisfaction at the territorial gains that
went with the new crown. Then the good feeling began to fade as it
became clear that the king's new dignity was an illusion.[48] Having sought
sovereignty, Bavaria instead found dependence, which the king's ministers could do little to mitigate. That their state had profited so hand-
somely from French patronage did not diminish their resentment at the
arrogance of their benefactor, nor did it reduce Montgelas's determination to protect the *AZ*, whose uninterrupted appearance throughout the
Napoleonic period helped preserve at least the semblance of Bavarian
autonomy in the eyes of Europe.[49]

If the goal of French policy had really been to publicize the "positive results of the emperor's operations," the agreement concluded in
1805 would have brought an end to the *AZ*'s troubles. In the long
run, though, Napoleon intended to reduce the European newspaper
press to an appendage of his new state system. He had reorganized the
French press to this end, each department being allowed one official
newspaper and no other. As further conflict with Austria became more
likely he made it known that he expected his German clients to follow
suit, by limiting themselves to a single official gazette published in their
capital cities.[50] Acceptance of this plan by Bavaria would have doomed
the *AZ*. Montgelas, however, declined to undertake any such general
reorganization.

Indeed, even less servile concessions, which might have led to the ex-
clusion of "unofficial" news from Bavarian papers, proved surprisingly
elusive. Between March 1808, when the Swiss took renewed offense at
the *AZ*'s coverage, and August 1810, when Napoleon personally ordered
his representative in Munich to "do something about this stupid newspaper from Ulm," Montgelas promised on three occasions to allow only
"official news from official sources" to appear in the *AZ*. Each time he
gave way before Stegmann's special pleading, as well as before the pro-

48. Dunan, *Napoléon et l'Allemagne*, pp. 35–40.

49. Bavaria's conduct during the Napoleonic period, like that of the other states of the
Rheinbund, has long been characterized as cravenly subservient to France. This view has
been substantially revised, in the Bavarian case at least, by recent work emphasizing the
dynamic character of Montgelas's domestic regime and the self-interested pursuit of independence and sovereignty that guided his foreign policy. See Quint, *Souveränitätsbegriff*,
pp. 100–275; Karl Otmar von Aretin, *Bayerns Weg zum souveränen Staat: Landstände und
konstitutionelle Monarchie, 1714–1818* (Munich, 1976), pp. 120–232; and Demel, *Bayerische
Staatsabsolutismus*.

50. Bitterauf, "Zensur der politischen Zeitungen," p. 321. On the French effort in the
occupied German lands, see Jeremy Popkin, "Buchhandel und Presse im napoleonischen
Deutschland," *Archiv für Geschichte des Buchwesens* 26 (1986): 285–96. Nothing comparable
exists for the states of the Rheinbund.

tests of his district governors, who complained that such a requirement was impossible to interpret.[51] As anyone familiar with the habits of provincial administrators might expect, the resistance of these local officials posed a formidable obstacle to the progress of French policy. Napoleon's insistence on the exclusive use of "official sources" sounds simple enough, but to those responsible for actually applying the rule it looked like a transparent ploy to force acceptance of a centralized ministerial press, a prospect that most of the district governors, in contrast to their chief, did not oppose. Short of complete acquiescence, however, lay chaos. There were strictly speaking only two "official" newspapers in all of Europe: the Parisian and Westphalian *Moniteurs*. Neither the French nor anyone else was prepared to say what, apart from the meager contents of these two journals, might appear in Bavarian newspapers, or which among the dozens of "semiofficial," "ministerial," and "government-friendly" periodicals might also be used as sources. This objection could not be ignored, and in the case of the *AZ* it repeatedly led Montgelas to withdraw by administrative memo what he had just granted by diplomatic note.

Even at the height of his power, Napoleon was unable to foresee, much less control, all the implications of his efforts to manipulate the German press. It was this inability, finally, that prevented his agents from "doing something" decisive about the *AZ*. His difficulties are well illustrated by a situation that arose as a result of the Treaty of Schönbrunn, which sealed the French victory over Austria in the fall of 1809. That agreement included a clause requiring Bavaria to cede Ulm to Württemberg in exchange for compensation at Austria's expense. Another clause required Austria to liberalize its press laws, so that the French point of view could be made clear to the Austrian public. That these provisions should have intersected at all seems peculiar. But they did, and Cotta made the most of it.

AUSTRIA AS ALLY

It may come as some surprise, in light of what has been said about the *AZ*'s conformity to the French line, to learn that Cotta's paper enjoyed cordial relations with Austria throughout the Napoleonic period. Karl Stegmann thought it was "truly bizarre that a paper universally considered pro-French by the enemies of France, and which as a consequence had to endure the greatest tribulations during the war [of 1798–1801] . . . should be banned in Paris, and welcomed in Vienna!"[52] Yet the welcome was real enough, if slow in coming.

51. Bitterauf, "Zensur der politischen Zeitungen," pp. 313–21. Bitterauf, as will be seen, is mistaken in supposing that Montgelas kept his third promise to Napoleon.

52. Stegmann to Cotta, [July 1805], in Heyck, *Allgemeine Zeitung*, p. 173.

Before the reorganization of the Empire by the Imperial Deputation, Austria's government had done almost nothing to counter the erosion of its influence in Germany. Its vendetta against the *Neueste Weltkunde* had been energetic, but it was not part of any general plan. The migration to Austrian soil of the brilliant counterrevolutionary journalist Friedrich Gentz might have made a difference in this respect, but he did not receive much official support or encouragement. Nor was he much interested, at this stage, in the newspaper press. Apart from Archduke Charles, no one at court thought the *AZ* worth cultivating until it had moved to Bavaria, at which point Johann Armbruster, a middle-level police official, stepped forward to act as Cotta's Vienna correspondent.[53] Armbruster's reports were the first systematic Austrian attempt to curry public favor in Germany, and compared to the emerging French program, it was a feeble effort: four letters per month, which, at Armbruster's insistence, could not be altered in any way or supplemented by other correspondence.

Despite Cotta's acceptance of this irksome condition, the *AZ* was not granted unrestricted entry to Habsburg territory until 1805. Before then only those willing to apply personally to the police had been able to read it. The new arrangement, Armbruster reported happily, allowed the *AZ* to be read "even in the coffeehouses," though he admitted this prospect was reduced by Austria's tariffs and stamp taxes, which raised the price of a year's subscription to thirty-six gulden.[54] Armbruster did his best to make Cotta's Austrian connection financially attractive. He arranged for a long-standing ban on the *Europäische Annalen* to be lifted,[55] and in 1807, when Cotta began publishing a literary magazine called *Morgenblatt für gebildete Stände*, he had it placed on the list of unrestricted periodicals.[56] Cotta did his part by arranging for copies of the *AZ* shipped to Austria to carry the imperial privilege, even though this was technically forbidden by the Rheinbund treaty.[57]

Both sides appreciated these gestures. Nevertheless, the real basis of Austria's grudging cordiality toward Cotta, despite his (equally grudging) ties to Napoleonic France, lay elsewhere: in Austria's utterly parochial press and in the strictness of domestic censorship, which assured the *AZ* an enthusiastic reception. It does not go too far to say that, under Austrian law, the government was responsible for literally every word published in its territory. This situation suited the crude suspicions of the emperor but not the real condition of the educated classes, to whom,

53. Johann Armbruster to Cotta, 28 Nov. 1803, CA.

54. Armbruster to Cotta, 10 June 1805, CA.

55. Armbruster to Cotta, 11 Sept. 1805, CA.

56. Armbruster to Cotta, 28 Aug. 1807, CA.

57. Montgelas to the Ulm District Government, 3 Jan. 1807, M Inn 25097/I; Armbruster to Cotta, 3 March 1807, CA.

as Police Minister Sumerau argued, newspapers had become "a genuine necessity," without which the country would fall into "a kind of apathy and insensibility that can only damage patriotic feelings."[58] As long as the domestic press remained moribund there was no choice but to favor a few foreign periodicals—in effect trading a guarantee of decent circulation for discretion in the handling of Austrian affairs. By 1806, despite its exorbitant price, Cotta's paper had found nearly four hundred subscribers in Vienna alone.[59]

Even this cautious approach could go awry: in 1807 the government almost banned the *AZ* because of an article by an official correspondent in the ministry of finance.[60] Austrian policy, moreover, was strictly defensive, tuned to domestic needs. To those familiar with conditions in southern Germany, it was clear that a little more care and consideration would be well repaid. In April 1806 an Austrian agent called Meyer reported that public sentiment in Swabia and Bavaria remained sympathetic to Austria, and that among editors and journalists in the region nothing was of greater interest than news from Vienna. Among the educated and the upper classes, he continued,

> the most important [journal] is without question the *Allgemeine Zeitung*. My first stop in Ulm was to see the editor of this journal, Stegmann . . . , who was manhandled by our troops during their last stay in Ulm and has taken it rather hard. Nevertheless, he spent an evening with me at the inn, and we parted on good terms. . . . I promised him reports for his paper, an offer that he accepted with thanks, since to him news of that kind is invaluable. Now I can only ask to receive such material myself, so I can prepare it for incorporation into the *AZ*, whose influence reaches throughout Germany. Meanwhile, I am leaving today for Tübingen, in order to come to an agreement with Cotta, who is the soul of the *Allgemeine Zeitung* and has extensive commercial activities that provide him with useful connections everywhere. If I am able to win him over—and here one must simply appeal to his interests as a businessman, which he is, heart and soul—then the path of publicity stands open to us, more than to any other party.[61]

Despite its limited scope, nothing came of Meyer's proposal (which was evidently written in ignorance of Armbruster's correspondence with Cotta). Two years later, Armbruster himself made much the same argument in a more extensive analysis of the German press, prepared at the request of his superiors, in which he urged that his relationship with the *AZ* be extended to other publications.[62] In contrast to Meyer, who,

58. Glossy, "Zeitungsgeschichte Alt-Österreichs," p. 134.

59. Armbruster to Cotta, 11 March 1806, CA.

60. Armbruster to Cotta, 2 March 1807, CA.

61. In Eckart Klessmann, ed., *Deutschland unter Napoleon* (Düsseldorf, 1965), pp. 75–76.

62. Glossy, "Zeitungsgeschichte Alt-Österreichs," pp. 134–43. Armbruster identified

like many others after him, was eager to diminish Cotta by insisting on his pecuniary motives, Armbruster believed that the political dangers that publishers now faced made it impossible simply to buy favorable coverage. For just that reason, however, truly reliable information had become more valuable than ever. Once Austria's version of the facts had been placed in a reputable journal, that version would spread quickly throughout Germany and, if the journal was the *AZ*, even into France (by a mechanism, of course, unknown to the Austrians). These recommendations were also ignored, though a less systematic propaganda campaign was undertaken toward the end of the year at the urging of those who favored renewal of the war.[63] The effort had barely begun, however, when Austria's defeat made it irrelevant.

When Metternich became foreign minister in the fall of 1809, he was determined that his earlier warnings about Austrian silence in the Century of Words would at last be heeded. But the creation of an effective political press now proved more difficult than it had seemed from his post in Paris. His personal ministrations could not save the hopelessly mundane *Oesterreichische Zeitung*, an organ of the war party edited by Friedrich Schlegel that finally appeared barely two weeks before the Battle of Wagram. In March 1810 Metternich and Schlegel tried again, and came up with the marginally less pedestrian *Oesterreichische Beobachter*. Like its predecessor, however, the *Beobachter* was badly outclassed by the *AZ*. It appeared only three times per week, and even at that there never seemed to be enough copy, since it all had to come from Metternich's ministry. The *Beobachter* was also an expressly ministerial newspaper, a genre that, by convention, was believed to speak for its government but not necessarily to speak the truth. At the end of six months, despite its low price, Metternich's house organ had only 256 subscribers.[64]

The alternative was to acquire greater influence over the *AZ*. In more normal times one might simply have banished Cotta's paper long enough for the *Beobachter* to take root. Austria's recent agreement with France, however, had required the government to remove most restrictions on foreign periodicals. The *AZ*, which the French were perceived to favor, could not be kept out—but it might be brought in, or so it seemed to Friedrich Gentz, who thought the contrast between the

---

eight periodicals besides the *AZ* through which his government might make its influence felt. Of these, four were Swiss; two appeared in Hamburg, the *Correspondent* and G. H. Schirach's *Politisches Journal*; the other two were Bavarian, the Nuremberg *Correspondent* and the *Bamberger Zeitung*.

63. Herbert Eichler, "Zur Vorgeschichte des *Oesterreichischen Beobachters*," *Jahrbuch der Grillparzer-Gesellschaft* 28 (1926): 172–77; and C. A. Macartney, *The Habsburg Empire, 1790–1918* (New York, 1969), pp. 186–87.

64. Eichler, "Vorgeschichte," p. 177.

French-inspired rigidity of the Rheinbund and the equally French-inspired liberality of the Habsburg lands would appeal to Cotta.[65] In Stuttgart the French were cordially hated, particularly by the remnants of the reform party, who had organized themselves around the crown prince into a quiet conspiracy based on the ideals of the old Empire.[66] Cotta, characteristically, remained on good terms with everyone. The French ambassador believed that "it would be difficult to find a man more devoted to France than Cotta,"[67] while the semiofficial *Journal de l'Empire* was pleased to describe the *AZ* as "one of the most esteemed newspapers in Germany."[68] But Cotta had also made himself useful on at least one occasion as a conduit for secret information between Metternich and Austrian agents in Württemberg.[69] In the summer of 1810, moreover, the transfer of Ulm to Württemberg meant that he would have to renegotiate the *AZ*'s arrangement with Bavaria, or move the paper elsewhere.[70]

In June, Cotta offered to transfer the *AZ* to Augsburg in exchange for additional commercial concessions and a renewal of Bavaria's beleaguered guarantee that the paper would appear subject only to "the personal supervision of the chief of the district government."[71] Despite a provisional agreement on these terms, however, Cotta's confidence that Bavaria could stand by its pledges had already been tempered by experience. It was probably further shaken later in the summer, when the *AZ* was again placed under the ban in France—a circumstance that made the large Austrian market that much more enticing.[72] At the same time, Montgelas, whose room to maneuver was shrinking with every

65. Gentz to Metternich, 24 Feb. 1810, in Wittichen and Salzer, *Briefe*, vol. 3, pt. 1, pp. 76–77.

66. August Fournier, *Historische Studien und Skizzen* (Prague, 1885), pp. 280–82; cf. Karl von Phull [William's adjutant] to Cotta, in Hölzle, *Württemberg im Zeitalter Napoleons*, p. 139.

67. Hölzle, "Cotta," pp. 581–82.

68. *Journal de l'Empire* [i.e., *Journal des Débats*], 10 Jan. 1810; cf. Stegmann to Cotta, 17 Jan. 1810, CA.

69. Enno Kraehe, *Metternich's German Policy* (Princeton, N.J., 1963–83), 1 : 232. When Austria's ambassador was forced to leave Württemberg three years later, following Austria's entry into the war against France, he considered Cotta a safe means of conveying his government's confidential assurances to the ministry, and of seeking information on how things stood in Stuttgart; see Eugen Schneider, *Aus der württembergischen Geschichte: Vorträge und Abhandlungen* (Stuttgart, 1926), p. 91.

70. Quite apart from the bad blood between Cotta and Frederick, censorship in Württemberg was far more repressive than in Bavaria. See Karlheinz Fuchs, *Bürgerliches Räsonement und Staatsräson: Zensur als Instrument des Despotismus, dargestellt am Beispiel des rheinbündischen Württemberg (1806–1813)* (Göppingen, 1975).

71. Cotta to Max Joseph, 25 June 1810, M Inn 25097/I.

72. Friedrich Engelbach [Strasbourg correspondent for the *AZ*] to Cotta, 29 Nov. 1810, CA; cf. Heyck, *Allgemeine Zeitung*, p. 170.

French victory, had finally given in to Napoleon's demand that Bavaria revise its tariffs in line with the rest of the Rheinbund. Similar conformity in press matters would certainly have forced the *AZ* out.

Cotta therefore continued to hold out the possibility of a move south well into the fall,[73] until it finally became clear that Bavaria would continue to honor the *AZ*'s special status rather than risk losing the journal altogether.[74] Austria settled for reorganizing the *Beobachter* as a daily under a new editor, Joseph Pilat, who arranged to supply the *AZ* with selected material from his own paper a day in advance of publication. Although Pilat understood that he was throwing away much of the circulation the *Beobachter* might have attracted outside Austria, it seemed an acceptable price to pay for a genuinely credible voice in Germany.[75]

By the end of 1810, then, at what proved to be the critical juncture in the *AZ*'s relations with France, a number of apparently unrelated forces, all motivated in one way or another by French efforts to regulate political discussion in Germany, had combined to create enough leverage for the *AZ* to survive. Cotta had made more concessions than he had won, but he had chosen his ground well. He had avoided ideological confrontation while demonstrating sufficient doggedness to discourage even Gentz, who had believed the *AZ* ripe for the picking, only to discover that Cotta would go to "any lengths" to retain control of his newspaper and that neither Cotta nor Stegmann would "entertain any connection either with the Bavarian government, or with any other quarter, aimed at perpetuating their paper in any altered form whatever."[76]

Institutionally speaking, this was true. In spite of everything, the *AZ* kept its private correspondents and its formal independence from the

---

73. See Carl Armbruster [Johann Armbruster's son] to Cotta, 30 Oct., 17, 21 Nov. 1810, CA.

74. On August 31, 1810 Montgelas informed the Augsburg District Government that the *AZ*, which would begin publication there the next day, should be forbidden to publish political news that was not "based on official sources." He received in reply a memorandum from Stegmann and a supporting letter from the district governor (both dated 3 Sept. 1810), which reviewed the earlier concessions to the *AZ* on this point and suggested that the paper might not be able to continue if the old arrangement was not restored. Montgelas then drafted new instructions (10 Sept. 1810) which specified, "in light of the extraordinary reputation that the *Allgemeine Zeitung* enjoyed in the rest of Germany," that private correspondence should continue to appear, subject to the discretion of the district governor—language taken verbatim from Stegmann's memo.

Two months later, Montgelas modified his instructions slightly, by advising the censor that reports of troop movements could come only from French authorities (29 Nov. 1810). Nevertheless, he specifically permitted the publication of an article sharply critical of the *Moniteur*'s reports on French colonial policy (1 Dec. 1810). All these documents are in M Inn 25097/I.

75. Joseph Pilat to Cotta, 7 July 1812, CA.

76. Gentz to Metternich, 14 Nov. 1810, in Wittichen and Salzer, *Briefe*, vol. 3, pt. 1, pp. 81–83.

state throughout the Napoleonic period.[77] But even so, the flood tide of official news still rose pretty high. Stegmann's skill at extracting dispensations from Montgelas could do only so much to arrest the *AZ*'s decline, since its day-to-day condition depended less on the promises of the ministry than on administrative procedures adopted at the district level. The resolute provincialism of the Bavarian bureaucracy helped save the *AZ* by unwittingly obstructing the French plan for centralized censorship, but it was no substitute for conscientious political support. Given the continuing stream of complaints from France and its allies, all of which required district officials to justify their actions to Munich, it is hardly surprising that they became less and less willing to assume personal responsibility in an ever more sensitive area of policy.[78] Censorship grew more cautious, and as it did the *AZ* became more predictable. By the end of 1812 its circulation had been cut in half, and it might have continued to decline but for the renewed interest in public affairs generated by the prospect of Napoleon's defeat the following year.

On balance there can be no doubt that Cotta's institutional victory came at the price of a substantial intellectual retreat. Rather than submit to being used by any single government, the *AZ* had survived by making itself useful to as many as possible. Cotta's peripatetic courtship of the French, the Austrians, and the Bavarians was a caricature of his original intentions. *Unparteilichkeit*, once a matter of high principle, had been transformed into a threadbare stratagem for staying in business. In the process it had been shorn of the intellectual integrity that was supposed to have been its distinguishing feature. The cultivated cosmopolitanism of the *AZ*'s early years slowly gave way to an almost incoherent chorus of conflicting reports, all certified by some distant authority to be true. The republican virtues in which Cotta had put such store had never counted for less, since they depended not just on the moral improvement of mankind, as he had originally supposed, but on the maintenance of political stability in Europe as well. Of all the hard lessons of the Napoleonic

---

77. The *AZ*'s privileges were not shared by other Bavarian papers. The *Bamberger Zeitung* was suppressed in 1809; the Nuremberg *Correspondent* was confined to strictly official sources and was not allowed to reprint material from the *AZ*. In one instance, however, the *AZ*'s independence has been overstated. The oft-repeated claim by Heyck (*Allgemeine Zeitung*, pp. 180–87, 299–300) that the *AZ* published reports by the banished Prussian minister, Baron vom Stein, is untrue. The articles in question, which appeared in 1809–10, seem on internal evidence to have been the work of a different Karl Stein, who was a professor at Weimar and a Prussian state councillor.

78. The Munich ministry was almost willfully ignorant of the problems faced by the *AZ*'s censors. In January 1812, for instance, a censor was reprimanded for letting Stegmann juxtapose two excerpts from the *Moniteur* in a way that called that journal's honesty into question. The poor fellow replied that he would be glad to compare all excerpts from the *Moniteur* with the original, if only he were allowed to subscribe to it himself (M Inn 25097/I).

period, this was the hardest, and the most salutary for the future of the Cotta press.

Napoleon was not the first to put diplomatic pressure on the German press. Political periodicals in central Europe had always been compelled by the fragmentation of their society to deal gently with the feelings of a multitude of neighboring states. Napoleon deepened and formalized this diplomatic hypersensitivity by promoting a uniform system of censorship that would make German journalists accountable to the German state system as a whole—a process whose fulfillment would come a few years later at Carlsbad, when the Austrians would complete the campaign to rationalize the regulation of public opinion begun by the French. Cotta, although he could not have suspected it at the time, would be the last publisher to exploit the "freedom of the Empire," the last to find in German particularism an underlying flexibility that could be made useful to intellectual liberty. His conduct, he later recalled, had combined "impartiality" and "fealty,"[79] an improbable synthesis, but one that allowed the *AZ* to survive a generation of war by assuming the role of messenger among the belligerents. Thereafter the paper remained immune to the claims of oppositional politics, a beacon of political enlightenment with a pronounced taste for service to the international community.

Although the *AZ* would go on to fill this role with great distinction, it was not precisely what Cotta had had in mind. As far as he was concerned, Napoleon had reneged on one of the central promises of the French Revolution: public opinion had acquired new importance in the calculations of Europe's statesmen, but it had not emerged as a force in its own right, certainly not one capable of securing the rights of the press. It was not inevitable that this should continue to be so. But Napoleon's eventual disappearance did not diminish the force of his example on the conservative regimes that succeeded him.

THE PEOPLE'S PRESS AT WAR

In the eyes of posterity, Germany's War of Liberation would one day acquire a kind of operatic grandeur and a moral power that were quite undetectable to even the most attentive reader of the *Allgemeine Zeitung*. As described in its pages, the struggle that began in East Prussia in January 1813 and ended in Paris sixteen months later was less a universal rising than a civil war, in which Germans fought on both sides and in which larger patterns of meaning were obscured by seemingly random violence. Ruthless censorship and shattered communications, two familiar consequences of Napoleonic warfare, insured that even the most stir-

79. Cotta to Bray, 24 Dec. 1828, in Heyck, *Allgemeine Zeitung*, pp. 253–55.

ring events would be deprived of their drama by the chaotic way they were reported.

In this respect the *AZ*'s treatment of the greatest battle of the war may stand for its coverage of the whole. The Battle of Leipzig, fought on October 16–19, 1813, was Napoleon's first decisive defeat while in personal command of his army. On that account alone it marked an epoch in the emotional lives of his opponents. Five days later, at the end of a long article describing engagements fought as early as September 6, the *AZ* reported that a battle of unknown scope had been fought near Leipzig and that, contrary to unspecified "earlier reports" (none of which had appeared in the *AZ*), the allies had won. The story, mostly copied from the *Bayreuther Zeitung*, emphasized Prussia's role in the fighting. Although the *AZ* had reported Bavaria's alliance with Austria a few weeks before, it did not mention the presence of Bavarian troops among the victors. Over the next ten days details of the French retreat began to emerge, included among reports of skirmishes that had in fact preceded the main battle. The first comprehensive account, taken from the *Leipziger Zeitung*, appeared on October 28–29 and implied that Napoleon had been badly beaten. On November 2–3 an equally detailed report claimed that the French had achieved substantial command of the field and had withdrawn only because they ran out of ammunition. Their march, it was said, took them through Leipzig proper, where, owing to bad luck, they were fallen upon by the battered allies, who subsequently gained "the appearance of victors."[80] This proved to be the *AZ*'s last word on the subject.

The source of the second story, which must have rung hollow to everyone who read it, was an official French bulletin, scarcely distinguishable from those Cotta had been publishing under mild duress since 1805. In practice, little had changed. Bavaria had been "liberated," but not the Bavarian press, which remained subject to strict legal restraint throughout the war.[81] In the case of the *AZ* this meant the editors were allowed to print the truth, but without distinguishing it from the equally plausible falsehoods that always accompanied it. Coverage of the fighting continued to be based on official bulletins and the ministerial press. All information was handled with self-effacing objectivity: in French reports "the enemy" was the allies; in allied reports "the enemy" was the French.

In a commercial sense the *AZ* could hardly have failed to benefit from the general revival of public-spiritedness that accompanied the war, and

---

80. *AZ*, 24 Oct.–3 Nov. 1813.

81. Bitterauf, "Zensur der politischen Zeitungen," p. 321; idem, "Zur Geschichte der öffentlichen Meinung im Königreich Bayern im Jahre 1813 bis zur Abschluss des Vertrages von Ried," *Archiv für Kulturgeschichte* 11 (1914): 31–69.

by the end of 1813 it had regained most of its lost circulation.[82] At
the same time, since the censor's attention was riveted on military matters, correspondence on other subjects was treated less rigidly. This allowed Cotta to recruit significant new contributors for the first time
in several years.[83] Their work did not compare to that of men like the
Prussian poet and journalist Ernst Moritz Arndt, who declined an invitation to write for the *AZ*, probably because he considered it politically
tainted,[84] but their contributions did help preserve the paper's reputation at a time when it might otherwise have suffered badly from northern competition. As it was, the *AZ*'s dispassionate style and "impure, un-
German, Frenchifying language"[85] were sometimes ridiculed by those
more openly committed to the patriotic cause. By the end of the war the
AZ had managed to regain some of its old perspicacity, but no one would
have mistaken it for the fifth ally against Napoleon. Such liberation as it
enjoyed was entirely undramatic. When the allies finally marched into
Paris, whatever feelings of exhilaration or relief Cotta and his associates
may have felt remained carefully concealed from their readers.

Despite these limitations, however, the War of Liberation was important to the history of the Cotta press in two respects: it inspired journalists everywhere in Germany with new confidence that they would soon
be granted their rightful share of political influence; and it encouraged
the emergence of a new attitude toward the press in Prussia, the one
power to remain indifferent to Cotta's newspaper throughout the Napoleonic period.

This indifference was entirely reciprocal. Neither Posselt nor his successors had ever devoted much space to Prussian affairs,[86] in part be-

82. The *AZ*'s circulation reached its historic low of 1,007 in 1812. At the end of the
following year it was back up to 1,801, and in December 1814 it reached 2,150 (Heyck,
Allgemeine Zeitung, p. 185; and *Druckauftragsbücher*, CA). The recovery was partly due to
increasing use of the *AZ* by the ministry to publish official announcements, a concession
that Cotta requested because circulation had fallen off dramatically after Napoleon banned
the importation of German newspapers into France in 1812 (Cotta to Max Joseph, 6 Feb.
1813; and Montgelas, Circular Memorandum, 4 March 1813, M Inn 25097/I).

83. During the first six months of 1814 Cotta recruited new correspondents in Berlin
(Wilhelm Scheerer, editor of a short-lived patriotic journal entitled *Deutschlands Triumph,
oder die entjochte Europa*), Hamburg (Johann Philip Nick, a censor during the French occupation and a future editor of the *Liste der Börsenhalle*), Brunswick (Rudolf Bosse, a phi-
lologist who eventually became a major source of material from northern Germany),
Mannheim (Eberhard Wächter, an artist), Milan (a man named Schätzler, apparently a
banker), and Paris (Konrad Oelsner, now a member of the Prussian legation).

84. Arndt to Cotta, 3, 12 Sept. 1814, in Ernst Moritz Arndt, *Briefe*, ed. Albrecht Dühr
(Darmstadt, 1972), 1:411, 417.

85. Joseph Görres, "Die teutschen Zeitungen," *Rheinischer Merkur*, 1 July 1814.

86. Heyck, *Allgemeine Zeitung*, p. 298. During the first fifteen years of the *AZ*'s existence
the government in Berlin took official notice of it only once, in 1800, when it protested an

cause Cotta had no luck recruiting a reliable correspondent there. The years of reform that followed the defeat of 1806 might have brought a change in this mutual disinterest had they not also been years of French domination. Many of the Prussian reformers, notably Wilhelm von Humboldt, who was given charge of censorship after 1809, believed than an informed public could be a useful adjunct to the reconstruction of the state.[87] But no one in authority regarded public opinion as an agent of change, and no one was prepared to risk Napoleon's wrath to foster it. Although the Prussian chancellor, Hardenberg, sometimes defended his policy in the Berlin and Königsberg papers, he generally preferred pamphlets for this purpose, because, as had long been recognized, they did not possess the institutional continuity of periodicals and did not raise the same expectations among their readers.[88]

The only significant private newspaper to appear in Prussia during the Napoleonic period, Heinrich von Kleist's conservative-oppositional *Berliner Abendblätter*, was ruthlessly harassed by the censors and soon ceased to count as a political force. Repeated schemes by private journalists to interest the government in some sort of official or semiofficial publication received mixed reactions but always failed to materialize.[89] The most elaborate of these, put forward by Adam Müller in 1810, called for the government to sponsor two complementary newspapers, both edited by himself: one an official exponent of policy, the other a bogus "opposition" journal intended to co-opt real critics of the government. Müller's plan was not a joke,[90] and it eventually won him an appointment as official publicist; but the job turned out to have no responsibilities to speak of. Reduced to its essentials, the goal of Prussian policy before 1813 was silence. Despite the emotional significance that appeals to the nation held for many of the reformers, there was broad agreement among them that public support was superfluous to their immediate task.

---

advertisement for a satirical biography of Frederick William II called *Saul dem Dicken, König von Kanonenland* (*AZ*, 23 March 1800 [Beilage]). Cotta was fined ten thaler as a result.

87. See, for instance, Humboldt's memorandum on press policy, 1 Dec. 1809, in Karl vom Stein, *Freiherr vom Stein: Briefe und amtliche Schriften* (Stuttgart, 1957–74), 3:240; and, more generally, Ruth Flad, *Der Begriff der öffentlichen Meinung bei Stein, Arndt, und Humboldt* (Berlin and Leipzig, 1929).

88. Paul Czygan, ed., *Zur Geschichte der Tagesliteratur während der Freiheitskriege* (Leipzig, 1909–11), 1:6.

89. Otto Groth, *Die Zeitung: Ein System der Zeitungskunde (Journalistik)* (Mannheim, 1928–30), 2:60–67.

90. It may, however, have been inspired by one: a facetious observation of Heinrich von Kleist's that the times demanded two kinds of newspapers, "one that never lies, and another that only tells the truth" ("Lehrbuch der französischen Journalistik," in Kleist, *Sämtliche Werke und Briefe* [Munich, 1961], 2:361–67). Cf. Müller's correspondence with Friedrich Staegemann, 29 Aug.–10 Oct. 1809, in Jakob Baxa, ed., *Adam Müller's Lebenszeugnisse* (Munich and Vienna, 1966), 1:116–31.

Systematic exploitation of the foreign press likewise did not exist, though the opportunities were there. As in Austria, the poor quality of Prussia's domestic press had insured that much of what had passed for public opinion there had for some years been published elsewhere.[91] A conspicuous example of this involved the work of Friedrich Buchholz, one of the most influential journalists living in Prussia, whose best writing appeared in Cotta's *Europäische Annalen* or in book form under the imprint of the Cotta Verlag and several smaller houses in Göttingen and Leipzig.[92] Prior to the Jena campaign, Hardenberg had considered recruiting Buchholz to prepare the public for the renewal of war with France;[93] once that war had been fought and lost, however, the government in Berlin was no longer in any position to make use of the kind of connection Buchholz enjoyed with Cotta.

Since the Peace of Basel Prussia had been the object of contradictory expectations on the part of Germans sympathetic to the Revolution (with which Prussia had been the first to make peace) and on the part of France's opponents (who expected Prussia to play a leading role in the nation's revival). This situation would have been difficult at any time, but after the defeat of 1806 it became quite impossible. While Austria might continue to cultivate papers like the *Allgemeine Zeitung* on a limited basis, if only as a way of influencing opinion in France, Prussia was simply too weak and dependent to contemplate any policy other than the most determined reticence. If Hardenberg had wished to cultivate the goodwill of the French through the press, Cotta's connections would have served him well: Buchholz might easily have done for Hardenberg what Joseph Pilat did for Metternich. But the service was not wanted, if only because the reformers most sensitive to the claims of public opinion were those who favored resistance to France, a project for which the greatest circumspection was essential.[94] Buchholz, who for much of this period was political editor of the *Vossische Zeitung*, never wrote a word for the *AZ*. Nor did anyone else with any standing in Berlin. Although Cotta eventually found a Prussian correspondent for his newspaper, this man's reports were anecdotal, uninteresting, and, according to Buchholz, inaccurate.[95] That this suited the authorities can scarcely be doubted. Under

91. Tschirch, *Öffentliche Meinung* 1:8.

92. Cf. Kurt Bahrs, *Friedrich Buchholz: Ein preussischer Publizist, 1768–1843* (Berlin, 1907); and the harsh comments in Tschirch, *Öffentliche Meinung* 2:76–89.

93. Ranke, *Hardenberg* 2:354–55.

94. See the outstanding study by Rudolf Ibbeken, *Preußen*, especially his discussion of "the party of action," pp. 91–116, and of public opinion generally, pp. 305–45; also Flad, *Begriff der öffentlichen Meinung*.

95. Buchholz to Cotta, 19 Jan. 1810, CA. The *AZ*'s best sources of material about Prussia were Philipp Nemnich and Dietrich von Bülow [the younger brother of the Prussian field marshall Heinrich von Bülow], both based in Hamburg and both, like Buchholz, well disposed toward France. Pro-French sympathies were also shared by two Prussian officers,

the circumstances it is not all that surprising that, as late as the end of 1809, an astute observer like Hegel, who had taken a lively interest in the Württemberg Reform Diet ten years before and who was himself a newspaper editor, could still be unaware of the existence of a reform movement in Prussia.[96]

Whether one attributes the detached public posture of the reformers to the inherently limited nature of their program[97] or simply to the repressive effects of the French alliance,[98] it is clear that, in the short term, their interests were best served by calling as little attention to their achievements as possible. When the time came to break with France, however, such a retiring public posture no longer made sense. Inevitably, this was not a moment that Frederick William's government could choose for itself, and when it came Hardenberg was obliged to master the new force of popular patriotism as best he could.

The press campaign of 1813–14 was the most elaborate Prussian attempt to influence European opinion since the Seven Years' War, when Frederick the Great had mounted a more modest effort, with somewhat different objectives. When, on the eve of that conflict, Frederick ordered one of his ministers to place fictitious reports of an Austrian mobilization in the Berlin papers, he pretty much exhausted the resources of European monarchs with respect to public relations in wartime. However vigorously such techniques might be employed, they were never intended to do more than inspire sympathy among neutral governments, and perhaps reassure civilians about the success of the army.[99] During the war against Napoleon, however, the press was supposed to mobilize the whole population—to encourage enlistment, incite sabotage and resistance, and persuade German soldiers fighting for France to lay down their arms.

The role of newspapers in all this should not be overestimated: the

August Rühle von Lilienstern and Christian von Massenbach, with whom Cotta was personally on good terms, presumably through Buchholz's mediation.

96. Franz Rosenzweig, *Hegel und der Staat* (Munich and Berlin, 1920), 2 : 62; cf. Hegel's early essay fragment on the Württemberg reform movement, "Daß die Magistrate . . ." [April–July 1797], in *Sämtliche Werke*, vol. 7: *Schriften zur Politik und Rechtsphilosophie*, ed. G. Lasson (Leipzig, 1913), pp. 150–54; and the discussion in H. S. Harris, *Hegel's Development: Toward the Sunlight, 1770–1801* (London, 1972), pp. 418–33.

97. Simon, *Failure of the Prussian Reform Movement*, pp. 237–39; and Ibbeken, *Preußen*, pp. 290–94.

98. These effects were by any standard considerable. Berlin was an occupied city until the end of 1808 and housed a French garrison again throughout the campaign of 1812. See Paul Czygan, "Über die französische Zensur während der Okkupation von Berlin und ihren Leiter, den Prediger Hauchecorne, in den Jahren 1806 bis 1808," *Forschungen zur Brandenburgischen und Preußischen Geschichte* 21 (1908): 99–137.

99. Ernst Consentius, "Friedrich der Grosse und die Zeitungs-Zensur," *Preussische Jahrbücher* 115 (1904): 220–49; and Groth, *Die Zeitung* 2 : 21–29.

War of Liberation was the last European war in which newspapers were not the chief means of public propaganda. Nevertheless, their new prominence is unmistakable. Since at least the end of the last century German journalists had been seeking a basis for partnership with the state; in the spring of 1813 it seemed to have emerged. Perhaps patriotism, founded on a sense of common cultural identity and galvanized by a decade of repression, might accomplish what Enlightenment and reformism had not: the creation of an authentically popular press with its own integrity—not an instrument of policy, but an ally in the struggle against a common enemy.

As the war progressed newspapers became part of the baggage trains of the allied armies. The sudden appearance of new periodicals, or the revival of old ones in patriotic dress, became part of the process by which the cities of northern Germany celebrated their independence. Although most such efforts were short-lived, to those concerned with the promotion of national values the brief flourishing of these new journals still presented a gratifying prospect, not least because the people's love of the Fatherland had finally found a means of expression that promised continuing progress in the future.

That promise could be realized, however, only if the liberated press survived the war. Take away the sound of the drums, and what was left? It was not until six weeks after the Treaty of Paris that anyone dared to ask this question in print. Writing in his *Rheinischer Merkur*, Joseph Görres argued that the distinctive characteristic of the wartime press had been, not its martial fervor, but its populism. The German people had "recovered their own history" through an act of collective will, and in the process had acquired a new voice. Newspapers, which before the war had been "sterile chroniclers of events," had become "the tribune[s] of the great majority, at once the voice of the people and the ear of the prince." Relations between journalists and the authorities, formerly suspicious or indifferent, had become voluntary and collaborative. It therefore followed that the liberated press would continue to be spared "the nervous, fearful censorship" of the past. But even if complete freedom was not forthcoming, Görres still felt confident that, now that the press had made itself worthy of the nation's trust, the people would honor it as their spokesman and "the shield of public opinion would save it from all harm." [100]

Even a cursory analysis of the social character of the liberated press reveals the falsity of Görres's claim to speak for "the great majority." The *Merkur* numbered its circulation in the low thousands and sold by quarterly subscription for more than a skilled worker could earn in a week. It is most unlikely that its readers were all that different from those of

100. Joseph Görres, "Die teutschen Zeitungen," *Rheinischer Merkur,* 1–3 July 1814.

the *AZ*. Yet Görres, like Cotta fifteen years before, recognized that the vitality of the press was mainly a political question. Their common aim had been to create newspapers whose contents were neither wholly in the hands of the state nor wholly isolated from it—newspapers that could function as organs of opinion without being out of touch with those who shaped events. Despite the persistence of censorship and other forms of official interference, it is fair to say that during the War of Liberation this problem was temporarily resolved, for the first time, in favor of the press.

It is on this account that the advent of modern journalism in Germany is usually dated from the war—modernity being synonymous with the appearance of newspapers intended to represent, rather than to indoctrinate, their audience.[101] The sense of a new departure is reinforced by the clear impossibility of explaining the rising of the press as a natural product of the reform movement that preceded it. No one who has read the official correspondence that attended the appearance of periodicals like the *Preussische Correspondent* and the *Rheinische Merkur* can fail to be struck by the mixed feelings with which Frederick William's ministers welcomed their new supporters.[102]

It is less commonly noted how much more readily the king's generals grasped the rising of the press for what it was: a natural response to the new conditions of Napoleonic warfare. The liberation of the press may have harmonized poorly with the bureaucratic values that had guided the civilian reformers, but it constituted a logical extension of the work of those who had labored to create a large army of motivated soldiers whose loyalty and initiative could be counted on. It is thus among the commanding officers of the allied armies that one finds the truest patrons of the new journalism. Some might not have gone as far as Johann von Thielmann, commander of a Prussian corps occupying Hamburg in 1814, who ordered his subordinates not to interfere with the civilian press on the grounds that "freedom of the press is the paladin of the nation's liberty, which all reasonable men will recognize as the finest jewel of our hard-won victory."[103] Nor can one doubt that many civilian leaders felt the same attraction to the patriotic cause as did those in uni-

101. There is no comprehensive study of the German press during the War of Liberation; Karl Wolff, *Die deutsche Publizistik in der Zeit der Freiheitskämpfe und des Wiener Kongresses, 1813–1815* (Plauen, 1934), has little to say about periodicals. There is a useful discussion in F. Schneider, *Pressefreiheit und politische Öffentlichkeit*, pp. 171–204.

102. Czygan, *Zur Geschichte des Tagesliteratur*, vol. 2, pt. 1, pp. 64–141; and vol. 2, pt. 2, pp. 299–377. See also Otto Tschirch, "Joseph Görres, der *Rheinische Merkur*, und der preußische Staat," *Preussische Jahrbücher* 157 (1914): 225–47; and Max von Lettow Vorbeck, *Zur Geschichte des Preussischen Correspondenten von 1813 und 1814* (Berlin, 1911; reprint Vaduz, Liecht., 1965).

103. Johann von Thielmann, "Korpsbefehl," 31 July 1814, in Salomon, *Geschichte des deutschen Zeitungswesens* 3:30.

form. But a military commander in wartime is entitled by his circumstances to seize opportunities and use available resources with a freedom and ruthlessness that would be impossible for a minister of the crown. Hardenberg thus found himself drawn to the head of a movement he would have preferred, not necessarily to oppose, but certainly to diffuse.

Ideally Hardenberg hoped to persuade the nation that it had risen in defense of universal peace, the balance of power, and the sacred person of the monarch.[104] This temporizing message did in fact find its way into the *AZ* and most other papers published outside the actual theater of operations. In the occupied territories of the north and west, however, it was soon lost in the flood of bulletins from the front, which appealed to the nation's honor and its accumulated sense of persecution and xenophobia in the frankest possible terms. The men who had guided the reconstruction of the Prussian army had not hesitated to adopt revolutionary methods of raising, training, and deploying their men, and they did not hesitate, when the time came, to employ what seemed an equally subversive form of journalism to further their cause.

Like the *Landwehr*, the liberated press existed to fulfill a military mission, which it accomplished well enough; but its constitutional standing and political future were no clearer for all that. Whether the "shield of public opinion" was fully forged by the end of the war remains a matter of dispute. What cannot be disputed is that the hand holding the shield was that of a soldier. Whether journalists would be able to lift it for themselves remained to be seen.

104. "Circular des Censors Schulz an die Redakteure der drei Berliner politischen Zeitungen," 6 July 1813, in Czygan, *Zur Geschichte des Tagesliteratur*, vol. 2, pt. 1, pp. 122–25.

FIVE

German Liberation

There are today some institutions—and freedom of the press is one of them— about which one is no longer called upon to decide whether they are good or bad. It is simply a question of whether one can stand firm against the tide of public opinion or not. But for a constitutional government to suppress such freedom would be an insulting anachronism—true insanity.

Mémorial de Sainte-Hélène, June 13, 1816

When Napoleon took the crown of France into his own hands at Notre Dame in December 1804, Cotta was forty years old, professionally successful, and a man of some importance in the political life of his country. When that crown was finally returned to its original owners, Cotta was two days past his fiftieth birthday. He had spent the intervening decade defending the achievements of his youth. That Cotta must have wished for Napoleon's downfall can scarcely be doubted: nothing less could have allowed Cotta to resume the public career on which he had embarked ten years before. As it was, Cotta had taken no part in Napoleon's defeat. The revival of the north German press inspired by news of the French failure in Russia found no audible response among the new monarchies of the south, where the strict controls of the Rheinbund years remained in force. Like so many of Napoleon's enemies, moreover, Cotta recognized that he and his fellow publishers owed their adversary a great deal. Napoleon's harassment of the press had done much harm, but it had also achieved two results that generations of journalists had sought in vain: it had made the freedom and vitality of the publishing industry into a national issue; and it had created conditions under which the interests of the press, the public, and, most especially, the princes could be seen to intersect.

Cotta's first opportunity to explore these new conditions would come at the Congress of Vienna, which marked the beginning of a period of intense political activity on his part, comparable in significance and complexity to the one that began with the founding of the *Neueste Weltkunde* in 1798 and ended with the eclipse of the Württemberg reformers after 1803. Technically, Cotta went to Vienna as a commercial lobbyist, to persuade the assembled delegates at long last to bring an end to literary piracy in Germany. Once there, however, he conducted himself like a man who expected to play a great role in his nation's affairs. In so doing he inadvertently did some damage to the cause he was sent to plead. He also did much that would help make his expectations a reality.

Even if the congress had not offered Cotta a chance to mend his fences politically, it would still have been a watershed in the history of the Cotta press. For the *Allgemeine Zeitung*, the war against Napoleon had not been a liberating experience; the congress was. It offered an ideal opportunity for the *AZ* to reassert its primacy among German newspapers and reclaim the standard of excellence that had once been its hallmark. When Cotta founded the *AZ* he had created a newspaper whose scope and values were self-consciously European. At Vienna, "Europe" was assembling for a public purpose of the highest importance. There could be no more effective demonstration that the cosmopolitanism of the *AZ*'s founder had retained its usefulness. At the same time, some of the decisions reached at the congress suggested that there would now be a place in Germany for equally sophisticated periodicals devoted to regional and national affairs, capable of contributing more directly to the constitutional debate the congress had begun. By the time Cotta left Vienna the problem of how to provide Germany with a political press appropriate to its new circumstances was already on his mind. The search for a solution would consume much of his energy for the next five years.

A PARIS FOR BOOKS

The Congress of Vienna, which met intermittently for eight months beginning in October 1814, was originally intended to be a mopping-up operation that would settle the territorial and political disputes left unresolved by the Treaty of Paris. It soon became clear that such a straightforward diplomatic exercise was out of the question. Since 1795 every attempt by the opponents of France to make peace with the Revolution had been scrutinized by the German public for constitutional implications—a tendency that Germany's statesmen had tried, for the most part successfully, to restrain. Rastatt, after all, had been a "congress" too, a word redolent with political significance, harking back to Westphalia. But only the *Neueste Weltkunde* had been in a position to cover that earlier meeting in detail, and the undertaking, as we have seen, eventually cost the editor his job.

At the end of twenty years of war, however, this sort of official disdain for public sentiment had become impossible. The War of Liberation had brought not just peace, but victory. Victors were supposed to get spoils. And to those whose political and military energies had been aroused by the war, the most coveted spoils took the form of further political and social reforms, like those that had helped defeat Napoleon. Even the

Allgemeine Zeitung, which had never gotten caught up in the excitement
of the war, took it for granted that the congress was destined to be more
significant than a strict reading of the Treaty of Paris suggested. Despite
repeated official denials, Stegmann and his colleagues followed the sum-
merlong migration of princes and ministers to the Austrian capital with
undisguised enthusiasm, heightened no doubt by the knowledge that
their own employer would be among those in attendance.

Cotta went to Vienna as a spokesman for the Publishers' Trade Association, to lobby for the enactment of what was anticipated to be an "imperial" copyright law in Germany. He was a natural choice for the job.
The cachet of his firm's literary list was unmatched anywhere, and it cast
a luster of cultural prestige on Cotta's person—a useful distinction at a
gathering where prestige would count heavily. He was also conceded to
possess the most scrupulous personal integrity and what one associate
described as "a distinct talent for confidential goings-on," a rare combination indeed.[1] Finally, Cotta was on his way to becoming a wealthy
man—a liability in one respect, since part of the argument for copyright
was that piracy impoverished legitimate publishers,[2] but also essential if
one was to hold one's own in the social whirl of the congress. Even grant-
ing money and culture their full weight, however, Cotta's credentials
were not the kind that would guarantee him a hearing. Heinrich von
Treitschke captured contemporary perceptions perfectly when he included Cotta's name only at the end of his survey of those in attendance,
after "the representative of German Jewry" and before a concluding reference to "an unending series . . . of place-seekers, eavesdroppers, and
toadies"[3]—all of whom had come to Vienna expecting a constitutional
convention for Europe, where grievances a generation in the making
would finally be redressed.

1. Carl Bertuch, *Tagebuch vom Wiener Kongress,* ed. Hermann von Egloffstein (Berlin,
1916), p. 248; cf. a police report dated 27 Oct. 1814, in August Fournier, ed., *Die Geheimpolizei auf dem Wiener Kongress: Eine Auswahl aus ihren Papieren* (Vienna, 1913), p. 206.

2. Other publishers viewed Cotta's financial success with ambivalence. In an essay on
the book trade published in 1816, Friedrich Perthes provides a detailed account of the
financial hardships he and his colleagues had suffered, which concludes, rather oddly, as
follows:

> Or should the case of the Cotta Verlag count here, instead of all the other examples
> we have given? Does anyone think of all the capital invested in that firm these last
> twenty years, or of the length of time over which this occurred? Do we consider how
> many works of scholarship and art would have been lost to our literature if this firm
> had not existed? But then, the owner of this house does not need anyone else to
> vindicate him: he can defend himself against reproach! (From *Der deutsche Buchhan-
> del als Bedingung des Daseyns einer deutschen Literatur,* in Widmann, *Der deutsche Buch-
> handel* 1:98.)

3. Heinrich von Treitschke, *History of Germany in the Nineteenth Century,* trans. Eden
Paul and Cedar Paul (New York, 1915–19), 2:17.

Like most of the others on Treitschke's list, Cotta viewed his mission in the broadest terms. Most educated people did not. The immediate obstacle in Cotta's way thus had little to do with the substance of the issues he wanted to see resolved; it was rather the prevailing sense that the copyright question was a parochial matter, of purely private, commercial interest and nothing more. Unless this atmosphere of indifference could be dispelled he would have no chance of success. Yet to dispel it meant confronting the political aspects of the book trade more directly than had been done in the past.

The group that Cotta represented originated in a meeting organized by the Potsdam publisher Carl Horvath in 1802, at which the heads of a number of leading firms, including Cotta, had gathered to discuss their common problems.[4] In its spirit (aggressively dignified) and membership (mainly older northern firms), the Publishers' Trade Association was recognizably a successor to the organization founded by Philipp Reich in 1764. But the difficulties it faced had grown significantly more complex. The cash-based fairs that Reich had promoted had gone some distance toward rationalizing the book trade and solving the problems of cash flow and inventory management that had perplexed Cotta as a young man. Like so many German institutions, however, the new fairs had eventually been overtaken by events. Since the early 1790s literary production in Germany had been on a war footing. The political excitement of the Revolution and the heightened sense of German cultural identity that followed in its wake had led to an enormous increase in the production of books and, more problematically, in the number of book dealers. In 1803 membership in the book trade was estimated to have grown by 25 percent in ten years, with even more dramatic increases in the north—Prussia was then supporting almost three times as many dealers as it had a generation before.[5] Some of these were pirates; others were not publishers at all but small-time retailers operating in towns that had never had bookstores before, who took advantage of the overproduction of books to scratch out a modest existence. The reformed fairs had made it possible for anyone with a little capital to make a living as a book dealer, and by the turn of the century it seemed as if almost anyone was. The result was ferocious competition, involving steep discounting and consignment-purchase schemes that eroded the profitability of even well-financed firms. The social consequences were equally disturbing: publishing was in danger of becoming one of those semirespectable trades one might recommend to a younger son who seemed unsuited to the liberal professions—exactly the outcome elite publishers like Cotta feared most.

4. F. Herm. Meyer, "Der deutsche Buchhandel," pp. 220–21, 231–33.
5. Kapp and Goldfriedrich, *Geschichte* 3:557.

The efforts of the new association were thus directed both against outright pirates and against discount retailers, who made use of the fairs to obtain credit and negotiate special deals that allowed them to undercut the regular selling price of legitimately published books. What was wanted, as always, were more rigid and fully elaborated regulations governing discount rates, credit, and admission to the fairs. What was needed, however, was someone to whom proposals of this kind might be submitted. As the aging Friedrich Nicolai replied when asked to endorse the group's program, "a law has no force if there is no sovereign to enact it"[6]—or, he might have added, if there are too many. The Imperial Deputation and the Rheinbund had between them eliminated most of the enclaves in which pirates had sheltered, creating instead a cluster of middle-sized states intensely jealous of their political and fiscal autonomy and better able than ever to resist appeals for national cooperation. Nor did the association's agenda dovetail well with the objectives of reformers in other quarters, most of whom were looking to loosen, not tighten, restraints on trade.[7]

With the return of war to northern Germany in 1806, the prospects for publishing reform were transformed. The immediate consequence of the French invasion was a decline in the number of books for sale at the Leipzig fairs. By the spring of 1807 the number of titles listed in the catalogue had fallen by 25 percent from the all-time high of 4,181 reached two years before. Although Cotta and his colleagues were inclined to attribute this depression to the effects of French tyranny, it was probably caused largely by wartime shortages of transportation and raw materials: 1808 and 1810 were years of peace in central Europe, and also of relative prosperity among publishers.[8] Moreover, the hardness of the times was felt most acutely by those marginal dealers whom the association's leaders considered "no better than fishwives" in any case.[9] Among the thirty-six signatories to the minutes of the association's founding meeting, only two were not around to endorse the instructions Cotta took to Vienna twelve years later.[10] At the end of the Napoleonic

6. Ibid., p. 581.

7. The rhetoric of free trade did not suit the program of the association, as can be seen in its most important programmatic statement, Georg Joachim Göschen's *Meine Gedanken über den Buchhandel und über dessen Mängel* . . . (Leipzig, 1802), which proclaims on its first page that "the book trade is a trade, . . . [and] trade, by its nature, must be free," and then proceeds to propose strict state regulation of prices, sales contracts, and credit. Even sympathetic governments could become confused as to where the industry's real interest lay. In 1810 Prussia repealed those portions of the *Allgemeine Landrecht* that protected copyright in order to promote free trade in books, a step precisely the opposite of what was wanted.

8. Kapp and Goldfriedrich, *Geschichte* 4:12–13.

9. Göschen, *Gedanken*, p. 6.

10. Cf. Kapp and Goldfriedrich, *Geschichte* 3:578; and "Actenstücke und Briefe zur Geschichte der Deputation der deutschen Buchhändler beim Wiener Congresse, im Jahre

period, concern about the social deterioration of the book trade was far less prevalent than at the start. It had been replaced, however, by a more acute sense of the industry's political vulnerability.

That vulnerability was brought home by the French press decrees of February 1810, the consequences of which for the periodical press were described in chapter 4. As applied to books the effects were almost as grave. Publishers in those German lands that had been (or would be) incorporated into France—comprising nine French departments along the left bank of the Rhine and up the Baltic coast as far as Lübeck—were subject to the reestablished *Direction générale de l'imprimerie et la librairie*, whose repressive powers were as extensive as anything western Europe had seen since the Counter-Reformation. Publishers elsewhere in Germany confronted stringent trade barriers, promulgated under the Continental system, which threatened to make interstate commerce in books a thing of the past. To this was added strict (if somewhat uneven) censorship, whose object was to crush political dissent but which had the effect of discouraging all forms of literary activity. By the end of 1812 book production had fallen another 20 percent from its prewar high, in part because the atmosphere had become so oppressive and uncertain that there were just not many books being written anymore.[11] Even Cotta, whose firm depended less than most on the regular appearance of new work, found himself so desperate that for a time he talked of giving up the book trade entirely.[12]

Although no unified regulatory agency was ever established for Germany, it was assumed that the full force of the French approach would eventually be felt there. Many informed observers, moreover, believed that only complete adoption of the new system could save German publishers from the destructive effects of those elements of it that were already in place. Accordingly, in the spring of 1811 Friedrich Perthes submitted a proposal to the king of Saxony calling for the establishment of a state-sponsored commercial bureau centered on the Leipzig fairs and with powers similar to those of the *Direction générale* in Paris.[13] Perthes believed that the French would prefer the oversight of a centralized agency modeled on their own to the patchwork of trade and censorship decrees promulgated during the past year. In return for the restoration

---

1814," *Börsenblatt für den deutschen Buchhandel* 4, nos. 50–54, 57, 58 (23 June–21 July 1837): col. 1099.

11. [Böttiger,] "Blike auf den Buchhandel im Jahr 1812," *AZ*, 19–23 Nov. 1812 (Beilage).

12. Friedrich Perthes to Görres, 19 Feb. 1812, in Widmann, *Der deutsche Buchhandel* 1:384.

13. Text in F. Herm. Meyer, "Der deutsche Buchhandel," pp. 243–45. Cf. Kapp and Goldfriedrich, *Geschichte* 4:29–31; and Albrecht Kirchhoff, "Ursprung und erste Lebensäußerungen der 'Leipziger' Buchhandlungs-Deputirten," *Archiv für Geschichte des deutschen Buchhandels* 16 (1893): 326–53.

of lost markets, German dealers would submit to having the fairs used to suppress illegal works, at the same time that they regulated prices, credit, and copyright, about which the French held very advanced views.[14] Leipzig would become "a Paris for books," the commercial and intellectual hub of a unified German culture.

Perthes submitted his memorandum in a pessimistic spirit that the progressive character of his cultural agenda can scarcely conceal.[15] As a resident of occupied Hamburg, he had felt the weight of the new system as heavily as any of his peers. Rather than cling to the wreckage of the old fairs, however, he preferred to gamble that Napoleon would be attracted by the organizational simplicity of his program and that the emperor's oft-affirmed sympathy for the native cultures of subject peoples was sincere. In this he was mistaken. As far as the government of Saxony was concerned, any program to restore the status and revenues that flowed from the Leipzig fairs was worth considering, and in due course a deputation was formed to pursue Perthes's proposal. The French, however, had no interest in promoting even the most benign forms of German national consciousness. Nor, given the substantial effectiveness of existing arrangements, did they care to experiment with new and needlessly subtle forms of political control. In the end the government in Dresden could do nothing to ease the publishers' situation, which continued to deteriorate until the spring of 1814, when the departure of the French at last permitted the convening of "the first real fair" since 1806.[16]

Perthes's proposal had not been officially endorsed by the trade association, nor did it command universal assent among his fellow publishers, some of whom felt that Perthes was "giving himself over to tyranny."[17] This fact was inadvertently highlighted by Karl Böttiger, who prepared the final memorandum for submission to the king. While doing so he took it on himself, in what Perthes rather charitably called a moment of "exceptional carelessness," to add the endorsement of some of Perthes's best-known associates, including Cotta, who had not seen the original document and subsequently felt obliged to repudiate it.[18]

14. Ludwig Gieseke, *Die geschichtliche Entwicklung des deutschen Urheberrechts* (Göttingen, 1957), pp. 124–26.

15. Perthes to Friedrich Bertuch, 23 Jan. 1811, in Ludwig Geiger, ed., "Buchhändler-briefe von 1786 bis 1816," *Archiv für Geschichte des deutschen Buchhandels* 8 (1883): 318–19; and Clemens Theodor Perthes, *Friedrich Perthes Leben* (Gotha, 1855), 1 : 202–6.

16. Karl Böttiger to Cotta, 15 Nov. 1813, in Fehling and Schiller, *Briefe an Cotta* 1 : 500.

17. Perthes to Friedrich Bertuch, 13 July 1811, in Geiger, "Buchhändlerbriefe," pp. 319–20.

18. Perthes to Bertuch, 14 Aug. 1811, ibid., pp. 320–21. Before the weight of the French system had made itself fully felt, Cotta also looked forward to the adoption of the French copyright law in Germany and to the establishment of a regulatory tribunal in Leipzig (Cotta to Goethe, 14 Sept. 1809, in Kuhn, *Goethe und Cotta* 1 : 198).

Yet despite its ambiguous reception in the trade, Perthes's formulation of the industry's problems is important to what follows, insofar as it marks the moment when two previously unrelated issues—copyright and censorship—converge.

Since the middle of the previous century the reform of the book trade had revolved around two questions: how to limit competition and how to balance the interests of producers and distributors without encouraging either piracy or cutthroat discounting. Why the state should become involved in either of these questions was not obvious. The preferred answer had been that Germany's princes had a responsibility to promote the national culture and, somewhat more controversially, to raise the intellectual level of their subjects. To this constellation of interests Perthes, following the French lead, had added the recently heightened desire of governments to regulate political life. The prospect that the same official mechanism might serve all these purposes was a new one, and once it had been raised it could not be ignored. Given the new atmosphere fostered by the War of Liberation, it might even be turned to good use, if only the state's interest in managing public life could be construed as favoring the elimination of censorship rather than its continuance.

This was Cotta's point of view, but it was not widely shared. The elimination of censorship had never been a goal of the trade association or its antecedent organizations, all of which had defined their objectives in economic terms. In this respect censorship had historically been less consequential than piracy, since it did not much affect the literary texts, devotional and technical manuals, almanacs, and reference works that formed the backbone of the book trade. Furthermore, to the extent that arguments for press freedom had an economic dimension at all, they tended to favor the deregulation of publishing. It seemed inconsistent to claim that, politically, publishing was just another business and did not warrant special attention from the authorities while insisting that, economically, it required an unusually high degree of official protection. The defenders of high culture were thus pitted against the advocates of political participation.

Whatever other lessons the recent past might hold, the publishers who gathered for the 1814 Easter fair were agreed that political agitation was bad for business and that it would be a mistake to hitch their wagon to any particular political system. They were also agreed that, if anything was ever to be done, the time was now. A new six-man deputation was therefore appointed, including three members from Leipzig—Paul Kummer, Carl Richter, and Friedrich Vogel—and three from outside—Johann Hartknoch from Dresden, Friedrich Bertuch from Weimar, and Cotta. These men were empowered in the name of "all fair-minded and ethical German publishers" to take whatever steps were necessary to insure the future health of the industry.[19] Kummer had already solicited an essay on the copyright question from the playwright and journalist August von Kotzebue, who provided a forceful if entirely conventional statement of the association's case.[20] This became the deputation's charter.

With the announcement of the congress at the end of May, moreover, it became obvious to whom this case might be presented. The deputation set about testing the waters. Since Saxony would not be represented in Vienna (the future of that state having been cast into doubt by the king's impolitic loyalty to Napoleon), Bertuch inquired directly of Hardenberg what his government's attitude on the copyright question would be. At Bertuch's request, too, Goethe wrote to Wilhelm von Humboldt urging him to support the association's program.[21] Both men received convincing assurances. On the Austrian side, though, the auspices were more clouded. Hartknoch presented his case to Metternich's secretary, Friedrich Gentz, and found the reply so discouraging that he withdrew from the deputation.[22] Perthes, in contrast, had already been assured of Metternich's sympathy by another of his subordinates, Joseph Pilat.[23] This Cotta confirmed during a private conversation with Metternich and Philipp Stadion later in the summer, at which he and Bertuch were invited to pursue the matter personally in Vienna.[24]

It soon became clear, however, that the two delegates were not agreed on how to proceed. Cotta seems to have been more than a little impatient with Kotzebue's account of the publishers' case, to judge by a report in the *Allgemeine Zeitung* in early October.[25] Kotzebue, like most opponents of piracy, focused on the question of "intellectual property" and on ex-

19. "Vollmacht," in "Actenstücke," cols. 1098–99.

20. August von Kotzebue, "Denkschrift über den Büchernachdruck; zugleich Bittschrift um Bewürkung eines deutschen Reichsgesetzes gegen denselben," in Johann Ludwig Klüber, ed., *Acten des Wiener Congresses in den Jahren 1814–1815* (Erlangen, 1815–35), 4:1–21.

21. Friedrich Bertuch to Paul Kummer, 24 Aug. 1814, in "Actenstücke," col. 1100; Goethe to Friedrich Bertuch, 29 Aug. 1814, in *Goethes Werke* (Weimar, 1887–1912), pt. 4, vol. 25, p. 29.

22. August Schürmann, *Die Rechtsverhältnisse der Autoren und Verleger sachlich-historisch* (Halle, 1889), p. 169; cf. Friedrich Bertuch to Hartknoch, 26 June 1814, in G. Legerlotz, ed., "Aus den Hartknoch'schen Geschäftspapieren," *Archiv für Geschichte des deutschen Buchhandels* 8 (1883): 329.

23. Perthes to Friedrich Bertuch, 30 Oct. 1814, in Geiger, "Buchhändlerbriefe," p. 322.

24. Friedrich Bertuch to Kummer, 24 Aug. 1814, in "Actenstücke," col. 1100.

25. "Buchhändlerdeputation an den Kongreß in Wien," AZ, 3, 4 Oct. 1814. It is likely that Cotta wrote this article himself; we know from Bertuch's letters to his father that Cotta reported regularly on the congress for the AZ (those articles labeled "*Wien"; see Carl Bertuch to Friedrich Bertuch, 30 Nov. 1814, in Bertuch, *Tagebuch*, pp. 248–50). Unfortunately, no editorial exemplar survives for the months when he was in Vienna (see Cotta to Stegmann, 8 May 1815, CA).

tending the common law of property to the world of ideas, in behalf of which he had brought forward an array of authorities ranging from Martin Luther to a past president of the Vienna censorship bureau. Although the *AZ* took nothing away from this, it did have something to add: repeated references to the suffering of Germany's publishers under Napoleon and to the contributions of Germany's writers to the War of Liberation, in which, in the words of the *AZ's* correspondent, "pen and sword had fought together to free Germany from the tyrant's yoke." In the *AZ's* account, copyright emerges as a question less of private property than of public right, one of the fruits of victory, which was owed not just to the literary elite but to the German people as a whole.

Cotta, moreover, was intent on using his invitation to Vienna to work both for copyright and against censorship. His overall approach was thus defined not by Kotzebue's essay, but by another work on the same subject, "Vom freien Geistes-Verkehr" by Heinrich Luden. Luden, a professor of history at the University of Jena, had been commissioned by Bertuch to write about the industry's problems at the same time that Kummer was approaching Kotzebue. Luden, however, adopted a much broader perspective, in which the central issue is not intellectual property but "intellectual commerce," to which piracy and censorship are equally inimical.[26] Although the association had considered adopting Luden's presentation as its official statement, it chose Kotzebue's more familiar presentation instead, a decision with which Bertuch agreed[27] but to which Cotta evidently did not feel bound.

Perthes, who had first brought these issues together under far different circumstances, was quick to note the danger in such a radical approach. Luden, he wrote Bertuch, was prone to say some things "too loudly, too clearly," a tendency that Cotta shared. "In actual practice," Perthes felt, Germany "had always had complete freedom of the press, since what could not be printed in Prussia could be published in Württemberg, and what might not appear in Hamburg could come out ten paces down the road in Altona." It was an arrangement to be tampered with only with the greatest care. "I am," he continued, "for clarity in all things; but, without being a Freemason or a Jesuit, I am likewise convinced that everything need not be spelled out unambiguously, still less set down on paper." Cotta, Perthes suspected, "saw many things from one side only"; nevertheless he was "honest, energetic, and determined to succeed."[28]

---

26. *Nemesis* 2 (1814), nos. 2: 211–59 and 3: 328–82. Luden's argument for copyright is summarized in the second half of the *AZ's* report, but his discussion of censorship is not mentioned.

27. Friedrich Bertuch to Kummer, 24 Aug. 1814, in "Actenstücke," col. 1100.

28. Perthes to Friedrich Bertuch, 30 Oct. 1814, in Geiger, "Buchhändlerbriefe," p. 322.

VIENNA

Cotta arrived in Vienna at the end of September, taking lodgings in a suite of rooms on the Graben. Friedrich Bertuch did not attend, owing to illness. In his place he sent his son, Carl, who had assisted his father in his business for several years and who also held a minor official post in Weimar. This change insured that Cotta would be the dominant partner in the delegation. The younger Bertuch's diary of the congress reveals him to be an industrious soul but definitely not at home in the elegant and highly charged atmosphere of the Austrian capital. A police agent described him as "much more open than Cotta, . . . well rounded, cultured, but something of a small-town type," who was "flattered to be the representative of such an obviously important cause."[29] His judgments of individuals were less than shrewd; he believed, for instance, that the emperor's physician had more influence over press policy than the "foreigner" Friedrich Gentz.[30] Despite their differences in experience and reputation, however, Cotta got along well with his young colleague, and they soon accomplished their minimum objective: to get the attention of those who would shape Germany's new constitution.

The responses they received were mixed. Baron vom Stein, who might have been expected to welcome any proposal to foster a sense of German national identity, reacted with impatience to Kotzebue's pedantic report and complained to Bertuch that the whole question of piracy was being blown out of proportion. Wilhelm von Humboldt doubted whether the matter would come up at the congress but promised his support if it did. Hardenberg repeated his earlier assurances. Wrede, from Bavaria, and Münster, from Hanover, were friendly but evasive. Wintzingerode, from Württemberg, was hostile and rejected any measure that would remove press policy from the hands of the states.[31] From the start, however, the one indispensable man was assumed to be Metternich, who expressed his regret that "false ideas" on the subject of piracy had prevailed in Austria and promised "to make the publishers' cause his own."[32]

To those waiting in Leipzig, Metternich's tacit approval seemed like half the battle won. Yet his support, having been promised in advance,

---

29. Fournier, *Geheimpolizei*, p. 181.

30. Carl Bertuch to Friedrich Bertuch, 4 Oct. 1814, in Bertuch, *Tagebuch*, p. 241.

31. These and other discussions with the main German plenipotentiaries are recounted in ibid., pp. 17, 27, 32, 43–44, and 90–91, and in Carl Bertuch's letters to his father, pp. 239–248.

32. Metternich heard the association's proposals for the first time during a private conversation with Cotta on October 1, and again on the eighth, when Cotta and Bertuch were granted a formal audience (ibid., p. 27; also Cotta to Kummer, 12 Oct. 1814, and Friedrich Bertuch to Kummer, 21 Oct. 1814, in "Actenstücke," cols. 1193–94). Metternich's sympathetic response eventually found its way into the *AZ*, 28 Oct. 1814.

should have come as no surprise; nor should its significance be over-estimated. Metternich's chancellery actually had no say whatever over copyright, which in Austria was a purely domestic matter. But Metternich was eager to expand his influence in internal affairs, in order to promote administrative reforms that would make it easier for Austria to carry out its international obligations.[33] Austria's encouragement of piracy was a symbol of commercial obsolescence whose original, mercantilist rationale—the conservation of specie—had vanished during the inflation of the Napoleonic period, when the crown had recalled most of the state's metal coinage and issued paper notes instead. These had since fallen below 50 percent of par, a collapse that made a general change of fiscal policy irresistible.[34] From Metternich's point of view the association's petition had come at an opportune moment: an agreement on copyright, as part of a comprehensive German settlement, would achieve a small but visible improvement in Austria's miserable trading posture and establish a precedent for further modification of the country's administration in line with its international position.

What almost no one except Cotta seems to have grasped, however, was that Austria could not consider any copyright settlement that did not include a parallel agreement on censorship. As far as the Habsburg lands were concerned, copyright really was a matter of "commerce" rather than "property." From a purely economic point of view Austria had a compelling interest in uniform press regulations, regardless of what degree of political freedom those regulations might afford. A federal copyright law would open up the Austrian market to publishers throughout Germany. If similar uniformity with respect to censorship were lacking, writers would obviously flock to those firms whose governments were the least troublesome, thus leaving tax-paying Austrian publishers in the lurch.[35] In 1810 Metternich had tried to take advantage of a temporary asymmetry between Austria's forcibly liberalized press laws and those of the *Bund* states to try to attract the *Allgemeine Zeitung* to Vienna. He was not likely to accept any comparable asymmetry at Austria's expense.

It had long been assumed that the key to copyright reform was persuading Austria to set an example for the rest of Germany.[36] Cotta did not think this strategy would work; he preferred instead to let "Germany break the path for Austria."[37] This did not mean that he expected Aus-

---

33. Arthur Haas, *Metternich: Reorganization and Nationality, 1813–1818* (Wiesbaden, 1963).

34. Adolf Beer, *Die Finanzen Oesterreichs im XIX Jahrhundert* (Prague, 1877), pp. 44–95; and Macartney, *The Habsburg Empire*, pp. 178–80, 194–96, 201–4.

35. Police report of 7 Oct. 1814, in Fournier, *Geheimpolizei*, pp. 160–61.

36. Friedrich Bertuch to Johann Hartknoch, 26 June 1814, in Legerlotz, "Geschäftspapieren," p. 329.

37. Cotta to Goethe, 30 Nov. 1814, in Kuhn, *Goethe und Cotta* 1 : 263–64.

tria to follow its smaller neighbors, but rather that Austria's interest in leading them could be turned to the book trade's advantage. It was on this basis that Cotta sought Metternich's support. For almost a month Cotta pursued these matters privately with the various delegates— though not so privately as to escape the notice of the police, who reported that most of those to whom Cotta spoke continued, despite his efforts, to view the publishers' petition as being directed to Austria alone.[38]

A more decisive step was necessary, and on November 1 Cotta and Bertuch took it, by publishing the full text of Kotzebue's essay, along with the following preface:

> ### Supplement to the Report of the Deputation of German Publishers Submitted to the Congress Assembled at Vienna
>
> The undersigned, as authorized representatives of the most enlightened segment of German publishers, having been called by the auspicious liberation of Germany to participate, as appropriate, in the proceedings of the Congress at Vienna, venture most humbly to offer for higher consideration the following recommendations, as being the most essential to the revitalization, purification, and better organization of German publishing.
>
> Given that it is of the utmost importance that Germany acquire both a secure internal order and a unified posture toward foreign lands, and that this shall be accomplished by means of a lawful constitution, it is necessary above all that *Freedom of the Press*, the one means whereby governments can be swiftly and accurately informed of the existing state of affairs, be legally established.
>
> This freedom, which serves the well-being of the whole people, achieves even greater force for the development of the public if it is permitted that all works of the intellect may be transmitted to the public without interference. If, in addition, writers, printers, and publishers are accorded security in their intellectual property by means of a legally enforced *Ban on Literary Piracy*, in the manner of the attached decree of September 22, 1814, issued by His Royal Highness, the sovereign prince of the United Netherlands, then the German constitution will have established all the measures whereby the benefits of freedom of the press can be realized, without suffering any of the disadvantages that it might entail.[39]

The effect of this statement, as intended, was to shift the ground of the association's case from copyright to censorship and, in so doing, to demonstrate its constitutional (as opposed to merely commercial) significance. By acknowledging the recent Dutch press law in their presentation, moreover, they added new specificity to what before had been a rather abstract argument.

As far as copyright went, the provisions of the Dutch decree were all

---

38. Fournier, *Geheimpolizei*, pp. 170–71.
39. Klüber, *Acten* 4:26–27; cf. Bertuch, *Tagebuch*, p. 39.

the trade association could have asked for: except for school books, Bibles, and other standard texts, all publications would be protected from piracy during the lifetime of the author and the first generation of heirs. The law's provisions with respect to press freedom were more circumspect, weighted heavily in favor of responsible opinion and against works that were provocative, ephemeral, or anonymous. Censorship as such was abolished, replaced by civil penalties that would apply to authors whose work offended private persons, public morality, or religion. All publications were required to bear the name of the author, editor, or printer and the date and place of publication. Special rules applied to political periodicals, which could appear only under a royal privilege, which in turn could be obtained only if the publisher could show he had at least three hundred subscribers lined up. The Dutch regent, in short, was prepared to establish "freedom of the press" as it was then understood, but not without reserving to himself very substantial means of regulating opinion.[40]

How far the Dutch law coincided with Cotta's private views is not clear. Cotta chose this decree to exemplify his program not so much because he endorsed all its provisions, but because he believed it was acceptable to the Austrians: it had already been published, with a favorable comment, in the *Wiener Zeitung*, a semiofficial organ of Metternich's chancellery.[41] Given vigorous Austrian leadership, and perhaps an explicit prohibition of seditious libel, this statute might well have served as a model for Germany. Metternich had led Cotta to believe that such leadership would emerge. It was, however, the settled conviction of Met-

40. The text of the Dutch decree is in "Actenstücke," cols. 1290–91. Its provisions approximate what might be called the official Enlightenment position on freedom of the press, which received an authoritative definition in William Blackstone's *Commentaries on the Laws of England* (Oxford, 1765–69):

> The *liberty of the press* is indeed essential to the nature of a free state; but this consists in laying no *previous* restraints upon publications, and not in freedom from censure for criminal matter when published. Every freeman has an undoubted right to lay what sentiments he pleases before the public: to forbid this is to destroy the freedom of the press. But if he publishes what is improper, mischievous, or illegal, he must take the consequences for his own temerity. . . . Thus the will of the individual is still left free; the abuse only of that free-will is the object of legal punishment. (4:151–52)

The unqualified language employed in the United States Constitution ("Congress shall make no law . . . ") tends to make this and other contemporary attempts to define the rights of the press seem parochial and mean-spirited. But even an undoubted democrat like Thomas Jefferson felt it reasonable, in his unadopted alternative to the First Amendment, to deny citizens the right to publish "false facts affecting injuriously the life, liberty, or reputation of others, or affecting the peace of the confederacy with other nations," a formulation whose spirit is not far from the kind of law Cotta wanted to promote.

41. Cotta and Bertuch, "Bericht über die von Seiten der Deputation des deutschen Buchhandels bis jetzt bey dem Congresse zu Wien geschehenen Schritte," in "Actenstücke," col. 1267.

ternich's chief, the emperor, that it would not. Francis had no stomach
for resuming single-handed his ancestral role as the leader of Germany,
and feared any undertakings that would open the Habsburg lands to
political innovation. He was also determined to defend Austria's commercial interests along the mercantilist lines set down by his uncle, Joseph II, a stance that enjoyed wide popular support. Finally, Francis did
not favor any blurring of the distinction between politics and administration of the kind implied by the Dutch decree. On this question he had
long followed the advice of the president of his general accounting office, Baron Anton von Baldacci, who openly opposed Metternich on the
copyright issue.[42] Immediately following the publication of the delegation's "Supplement," Pilat was dispatched to Cotta with the news that
Francis "wanted to hear nothing about press freedom, constitutions, or
special limitations on property."[43]

For practical purposes, the emperor's obstinacy meant an end to Austrian support for Cotta's mission. Metternich remained politely sympathetic throughout the congress and in January supported Cotta and Bertuch in their efforts to rebut the attack of a Viennese pirate who
reprinted a corrupted, polemically annotated version of Kotzebue's essay.[44] But beyond this he would do nothing. Neither of the constitutional
drafts submitted by Austria that spring included any language touching
the issues of copyright or press freedom.[45]

Metternich's receptivity to Cotta's proposal reveals a convergence of
interests—in the clarity and consistency of press regulations—but not of
values. Metternich had not yet assumed his future role as scourge of the
German press, and unless one credits him with the most absolute cynicism, it seems likely that he was prepared at this juncture to contemplate
the disappearance of censorship in exchange for the creation of a larger
regulatory structure that Austria could expect to control.[46] But he was
never persuaded that the modest liberalization reflected in the Dutch
press law offered any prospective benefits to Germany's rulers. A system
of civil penalties of the kind put forward by Cotta, no matter how se-

42. Fournier, *Geheimpolizei*, p. 378.

43. Bertuch, *Tagebuch*, p. 47.

44. Cotta and Bertuch, "Bericht," in "Actenstücke," cols. 1267–68. The association's
efforts attracted other replies, and other defenses. See Hans Widmann, "'Die Krisis
des deutschen Buchhandels': Bemerkungen zu einer Apologie für den Büchernachdruck
aus dem Jahre 1815," *Gutenberg-Journal* (1968): 257–61; and Jean Paul Friedrich Richter,
"Sieben letzte oder Nachworte gegen den Nachdruck," *Morgenblatt für gebildete Stände*,
17–22 April 1815.

45. Klüber, *Acten* 2:1–5, 308–14; cf. Bertuch, *Tagebuch*, pp. 195, 257–59.

46. This proposition is expressly denied by Metternich's most distinguished biog-
rapher, Heinrich Ritter von Srbik, *Metternich: Der Staatsmann und der Mensch* (Munich,
1925–54), 1:348, 494, who does not, however, consider Metternich's negotiation with
Cotta; but cf. Enno E. Kraehe, *Metternich's German Policy* (Princeton, N.J., 1963–83), 2:189.

verely it might be framed, necessarily establishes the state and the press as equal parties before the law, and subjects the actions of the government to public scrutiny in ways that are barred by even the most tolerant censorship. This was a distinction to which Metternich's chief political advisor, Friedrich Gentz, was acutely sensitive, and his distrust of what were called "English principles,"[47] combined with the emperor's reflexive distrust of public opinion, far outweighed whatever marginal advantage Metternich might have detected in the trade association's initiative.

Cotta therefore turned to Prussia to champion his industry's cause, a choice that was in some ways less desirable. On the one hand, Prussia did not harbor many pirates, so the enactment of copyright there would be inconsequential in itself and would carry little weight as an example to others.[48] On the other hand, Frederick William's ministers had acquired a reputation for generosity toward the press during the War of Liberation. The Prussian delegation also experienced no disagreement about the need for federal regulation. The so-called Forty-one Articles drafted by Humboldt and Hardenberg prior to the congress had already contained a provision for "freedom of the press subject to modifications still to be determined,"[49] a formulation reflecting a much broader common purpose than any Cotta might have shared with Metternich. As Austrian interest began to wane Cotta found himself drawn to Hardenberg and his associates, in whose company he passed much of November and December,[50] a time when the major powers were preoccupied with an entirely different matter (about which there will be more to say later on)—the competing claims being advanced against the territories of Saxony and Poland.

Cotta had come to Vienna prepared to wait as long as necessary to see the questions that had brought him there resolved.[51] His stay was cut short, however, by the arrival of news from Stuttgart that the king had proclaimed a constitution for Württemberg and that a Diet would be convened to receive it. This announcement was followed by word that Frederick, who had long held that "anyone who buys a book is free to reprint it," had also given in on the copyright question.[52] To those look-

47. Friedrich Gentz, "Pressefreyheit in England," *Wiener Jahrbücher der Literatur* 1 (1818): 210–55; in *Schriften von Friedrich von Gentz,* ed. Gustav Schlesier (Mannheim, 1838–40), 2:39–115.

48. Carl Bertuch to Friedrich Bertuch, 26 May 1815, in Bertuch, *Tagebuch,* p. 198.

49. Klüber, *Acten,* vol. 1, pt. 1, p. 47.

50. Fournier, *Geheimpolizei,* p. 374. Cf. Cotta to Friedrich Schelling, 26 Nov. 1814, in Horst Fuhrmans and Liselotte Lohrer, eds., *Schelling und Cotta: Briefwechsel, 1803–1849* (Stuttgart, 1965), p. 94; and Carl Bertuch to Friedrich Bertuch, 30 Nov. 1814, in Bertuch, *Tagebuch,* p. 248. These consultations went well beyond Cotta's mission for the trade association, as will be seen in the next chapter.

51. Cotta to Goethe, 11 Jan. 1815, in Kuhn, *Goethe und Cotta* 1:266.

52. Kapp and Goldfriedrich, *Geschichte* 4:73–74; cf. *AZ,* 7 March 1815.

ing forward to a new order in Germany it seemed a remarkable and, considering its source, wholly unexpected victory.[53] It was not. On the contrary, Frederick's unilateral action revealed the limits of the congress's power, as well as the continuing determination of the lesser princes to maintain control of their own affairs. The underlying premise of Cotta's mission—that resistance from this quarter had been swept away by the War of Liberation—was thus proved wrong, albeit in a way that was not apparent at the time. Yet even if Cotta had grasped this fact at once, it would not have made any difference. Frederick's announcement would still have forced him to choose between staying at the congress and returning home to stand for election to the new Diet. After four months of steady effort, Cotta was ready to believe that he had done all he could, and on February 10, after securing a promise of continuing support from Humboldt, he left Vienna.[54]

Bertuch stayed until the end, and found the Prussians as good as their word. Humboldt's draft constitution, made public toward the end of February, included precise language restraining both piracy and censorship. Its press clauses were included in a compromise worked out with the Austrians in May, and from there they made their way, in revised form, into the Special Stipulations of the Federal Act. The revision, however, was fundamental. In the end Hardenberg was unable to resist the demand of the middle-sized states that the final definition of the press's rights be postponed.[55] Instead of a guarantee of rights, the press was given a promise of further action, to the effect that "the Federal Diet will, at its first meeting, occupy itself with the formulation of uniform ordinances respecting freedom of the press and the protection of writers and publishers against illegal reprinting."[56]

Like Frederick's constitution a few months before, this promise was taken to be a victory for the good cause, and Bertuch was happy to receive the congratulations of the delegates he had lobbied so tirelessly.[57] Even at the time, however, this language should not have been all that reassuring. What Cotta and Bertuch had achieved was a promise not of freedom and security but of uniformity, which Napoleon had already

53. Wintzingerode reported that Stein, who loathed Frederick, embraced Cotta warmly and declared that Württemberg had now set an example for the rest of Germany (Hölzle, *Württemberg im Zeitalter Napoleons*, p. 191). Cotta felt entitled to take indirect credit for Frederick's concession (Friedrich Bertuch to Kummer, 8 March 1815, in "Actenstücke," cols. 1266–67).

54. Carl Bertuch to Friedrich Bertuch, 15 April 1815, in Bertuch, *Tagebuch*, pp. 256–57.

55. Kraehe, *Metternich's German Policy* 2:383. The key opponent of Prussia on this issue was Bavaria; see Aretin, *Bayerns Weg zum souveränen Staat*, pp. 128–74.

56. Article 18d, in Klüber, *Acten* 2:613; for the intervening Prussian drafts, see 2:46–47, 62, 305, and 4:109–10.

57. Bertuch, *Tagebuch*, p. 197; also the optimistic report by Böttiger in the *AZ*, 11 April 1815 (Beilage).

shown could be turned to all sorts of dangerous purposes. They had also managed to link together the issues of piracy and censorship more intimately than ever before, which would prove to be a distinctly mixed blessing in itself.

When, in March 1817, the Federal Diet finally turned its attention to a new press law, it found itself unable, despite the urging of the trade association, to disentangle the question of "intellectual property" from the increasingly vexed question of intellectual freedom.[58] Metternich remained convinced of the mutual dependency of censorship and copyright long after his brief flirtation with the industry's reformers had been forgotten, and continued to pursue these issues in the same order, both logical and political, in which Cotta had presented them. The press decree adopted at Carlsbad in 1819, in which Cotta's efforts at Vienna can be said to have found their heterodox fulfillment, was supposed to have been part of a more inclusive settlement, involving the establishment of a federal bureau to oversee all phases of publishing. The logic of this proposal, submitted to the Vienna Ministerial Conference in the spring of 1820, bears a perverse but recognizable resemblance to the supplement Cotta and Bertuch attached to Kotzebue's essay: "The *authority* of the Federation to prevent misuse of the press," it was now argued, "flowed from one and the same source [as] . . . its *obligation* to protect printed works from piracy."[59] The source, however, was no longer the "auspicious liberation of Germany," as Cotta had imagined, but the defense of the status quo against revolution. But even Metternich at the height of his power could not force this scheme through the Diet, and serious copyright legislation was again postponed. Cotta would not live to see its enactment.[60]

Despite this sorry sequel, Cotta always regarded his trip to Vienna as

58. Ludwig Gieseke (*Geschichtliche Entwicklung*, pp. 131–33) argues that the "apparent relationship" between copyright and censorship established in the Federal Act was a hindrance to further progress on copyright. Karin Hertel ("Der Politiker Johann Friedrich Cotta: Publizistische verlegerische Unternehmungen, 1815–1819," *Archiv für Geschichte des Buchwesens* 19 [1978], cols. 394–95) rejects this conclusion. She explains Cotta's linkage of these two issues as a reflection of his desire to appeal to the "national interests" of the German delegates, which she regards as a success. She goes on to observe that spokesmen for copyright in the Federal Diet distinguished their cause from that of press freedom, as did the major spokesmen in the trade. However cogently this intellectual distinction might have been maintained, however, it is still true that, politically, it could not be sustained. Detailed accounts of these subsequent deliberations are in Kapp and Goldfriedrich, *Geschichte* 4:80–121; and Leopold Friedrich Ilse, *Geschichte des Deutschen Bundesversammlung, insbesondere ihres Verhaltens zu den deutschen National-Interessen* (Marburg, 1861–62), 2:288–95.

59. Heinrich Eduard Brockhaus, "Metternichs Plan einer staatlichen Organisation des deutschen Buchhandels," *Archiv für Geschichte des deutschen Buchhandels* 1 (1878): 91–119. Brockhaus identifies the author of this document as Adam Müller.

60. Serious progress on copyright resumes in the mid-1830s and reaches fruition in 1845; see Gieseke, *Geschichtliche Entwicklung*, pp. 145–56.

a personal and political success. Indeed, it would be asking a great deal for him to have anticipated all the perversities the future had in store. He certainly never shared Friedrich Perthes's reservations about the dangers of clarity. In politics as in literature, Cotta's tastes ran to the classic; his sense of proportion demanded that large questions be resolved as far as possible by reference to large principles. Neither, however, would he again play a leading role in the politics of his profession. In the spring of 1817 he went to Frankfurt at Bertuch's request to lobby the Federal Diet,[61] and he later wrote to Hardenberg urging him to raise the copyright issue there again.[62] But apart from these incidental efforts he kept more or less to himself, and he felt personally affronted when, a few years later, he was attacked in the Württemberg Diet for supporting copyright legislation that might have benefited his firm.[63] This, too, was for him a matter of principle—a conviction that public men should conduct themselves with almost inhuman detachment. Cotta's feelings on this matter had deep roots, extending back to his reflections on "true republicanism" twenty years before. That he was able to set such scruples aside for the duration of the congress is testimony to his appreciation of the unprecedented gathering in which he found himself.

THE CONGRESS AS NEWS

Shortly before he left Vienna, Cotta was involved in an episode that, while not so unpleasant as to hasten his departure, may have given him something to think about on his way home. On January 29 the *Allgemeine Zeitung* published a long, derisive review of a recent book about Stein's wartime *Zentralverwaltung*, in which Stein himself was handled roughly.[64] The article attracted widespread attention, and although Stein person-

---

61. Kapp and Goldfriedrich, *Geschichte* 4:96.

62. Hardenberg to Cotta, 16 Jan. 1820, CA.

63. *Die Debatten über den Bücher-Nachdruck, welche in der Württembergischen Kammer der Abgeordneten stattfanden* (Stuttgart, 1822). Cotta also refused to help Friedrich Brockhaus to take legal action against a local pirate (Heinrich Eduard Brockhaus, *Friedrich Arnold Brockhaus* [Leipzig, 1872–81], 2:3–5). See also chapter 7 below.

64. "*Von den Donau," *AZ*, 29 Jan. 1815. The article contains a number of passages like the following:

> On first reading [the book in question] one thinks one sees again the *ami du peuple*. Upon reflection, however, the resemblance fades more and more. Just as a wild ape will mimic whatever gestures are put to him with grimaces in which the original is barely discernible, so Germans, in imitating the French, know how to dispense with the charms of novelty, which they replace with systematic thoroughness. In this way they recover at least the form of originality. And in just this way does the deeply laid plan of Stein and his followers differ from the insane inspirations of the Jacobins in 1793. . . . Baron vom Stein shares only one (admirable) characteristic with the French revolutionaries: the courageous frankness with which he has told the German princes what he has in mind for them.

ally took no offense, it contributed to the decline of his prestige at the congress. A few days after its appearance Cotta was publicly confronted with a demand for an explanation by Stein's chief patron, the czar. Cotta replied that the report had been published at the order of Bavaria's chief minister, Montgelas.[65]

Two aspects of this affair were instructive. First, all the offensive passages in the *AZ*'s report were identified as having been excerpted from the Munich journal *Allemannia*, over which Montgelas was known to wield continuous influence and in which the comments had attracted no attention whatever. The *AZ* had obviously broadened the article's original distribution, but the exceptional reaction that Cotta encountered suggested that the original meaning had been changed too: by virtue of their appearance in the *AZ*, Montgelas's views had been accorded a kind of public standing they had not enjoyed when they were confined to a provincial periodical.

Second, and even more unexpectedly, Cotta's attempt to defend himself by deferring to "higher authorities" did not win him any sympathy, from the czar or anyone else. Karl von Phull, general adjutant to Württemberg's Prince William, reported that in Stuttgart it was felt that "one could hardly have compromised and prostituted oneself more than Cotta has in this affair" and that a man of honor would have refused such an article, regardless of its source, or fired the editor who accepted it.[66] In light of the experience of the preceding ten years, such a remark seems almost insane. Yet in one respect it was fair enough: Cotta had wanted to create a newspaper with unique intellectual authority; now, after no end of trouble and expense, he had done it. His success would limit the *AZ*'s freedom from now on. If his newspaper was to continue to occupy the special place in Germany's public life that he had staked out for it, it would have to stand on its own feet. Responsibility could no longer be deflected downward to less distinguished periodicals, or upward to the king's ministers. It was a sobering prospect: however bright the future might seem in relation to the past, the road ahead was by no means free of pitfalls.

Six months earlier one would have had to forgive Cotta for feeling that the Congress of Vienna was the story the *Allgemeine Zeitung* had been destined to cover. From the moment of its appearance Cotta's newspaper had devoted itself to describing what Ernst Posselt had identified as the two great processes of contemporary history: the reorgani-

---

65. Fournier, *Geheimpolizei*, p. 381; cf. an earlier report by Cotta himself, in which the book is warmly recommended ("*Wien," *AZ*, 7 Dec. 1814).

66. Fournier, *Geheimpolizei*, pp. 372–73. Although there is no record of Cotta's ever attempting to deflect responsibility for a decision onto his editors, Stegmann had in fact published this article without consulting Cotta, and Cotta was duly annoyed; see Police Director Wirschinger to Montgelas, 13 May 1815, M Inn 25097/I.

zation of the European state system, and the emergence of a popular political culture capable of challenging the hierarchical order of the past. The congress was expected to provide an arena where these questions could finally be addressed without resort to force and with some recognition of the public's interest in their resolution. Exactly how far the public's interest should reach was, of course, a difficult question. The *AZ* gave little space to the notion that the congress itself was a natural outcome of the War of Liberation. In contrast to the Rhenish press, it paid little attention to popular celebrations of the anniversary of the Battle of Leipzig, discounting their political significance.[67] The report on Cotta's mission that appeared in October, while emphatic in its tone, was almost unique in treating political reform as a reward for the popular rising against France. For the most part the congress loomed as an affair of the great powers, at which the public's newly awakened political energies would be unrepresented.

Like most German newspapers, the *AZ* anticipated the enactment of a national constitution based on that of the Holy Roman Empire.[68] Most contributors identified social and constitutional progress with the revival of the territorial estates, as Cotta did.[69] At the same time, the abolition of serfdom, religious toleration, tariff reform, and freedom of the press were all approved almost unreservedly. Overall, however, emphasis fell on the need for a comprehensive structure that would express Germany's national identity while still maintaining continuity with the past. The *AZ*'s coverage of local or regional initiatives was thus generally unsympathetic. The taste for grass-roots activism left behind by the war seemed more likely to deepen Germany's particularism than to bring about real reform.[70] Constitutional progress, it seemed, depended on the avoidance of political tension.

It would have been out of character for the *AZ* to offer any summary judgment on the proper relationship of public opinion to the proceedings at Vienna. The ideal, to which many contributors referred, was the English press, which was admired both for its variety and for its wide circulation.[71] But when this distant model was set against the up-close

---

67. "Deutschland," *AZ*, 26 Oct. 1814; a more sympathetic article appeared a few weeks later (8 Nov. 1814 [Beilage]). On the general state of public opinion in the Rhineland, which contrasted sharply with that in the south (as the *AZ* repeatedly pointed out), see Karl-Georg Faber, *Die Rheinlande zwischen Restauration und Revolution: Probleme der rheinischen Geschichte von 1814 bis 1848 im Spiegel der zeitgenössischen Publizistik* (Wiesbaden, 1966), pp. 21–109.

68. For instance Böttiger's review of recent political writing, *AZ*, 6 Sept. 1814 (Beilage).

69. See chapter 7.

70. Cf. "Deutschland," *AZ*, 13, 21 Sept. 1814; and an article on the new municipal constitution in Frankfurt, 17 Sept. 1814 (Beilage).

71. For instance Böttiger's essay on English newspapers and magazines, *AZ*, 11 July 1814 (Beilage).

reality of an aroused public, the results were not entirely reassuring. The *AZ* liked to identify with the public, but it did not on that account trust it completely. Nor, for that matter, did it trust the press, particularly those newer journals, like Joseph Görres's *Rheinischer Merkur*, which sought their audience among the most politically dissatisfied groups in Germany.[72] As admirable as the English example might be, there was no guarantee the German press could perform as well.[73] Its role in the formulation of policy was unclear, and the present moment, precisely because it was so ripe with hopes, was not a good one for experimentation. On balance, the congress would function best if the public's expectations were tempered by patience and a sense of the common weal.[74] As a demonstration of statecraft the deliberations at Vienna would contribute to the nation's political education, but they would not mark its maturity.

The *AZ* reported on the congress regularly and in detail. Most stories were a composite of official bulletins and excerpts from other newspapers; these were supplemented by letters from Cotta, whose contributions seemed to his colleague Bertuch to be the most accurate political coverage available.[75] The contrast between Cotta's reports and Stegmann's secondhand sources could be stark. In the issue of October 11, 1814, for instance, a breathless discussion of court etiquette taken from a Vienna paper is followed by an article by Cotta that begins, "The political horizon is still shrouded in darkness." Despite its reliance on other newspapers, the *AZ* was openly critical of them, most scathingly of the widely quoted *Chronik des Wiener Kongresses*, of which Cotta wrote that, when the real history of the congress finally became known, not one in a hundred of its reports would prove to have been true.[76] In spite of his sometimes brusque tone, however, Cotta was not a critic of the congress itself. When he could not report visible progress he turned to dispelling rumors that talks were breaking down or that some key person was on the verge of departure. Throughout his stay he remained publicly confident that the powers would supply Germany, "as a whole and in its parts," with a constitution that would secure the rights of the people and unite the several states against all "internal and external enemies."[77]

Yet it was precisely on constitutional questions that the congress proved most reticent in communicating with the public. As so often in the past, the *AZ*'s editors again found a kind of substitute in the affairs of the Swiss Confederation. The expulsion of the French from Switzer-

72. "Oesterreich," *AZ*, 13 July 1814; reprinted from the *Oesterreichische Beobachter*.

73. "Oesterreich," *AZ*, 28 Oct. 1814.

74. "Deutschland," *AZ*, 10 Sept. 1814, is representative.

75. Carl Bertuch to Friedrich Bertuch, 30 Nov. 1814, in Bertuch, *Tagebuch*, pp. 248–50.

76. "*Wien," *AZ*, 6 Dec. 1814.

77. "*Wien," *AZ*, 16 Oct. 1814; see also 6, 30 Nov. 1814.

land at the end of 1813 had allowed the reemergence of the old struggle between cantonalists and unionists, in which the tension between local autonomy and federal cohesion that was preoccupying the congress's "German committee" was clearly mirrored. The *AZ*'s correspondents, again led by Paul Usteri, unanimously favored a strong federal union, whose members would cede substantial rights to a national assembly. These reports inspired a number of formal protests from the government in Bern, which rivaled in vehemence those being lodged simultaneously by Max Joseph's government against Görres's *Merkur*. Montgelas nevertheless treated the matter routinely, since the relevance of these reports to Germany's circumstances was not so explicit as to be embarrassing. This judgment was confirmed by the refusal of Austria, which supported the cantonalists, to back the Swiss protests. There were limits to how far the *AZ*'s indirect approach could carry it, however, and in the spring of 1815, when the congress finally got down to serious work on the Federal Act, Montgelas's warnings to Stegmann became noticeably more blunt. A few articles were suppressed at his insistence.[78]

Montgelas's patience was even more sorely tried by the *AZ*'s role in what proved to be the most important public controversies of the congress: the reconstitution of Poland and the partition of Saxony. The centrality of these questions had been widely anticipated, since it was assumed that Russia would claim the territory of the former Kingdom of Poland as a protectorate, as a reward for liberating Europe, and that Prussia would choose Saxony as the compensation promised by the Treaty of Paris. England and Austria were determined to resist both these claims as being incompatible with the restoration of the balance of power. The negotiations to break the deadlock were intricate and secret, hence entirely mysterious to the press, which was left to reflect as best it could on the moral qualities of the claimants and their proposed solutions. Since the negotiations were also protracted over many months, during which time nothing else could be decided, these questions above all defined the public posture of the congress and eventually supplied the official rationale—respect for "legitimacy"—for its work as a whole. The crux of the matter lay with Prussia, the only state with territorial claims in both Poland and Saxony, and the only one not physically in possession of its special prize. Prussia was thus the most dependent on the force of argument, and the most eager for public support.

To the extent that the *AZ* displayed any predisposition at all on these issues, its contributors generally preferred that Prussia accept alternative compensation in the Rhineland, in order to stabilize that volatile area.

78. The Swiss complaints and the responses they received are in M Inn 25097/I. See particularly Montgelas's notes to the district government in Augsburg, 6 Dec. 1814, 27 March 1815; and Baron Seida to Montgelas, 1 April 1815.

Despite the failure of Saxony's king to give up his French alliance in a timely fashion, the evident desire of the Saxons to have him restored to them could not be discounted. This public sentiment, together with the antiquity of Saxony's ruling house, seemed to override the claim established by Prussia's leadership in the war against Napoleon.[79]

Once Cotta had made personal contact with the Prussian delegation, however, their point of view was accorded more respect, particularly after Prussia assumed the military governorship of Saxony in November.[80] An open letter from the king of Saxony, reasserting his rights, was immediately rebutted by reports that the annexation of Saxony by Prussia and the establishment of a Russian viceroyalty in Poland were "as good as done."[81] There followed two long defenses of Prussian policy as being in the interest both of the Saxons, who would otherwise be consigned to political insignificance, and of Germany as a whole, since the consolidation of Prussia's position in the north would add to the nation's security and favor constitutional reform.[82] By the first of the year rumors of war were widespread, and Prussia's isolation was evident. But even as the danger subsided the *AZ* continued to review Prussia's original claims, and as late as January 26 reported that Prussia would accept compensation only if it included the whole of Saxony.

The dispute over Saxony marked a significant step in the awakening of German public opinion. Among journalists, the controversy revived some of the fervor of the War of Liberation, and redirected it toward a more concrete concern with Germany's future organization. The debate produced pamphlets and articles without number and appears in retrospect as the opening round of the constitutional struggle that would preoccupy the press for the next five years.[83] The congress's oft-criticized indifference to public sentiment, which accounts for much of the inaccuracy and irrelevance of the coverage it inspired, did not extend to this issue. The British plenipotentiary, Viscount Castlereagh, even professed to regard the overwhelming popular support for Saxony's preservation as decisive.[84] Hardenberg's desire to win the favor of the *AZ* and its readers was thus by no means casual. Having realized that publicity in this matter was inevitable, he decided that, since it was "not in accord with the spirit of [Prussia's] government" to suppress hostile reports, the only alternative was to fight it out in the open.[85]

79. "Deutschland," *AZ*, 9 July, 7, 22 Oct. 1814.

80. "Deutschland," *AZ*, 12 Nov. 1814.

81. "Deutschland," *AZ*, 29 Nov., 1 Dec. 1814; "*Wien," *AZ*, 7 Dec. 1814.

82. "*Wien," *AZ*, 19 Dec. 1814; "Preussen," *AZ*, 22–23 Dec. 1814.

83. Czygan, *Zur Geschichte des Tagesliteratur*, vol. 2, pt. 2, pp. 39–64, 74–83.

84. John Robert Seeley, *Life and Times of Stein* (Cambridge, 1878), 3 : 297.

85. Hardenberg to the General Government of Saxony, 21 Dec. 1814, in Czygan, *Zur Geschichte des Tagesliteratur*, vol. 2, pt. 2, p. 105; also Hardenberg to Privy Councilor Friedrich von Raumer, 21 Nov. 1814, ibid., p. 81.

The evolution of the *AZ*'s coverage was of course immediately noted by those on the other side of the issue, including the Austrian police, who took it for granted that "the important articles on the congress in Cotta's *Allgemeine Zeitung* are drafted in Prince Hardenberg's chancellery."[86] This state of affairs, as it turned out, caused more concern in Munich than Vienna. None of the delegates to the congress ever complained about the *AZ*'s coverage of their activities. Nonetheless, Montgelas felt that any compromise of Saxony's sovereignty was detrimental to Bavaria's interest—which likewise focused on the preservation of sovereignty—and that the level of *raisonnements* being displayed in the *AZ* and other Bavarian papers was too high. In January he wrote to his district governors reminding them about requirements respecting the use of official sources, and affirming (in complete disregard of their contradictory contents) that all the press edicts promulgated since 1799 were still in effect.[87] Most of the material Cotta brought back with him from Vienna, including one report by Hardenberg himself, was suppressed,[88] and it is reasonable to assume that a few vehemently anti-Prussian reports, similar to the article on Stein discussed earlier, stemmed from Montgelas's ministry.[89]

Despite Montgelas's efforts, however, Hardenberg had good cause to be satisfied with Cotta. The *AZ* was the only Bavarian paper, and one of very few anywhere in the south, that did not adopt an anti-Prussian line during the congress.[90] In matters of substance Stegmann's treatment of the Saxony question was not decisively different from that of the *Rheinische Merkur*, which appeared under Prussian auspices in Coblenz. Like the *Merkur*, the *AZ* found some justice on both sides of the issue, while leading readers to sympathize for the most part with Prussia. But neither Görres nor Stegmann considered Prussia's claims compelling enough to justify talk of war, and in the end neither expressed any regret when Frederick William's government was forced to give way.

In matters of rhetoric and style, though, the distance separating the *AZ* from ideologically assertive journals like the *Merkur* was unmistakable.[91] The dispute over Saxony had pitted the claims of Germany's recent past, a past defined by successful resistance to Napoleon, against an

86. Fournier, *Geheimpolizei*, p. 374.

87. Montgelas, Circular Memorandum, 7 Jan. 1815, M Inn 25097/I.

88. Bitterauf, "Zensur der politischen Zeitungen," pp. 324–25.

89. For instance the reports labeled "*Leipzig," 30 Dec. 1814, 16 Jan., 5 Feb. 1815.

90. Hardenberg to Raumer, 21 Nov. 1814, and the General Government of Saxony to Hardenberg, 11 Dec. 1814, 8 Jan. 1815, in Czygan, *Zur Geschichte des Tagesliteratur*, vol. 2, pt. 2, pp. 81, 105, 128–29.

91. Precisely for this reason, however, the degree of official influence exerted over periodicals like the *Merkur* is easily forgotten. See the careful study by Esther-Beate Körber, *Görres und die Revolution: Wandlungen ihres Begriffs und ihrer Wertung in seinem politischen Weltbild, 1793 bis 1819* (Husum, 1986), pp. 66–71.

older cosmopolitanism to which the *AZ* remained loyal. Even at the height of the Saxony crisis Stegmann rarely devoted as much as half of any issue to the congress, which had to compete for space with reports from all over the continent. Some of these reports might bear on Germany's predicament (some, like those from Switzerland, were obviously selected with this end in mind), but such considerations could never be more than incidental to the *AZ's* larger mission, which continued to embrace Europe as a whole.

The *AZ*, in short, was simply incapable of devoting itself to German affairs with the same decisiveness and clarity that came so naturally to a new generation of political periodicals. Within the limits imposed by its origins, the *AZ's* coverage was neither passive nor naïve. Cotta and Stegmann were not blind to the cynicism of Prussia and the other powers. There is scarcely any mention of "legitimacy" as a significant theme of the proceedings, and Cotta was personally appalled by the capriciousness with which Saxony was finally carved up.[92] Just the same, the congress accomplished much that Cotta applauded, including the establishment of a Federation in which the press could hope to play its part and through which its rights might be acknowledged and protected. In Prussia, moreover, Cotta had found a likely partner for future efforts to take advantage of these new circumstances—a state whose interests seemed to favor a strong and stable federal union and whose leadership was known to be friendly to reform. Like Cotta's other political attachments, however, this one was unsentimental. The idea, frequently voiced in the northern press, that Prussia had somehow become "the state that had proven itself in every respect the most German" seemed to him nonsensical. "The definition of the concept and meaning of German-ness," he replied, "ought to be made the subject of an academic competition. It is true, however, that in southern Germany, where words in general are less blinding, we are more or less clear about this—thus the coolness with which the *people* greeted the anniversary of Leipzig. We want to wait and see what really comes of Germany's liberation."[93]

It is thus no easy thing to determine Cotta's political direction at the moment of his departure from Vienna. On the one hand, he was on his way home to refight old battles; on the other, he had formed important new attachments in northern Germany. Whatever may have been on his mind during his return journey, however, there can be no doubt that he left Vienna with his realism and his idiosyncratic Swabian patriotism fully intact.

92. Cotta to Goethe, 11 Jan. 1815, in Kuhn, *Goethe und Cotta* 1 : 266; Cotta to Charlotte von Schiller, 7 Feb. 1815, paraphrased in Vollmer, *Briefwechsel*, p. 565.

93. "*Wien," *AZ*, 12 Dec. 1814. Cotta neglects to mention that celebrations of the anniversary of Leipzig were illegal in Bavaria and Württemberg; like other journalists, he was not immune to the temptation to attribute his own feelings to the public at large.

SIX

Reconstruction: The Federation

Who now can take the announcement of a new journal into his hands without a smile or a sigh? Not even the most good-natured reader, if he is a German. To him the endless discussion of the nation's business is not the natural, steady breathing of a free and healthy soul, but the groaning of one whose breast is constricted—an unwelcome sign of his indisposition, which only betrays his oppression.

Ludwig Börne, Advertisement for
the *Wage*, May 26, 1818

Among the results of the Vienna Congress, Cotta believed the most important was the stimulus it provided to constitutional reform in the German states.[1] It also altered the surrounding political landscape in a way that promised him new political and commercial opportunities. Prussia's failure to gain possession of a compact bloc of land in the east left it with a collection of prosperous but disconnected territories, whose inhabitants were collectively more German, more urban, and more politically sophisticated than those of the Polish and Slavic lands that had been lost. Most had grown up in small, autonomous principalities of the Holy Roman Empire. Some had been French citizens for a generation. These newly subject populations totaled about two million souls, and their political reeducation as Prussian citizens could not be put off. At the same time, the location of these new provinces, bracketing Germany's northern frontier as the Habsburg lands had once bracketed the Empire, suggested that Prussia would have a special stake in the vitality of the new Federation. The Federal Diet, finally, seemed certain to be a major focus of public interest and, if the promise incorporated into the Federal Act could be credited, a friend of the press.

This complex of possibilities defined Cotta's political agenda. To his eye they presented a unified prospect, and they gave rise to a variety of projects whose common aim was to promote constitutional government and, secondarily, to affirm the existence of a natural alliance between parliaments and the press. In retrospect, however, Cotta's efforts fall easily into two groups: those that drew him deeper into the politics of his native Württemberg, and those that led him outward, into the un-

1. Cotta to Charlotte von Schiller, 7 Feb. 1815, paraphrased in Vollmer, *Briefwechsel*, p. 565.

tested waters of northern Germany and the Federation. Such a distinction risks oversimplification, but the gain in clarity is considerable. We will therefore defer consideration of Cotta's role in Württemberg's constitutional debate to the next chapter and focus for now on his attempts to operate in the new federal arena the congress created.

THE *DEUTSCHE BEOBACHTER*

With only one exception, Cotta was personally responsible for the creation of all the political journals he published. The exception was the *Deutsche Beobachter*, which Cotta took over at Hardenberg's request while still in Vienna. Like most exceptions, this one casts a useful light on the rule from which it deviates.

The *Deutsche Beobachter* first appeared in Hamburg in April 1813 under the auspices of the Russian general Friedrich von Tettenborn, who had captured the city from the French a few weeks before. Tettenborn ordered his secretary, Bendix Daevel, to mobilize the local press. Daevel, whose most recent job before meeting Tettenborn had been as a bookshop assistant in Vienna, immediately took charge of the Hamburg *Correspondent*, but was soon persuaded by the owners to accept a cash settlement in return for leaving them in peace. Daevel used the money to establish the *Beobachter* as an organ of the liberation movement, in opposition to the *Correspondent*, which remained sympathetic to France. Daevel was a striver, and he hated the French; but he had none of the equipment one normally looked for in a newspaper editor. He knew no language other than German and nothing whatever of business. The editor of the *Correspondent*, having narrowly escaped unemployment at Daevel's hands, branded his new rival a mercenary and intrigued against him with the city fathers. Daevel had neither the experience nor the money to ride out the storm, and when the war ended the *Beobachter* shut down, apparently for good.[2]

Despite the brevity of its life, Deavel's newspaper had made itself felt. Joseph Görres numbered it among the best journals in the north,[3] and Friedrich Gentz considered it an important opponent of Austria's relatively accommodating policy toward France.[4] Apart from Daevel, the *Beobachter*'s guiding spirit had been Varnhagen von Ense, one of Tettenborn's staff officers, whose acerbic commentary on articles from the

2. On the early history of the *Beobachter*, see Heinz Bergmann, "Der *Deutsche Beobachter* und die deutsche Verfassungsbewegung am Beginn der Befreiungskriege bis zum Ausgang des Wiener Kongresses," Ph.D. diss., Cologne, 1940, pp. 7–33; and Hertel, "Cotta," cols. 403–13.

3. "Die teutschen Zeitungen," *Rheinischer Merkur*, 1 July 1814.

4. Gentz to Pilat, 15 Jan. 1814, in *Briefe von Friedrich von Gentz an Pilat: Ein Beitrag zur Geschichte Deutschlands im XIX. Jahrhundert* (Leipzig, 1868), 1 : 100.

Moniteur was a regular feature. Varnhagen had introduced Daevel to Tettenborn, and subsequently urged the creation of the *Beobachter*. Its disappearance had been doubly disappointing, since, apart from the fact that Varnhagen was still owed money for his contributions, Daevel's paper had collapsed just a few weeks before Varnhagen was chosen to serve as Hardenberg's chief press aid in Vienna. Varnhagen therefore urged Daevel to seek help from Cotta, whom Varnhagen had met while studying at Tübingen some years before.[5]

Daevel's appeal was straightforward. He still possessed the legal right to publish a newspaper in Hamburg. He also possessed a political past characterized by patriotism and resistance to tyranny, of which he was certain Cotta approved.[6] Cotta needed no instruction as to the value of this first credential.[7] As to the second, although he had no reason to question Daevel's intentions, he felt the need for more details.[8] He also consulted with Varnhagen, who felt that he could express himself more freely in Daevel's *Beobachter* than almost anywhere else and endorsed the plan warmly.[9] When Daevel replied to Cotta's inquiries by returning a prospectus, Varnhagen rewrote it at Cotta's request.[10] He declined to accept a formal editorial role,[11] but his enthusiasm was otherwise unqualified. It was quickly seconded by his chief, Hardenberg, who recalled the *Beobachter*'s "invaluable service" during the war and declared that "on Prussia's side the establishment of such a worthy organ of public opinion in northern Germany can only be looked upon favorably."[12] Cotta thus felt himself on firm ground and replied to Daevel's prospectus with a check to cover immediate expenses and a letter of encouragement.[13] He did not send a contract; despite the richness of the Hamburg market, this was primarily a political arrangement.

Announcements of the *Beobachter*'s revival appeared late in December of 1814 in the *Allgemeine Zeitung* and, perhaps as a challenge, in the Hamburg *Correspondent*.[14] Daevel is identified as the paper's "editor and

5. Bergmann, "Der *Deutsche Beobachter*," pp. 31–32.

6. Bendix Daevel to Cotta, 17 Sept. 1814, CA.

7. Cotta knew the value of a Hamburg newspaper privilege. Some years before, when Cotta was considering moving the *Neueste Weltkunde* to that city, he was warned off by his friend Archenholz, who feared that Cotta could expect only about four thousand subscribers there—a level the *Allgemeine Zeitung* had still not achieved when Daevel made his offer (Archenholz to Cotta, 7 Nov. 1798, CA).

8. Cotta to Daevel, 15, 20 Oct. 1814, in Bergmann, "Der *Deutsche Beobachter*," p. 43.

9. Karl August Varnhagen von Ense to Friedrich Perthes, 22 June 1814, in Carl Misch, *Varnhagen von Ense in Beruf und Politik* (Gotha, 1925), p. 168.

10. Daevel to Cotta, 11 Nov. 1814, in Bergmann, "Der *Deutsche Beobachter*," p. 43.

11. Varnhagen von Ense to Cotta, 18 Jan. 1815, CA.

12. Hardenberg to Cotta, 13 Jan. 1815, in Heyck, *Allgemeine Zeitung*, pp. 301–2.

13. Bergmann, "Der *Deutsche Beobachter*," p. 44.

14. *AZ*, 30 Dec. 1814 (Beilage), and Hamburg *Correspondent*, 21 Dec. 1814; cf. Daevel to Cotta, 16 Dec. 1814, CA.

owner," with Cotta as his "closest associate," who had committed "all the resources at his disposal" to the *Beobachter* and whose reputation would guarantee its quality. What this meant to Daevel can be inferred from his correspondence. He expected Cotta to provide him with an additional editor, "only the best" correspondents from among the contributors to the *AZ*, and exclusive reports on the congress, which would give his paper an immediate edge on the competition.[15] Given this level of support, Daevel looked forward to good times: fine clothes, a house, a rich wife, and respect.[16] The *Beobachter* would become something like the *London Times*, with other, equally distinguished enterprises to follow.[17]

Before any of this could happen, however, it would be necessary to overcome the local animosity that had brought Daevel's newspaper to ruin once before. Cotta's good name was supposed to be part of the solution to this problem. The rest would take the form of direct Prussian protection, which Cotta was expected to deliver.

Through all the vicissitudes of German politics since the accession of Frederick the Great, one of the constants of public life had been the hostility of the Hamburg press toward Prussia. This dislike was rooted in commerce (the city's preference for England as a trading partner) and geography (the natural distrust of a small, peaceful, urban polity for a large, well-armed, agrarian neighbor) and had remained unaffected by Prussia's role in freeing the city from the French. Prussia had made a few efforts to rebut its critics at the end of the last century, among French-speaking readers via the Clèves *Courier du Bas-Rhin* and among Germans via Schirach's *Politisches Journal*—to which Frederick William II's foreign minister, Hertzberg, had been an important contributor.[18] As the public debate inspired by the Vienna Congress heated up, there was reason to try again. For this purpose, the Berlin papers were of no use: they were so closely censored that they could not even report the ministry's point of view correctly (apart from official bulletins, political coverage consisted mainly of excerpts from the *Oesterreichische Beobachter*),[19] and they were not widely read outside Prussian territory.

Daevel's paper promised to be a more useful instrument, less personal in tone than Joseph Görres's *Merkur*, more open to direct advocacy than the *AZ*, and located in the most important press center in Germany. Daevel's constitutional-federalist sympathies were also well within the

15. Daevel to Cotta, 8 Nov., 9 Dec., 30 Dec. 1814, CA.

16. Daevel to Varnhagen von Ense, 8 Nov., 13 Dec. 1814, in Bergmann, "Der *Deutsche Beobachter*," pp. 45–46.

17. Daevel to Varnhagen von Ense, 8, 18 Nov. 1814, ibid., p. 43.

18. My thanks to Jeremy Popkin for alerting me to this aspect of Prussian policy.

19. Hardenberg to Johann Heinrich Renfer [head of newspaper censorship in Berlin], 14 Nov. 1814, in Czygan, *Zur Geschichte des Tagesliteratur*, vol. 2, pt. 2, pp. 88–90.

range tolerated by the city's censorship. But even so, it seemed expedient, given his treatment by the local establishment the previous year, to ask for a formal statement of Prussian support. Cotta relayed the request to Hardenberg, who instructed Prussia's representative in Hamburg to inform the Senate that "any favors that might be bestowed on this enterprise . . . will be viewed with special satisfaction by the Prussian government."[20] Exactly how this announcement was received is not recorded. But about a month later the *Beobachter* was placed under a temporary ban, and Daevel was thrown in jail.[21]

Here was a sensation: a licensed editor imprisoned for publishing an article approved by the censors. The sense of scandal was heightened by the improbability of the alleged offense: an insult to the king of Spain contained in a report from Paris.[22] In the end Daevel served only a few days of his sentence, and the *Beobachter* reappeared immediately after his release. Daevel insisted the incident had been concocted by the competition, and Cotta supported his demand that some sort of retribution be exacted, preferably a reciprocal ban on the *Correspondent* in Prussia.[23] Cotta also approached another of Hardenberg's aides, Friedrich Staegemann, about giving Daevel a Prussian title in order to obtain "a little more respect from the philistines of Hamburg."[24] Neither of these proposals was taken up, however, since either one would have created the impression that Prussia was assuming responsibility for a paper over which it had no effective authority.

To Varnhagen, the *Beobachter*'s easy suppression illustrated a larger problem: the difficulty of carrying on a press campaign by means of foreign periodicals. The reasons for doing so had always been to combine credibility with political distance and, secondarily, to allow governments to address outsiders in terms they might hesitate to use with their own people. During the first weeks of its existence Varnhagen had made the *Beobachter* his chief weapon in contesting the Saxony question, using moralistic, patriotic arguments that could not possibly have appeared in Prussia or, for that matter, in the *AZ* (where Prussia's case was presented as a matter of geo-political expediency rather than of moral entitlement). It had doubtless been these articles, and not some supposed insensitivity to the dignity of Spain, that had landed Daevel in jail. The alternative, as Varnhagen saw it, was to establish a ministerial newspaper in Berlin and give it the freedom necessary to defend the government.

20. Hardenberg to Cotta, 13 Jan. 1815, in Heyck, *Allgemeine Zeitung*, pp. 301–2.
21. Senate Decree of 17 Feb. 1815, in Bergmann, "Der *Deutsche Beobachter*," pp. 64–65.
22. Ibid., p. 65.
23. Ibid.
24. Cotta to Friedrich Staegemann, 3 March 1815, in Franz Rühl, ed., *Briefe und Aktenstücke zur Geschichte Preussens unter Friedrich Wilhelm III, vorzugsweise aus dem Nachlass von F. A. von Stägemann* (Leipzig, 1899–1902), 1:326.

Most of those around the Prussian throne, however, were not prepared to go this route, or to concede its underlying premise, self-evident to Varnhagen, that "public opinion, once awakened, cannot simply be put back to sleep."[25] Ever since the war Prussia's professed sympathy for "the spirit of liberty and intellectual freedom"[26] had concealed significant confusion about the goals of press policy, particularly as to how far the ministry's need to influence foreign opinion (which seemed essential) should be allowed to stimulate domestic controversy (which seemed pernicious). Until this question could be resolved Prussia's conduct toward the press would remain opportunistic, sometimes zealous, sometimes diffident, but in any event unpredictable.[27]

To Cotta, Daevel's arrest illuminated roughly the same problem, but in a different light. Cotta had anticipated that Daevel's enemies might seek an opportunity to embarrass his Prussian sponsors[28] but probably not that the Prussian response would be so half-hearted. In any event, he had already taken steps to adjust the *Beobachter*'s political course, by hiring Friedrich Hartmann as the co-editor Daevel had requested.[29] Cotta had known Hartmann for some time, as a member of a socially prominent Württemberg family and, more to the point, as assistant editor of the *Oesterreichische Beobachter*, to which he had brought a dispassionate professionalism that its editor-in-chief, Joseph Pilat, lacked. Cotta hoped Hartmann might do the same for Daevel. But this hope only betrayed Cotta's ignorance of the real state of affairs in Hamburg, on which Hartmann reported in the bleakest terms shortly after his arrival.

Hamburg, in Hartmann's view, had become a terrible place to do business. Stamp duties and printing costs were inflated, postal service had been left a shambles by the French, and the competition was as fierce as everyone said. The local audience, moreover, had long ago come to put a premium on speedy reporting, an area in which the *Beobachter* was at a hopeless disadvantage, since its tiny staff could not even keep up with the flow of foreign newspapers into the city. If the paper was to survive, it would have to appear every day (as against the present schedule of every other day), in a more flexible format, and have a larger staff and continuous access to a print shop. Furthermore—and just as

25. Varnhagen von Ense to Hardenberg, 9 March 1815, in Czygan, *Zur Geschichte des Tagesliteratur*, vol. 2, pt. 2, pp. 196–98.

26. Hardenberg to Cotta, 13 Jan. 1815, in Heyck, *Allgemeine Zeitung*, pp. 301–2.

27. See Varnhagen von Ense to Cotta, 6 Nov. 1815, in Fehling and Schiller, *Briefe an Cotta* 2:4–5; and, more generally, Friedrich Kapp, "Die preussische Pressgesetzgebung unter Friedrich Wilhelm III (1815–1840)," *Archiv für Geschichte des deutschen Buchhandels* 6 (1881): 185–90.

28. Daevel to Cotta, 30 Dec. 1814, CA.

29. Friedrich Hartmann to Cotta, 13 Jan. 1815, CA.

urgently—Daevel would have to go. His reputation as an interloper rivaled that of "Bonaparte's brothers." Further problems were therefore guaranteed.[30]

Hartmann did not presume to say whether Cotta should put up the money necessary to save the *Beobachter*; but he was certain he did not have the strength to lead the effort, and resigned.[31] Cotta accepted his departure reluctantly and then demanded that Daevel present an accounting of the paper's finances. Daevel was surprised and annoyed. He replied that Hartmann was lazy and incompetent, with no credentials as a businessman.[32] Varnhagen also intervened on Daevel's behalf.[33] Cotta therefore decided to carry on, though only after fixing more formal financial arrangements between Daevel and himself, a step Daevel vigorously resisted.[34]

Thereafter, Daevel made a point of providing Cotta with regular, invariably optimistic reports on the *Beobachter*'s condition, which did in fact improve as time passed and as the personal friction between Daevel and his fellow journalists in Hamburg eased. Even so, circulation never rose above four hundred copies,[35] and Daevel never overcame his resentment at Cotta's insistent curiosity about a venture for which Daevel, who still held the *Beobachter*'s privilege, had assumed all the legal risks.[36] Cotta, on his side, continued to receive disconcerting reports on his editor's performance.[37] In the fall of 1816, moreover, the accession of Cotta's old ally William to the throne of Württemberg presented Cotta with his first opportunity in almost fifteen years to publish a political journal in his hometown. The commonality of interest that had first led him to take up the Prussian cause had in any case grown cloudy—Prussia had frowned on Württemberg's constitutional initiative,[38] and with the suppression of the *Rheinische Merkur* at the start of 1816 its record with respect to the press had become decidedly mixed. Some warm feeling remained, but it was no longer enough to offset the expenses Cotta had

30. Hartmann to Cotta, 7 May 1815, in Hertel, "Cotta," cols. 407–9.

31. Hartmann to Cotta, 24 June 1815, ibid., col. 409.

32. Daevel to Cotta, 18 Nov. 1815, CA; on Hartmann, see Daevel to Cotta, 5 July, 7 July, 15 July, 9 Dec. 1815, CA.

33. Varnhagen von Ense to Cotta, 30 June, 19 Sept. 1815, CA.

34. Contract dated 13 Dec. 1815, in Hertel, "Cotta," cols. 479–82; cf. Daevel to Cotta, 18, 21 Oct., 4 Nov. 1815, CA.

35. "Uebersicht wie das Institut von Quartal zu Quartal Fortgeschritten ist," [1817,] among Daevel's letters, CA.

36. Daevel to Cotta, 11, 15 Nov. 1815, 31 Jan., 7 Dec. 1816, CA.

37. Friedrich Perthes to Cotta, 2 May, 10 Dec. 1816, and Heinrich Struve [Hamburg correspondent for the *AZ*] to Cotta, 24 June 1816, CA.

38. Wilhelm Adolf Schmidt, *Geschichte der deutschen Verfassungsfrage während der Befreiungskrieg und des Wiener Kongresses 1812 bis 1815*, ed. Alfred Stern (Stuttgart, 1890), p. 427.

been incurring on Prussia's behalf. Cotta therefore decided that, with the start of the new year, Daevel would have to fend for himself.[39]

During the years that Cotta owned the *Deutsche Beobachter*, it came in for its share of political criticism. The paper was (more or less by design) a constant aggravation to Austria and attracted repeated complaints from the emperor's representative in Hamburg, Baron von Hoefer.[40] These complaints were echoed by Adam Müller, Austria's consul general in Leipzig, who urged his government to do something to counteract the paper's influence in the north.[41] On one occasion Friedrich Gentz wrote about "the damned *Deutsche Beobachter*" so off-handedly as to suggest that he had grown accustomed to describing it in those terms.[42] But despite the preponderance of pro-Austrian sympathy among Hamburg's leaders, none of these missiles found its mark. Bavaria, which also had reason to dislike the *Beobachter*'s Prussophilism, did not have to rely on the local authorities to retaliate: it might simply have held the *AZ* hostage for Daevel's good behavior. Like Austria, however, Bavaria was mainly concerned with the state of domestic opinion, and Montgelas was satisfied to prevent the *AZ* from reprinting the *Beobachter*'s attacks on his government.[43]

In the absence of compelling political pressure, it seems fair to assume that Cotta's reason for giving up the *Beobachter* was the obvious one: he was losing a lot of money and gaining little in the way of influence or prestige. Daevel's share of the blame, in this view, is large: he had begun, as one observer recalled, as "a poor *colporteur* who approached Cotta in order to have something warm to eat,"[44] and he consistently lied to his benefactor about money, until Cotta's patience simply ran out. Although this explanation is not entirely wrong, it is incomplete, in that it fails to account for the *Beobachter*'s rapid recovery of vigor and solvency after Cotta abandoned it. Daevel soon found another partner, Johann Benzenberg, an able journalist from the Rhineland, and under their joint

39. Hertel's assertion ("Cotta," col. 411) that Cotta lost twenty-two thousand marks on the *Beobachter*, based on a comment by Johann Benzenberg, is misleading, not least in that it could be taken to refer to Cologne marks, in which case the sum involved would indeed be, as Hertel says, "monstrous." Cotta's transactions with Daevel were conducted in Kurantenmark, which were valued at roughly 1.4 to the Rhenish gulden. Cotta invested a total of twenty-two thousand Kurantenmark in the *Beobachter*, which was partly offset by the paper's gross income (about seven thousand Kurantenmark). In all Cotta lost something over ten thousand gulden in two years. Cf. Daevel's summary of "Gelduebermachungen des Herrn Doctor Cotta in Stuttgart," and Cotta's ledgers, among Daevel's letters, CA.

40. Baasch, *Geschichte des hamburgischen Zeitungswesens*, p. 17n.

41. Müller to Metternich, 24 Nov., 22 Dec. 1815, 17 March 1816, in Baxa, *Adam Müller* 1:1118–20, 1128–30, 1148–50.

42. Gentz to Pilat, 2 Sept. 1816, in Gentz, *Briefe an Pilat* 1:237.

43. Police Director Wirschinger to Montgelas, 13 May 1815, M Inn 25097/I.

44. J. F. Benzenberg, cited in Hertel, "Cotta," col. 411.

leadership the *Beobachter* enjoyed a modest prosperity for another two years.[45] Cotta's role in the paper's history thus merits a little more thought.

The *Beobachter* had begun its new life under Cotta's proprietorship by adopting the same combative style it had employed during the war. This was in accord with Varnhagen's immediate interest vis-à-vis Saxony, but not with Daevel's long-term ambition, which was to produce something "distinguished and durable," in contrast to papers like Görres's volatile *Merkur*, which Daevel believed had no future.[46] Although Daevel resented Hartmann's criticism, Hartmann's recommendations were actually in accord with these aspirations. And although Cotta never formally adopted Hartmann's program—the *Beobachter* never became a daily, for instance—the general course of the paper's development over the next two years was close to what Hartmann had envisioned. By the end of its first year, the *Beobachter*'s tone had moderated a good deal. Its promotion of constitutionalism under Prussian leadership had become less vehement—an accurate reflection of the drift of Prussian policy—and increasingly diluted by reports from Vienna, Prague, Warsaw, and Paris that bore no relation to this dominant theme. Its coverage of the French and British parliaments expanded, as did its use of excerpts from other newspapers. The *Beobachter*, in other words, had begun to resemble, not the *London Times*, as Daevel hoped, but the *AZ*.

This was Daevel's own doing, not Cotta's. The *Beobachter*'s evolution reflected his craving for the kind of respectability a connection with Cotta promised. Cotta did not dictate political terms to his editor; but then, he did not need to. Daevel was already intent on making the *Beobachter* into the kind of paper he had every reason to suppose Cotta wanted. Cotta ignored Daevel's desire to link the *Beobachter* directly to the *AZ*, since the gain in day-to-day control that such an arrangement offered was more than offset by the added risk it would have posed to the more established paper. But Cotta was prepared to underwrite his editor's obsessive urge to outdo the *Correspondent*, the paper that, more than any other, embodied the matter-of-fact, quotidian journalism of the Old Regime. To compete on the *Correspondent*'s terms required just the kind of steady investment Cotta provided, most of which went to pay for correspondents, assistant editors, and subscriptions to foreign periodicals. Over two years this investment came to a good deal of money—enough to snuff out the ideological fire the *Beobachter* had displayed during the war, but not enough to save it from the competition

45. Julius Heyderhoff, *Johann Friedrich Benzenberg: Der erste rheinische Liberale* (Düsseldorf, 1909), pp. 69–100.
46. Daevel to Cotta, 15 Nov. 1814, CA.

Daevel had imprudently chosen for himself. By the time Cotta gave up the *Beobachter*, it was locked into a struggle it had no hope of winning.

Ideally, Cotta's collaboration with Daevel might have produced a newspaper that combined the professionalism and polish of the *AZ* with an overriding dedication to German affairs. This, surely, was Cotta's hope. Instead the *Beobachter* became an unsatisfying hybrid with no natural audience, caught between the nonpartisan tradition of the Cotta press and the political engagement of the War of Liberation. The paper's fortunes improved under Benzenberg only because he adopted an approach sharply at odds with Cotta's. Benzenberg sought his constituency not among the readers of the *Correspondent* but among those left hanging by the suppression of the *Rheinische Merkur* and by the financial failure of other, smaller papers established during the war. He dispensed with paid correspondents and relied instead on personal letters from his friends. He cut the publication schedule in half and eliminated most excerpts from other periodicals and parliamentary proceedings; instead each issue was dominated by a lead essay by one of the editors. The *Beobachter* thus became a journal of opinion with an identifiable point of view, openly supportive of constitutionalism and social reform. It was well suited to a region where traditional loyalties had suffered serious erosion since the Revolution and where habits of political criticism were particularly pronounced. By the middle of 1817 circulation had doubled, and the *Beobachter*, for the first time in its history, was running in the black.[47]

The *Deutsche Beobachter* remained a losing proposition during the years Cotta owned it because it could find no niche for itself in a crowded, relatively sophisticated market—a market distinctly unlike the virtual vacuum in which Cotta had founded the *AZ*. Finding that niche, moreover, required political assumptions that Cotta did not share. For Benzenberg and most other journalists of the rising generation, the press was a means of fostering political independence and equipping the public to influence government policy. This was Cotta's view too, but his approach to the problem of political education was more indirect, and more intellectually complicated, than that of his younger contemporaries.

The reformation of public life, as Cotta understood it, was not simply a matter of freeing people from the tutelage of the state; it required the active cooperation of those in power, who continued to possess a monopoly on political initiative and information. For the press to succeed in its educational mission, it needed more than the incidental tolerance of friendly regimes: it needed to become part of the nation's constitu-

47. Heyderhoff, *Benzenberg*, pp. 72–74.

tion. Cotta always assumed the press could serve the public best if it could also be made useful to government. The collapse of the *Beobachter* as an organ of officially inspired reformism, and its rebirth as an organ of political opposition, provided Cotta with his first indication of how difficult the reconciliation of these competing demands would prove to be, and describes a course that would recur repeatedly in the subsequent history of the Cotta press.

A VOICE FOR THE DIET

The most direct road to constitutional standing for the press lay through Frankfurt, seat of the new Federal Diet. Like Hamburg, Frankfurt was a historically important press center, whose journalistic establishment had suffered under the French, and was slowly recovering its nerve. That the local press would take a strong interest in the Diet seemed certain; its attitude was not. The city of Frankfurt was an independent member of the Federation; its traditions were progressive and particularist, and although its press was not as reflexively hostile to Prussia as that of Hamburg, it could not be relied on to sympathize with Prussia's interests. This, at any rate, was the impression drawn by Prussia's representative in Frankfurt, Friedrich von Otterstedt, who urged his government to support the establishment of an independent journal devoted to federal politics. He found Hardenberg "uncommonly receptive" to this idea, as well as to Otterstedt's nomination of Cotta as its executor.[48]

Politically, Otterstedt's views were close to those of Varnhagen, with whom he was on friendly terms. A self-described republican, Otterstedt had spent most of the Napoleonic period in Paris, returning to Germany during the War of Liberation to assume a post in the Middle Rhine district of Stein's *Zentralverwaltung*. His performance earned him the confidence of Württemberg's Crown Prince William, and it was probably through William that he met Cotta. Otterstedt was also in touch with another junior member of the Prussian diplomatic service, Konrad Oelsner, whom he proposed to Cotta as a possible editor for the new journal. Oelsner, who was now a member of the Prussian legation in Paris, was known to Cotta as a correspondent for both the *Allgemeine Zeitung* and the *Deutsche Beobachter*. So was Franz Wilhelm Jung, an old friend of Ernst Posselt's whom Otterstedt recruited as Oelsner's associate.

Planning for the new journal proceeded by way of correspondence among these four men through the summer and fall of 1815.[49] The most immediate obstacle—obtaining a newspaper privilege in Frankfurt—was to be overcome through the purchase of a patent held by the *Frank-*

48. Friedrich von Otterstedt to Cotta, 8 Oct. 1815, CA.
49. Hertel, "Cotta," cols. 413–16.

furter Journal.[50] It was also agreed that a Frankfurt publisher, Franz Wilmans, would be brought in to diffuse whatever local resentment the new venture might arouse. In October, Jung received an explicit blessing from Hardenberg's hand—slightly more temperate than the one bestowed on the *Deutsche Beobachter* ten months before, but reassuring nonetheless.[51] The gravest obstacle of all, however, was the failure of the Diet actually to meet: its convening, originally anticipated for the fall, had been put off while the second Peace of Paris was being negotiated, and no new date had been set. But given that the Diet would come along in good time, there was no reason not to go forward, and at the end of December a contract was signed by Cotta, Jung, Oelsner, and Wilmans, calling for the creation of a newspaper called the *Deutsche Bundeszeitung.*[52]

As compared to the *Deutsche Beobachter*, the *Bundeszeitung* must have seemed a very safe bet. Among the recognized uses of newspapers, one of the least controversial was the reporting of parliamentary proceedings. In contrast to the inner processes of government, the acts of representative bodies had lately been conceded to have a public dimension. This had not always been the case. For most of their history, European diets, however constituted, had conducted their business in private, and any violation of the members' confidentiality was treated as a crime (it was only in the 1770s, for example, that the British House of Commons ceased trying to prosecute individuals who published accounts of its debates). More recently, however, attitudes had begun to change, owing to the persistence of journalists and, in England and America, to a growing interest in parliamentary reform. The United States Constitution required both houses of Congress to publish their proceedings, and since 1789 the various French assemblies had all conducted their business under the public eye. The *Moniteur*, despite its debasement under Napoleon, remained the most authoritative governmental organ in Europe, though it was now more than matched in bulk by Hansard's (unofficial) *Parliamentary Debates*, which first appeared in 1803. In Germany, where parliamentary life was inconsequential, every newspaper with pretensions to political significance paid close attention to these foreign assemblies, recounting the most telling exchanges word for word. Such material did not necessarily make lively reading, even when it originated close to home; Cotta's earlier attempt at parliamentary journalism, covering the Württemberg Reform Diet of 1797–98, had clearly fallen victim to tedium. But neither Cotta nor his associates supposed anything like that could happen again.

50. Franz Wilhelm Jung to Cotta, 23 July 1815, CA.
51. Hardenberg to Jung, 21 October 1815, in Hertel, "Cotta," col. 415.
52. Ibid., cols. 484–87.

The first advertisement for the *Bundeszeitung*, based on a draft prospectus by Otterstedt, appeared in the *Deutsche Beobachter* in January 1816.[53] As compared to the *Beobachter*'s own announcement a year before, it was a model of deference and restraint. Varnhagen and Daevel had spoken in emphatic terms about the "tumult of arms" that had created the *Beobachter*, and about the power of public opinion to influence events.[54] The *Bundeszeitung*'s editors, conversely, directed their readers' attention toward the highest ideals of political life: Truth, Justice, Dignity, and Love. This orientation was in accord with the solemnity of the occasion as they understood it; for the convening of a German diet signified "a fundamental change in the condition of the Fatherland," a change that the *Bundeszeitung* would report and clarify. It would do this by paying close attention to the Diet's deliberations (the paper would appear daily except Sunday, in large quarto format) and by placing them in a European context—a somewhat surprising announcement, given the paper's explicitly "national" focus. The *Bundeszeitung*, in short, would be a characteristic Cotta production, with comprehensive reporting from all over and an evenhanded approach to controversy, all done in fine style.

Equally characteristic was the subtle activism at the heart of a putatively nonpartisan program. What effect, after all, could the *Bundeszeitung* be expected to have on the Diet itself? This question the editors were reluctant to address directly; yet it must have been of paramount interest to all the principals, including Hardenberg. Political publicity is always reciprocal: any institution whose activities are systematically reported to the public will be changed in the process. By routinely informing the nation of the Diet's proceedings, the *Bundeszeitung* would at least create a presumption that the public was entitled to be so informed—a relationship of tacit public responsibility the Diet had no mandate to assume. The *Bundeszeitung* did not presume, in the manner of the wartime press, to address the Diet in the name of the people. It did not need to. Simply to address the people in the name of the Diet would create a new kind of political leverage, of which no account had been taken in the Federal Act. The future of the *Bundeszeitung* was thus dependent on who, if anyone, would find this sort of leverage useful.

As far as the Prussian government was concerned, a publication like the *Bundeszeitung* was not essential. Hardenberg personally would have preferred to pursue Varnhagen's proposal for a ministerial newspaper in Berlin. In November, when it became clear that the Diet would not be

53. "Nachricht aus Frankfurt," *Deutscher Beobachter*, 5 Jan. 1816; the draft prospectus was included with Otterstedt to Hardenberg, 30 Dec. 1815, in Czygan, *Zur Geschichte des Tagesliteratur*, vol. 2, pt. 2, pp. 405–6.

54. *AZ*, 30 Dec. 1814 (Beilage).

meeting for some time, he offered the editorship of such a paper to Oelsner, in lieu of the position with Cotta.[55] Further progress along this line proved impossible, however, owing to what Varnhagen called "the uncertain development of our internal conditions."[56] But in any event, Prussia could not remain indifferent to the creation of a federal newspaper, which seemed certain to appear whether Hardenberg's government participated or not.

The *Bundeszeitung*'s other likely patron was, of course, Austria. With Napoleon safely dispatched to his second, indubitably final exile, Metternich knew that Germany's constitutional debate would revive in earnest. Even before returning home from Paris he instructed his subordinates to prepare themselves for "polemic and war," for which purpose he was prepared to accord the *Oesterreichische Beobachter* far more freedom than it had enjoyed in the past.[57] He also sent Friedrich Schlegel and Adam Müller to Frankfurt and Leipzig, respectively, with instructions to see to it that Austria's point of view was not slighted. Müller was empowered to publish a journal of his own, as a kind of clandestine organ of Metternich's chancellery.[58] Schlegel had similar plans, which involved gaining control of the widely read (though not widely respected) *Frankfurter Oberpostamtszeitung*.[59] By the start of the new year, however, whatever independent effort Austria might have made in Frankfurt had been shelved, and the *Bundeszeitung* was left without competition.

The achievement of this compromise was Cotta's distinctive contribution to the whole venture. As Oelsner reported to Hardenberg, "Dr. Cotta strode into the middle of the affair and, with his own particular dexterity, though not without difficulty, leveled the field."[60] The dexterity required should not be underestimated. At this point all knowledgeable observers of the press—Gentz, Varnhagen, Müller, even Daevel—were agreed that, to be effective, political journals could not appear to be the private instruments of any government. In the case of the *Bundeszeitung*, however, it was not enough to manipulate appearances; to succeed as an organ of the Diet, the paper really would have to be independent of the member states. The problem was complicated by

55. Hardenberg to Oelsner, 18 Nov. 1815, in Peter Kuranda, "Konrad Engelbert Oelsner," *Schlesische Lebensbilder* (Breslau, 1931), 4:224.

56. Varnhagen von Ense to Cotta, 6 Nov. 1815, in Fehling and Schiller, *Briefe an Cotta* 2:4–5.

57. Gentz to Pilat, 26 Nov. 1815, in Gentz, *Briefe an Pilat* 1:214–16.

58. Baxa, *Adam Müller* 1:1086–94.

59. Schlegel, "Erster Bericht über die Zeitungen," 17 Jan. 1816, in Jakob Bleyer, *Friedrich Schlegel am Bundestage in Frankfurt* (Munich and Leipzig, 1913), p. 135.

60. Oelsner to Hardenberg, 30 Dec. 1815, in Czygan, *Zur Geschichte des Tagesliteratur*, vol. 2, pt. 2, pp. 404–5; cf. Oelsner to Friedrich Staegemann, 30 Dec. 1815, in [Wilhelm] Dorow, ed., *Briefe des Königl. Preus. Legationsraths Karl E. Oelsner an den wirkl. Geheimen Rath Fr. Aug. von Staegemann aus den Jahren 1815–1827* (Leipzig, 1843), pp. 1–2.

mutual suspicions on the part of the paper's likely sponsors: although there was some hope on the Prussian side that a federal newspaper would improve Austro-Prussian relations,[61] both governments were wary of the other's efforts to control public perceptions. The agreement that Cotta achieved, at the cost of a trip to Frankfurt, was really a kind of partition. Schlegel agreed to take over the *Bundeszeitung*'s coverage of Austrian and Italian affairs, while Oelsner agreed to step down as editor-in-chief in favor of Jung, who was thought to be less beholden to Hardenberg. Cotta also engaged Schlegel to report on the Diet for the *AZ*,[62] insuring that Austria's point of view would receive an authoritative airing regardless of the *Bundeszeitung*'s fortunes. Finally, as if to seal the deal, Cotta persuaded Austria's senior representative in Frankfurt, Baron von Wessenberg, to support the group's effort to buy a newspaper privilege, by writing to the Frankfurt Senate on their behalf.[63]

If the Federal Diet had convened early in 1816, as expected, the *Bundeszeitung* would certainly have appeared. But the Diet did not convene, and with the coming of spring Cotta's arrangements began to unravel—in part because all interested parties had not been included. The announcement of the *Bundeszeitung* (which appeared three times in as many weeks in the *Oesterreichische Beobachter*)[64] brought immediate resistance from the representatives of the middle states, who were opposed to any institution that might enhance the corporate reality of the Federation. Their hostility in turn alarmed the local authorities and the local publisher Wilmans, who did not wish to be a party to anything unpleasant. When the city magistrates finally declined to award the paper an "unrestricted" privilege,[65] Wilmans withdrew. Schlegel followed suit.[66] By the time the Diet finally convened in October, the *Bundeszeitung* had been dead for some time.

Jung, Oelsner, and Otterstedt were unanimous in blaming Schlegel for the paper's demise, which, they insisted, he had brought about by intriguing with the municipal authorities and with Wilmans, whose departure he was supposed to have encouraged.[67] Schlegel had always been less favorably disposed to the project than the others; he suspected that, despite Cotta's efforts at mediation, the publication would still favor

61. Oelsner to Varnhagen von Ense, 7 Aug. 1815, in Ludmilla Assing, ed., *Briefwechsel zwischen Varnhagen von Ense und Oelsner, nebst Briefen von Rahel* (Stuttgart, 1865), 1:3.

62. Schlegel to Cotta, 18 Nov. 1815, 19 May 1816, in Fehling and Schiller, *Briefe an Cotta* 2:356–61.

63. Schlegel, "Erster Bericht," p. 135; Otterstedt to Hardenberg, 30 Dec. 1815, in Czygan, *Zur Geschichte des Tagesliteratur*, vol. 2, pt. 2, pp. 404–5.

64. 9, 18, 31 January 1816.

65. Jung to Cotta, 1 March 1816, CA.

66. Schlegel to Cotta, 19 May 1816, in Fehling and Schiller, *Briefe an Cotta* 2:358–59.

67. Hertel, "Cotta," cols. 419–21.

Prussia decisively.[68] In Schlegel's view, however, the *Bundeszeitung*'s chief defect was not its potential biases, but rather its ambiguous status. His first reaction to Cotta's proposal had been concern that the *Bundeszeitung* would be viewed as authoritative by the public without being truly official—a status that could not exist in the absence of a federal press law. The risk that the paper might yield some marginal advantage to Prussia paled alongside the possibility that it might achieve significant public standing as the voice of the Diet, without being firmly under its control. Yet in this case, such control required a legal and administrative apparatus that the Diet did not possess.[69]

What finally killed the *Bundeszeitung* was a decision on the Prussian side that Schlegel was right. Cotta was perfectly prepared to continue in the absence of Austrian support, provided Hardenberg held fast; but he did not. Although Prussia's ambassador, Wilhelm von Humboldt, was personally sympathetic to the project,[70] as a matter of policy he considered the venture neither fish nor fowl. He could envision a federal newspaper in one of two modes: either an official journal, published in the Diet's name and dependent upon it, or an independent journal of opinion, published outside the city of Frankfurt and treating the Federation as a whole. The latter sort of journal, Humboldt believed, might prove interesting, but it would have to make its own way. If Cotta intended to publish something like the *Moniteur* (as he clearly did), with a mixture of official and unofficial elements and regular consultation with members of the Diet, then Humboldt could not help him. There was nothing else to say.[71]

To the extent that it has been noticed at all, the failure of the *Bundeszeitung* to materialize has been attributed to Austro-Prussian rivalry.[72] More accurately, however, its collapse can be seen as an early sign of the "peaceful dualism" that would dominate German politics through the middle of the century. Although both Austria and Prussia were attracted to the idea of a federal newspaper, neither side, on reflection, was sure it knew the answer to the question, posed earlier, of how such a venture would affect the Diet itself. Schlegel and Humboldt were both prepared to tolerate a federal newspaper of less imposing character.[73] Indeed, such a journal did appear, edited by Oelsner, published by Wilmans

68. Schlegel, "Erster Bericht," p. 136.

69. Ibid.

70. Humboldt to Cotta, 13 June, 15 Sept. 1816, CA.

71. Humboldt to Cotta, 29 Aug. 1816, in Fehling and Schiller, *Briefe an Cotta* 2:359n.

72. Hertel ("Cotta," cols. 413–22) argues that the venture was suppressed because of its "national-liberal Prussian standpoint" (col. 413).

73. Cf. Schlegel to Cotta, 19 May 1816, in Fehling and Schiller, *Briefe an Cotta* 2:358–59; Humboldt to Cotta, 29 Aug. 1816, ibid., p. 359n; and Humboldt to Cotta, 13 June 1816, CA.

(who evidently felt safer in obscurity), and entitled the *Bundeslade*; it was left entirely unmolested and survived for two issues, long enough to declare the Federal Diet a nonentity[74] and so confirm Cotta's judgment that no newspaper devoted to the Diet could survive without the cooperation of the Diet's members.

The reporting of parliamentary proceedings would remain a staple of German political journalism throughout the nineteenth century. At the same time, publicity would become an important means by which the legislative assemblies created after 1815 would try to secure their own share in government. This mutual support depended on the perception of a shared constituency, whose interests could be symbolized by press and parliament alike. The very absence of such a shared constituency is what finally makes the *Bundeszeitung* such an implausible project—more so, in retrospect, than a superficially riskier venture like the *Deutsche Beobachter*. The Diet was neither a modern legislature nor a traditional assembly of estates. As such, it was scarcely a proper vehicle for demonstrating the constitutional role of the press. The public the *Bundeszeitung* would have been addressing was not represented even in principle by the delegates at Frankfurt, who acted only as agents for Germany's reigning princes. Cotta and his colleagues were resolved to work against this tendency—to aid the evolution of the "German Federal Diet" into a "federation of Germans," a true national assembly.[75] But after being instructed by Humboldt, representing the government that first sought their services, to "look with care to [their] own resources," it is hardly surprising that those resources were found wanting.

MEDIATION AND OPPOSITION

A few months after the failure of the *Bundeszeitung*, Cotta was drawn into a third attempt to create a newspaper that would advance the cause of reform, which was still thought to be better cared for in Berlin than elsewhere. The instigator was again Friedrich von Otterstedt, who urged Cotta to adapt the *Deutsche Beobachter* to the *Bundeszeitung*'s mission by replacing Daevel with a Frankfurt journalist named Stiefel.[76] A contract was drawn and signed,[77] but it became a dead letter when Cotta decided

74. "Der Deutsche Bund," *Bundeslade*, no. 1 (Jan. 1816): 22–24. In part because of the events discussed here, publicity attending the Diet in its early years (the only years when it attracted much public interest) was extremely haphazard. It is surveyed in Rolf Darmstadt, *Der Deutsche Bund in der zeitgenössischen Publizistik* (Frankfurt am Main, 1971).

75. Prospectus, with Otterstedt to Hardenberg, 30 Dec. 1815, in Czygan, *Zur Geschichte des Tagesliteratur*, vol. 2, pt. 2, pp. 404–5.

76. Otterstedt to Cotta, 9 Jan. 1817, CA. Little is known about Stiefel, except that he was a regular contributor to the *Frankfurter Journal*, a respected independent newspaper that had been suppressed by Napoleon in 1810, and reemerged, badly damaged, in 1813.

77. Contract dated 13 Jan. 1817, in Hertel, "Cotta," cols. 482–84.

to give up the *Beobachter* altogether. Otterstedt and Stiefel then proposed an entirely new venture: a "ministerial" newspaper published in the Hessian town of Offenbach and tentatively titled the *Unparteiische Beobachter*.[78]

To a greater extent than either of its predecessors, Otterstedt's new proposal exposed the shaky ground on which journalists in Germany had recently been operating. The *Unparteiische Beobachter*'s stated purpose was to check the spread of "oppositional" journalism in Germany by creating a vehicle to publicize the "excellent and noble actions of governments"[79]—"governments" in this instance being the one in Berlin and, more problematically, the one in Frankfurt. The delicacy demanded for such a seemingly unimpeachable project can be judged by the impossibility of publishing the journal in either of those cities. Offenbach was chosen as the journal's home because it was close enough to Frankfurt to allow decent coverage of the Federal Diet and far enough from Berlin to preserve some hope of gaining Hardenberg's favor, which the chancellor would never have bestowed on any journal he couldn't repudiate if necessary. In themselves, compromises of this kind were by no means unusual; they had been a part of Cotta's political life from the start. As applied to a paper styled "ministerial," however, such cunning seemed out of place, and it raised questions in Cotta's mind that the *Beobachter*'s promoters found difficult to answer.

Ministerial newspapers usually involved a compromise of a different sort, between the public's disbelief in "official" journalism on the one hand and the state's desire to manage public opinion on the other. As compared to official publications, ministerial journals could be relatively opinionated, even inflammatory, and hence interesting. The views expressed were understood to enjoy the general approval, though not the absolute sanction, of the sponsoring government. Such "ministerial" relationships were intrinsically ambiguous, but not secret. Adam Müller's repeated proposals for a clandestine ministerial press were in fact a little peculiar, since, apart from being difficult to realize in practice, they would have deprived the ministerial press of its presumptive if somewhat vague political authority. The archetype of the genre was the *Oesterreichische Beobachter*: the unofficial voice of official Austrian opinion, published in a capital city with the political support and financial assistance of the government.

Otterstedt's *Unparteiische Beobachter* diverged from the norm mainly in its assumption that a newspaper could speak for "governments" in general. This point of view had something to recommend it, for not only did it reflect the new governmental solidarity symbolized by the Federa-

78. Stiefel to Cotta, 11 Feb. 1817, and Otterstedt to Cotta, 12 Feb. 1817, CA.
79. Otterstedt to Cotta, 12 Feb. 1817, CA.

tion, but it also responded to the impatience displayed by the "oppositional" press at the ever-slower pace of reform. It was also obvious, however, that individual regimes would deal with such a journal solely in
light of their own interests. How would the editors manage in those cases
where, in praising one policy, they found themselves condemning another? To an experienced practitioner of "unparteilich" journalism, no
question was more vexed than this one. Cotta therefore decided, for the
first (and only) time in his career, that he could do nothing without seeing a sample issue.

This Stiefel refused to produce. But he was prepared to accept any
"ground rules" Cotta might wish to impose, with the sole proviso that
"the editor's hands not be tied," so that, "with due deference, he might
speak of the bad as often as the good."[80] This point of view was elaborated a few weeks later in a letter from one of Stiefel's associates on the
Frankfurter Journal, Ludwig Börne, whom Otterstedt and Stiefel wished
to bring into the project as coeditor. A ministerial newspaper, Börne
argued, should "defend government against *unjust* opposition" and
show how "even the expedient and equitable claims of the people's representatives cannot be fulfilled *all at once*." At the same time, part of the
press's role was also to show that both "the maximum and the minimum
of submissiveness led to despotism." It was hardly a sign of political
health, after all, if people "only felt comfortable when the heat of loyalty
reached a fever pitch." A ministerial newspaper should therefore include a broad spectrum of responsible opinion, including views that
were "antiministerial." Only the commonplace should be excluded.[81]

A few days later Stiefel and Börne arrived in Stuttgart to pursue these
matters in more detail, bringing with them two drafts of a prospectus
for their journal, now called the *Vermittler*.[82] In both drafts, the emphasis
was on the constructive management of political diversity, which was
envisioned alternatively as a "court of public opinion" or a "marketplace
of ideas." At the common center of both versions was the assertion that
popular pressure, rising out of the struggle against France, had made
"new forms of legislation and . . . a freer relationship between the people
and government" inevitable. The choices that remained had to do with
means rather than ends, and in the definition of political means the
press would play a decisive part, not simply as an observer, "an echo of
the last syllable of history," but as an independent arbiter, a defender of
"clarity and reason, to which alone allegiance is due . . . against the usur-
pation of fraud and egoism." The two men's aim, in short, was "to rec-·

80. Stiefel to Cotta, 19 Feb. 1817, CA.
81. Börne to Cotta, 2 March 1817, in Börne, *Sämtliche Schriften* 5:622–25.
82. Both versions are in ibid., pp. 626–31.

oncile the opposing or competing claims and expectations of the various classes of civil society, and to bring the uncertain relations of the people and the government into sharper focus; and to unify and blend their various requirements, in light of the high and universal needs of the state, so as to produce satisfaction on all sides."

Cotta's first reaction was to submit the drafts to his friend and political ally Karl von Wangenheim for advice.[83] Wangenheim, at that time a key member of the government in Stuttgart, was already collaborating with Cotta on a ministerial journal of more conventional stripe, directed against the conservative opposition in the Württemberg Diet.[84] He found the new project admirable: similar in spirit to the one he and Cotta had already undertaken, and perhaps serviceable in the same cause.[85] Cotta, however, remained unconvinced. He had already decided to withhold his name from the venture—though whether out of prudence or from a desire to make better use of the *Vermittler* within Württemberg is impossible to say.[86] On being presented with a draft contract by Stiefel, he amended it in detail. Although most of the changes were technical, Cotta also insisted on approving all the *Vermittler*'s correspondents himself. And he inserted language obliging the editors "to comply with the goals of this journal, as set forth in the prospectus; in no way to impugn the honor and worth of governments or their agents; and above all to avoid whatever might give occasion for substantive reproach . . . [so that] the legal burden should under no circumstances fall to the publisher."[87] It is hard to imagine that this last addition, tantamount to a loyalty oath, did not cause some hard feelings. In the end the contract remained unsigned.

It would be wrong to attribute the collapse of the *Vermittler* to any disagreement between publisher and editors on matters of principle. All three men shared a common vision of the press as being situated between the public and the state. The balance that Börne and Stiefel struck was just a little different from Cotta's: despite their claim of "ministerial" affiliation, they portrayed the *Vermittler* as accountable mainly to the public. They may also have construed their mediating role more broadly than Cotta did; there is little mention elsewhere in the Cotta press about reconciling the various classes of civil society. Certainly Börne and Stiefel were less impressed than Cotta by the moral and intellectual authority of "history," and more willing to assign the press a positive role in political decision making. But these nuances aside, there is no reason to sup-

83. Cotta to Wangenheim, 8 March 1817, CA.
84. *Für und Wider*; see chapter 7 below.
85. Wangenheim to Cotta, [9 or 10 March 1817,] CA.
86. Wangenheim to Cotta, [8 or 9 March 1817,] CA.
87. Draft contract dated 8 March 1817, in Hertel, "Cotta," cols. 487–90.

pose the ideas expressed in their draft advertisements exceeded Cotta's own political aspirations. They probably did mark their limit, however, beyond which Cotta would not go—hence his willingness to accept his editors' principles only if they swore to stick to them absolutely.

There is also a personal element to be considered, at least as far as Cotta's relations with Ludwig Börne are concerned. Börne was one of the ablest political writers ever to cross Cotta's path, and Cotta immediately recognized his talent. Both men were eager to make up for the disappointment of their first meeting.[88] Yet despite years of trying, they never managed to become as useful to each other as they might have. Cotta sensed at once that Börne was a man destined to test the boundaries of contemporary political discourse, but his efforts to describe those boundaries to his less experienced friend were never entirely successful.[89] Beginning in 1819 Cotta paid Börne an annual retainer against future contributions to various Cotta periodicals;[90] but apart from some translations and theater criticism for the literary *Morgenblatt für gebildete Stände*, most of what Börne sent in proved unpublishable. By the end of 1825 his debt to Cotta was approaching five thousand gulden, and his feelings of resentment and frustration had grown accordingly.[91] The two men's differences were matters of style and character rather than of underlying values. Cotta was convinced that "you can say anything if you employ the necessary circumspection";[92] but Börne rarely achieved the appropriate degree of tact. What Cotta needed above all was "sober but intelligent" writing;[93] Börne, however, could write well only if he wrote "from the heart."[94] Even in 1817 Cotta was already finding this a luxury he could not afford. The price would only go up.

The underlying cause of the *Vermittler*'s failure, however, was not personal differences among the men involved, but the uncertain political context in which it was conceived. Cotta told Wangenheim that he had finally decided that "neither time nor place nor circumstances nor trade" was right,[95] and it may well have been just such a generalized feeling of unease that tipped the balance. It is hard to believe Cotta could have put

88. Börne to Cotta, 9 March 1817, in Börne, *Sämtliche Schriften* 5:631–32; Cotta to Börne, 9 March 1817, Stadt- und Universitätsbibliothek, Frankfurt am Main, Börne-Nachlass, letter 109.

89. Cotta to Börne, 25 Nov. 1819, 7 April, 18 Oct. 1820, 26 Jan. 1824, Börne-Nachlass, letters 112, 113, 114, and 119.

90. Cotta to Börne, 2 Nov. 1819, ibid., letter 110.

91. Cotta to Börne, 3 Jan. 1826, ibid., letter 121; cf. the editors' introduction to Börne's *Sämtliche Schriften* 4:lxxv–xciv.

92. Cotta to Börne, 2 Nov. 1819, Börne-Nachlass, letter 110.

93. Cotta to Börne, 18 Oct. 1820, ibid., letter 114.

94. Börne to Cotta, 25 Oct. 1820, in Börne, *Sämtliche Schriften* 5:659–60.

95. Cotta to Wangenheim, 9 March 1817, CA.

much faith in Otterstedt's assurances that the project had the "strong support" of the middle states in the Diet, in addition to Prussia.[96] Neither Hardenberg nor anyone else had offered any guarantee so strong that it could not be withdrawn at the first sign of controversy. Nor was it certain that even sympathetic governments were ready for the paper Cotta was actually being asked to publish. Otterstedt had promised them an "impartial observer." Börne and Stiefel, however, were preparing a "mediator," one that might even lend itself to the opposition on occasion.

The *Vermittler* was the last periodical Cotta considered publishing at the behest of Hardenberg's ministry. It is easy to forget that a newspaper whose professed values so nearly approached those of the "oppositional" press it was intended to check should have been inspired by Prussia's desire to improve its standing with the German public. From the Prussian point of view, the *Vermittler*'s failure was a temporary setback: in 1819 the government finally established a ministerial newspaper of the conventional sort, the *Allgemeine Preussische Staatszeitung*, published in Berlin under the direction of Friedrich Staegemann.[97] But the *Staatszeitung*, which was closely modeled on its counterpart in Vienna, did not represent an alliance between the government and the press of the kind envisioned by Varnhagen, who had argued, in common with most progressive opinion of the time, that the state should concede freedom of the press in order to use it itself.[98] It seemed a simple enough idea. But Cotta's experience revealed it to be fraught with difficulty, because those in power did not trust their subjects, because journalists and their audience both suffered from inflated expectations about how quickly conditions could change, and, most fundamentally, because the constitutional position of the press at the national level remained hostage to the rivalry of the German states.

As a stage in the evolution of the Cotta press, the step from "observer" to "mediator" represented by the *Vermittler* would seem natural, akin to the transition from the naïve objectivity of eighteenth-century newspapers to the analytic impartiality of the *Allgemeine Zeitung*. Indeed, as a description of the press's constitutional role as Cotta saw it, "mediation" was entirely apt. But as Börne and Stiefel inadvertently demonstrated, the distinction between the mediating and the opposing voice was in practice a fine one, requiring a firm political frame of reference if it was to be maintained. This was not available in Frankfurt, and it could not

96. Otterstedt to Cotta, 12, 23 Feb. 1817, and Cotta to Wangenheim, 9 March 1817, CA.

97. Groth, *Die Zeitung* 2:99–100.

98. Varnhagen von Ense to Hardenberg, 9 March 1815, in Czygan, *Zur Geschichte des Tagesliteratur*, vol. 2, pt. 2, pp. 196–98; see also the pamphlet by M.K.F.W. Grävell, *Drei Briefe über Preßfreiheit und Volksgeist* (Berlin, 1815).

simply be imported from Berlin. In Stuttgart, however, it appeared to be ready to hand. The natural step would therefore be taken, but closer to home.

On January 18, 1817, four months after the collapse of the *Bundeszeitung* and a few days after he had decided to give up on the *Deutsche Beobachter*, Cotta was made a Prussian privy councillor by Frederick William III.[99] This title was the first of several such honors he would receive, and it must have seemed a little ironic even then that it should have come from a government for whom Cotta's efforts had borne such meager fruit. The irony would only grow more apparent. Hardenberg's goodwill, sincere at the start, proved to be a wasting asset. As Prussia moved toward rapprochement with Austria he did not hesitate to deliver exactly the same kind of veiled but trivial threats that Cotta was long accustomed to receiving from Vienna.[100] With Hardenberg's passing Frederick William's government lapsed once more into that resentful diffidence toward the press that had characterized its early years. As far as Cotta was concerned, Prussia again became the least of the Great Powers; it would be ten years before he would renew his involvement in its affairs.

Nevertheless, the title that he received in 1817 was not supposed to be a consolation prize; it was supposed to symbolize a common purpose and set the seal on a relationship with a future. And some have argued that the common purpose, at any rate, was real. The result has been what might be called the "kleindeutsch" interpretation of Cotta's career, a no doubt inevitable response to Heinrich von Treitschke's early identification of Cotta as a tool of Metternich's chancellery.[101] The gist of this interpretation is that, with the defeat of revolutionary France, Cotta found Prussia the natural focus for his progressive ideals, both because of the personal qualities of its leadership and because it represented the only possible basis for a national solution to Germany's constitutional dilemma.[102] This view draws its support from Cotta's conduct during and after the Congress of Vienna as well as at the end of the 1820s, when he would help pave the way for the founding of the customs union a few years later. Erwin Hölzle has also cited several passages from Cotta's letters to Varnhagen von Ense in which Cotta refers to Prussia as, among other flattering things, Germany's "guardian angel."[103]

99. "Patent des Geheimer Hofrath für den Doctor Cotta zu Tübingen," CA.

100. Hardenberg to Cotta, 31 Jan. 1821, CA.

101. Treitschke, *History of Germany*, 2:17.

102. This view is forcefully presented in Hölzle, "Cotta," pp. 576–96. The same approach is evident in Bergmann, "Der *Deutsche Beobachter*" (Cologne, 1940); and Hertel, "Cotta."

103. Cotta to Varnhagen von Ense, 23 Dec. 1830, in Hölzle, "Cotta," p. 594. A slightly longer excerpt, in Erwin Hölzle, "Der Deutsche Zollverein: Nationalpolitisches aus seiner

On balance, however, the image of Cotta as a kind of premature National Liberal is too anachronistic to be persuasive. Hölzle himself admits that, in view of Cotta's attachment to Prussia and its presumptive "national mission," his continued involvement in the politics of the middle states seems "blind" and "incomprehensible."[104] But this is so only if we assume that the members of the reform generation were destined to travel an ascending path, from Empire to nation-state, from traditional liberties to modern liberalism. If one judges Cotta's career by how closely it approximates this theoretical norm, there are indeed moments when he appears to be decidedly at sea. But he never felt that way himself. His political loyalties were complex, but that does not make them blind or incomprehensible. On the contrary, his support of Prussia in federal matters coexisted quite peacefully with his deepening involvement in the politics of his homeland, to which we now turn.

Vorgeschichte," *Württembergische Jahrbücher für Statistik und Landeskunde* 33 (1932–33): 145, includes important reservations about Prussia's failure to enact a constitution.

The Varnhagen papers, including 125 letters from Cotta (Ludwig Stern, *Die Varnhagen von Ensesche Sammlung in der Königlichen Bibliothek zu Berlin* [Berlin, 1911]), were believed lost after 1945. They have since reemerged at the Jagiellonian University Library in Krakow (Deborah Hertz, "The Varnhagen Collection Is in Kraków," *American Archivist* 44 [1981]: 223–28). Access remains difficult.

104. Hölzle, "Cotta," pp. 588–89.

SEVEN

Reconstruction: Württemberg

The king has given his explanation. We have given ours. I can say Yes or No.
I say Yes.

Ludwig Uhland, Speech in the
Württemberg Chamber of Deputies, 1819

It is characteristic of police informers that they should try to make the people they spy on seem important. On that account one might simply dismiss the report of an Austrian agent named Hebenstreit, who identified Cotta as the "central point" of the Württemberg delegation to the Vienna Congress.[1] The key figure in that group was of course not Cotta but King Frederick, under whose stewardship Württemberg had at last acquired the centralized institutions of an absolutist state. Next to Frederick was his son William, who arrived in Vienna thrice blessed in the eyes of his people: as a hero of the War of Liberation, as fiancé to the czar's sister, and as living proof that the present regime would not last forever. Cotta had no official connection to the delegation and no sympathy for its purpose, which was to obstruct any measures that would limit the king's authority. As a defender of the estates against the crown, Cotta had been excluded from domestic politics for more than a decade, but he had remained William's friend and had become one of Frederick's most prominent subjects. Although the congress provided no formal occasion for Cotta to air his views on Württemberg's future, it did allow him to position himself to participate in the political debate that was sure to follow.[2]

In the fall of 1814 Württemberg was entering the tenth year of a constitutional hiatus, during which it had undergone far-reaching change. Under French protection Frederick's kingdom had more than doubled in size, by incorporating most of the ecclesiastical benefices,

---

1. Fournier, *Geheimpolizei*, p. 136.
2. Cotta to Friedrich Schelling, 26 Nov. 1814, in Fuhrmans and Lohrer, *Schelling und Cotta: Briefwechsel, 1803–1849* (Stuttgart, 1965), p. 94; Carl Bertuch to Friedrich Bertuch, 30 Nov. 1814, in Bertuch, *Tagebuch*, p. 248.

Free Cities, and imperial lordships that had comprised the Holy Roman Empire's Swabian Circle. The machinery of state had also been retooled to concentrate legal, financial, and administrative authority in the hands of the king. The result was a regime more efficient, less corrupt, and more autocratic than any Württemberg had known before.[3] These innovations were the work of one man, Frederick, who, unlike Bavaria's Max Joseph, had not been disposed to promise his people a constitution as the culmination of reform; on the contrary, Frederick had acted in studied disregard of a constitutional tradition based on centuries of precedent. With the eclipse of Napoleon's power in Germany, however, Frederick had lost the chief prop to his ambitions, even as his domestic opponents were preparing to reclaim their rights, if necessary by installing the crown prince on the throne of his father. It was in response to this threat, and in order to avoid submitting to a settlement dictated at Vienna, that Frederick proclaimed a constitution of his own. The ensuing crisis lasted five years and proved to be the most exhausting struggle of Cotta's political career. It was also the first and only time that he fully committed his resources as a publisher to support his own cause.

THE KING AND PARLIAMENT

The constitution that Frederick tried to impose in January 1815 was typical of its time. It called for a departmentally organized cabinet responsible to the king, centralized legal and fiscal bureaus, and a unicameral assembly with power to approve taxes, consult on legislation, and petition the crown. There was also a section detailing the civil rights of citizens, most of which were contingent on subsequent legislation. According to a supplementary electoral decree, males over the age of twenty-five were allowed to vote, provided their income from real property was at least two hundred gulden per year. It was under these terms that Cotta first stood for office, to represent the *Oberamt* of Böblingen.

In an election in which most seats were won unanimously, Cotta gained his by a narrow majority, over the opposition of a local notable who attacked Cotta as an "outsider."[4] Technically, this charge was true: Cotta owned some land in his district but had never lived there. More damaging, however, was the insinuation that Cotta's far-flung enterprises had made him insensitive to Württemberg's traditions. This was untrue. Like most of those excluded from power by the abrogation of the Old Law, Cotta had viewed the king's authority under the Rheinbund as de facto and illegitimate. He greeted Frederick's constitution cheerfully only because he thought it represented a healing concession.

3. Hölzle, *Württemberg im Zeitalter Napoleons,* pp. 52–129.
4. Albert Schäffle, *Cotta* (Berlin, 1895), p. 91.

Nonetheless, he continued to believe that, one way or another, "what has been taken from us must be restored to us."[5] When the new constitution was submitted to the Diet in March, Cotta was one of the first to speak against it.

The Diet's opening session was dominated by two men, Cotta and Count Georg von Waldeck, a joint appearance that reflected Frederick's knack for unifying opposition against himself. Waldeck spoke for the "mediatized" nobility, former subjects of the emperor who were now attending their first territorial Diet and at whose expense the growth of royal power under the Rheinbund had largely occurred: once incorporated into Frederick's kingdom, their estates had been treated more or less as crown lands. Even though Waldeck had never enjoyed the protection of the Old Law, he recognized that it embodied the principle of divided sovereignty, which would have to be preserved if the nobility was ever to reclaim the rights it had exercised under the Empire. Cotta, in contrast, spoke for the *Ehrbarkeit* of old Württemberg, a group that included both strict traditionalists, who were prepared to tolerate a high level of administrative chaos as long as their prerogatives were protected, and more progressive types, heirs to the Reform Diet of 1797 who hoped the Old Law could be revised to make the state's institutions more equitable.

To many in his audience Cotta also represented a much larger constituency: the readers of his newspaper. That the proceedings of Württemberg's Diet were of interest to outsiders was doubted by no one. Yet it is one thing for a legislator, unaccustomed to the public eye, to know in a general way that his words are a matter of record, and another for him to see them in print, a week or so later, in a national newspaper. Right from the start, Cotta kept the *Allgemeine Zeitung* fully apprised of the Diet's activities, to all appearances unaware of the conflict of interest this behavior implied. As long as his reports served to put pressure on the crown, his colleagues found them congenial enough; later on, however, when circumstances had changed, these same colleagues would prove a good deal less sympathetic.[6]

From the point of view of the government, the history of the next

5. Cotta to Charlotte von Schiller, 15 Feb. 1814, paraphrased in Vollmer, *Briefwechsel*, p. 565; cf. Ernst Ludwig Marschall von Bieberstein [first minister of Nassau] to Stein, 16 Jan. 1815, in Stein, *Briefe und amtliche Schriften* 5:243.

6. The proceedings of the Diet were published irregularly as *Verhandlungen in der Versammlung der Landstände des Königreichs Württemberg*, ed. Dr. Schott and Procurator Feuerlein (Heidelberg, 1815–19). The *AZ's* reports were selective but accurate, and must have been based on official minutes. Cotta is almost always identified in the editorial exemplar as the source of these reports; he clearly supervised the *AZ's* coverage of Württemberg closely, to the point where Stegmann began to feel his independence was compromised (Cotta to Stegmann, 2 March 1816, and Stegmann to Cotta, 10 May, 23 Dec. 1816, CA). On the opening session, cf. *Verhandlungen* 1:15–17, and the *AZ*, "Stuttgart," 22, 23 March 1815.

four years can be described as a series of attempts to divide the coalition represented by Cotta and Waldeck. From the Diet's perspective, conversely, each new offer from the crown meant a new temptation to accept concessions on matters of detail—taxation, judicial privileges, military exemptions, and so forth—in lieu of a more fundamental recognition of the assembly's collective rights.[7] It was toward this larger issue that Cotta and Waldeck addressed their opening remarks. Since the two men did not share the same past, they did not dwell on its glories. Instead they united in disputing the constituent power of the king.

The impasse was one with revolutionary overtones. As in France in 1789, an elected assembly was refusing to conduct the state's business by denying the force of the royal act under which it had been convened. Frederick, furthermore, faced a financial crisis that probably seemed as terrible as Louis XVI's. On March 1, Napoleon had returned from Elba; by the time the Diet got down to business, the tricolor was again flying from Notre Dame. War was certain, and Frederick was hopelessly in debt, for which the only remedy was new taxes, which required the Diet's consent. There was, of course, no physical danger, but failure to join the rest of Europe in putting down the usurper would have denied Württemberg any share in the fruits of victory and blackened Frederick's name among patriots everywhere.

The Diet temporized until March 28, when Cotta broke the deadlock by proposing that Württemberg respond to Napoleon's return by arming the whole population, for which the Diet would raise the necessary funds.[8] This was a shrewd idea, and less provocative than it sounds. A sense of intimate connection between military service and constitutional government was a cherished element of the Old Law, as well as being one of the most unsettling legacies of the War of Liberation. The willingness to bear arms had been a requirement of citizenship in Württemberg since 1515.[9] Reliance on popular militia had been an important expression of the estates' power as late as the 1790s,[10] and resistance to the

7. The discussion that follows does not pretend to do justice to all the issues and personalities involved in Württemberg's constitutional debate. Among more comprehensive treatments, see Friedrich Wintterlin, "Die württembergische Verfassung, 1815–1819," *Württembergische Jahrbücher für Statistik und Landeskunde* 104 (1912): 47–83; Albrecht List, *Der Kampf um's gute alte Recht (1815–1819), nach seiner ideen- und parteigeschichtlichen Seiten* (Tübingen, 1913); Hölzle, *Württemberg im Zeitalter Napoleons*, pp. 186–275; and Grube, *Stuttgarter Landtag*, pp. 489–508.

8. "Stuttgart," *AZ*, 5 April 1815; cf. Schäffle, *Cotta*, pp. 101–2.

9. "Second Territorial Ordinance," 10 April 1515, in Reyscher, *Württembergische Gesetze*, vol. 19, pt. 1, p. viii.

10. Cotta to Reinhard, 16 Nov. 1798, CA. The overturning of the military constitution of the Swabian *Reichskreis* was one of the chief objectives of Frederick's policy, once the reformers in the Diet had been silenced. See Heinz-Günther Borck, *Der schwäbische Reichskreis im Zeitalter der französischen Revolutionskriege (1792–1806)* (Stuttgart, 1970), pp. 184–250.

crown's demands for a standing army was a perennial theme of domestic politics. Although the Revolution removed all the antique charm from the ideal of the people in arms, it was only in 1809 that Frederick actually disarmed his subjects.[11] His decision became a symbol of bad faith between ruler and ruled, the more so in light of the performance of the Prussian *Landwehr* four years later, when it proved itself militarily useful and politically reliable.

The conditions that had given rise to Württemberg's old civil guard were dramatically different from those created by the War of Liberation. For Cotta to have explored these conditions in his speech would have not only alarmed the king but also exposed all the latent divisions in the Diet. For his purpose, however, what mattered most was the emotional connection between military service and political participation, and between the recent and the more distant past. It was, in Cotta's view, unrealistic to demand further sacrifices except under the security of the "existing" (that is, the old) constitution. That Frederick might fear unrest in the countryside, which was perceived to favor the Diet, was to Cotta unfortunate.[12] But that fear could be put aside if the king and the assembly joined hands. Frederick agreed, and a few weeks later Cotta and three others were appointed to a joint committee to work out a cooperative policy.

As it turned out, the financial embarrassment caused by Napoleon's return proved fleeting. Before Cotta's committee could even meet Frederick had secured an English subsidy for his army.[13] This arrangement posed no lasting threat to the domestic political balance, but Cotta still tried to block it, going so far as to present the English ambassador with an appreciation of Württemberg's constitutional predicament authored by Karl von Wangenheim, the curator of Tübingen University. Wangenheim, who had known Cotta for some time, had hopes of higher office, for which this as yet unpublished book would be an important credential, and he was understandably annoyed that his friend had made use of his work in a cause that seemed to him unpatriotic.[14] But Cotta was not chastened; even after the subsidy had been granted, he attacked it in print, arguing that the funds needed to outfit ten thousand regular troops might have equipped a *Landwehr* of eighty thousand and aided the country's "moral rearmament" as well.[15]

11. Wilhelm Wendland, *Versuche einer allgemeinen Volksbewaffnung in Süddeutschland während der Jahre 1791 bis 1794* (Berlin, 1901); Paul Sauer, *Revolution und Volksbewaffnung: Die württembergischen Bürgerwehren im 19. Jahrhundert, vor allem während der Revolution von 1848/49* (Ulm, 1976), pp. 25–35.

12. "Stuttgart," *AZ*, 29 April 1815.

13. Cotta to Stein, 7 May 1815, in Stein, *Briefe und amtliche Schriften* 5:309–10.

14. Wangenheim to Cotta, 6 April 1815, CA.

15. "*Vom Neckar," *AZ*, 15 May 1815. This article provoked an unavailing protest to the Bavarian censors (Count Ulrich von Mandelsloh [Minister-President of Württemberg]

Still, however warmly Cotta may have felt about the matter, he did not let it blind him to the larger task of bringing the Diet and the crown together. To some extent the simple existence of a joint committee legitimized the assembly's position, since it implied that, on constitutional questions, more than one point of view was possible.[16] Once the right to negotiate had been conceded, Cotta's personal objectives were modest. To Baron vom Stein, who had taken an interest in Württemberg's affairs at Vienna,[17] Cotta wrote reassuringly that substantial changes were possible, as long as they were achieved "contractually":

> Any demand that would overstep the proper relationship between the ruler and the estates is remote from our purposes. In this respect we will certainly follow the ideas and teachings of great statesmen like yourself and gladly renounce everything in the Old Law that might compromise that relationship. In particular we will willingly dispense with any structure that could be used for private purposes, such as, for instance, an independent treasury for the estates. We have, God knows, nothing but the welfare of the Fatherland before our eyes.[18]

But Cotta's colleagues on the committee were not so flexible. Their agenda, which Cotta presented to the Diet on April 30, embraced all sorts of "private purposes," including the right of "self-taxation" to support a *Ständekasse*; an apportionment scheme under which "all classes of subjects would be represented with relative equality"—that is, as classes, not as individuals; and the reestablishment of an executive committee to protect the estates' prerogatives.[19] The whole program was in the strictest sense reactionary, and some weeks later Cotta attacked its fiscal provisions as incompatible with the idea of a unified state. He also warned his colleagues that the government's representatives would not even discuss such a plan.[20] But he was not heeded, and at the end of July the Diet was suspended by the king.

Such chance of a settlement as still existed lay with Frederick's son William. Despite the crown prince's more accommodating nature, Frederick was confident that the heir to the throne would protect those rights he would one day wish to exercise himself.[21] William was also well regarded in the Diet, having helped convince Frederick to accept Cotta's

---

to Max Joseph, 19 May 1815, and Montgelas to Mandelsloh, 29 May 1815, M Inn 25097/ I). Although Montgelas assured Frederick that he was "always glad to suppress material offensive to Württemberg's government," he seems never to have done so.

16. "Stuttgart," *AZ*, 29 April, 3–4 May 1815.

17. Gerhard Ritter, *Stein: Eine politische Biographie* (Stuttgart and Berlin, 1931), 2:281; Seeley, *Stein* 3:364–66.

18. Cotta to Stein, 18 March 1815, in Stein, *Briefe und amtliche Schriften* 5:286–88. The *AZ* published this letter on March 24, as a comment on the opening session.

19. Wintterlin, "Württembergische Verfassung," pp. 57–60.

20. "*Stuttgart," *AZ*, 23 July 1815.

21. Cotta to Goethe, 8 April 1815, in Kuhn, *Goethe und Cotta* 1:274–75.

proposal for a joint committee. Now that negotiations had failed, he further persuaded his father to turn to Cotta's friend Wangenheim for assistance.

Among Württemberg's civil servants, Wangenheim is the only one who bears comparison with the Prussian reformers, with whom he shared a concern for reconciling centralizing and decentralizing political forces and for creating a state that could serve the needs of free individuals.[22] A Thuringian by birth, Wangenheim had been named president of Württemberg's *Oberfinanzkammer* in 1806, though he subsequently withdrew to the university because his sometimes visionary politics were out of step with the pragmatism of the new king. His analysis of Württemberg's constitutional dilemma, which Cotta had appropriated to lobby the English ambassador, appeared toward the end of the Diet's spring session[23] and established its author as an authoritative voice on domestic affairs. Wangenheim believed that, whatever the Old Law's merits, its historically conditioned character meant that it could not be summarily extended to the monarchy's new lands, as its more conservative proponents insisted. Instead Wangenheim urged the creation of "mediating structures," like those described in Montesquieu's *De l'esprit des lois*, which would soften the king's authority and foster a sense of political participation, but without reintroducing the baroque refinements of the past. The most important of these structures was an upper legislative house, which, it was hoped, would break the deadlock in the Diet by compensating the former imperial nobility for the loss of their autonomy and isolate the die-hard representatives of the old lands.

Even with the Diet in suspense, pressure to find a solution continued to mount. Throughout the spring there had been sporadic demonstrations against the government, which had led Wangenheim to conclude that "everything comes down to having public opinion united on your side."[24] Cotta repeated this statement on the floor of the Diet a few weeks later as a warning to both sides.[25] But neither Cotta nor Wangenheim was prepared for the widespread disturbances that followed the return of the delegates to their districts. The threat that the estates would raise the countryside against the crown was palpable, and it soon gave rise to what Cotta believed would be the decisive concession: a

22. Heinrich von Treitschke, "Karl August von Wangenheim," in *Historische und politische Aufsätze*, 7th ed. (Leipzig, 1911), 1 : 199–268. The only biography, which sticks very close to the documents, is Oswald Isey, "Untersuchungen zur Lebensgeschichte des Frhrn. Karl August von Wangenheim," Ph.D. diss., Freiburg, 1954.

23. Karl von Wangenheim, *Die Idee der Staatsverfassung in ihrer Anwendung auf Württembergs alte Landesverfassung und den Entwürf zu deren Erneurung* (Frankfurt am Main, 1815).

24. Wangenheim to Cotta, 31 May 1815, in Fehling and Schiller, *Briefe an Cotta* 2 : 67.

25. Speech of 23 June 1815, *Verhandlungen* 7 : 139.

pledge from the king to negotiate a new constitution and to accept the Old Law as the basis for discussions.[26]

In the fall the Diet reassembled to receive a new proposal, incorporating most of the recommendations in Wangenheim's book. This new version acknowledged the constituent role of the estates and provided for joint review of all legislation passed since 1805. Although there was no mention of a *Ständekasse* or an executive committee, the proposal did guarantee that, should the estates and the crown fail to agree, the lands of old Württemberg would continue to be ruled according to established custom.[27] It seemed a skillful compromise. Baron vom Stein is supposed to have "cried tears of joy" on hearing of it, while Friedrich Gentz wrote to Metternich that the new draft was "a masterpiece of our time."[28] Within the assembly, however, Wangenheim's program stood no chance. With the public on its side, the estates were not about to give up the fiscal and administrative bases of their power in return for theoretical concessions.

Nor were many additional sources of leverage available to the crown. In the past, Württemberg's constitutional problems had routinely been settled by appeals to outside powers, but the prospect of having to do so again made both Wangenheim and Cotta uneasy, even if the outside power was the Federation itself.[29] Wangenheim preferred to appeal in a general way to the Diet's German patriotism, which was a staple theme of its public rhetoric, and he asked Cotta to write to Stein seeking his endorsement of the king's program.[30] Hitherto Stein had shown a pronounced distaste for Frederick and all his works; during the War of Liberation he had actively sought Frederick's deposition,[31] and he had already asked the czar to intervene on the side of the estates.[32] But Stein also shared Cotta's fear that failure to achieve a quick settlement in Württemberg would blunt constitutional initiatives elsewhere. He therefore agreed to urge the Diet to accept the government's new formula.[33]

26. Cotta to Schelling, 31 Aug. 1815, in Fuhrmans and Lohrer, *Schelling und Cotta*, p. 101; Wangenheim to Cotta, 1 Sept. 1815, in Fehling and Schiller, *Briefe an Cotta* 2:68–69.

27. *Reskript* of 13 Nov. 1815, in *AZ*, 17–19 Nov. 1815.

28. Varnhagen von Ense to Cotta, 17 Nov. 1815, in Fehling and Schiller, *Briefe an Cotta* 2:5–6; Gentz to Metternich, 22 Dec. 1815, in Wittichen and Salzer, *Briefe*, vol. 3, pt. 1, p. 315.

29. Wangenheim to Cotta, 31 May, 5 Sept. 1815, in Fehling and Schiller, *Briefe an Cotta* 2:64–69.

30. Wangenheim to Cotta, 21 Nov. 1815, in Georg Heinrich Pertz, *Das Leben des Ministers Freiherrn vom Stein* (Berlin, 1854), 5:9–11.

31. Hölzle, *Württemberg im Zeitalter Napoleons*, pp. 143, 161–62.

32. Ibid., p. 192.

33. Stein to Cotta, 17 Nov. 1815, and Cotta to Stein, 21, 23, 28 Nov. 1815, in Stein, *Briefe und amtliche Schriften* 5:444–47.

He also forwarded a letter from Cotta to Joseph Görres, asking that the *Rheinische Merkur* aid the cause of compromise by moderating its criticism of Frederick.[34]

None of these efforts had the slightest effect. It must have come as a shock to Cotta, who regarded Stein as a great man, to hear the young Count Waldeck pretend to question the authenticity of one of Stein's letters.[35] Incidents of this kind would prove common enough in the next few years, however; all rhetoric to the contrary, by the end of 1815 the national cause, which at Vienna had seemed integral to the whole constitutional movement, had ceased to count for much in Württemberg.

Whether the Diet could be made to yield to more direct pressure was another matter. The larger purpose of Stein's visit, after all, had been to "use the power of public opinion to bring the estates, and particularly the nobility, to their senses."[36] Cotta had already been doing his share to keep Württemberg's affairs in the public eye. The *AZ*'s coverage had been scrupulously factual, with some leavening of historical commentary to elucidate the more obscure passages from the official minutes. Within this objective framework, however, the *AZ*'s reports managed to evoke a good deal of sympathy for the estates. Here, for instance, is a description of the assembly's last meeting, as its members awaited an answer to their final appeal to the king:

> No answer came. Finally one had to give up hope that one would ever come. This, then, was the end of an assembly, composed of the most diverse elements, which will forever mark an epoch in our history—because of its unanimity and steadfastness, because of the dignity of its behavior, because of its renunciation of all personal interests, and because of the deference it displayed toward its king—even though it was unable to achieve any of the goals for which it gathered.[37]

Passages of this kind left little doubt that the Diet had become the center of the state's political life.

With the presentation of Frederick's compromise four months later, however, Cotta's paper adopted a different tone:

> The king of Württemberg was one of the first German princes to grasp the spirit of the times and guarantee his people a truly living constitution, in tune with the current state of human culture. But he did not rest content with a mere promise. He actually produced the draft for such a charter in March of this year. And, however one may judge his effort, all unbiased men are agreed that it contained the organic germ of a good constitution. The notables from the old and new lands whom the king

34. Cotta to Görres, 23 Nov. 1815, in Pertz, *Stein* 5 : 13–14.
35. Cotta to Stein, 21 Nov. 1815, in Stein, *Briefe und amtliche Schriften* 5 : 445.
36. Wangenheim to Cotta, 21 Nov. 1815, in Pertz, *Stein* 5 : 9–11.
37. "Stuttgart," *AZ*, 15 Aug. 1815 (Beilage).

called together had no choice but to acknowledge the virtues of that draft. But they nevertheless believed that they had a right, on the basis of the old contractual constitution of the Duchy of Württemberg, to put forward modifications that they deemed necessary. The debate on these matters has attracted the attention of all of Germany. Now the king has offered a remarkable, indeed a decisive reply, . . . [in light of which] a successful outcome can no longer be in doubt.[38]

The Diet was bewildered. It had looked to public opinion to justify its resistance to the king, but it was not prepared to have the same weapon turned so forcefully against itself. On December 5, Waldeck attacked Wangenheim (whom he assumed, correctly, to be the author of this and similar pieces) for misleading the people and moved that all delegates and ministers refrain from airing their views in the press—a suggestion Karl Stegmann ridiculed while at the same time defending the credibility of his new (and ostensibly anonymous) contributor.[39] Opposing views were welcomed; but to men unused to publicity this seemed an empty offer, one which scarcely offset the fact that Cotta and his newspaper had changed sides.

In any event, the swift settlement that Wangenheim predicted did not materialize. The king's proposal shattered the unanimity of the Diet, but it did not break the will of the majority—a coalition of "Old Württembergers" and the mediatized nobility—to defend themselves. Cotta was now branded the government's man, excluded from the negotiating committee, and cast in the unaccustomed role of factional leader. Over the next eighteen months he and the *AZ* would themselves become issues in the debate, which proceeded in an atmosphere of mounting public tension.

THE KING'S FLUNKY

Cotta's remarkable about-face in the fall of 1815 raises questions about his earlier conduct. It has been argued, for instance, that Cotta was not a sincere defender of the Old Law but rather a German patriot whose call to arms in the spring was perverted by others into a negotiating ploy.[40] Cotta certainly viewed Württemberg's problems in a national context: he would have preferred to postpone action on Frederick's constitution until the conclusion of the Vienna Congress, and he was duly irritated when Prussia's Frederick William failed to produce the pathbreaking constitution he had promised his people in May.[41] But Cotta was also determined that Württemberg should settle its own fate, in or-

38. "Stuttgart," *AZ*, 17 Nov. 1815; cf. *AZ*, 1 Dec. 1815.
39. "Deutschland," *AZ*, 18 Dec. 1815; "*Stuttgart," *AZ*, 24 Dec. 1815.
40. Hölzle, *Württemberg im Zeitalter Napoleons*, pp. 196–97.
41. Hölzle, "Cotta," p. 586.

der to provide an alternative to whatever constitutional models might
come out of Vienna and Berlin.[42] His call to arms was heartfelt, but so
was his insistence that the Diet's rights be recognized: Cotta personally
drafted the resolution declaring that military cooperation would depend
on Frederick's acknowledgment of the Old Law.[43] There is thus no mistaking his intention. Cotta was ready to sit out the climactic struggle with
France rather than simply fall in line behind the king—a tactic whose
desperation makes his subsequent support of the crown all the more
striking.

Cotta's readiness to back the government once it had given in on the
question of the estates' constituent power does, however, suggest that in
the years since the Reform Diet he had come to value the Old Law less
for its content than as a symbol of the republican virtues he always
thought he saw there. More than anything else, it was the desire to limit
the power of the imperial nobility—whose rights he had once defended—that now bound Cotta to his old adversary Frederick.[44] There
is no question that Cotta's early appearance with Waldeck was purely
tactical. As far as Waldeck's supporters were concerned, Cotta's apparently old-fashioned views were corrupted by other, less attractive sentiments. Alone among Wangenheim's allies, for instance, Cotta wanted to
preserve the unicameral assembly of the Old Law, as a symbol not of the
ancient unity of the estates but of equality before the law. A bicameral
legislature did not seem to him to express the new autonomy of the
Third Estate (as it did to Wangenheim); rather, it stood for the pride of
the higher nobility, who "wanted to know nothing about the lower orders."[45] It is also clear that Cotta hoped for a diet, however constituted,
that would be of more than symbolic significance and more than a brake
on the actions of the crown. From the beginning he urged his colleagues
to think of themselves as representatives with real constituents, whom
they should consult before negotiating with the king.[46]

42. Cf. Wangenheim to Cotta, 14 Sept. 1815, CA.

43. "Antwortsaddresse," 17 April 1815, CA.

44. On the constitutional and administrative problems posed by the incorporation of
so many of the Swabian imperial lordships into Württemberg, see Günther Zollmann,
"Adelsrechte und Staatsorganisation im Königreich Württemberg 1806 bis 1817," Ph.D.
diss., Tübingen, 1971.

45. Varnhagen von Ense to Cotta, 1 March 1816, in Fehling and Schiller, *Briefe an Cotta*
2:9–11. Cotta's preference for a unicameral diet was shared by Hegel, who also had been
a supporter of the Reform Diet in his youth, only to find that Frederick's program of legal
and fiscal rationalization had much to offer. See Hegel's (originally anonymous) essay,
"Beurteilung der Verhandlungen in der Versammlung der Landstände des Königreichs
Württemberg im Jahre 1815 und 1816," *Heidelbergische Jahrbücher der Literatur*, nos. 66–68,
73–77 (1817); reprinted in *Werke*, ed. Eva Moldenhauer and Karl Markus Michel (Frankfurt, 1970–79), 4:462–597.

46. "*Stuttgart," *AZ*, 10 May 1815.

In retrospect it is easy to see that the Württemberg Diet, whether housed in one chamber or two, could not function as a modern parliament and still fulfill its historical role as a symbol of what Otto Hintze called "the manifold private interests of society."[47] The distinction between "landständisch" and "repräsentativ" institutions was never addressed in Württemberg's Diet, but the significance of the latter concept for the contending parties is readily inferred. For Frederick, representative bodies would complement the unified administrative structure he had already created. For most of his opponents, the Diet was representative in Hintze's sense: it embodied the social hierarchy and insured its continuance. To Cotta, Wangenheim, and their allies, finally, representative bodies had a function akin to that of the press: they bound the people to the state, thus improving administration, fostering patriotism, and keeping the government informed of its citizens' needs. But neither Cotta nor anyone else in a position of influence was prepared to go further—to argue that representation legitimized authority, still less that sovereignty lay with the people or the parliament. It is for this reason that, in Württemberg and elsewhere, the most vigorous defenders of the rights of the assembly were traditionalists, who alone accorded the estates truly equal standing with the prince. More sophisticated and progressive men like Cotta, who wanted to begin integrating representative institutions with the other machinery of government, tended in the end to concede the logical supremacy of the crown. Thus was born the alliance between reformism and the "monarchical principle," whose triumph would prove to be the most durable result of the constitutional movement in southern Germany and a prominent feature of Cotta's later career.

Yet Cotta did, however improbably, fight hard for one specific aspect of the Old Law: the rearming of the countryside. One would not have expected it. As a publisher Cotta had shown no inclination to appeal to a popular audience, and he was as distressed as anyone by the civil disturbances that punctuated the Diet's deliberations. Yet in the spring of 1815 a return to the Old Law and the establishment of a *Landwehr* had become for him virtually one and the same issue, with implications

---

47. Otto Hintze, "The Preconditions of Representative Government in the Context of World History," in *The Historical Essays of Otto Hintze,* ed. Felix Gilbert (New York, 1975), p. 305. The scholarly literature on this subject, which Hintze did much to define, is enormous. The notes to a recent essay by Eberhard Weis, "Kontinuität und Diskontinuität zwischen den Ständen des 18. Jahrhunderts und den frühkonstitutionellen Parlamenten von 1818/1819 in Bayern und Württemberg," in *Festschrift für Andreas Kraus zum 60. Geburtstag,* ed. Pankraz Fried and Walter Ziegler (Kallmünz, 1982), pp. 337–55, may serve as a guide. For a comprehensive, theoretically sophisticated discussion, see Hartwig Brandt, *Landständische Repräsentation im deutschen Vormärz: Politisches Denken im Einflußfeld des monarchischen Prinzips* (Neuwied am Rhein and Berlin, 1968).

reaching to the heart of constitutional life. "It may be all the same to us," he declared,

> whether Napoleon rules in France or not. It is military government itself that moves us so forcefully to draw the sword in our own defense. We must therefore become soldiers, we must arm the whole people and procure whatever is necessary through a levy. But we cannot support this without a guarantee, and we know where to find one only in the ways of the old constitution. The honest monarch ought not hesitate to arm his worshipful subjects.[48]

"It is military government itself that moves us"—here, certainly, the Old Law and the new politics speak with one voice. In Cotta's eyes the new monarchies left behind by Napoleon had rested on a monopoly of force, to which he now opposed the claims of history and community. The compromise that Wangenheim persuaded Frederick to accept included no sharing of military power, but it did repair lost continuity with the past and reaffirmed the contractual relationship between the government and the people. To Cotta, who had suspected that he might have to "be satisfied with a little,"[49] this was enough.

By the end of 1815, however, the achievement of any sort of compromise seemed beyond the power of the parties involved. If public opinion had become the only feasible source of political leverage, what leverage existed was not very great. The Diet, in bare majority an elected body, was directly accountable only to the two-hundred-gulden freeholders enfranchised by the king.[50] A few members might exploit incidental violence to pressure the government, but none was ready to lead a general movement against the crown, even if such a movement could somehow have been called into existence. The means of mobilizing the people were meager. The Diet's proceedings were a matter of public record, but these minutes were not widely or regularly distributed, nor were their contents the stuff to ignite the countryside. Frederick, for his part, was no friend of the press, whose influence during his reign had shrunk from modest to negligible. The French-inspired press law under which Wangenheim was forced to operate was so restrictive as to insure that most significant commentary on Württemberg's affairs appeared outside its borders.[51] In all, the publicizing of Württemberg's constitutional debate consumed far more energy than it produced.

48. Speech of 4 April 1815, in Schäffle, *Cotta*, p. 103; also Cotta's speech of 17 April, in "Stuttgart," *AZ*, 29 April 1815.

49. Cotta to Charlotte von Schiller, 7 Feb. 1815, paraphrased in Vollmer, *Briefwechsel*, p. 565.

50. Of the Diet's 125 members, 72 were chosen by general election. The rest were appointed spokesmen for the nobility, the university, and the church.

51. Apart from the *Hofzeitung*, Württemberg's only political periodicals were the "semi-ministerial" *Schwäbische Merkur* and three local gazettes: the *Ulmer Landbote*, the *Ried-*

During the periods when the Diet was in session, about one in five issues of the *AZ* included significant coverage of its proceedings—thorough treatment by contemporary standards, the more so in view of the glacial pace of events. This material was distinctive in several respects. The ratio of *raisonnements* to straight reportage was high. Although some reports favored the Diet, these were generally accompanied by disingenuous footnotes claiming that the article's appearance was a demonstration of the editor's impartiality.[52] More striking is the antiaristocratic tone of those articles that favored the crown, a tendency entirely in accord with Cotta's feelings and one that probably would have been even more pronounced but for the restraint applied by the Bavarian authorities.[53] Württemberg was alleged to be in the grip of an aristocratic *partie souterraine*, not unlike that which had existed in revolutionary France[54]—an improbable idea in itself, since Frederick clearly had opponents among the representatives of old Württemberg, as well as the support of the less prosperous nobility. But the pretensions of the aristocratic opposition were especially vexing to Cotta, since they transgressed both the ideal of civic virtue embodied in the Old Law and the modern concept of legal equality. His aggressive speeches on these themes were regularly reported by the *AZ* as news,[55] and in turn were pilloried by his opponents as "insolent"[56] and "more worthy of a Jacobin club than a German Diet."[57]

---

linger *politische Zeitung*, and the Heilbronn *Neckarzeitung*. Cotta's *Europäische Annalen*, although published in Tübingen, did not concern itself with domestic issues. Far more important than any of these journals was the *Rheinische Merkur* in Coblenz, which vigorously supported the estates. The most significant book inspired by the conflict, Wangenheim's *Staatsverfassung*, was published in Frankfurt. The venue of more ephemeral works is difficult to establish. Many are listed in Wilhelm Heyd et al., eds., *Bibliographie der württembergischen Geschichte* (Stuttgart, 1895–1965), 1:156–57, 3:62–69. Württemberg's constitutional crisis eventually attracted the attention of quite distant observers; see, for instance, the witty (if entirely serious) defense of the nobility in the *Edinburgh Review*, "Verhandlungen in der Versammlung der Landstände des Königreichs Würtemberg," vol. 29, no. 58 (Feb. 1818): 337–63, in which Frederick's treatment of the estates is likened (with somewhat ambiguous effect!) to the cruelty of "a chimney-sweeper drubbing his jack-ass."

52. For instance "Stuttgart," *AZ*, 8 April, 29 June, 9 Oct. 1816.

53. Cf. Alois von Rechberg [Bavarian foreign minister] to Karl von Gravenreuth [district governor in Augsburg], 19 May 1817, and Gravenreuth to Rechberg, 26 July 1817, M Inn 25097/I.

54. "*Aus Schwaben," *AZ*, 22 Aug. 1816; cf. "*Aus dem Württembergischen," *AZ*, 5 May 1816.

55. For instance "Deutschland," *AZ*, 18 July 1816 (Beilage), and "*Stuttgart," *AZ*, 8 Oct. 1816.

56. "*Stuttgart," *AZ*, 8 Oct. 1816.

57. *Verhandlungen* 31:68. Hegel, reviewing the proceedings of the Diet's first two years, noted that these periodic attacks on Cotta were the only occasions for spontaneous debate in an assembly in which most speeches were set pieces prepared in advance ("Beurteilung," in Hegel, *Werke*, p. 516).

In March 1816 resentment of Cotta's conduct had already given rise to an ugly scene, at a party celebrating the name day of one of the king's ancestors. After dinner songs were sung, including some extemporaneous verses apostrophizing the "king's flunkies." Cotta refused to sing or to drink the health of the song's author. Harsh words were exchanged, including some on Cotta's part that amounted to a challenge to a duel. But the challenged party, a former imperial count, declared himself offended that he had been called out by a commoner and refused to fight.[58] By the fall, Cotta's isolation in the Diet was almost complete: a debt amortization scheme that he championed on behalf of the crown was rejected with but two dissenting votes, Cotta's and that of the representative from Stuttgart, Ludwig Griesinger.[59]

This defeat came hard because it compromised other efforts (in which Cotta was also involved) to provide relief to people suffering from that year's poor harvest.[60] It was followed by another, some weeks later, when Cotta's opponents successfully moved for the appointment of a committee to "investigate" the *AZ*'s reports and bring their "promulgator" to justice. The *AZ* reprinted this attack verbatim, as a "tribute to the freedom of the press."[61] Cotta's personal response was likewise defiant: he lectured his colleagues roundly for their intolerance and spitefulness and, above all, for allowing "everything to incline toward the personal" at a time when only the common interest was important. Having been challenged, in effect, to resign, he announced instead that he would resume his seat "with a clear conscience and an untroubled heart."[62]

Despite the *AZ*'s promotion of Wangenheim's program, the Diet and the crown were no nearer agreement than they had been a year before. Cotta's exertions had not even won him the favor of his old nemesis Frederick, who found the antiaristocratic tenor of the *AZ*'s coverage distasteful and reflexively despised the press even when it was on his side.[63] Cotta's public responsibilities were also taking their toll in other areas of his life. He had missed the Leipzig book fairs for two years running, something he could not continue to do indefinitely. To Goethe, who regularly urged him to devote himself to the world of letters, Cotta wrote wistfully of the joys of a life outside the public eye and of his longing to "give up my thorny political career" in favor of his old friend's

58. "Deutschland," *AZ*, 24 April 1816.

59. "*Stuttgart," *AZ*, 6 Sept. 1816.

60. Cf. two critiques of the Diet's position [by Wangenheim], *AZ*, 31 Aug. 1816, 18 Sept. 1816 (Beilage).

61. "Stuttgart," *AZ*, 9 Oct. 1816.

62. "*Stuttgart," *AZ*, 8 Oct. 1816.

63. At the very height of the *AZ*'s support for his government, Frederick threatened to ban its importation if it ever compromised his interests (Christian Vellnagel [Frederick's secretary] to Cotta, 15 May 1816, CA).

brilliant company.[64] Indeed, if Cotta's political fortunes had continued on their present course, he might well have had no other choice. On the morning of October 30, however, all thoughts of retirement were rendered moot by the unexpected news that Frederick had died in his sleep.

FÜR UND WIDER

William's accession to the throne promised a dramatic improvement in Cotta's position. Here, Cotta believed, was a prince of "the most admirable sentiments . . . [who] understands my actions and desires."[65] Overnight Cotta was an insider again, a potential minister, full of energy and expectations.[66] Wangenheim was less sanguine. He found William "a very upright man . . . [who] in the best case will do what he must do, but *contre coeur.*" Although he lacked his father's autocratic manner, he was still a king, whose progressive instincts would carry him only so far. The chances that Germany would receive a "model constitution" from Württemberg had therefore improved, but they still depended on the power of public argument[67]—a burden the *AZ* clearly could not bear alone.

Three years earlier, while he was still curator at Tübingen, Wangenheim had urged Cotta to publish a more specialized political review focusing on constitutional questions. The journal was to have been the work of a small group, men of the center, who would defend constitutional monarchy against "Jacobinical republicans" and reactionaries alike.[68] There had been little chance that such a venture could have prospered under Frederick's Board of Censors—Friedrich List's conceptually similar *Württembergisches Archiv* was published in Heidelberg for just this reason. Within a month of Frederick's death, however, Cotta applied to the board for permission to publish a journal outside its supervision, only to be turned down, despite the support of the new king.[69] In January, though, Cotta and Wangenheim persuaded William to enact a new press law, abolishing the board and placing the press under ordinary civil law—the crucial reform for which Cotta had lobbied at Vienna.[70]

64. Cotta to Goethe, 26 Sept. 1816, in Kuhn, *Goethe und Cotta* 2:26–27.

65. Cotta to Goethe, 16 Nov. 1816, ibid., p. 30; cf. Cotta to Goethe, 27 Dec. 1816, ibid., pp. 32–33.

66. Hölzle, "Cotta," p. 587.

67. Wangenheim to Cotta, 30 Nov. 1816, CA.

68. Wangenheim to Cotta, 14 May, 2 Aug., 21 Aug. 1814, CA.

69. Hertel, "Cotta," cols. 493–98.

70. Press law of 30 Jan. 1817, in Reyscher, *Württembergische Gesetze* 15:875–77. This legislation was quite modern in character, and proved remarkably durable; after being superseded for twenty years by the Carlsbad decrees, it was revived unchanged in 1848 and remained in force until 1931. Its place in the evolution of Württemberg's press laws is discussed in Gregor Richter, "Der Staat und die Presse in Württemberg bis zur Mitte des 19. Jahrhunderts," *Zeitschrift für württembergische Landesgeschichte*, n.s., 25 (1966): 404–12.

Cotta's contribution to the ensuing flood of publicity was a series of octavo volumes entitled *Für und Wider* and bearing the motto "Examine everything and keep the good."[71] The first two issues, 368 pages between them, appeared simultaneously early in February and consisted of essays by individuals sympathetic to the government. These gentlemen were not entirely of one mind. Heinrich Paulus, a professor of theology at Heidelberg who had written an early draft of Frederick's constitution, regarded Wangenheim's views as oligarchical.[72] Heinrich Kessler, a collaborator of List's, criticized the Old Law in light of a legendary *uralte Recht* to which other contributors were indifferent. Kessler's sympathy for the poor was more pronounced than theirs as well.[73] The virtues of a unicameral assembly were also given a fair hearing.[74] But these differing emphases scarcely justified the new journal's title. More than any of Cotta's other ventures, *Für und Wider* was a party organ, whose contents consistently favored a unified, monarchical-bureaucratic *Rechtsstaat* of the kind that William was expected to establish.

Thematically, *Für und Wider* intensified the campaign already under way in the *AZ*.[75] It criticized the Old Law in familiar terms, as an honorable anachronism too ridden with privilege to accommodate the popular desire for freedom and progress stimulated by recent events. Unlike the *AZ*, though, *Für und Wider* was designed to place these arguments in relatively few hands. At the time of the negotiations to publish the *Vermittler*, Cotta had expressed an interest in publishing something that would "work powerfully and steadily on the masses."[76] But *Für und Wider* was not it. While not expensive—it sold for forty-eight kreuzer per issue, far less, page for page, than the *AZ*—it consisted almost exclusively of long articles by scholars and was distributed only through the Cotta bookshops in Tübingen and Stuttgart. It also appeared irregularly—a sign that its commitment was to its subject, not its audience. It

71. Between 1817 and 1819 at least ten new political periodicals appeared in Württemberg (Walter Kissling, "Württemberg und die Karlsbader Beschlüsse gegen die Presse: Ein Beitrag zur württembergischen Pressezensur–Pressegesetzgebung," Ph.D. diss., Munich, 1956, p. 17).

72. See Paulus's earlier review of Wangenheim's *Staatsverfassung* in the *Heidelberger Jahrbücher der Litteratur* 10 (1817): 145–83.

73. "Bemerkungen," *Für und Wider*, no. 1 (1817): 191–206; and "Politische Predigt über ein Text von Johannes von Müller," *Für und Wider*, no. 2 (1817): 95–120.

74. See Heinrich Kessler, "Die Trennung der Volksvertretung in zwey Abtheilungen," *Für und Wider*, no. 2 (1817): 95–120; and J. Jaumann, "Die Vereinigung des Adels und der Gemeinen in einen Kammer," *Für und Wider*, no. 2 (1817): 33–87.

75. The mutual support of the two journals was evident. Cf. "Replik des Verfassers der Vermittlungsworte auf den vom Herrn Dr. Zahn . . . ," *Für und Wider*, no. 2 (1817): 2–118 and no. 3 (1817): 135–50; and "Worte zur Vermittlung in der landständischen Angelegenheiten in Württemberg," *AZ*, 21, 27 Oct., 7 Nov. 1816 (außerordentliche Beilage).

76. Cotta to Wangenheim, 9 March 1817, CA.

seems unlikely that many issues made it across Württemberg's borders, or into the coffeehouses and cafés that subscribed to the *AZ*. This new effort was thus aimed at a very exclusive audience: the members of the Diet and the narrow, politically enfranchised class it represented.[77]

Für und Wider was well conceived to complement Cotta's newspaper. Its appearance restored some semblance of the time-honored distinction between *Zeitungen* and journals of opinion and relieved the *AZ* of some of the didactic material that had bred such hard feelings among Cotta's colleagues. Almost inevitably, however, it was overshadowed by the sheer volume of the *AZ*'s coverage, which with the reconvening of the Diet escalated from thorough to relentless: three out of four issues now included a report on Württemberg. And although the reporting was more documentary and evenhanded as compared to the previous year, overall the *AZ*'s attitude had not changed. When William presented his new constitution early in March, it was found to incorporate every concession the estates could justly ask.[78]

Despite the new king's more generous nature, compromise remained out of reach. As so often in the past, debate on matters of principle quickly hardened into a disagreement over procedures, thus compounding paralysis with the appearance of triviality. In the present case, however, the procedural issue at stake was a grave one. William's constitution, like his father's, required the estates to give up many traditional rights. In reply, the king's opponents now argued that only delegates from old Württemberg should be allowed to vote on such concessions, since only they had exercised the rights to begin with. As a practical matter, adoption of this procedure would have reduced the Diet, in Cotta's words, to "a semblance of the Polish *Reichstag*";[79] it would also have opened the door to all those distinctions of status that Cotta rejected. There was, in other words, no room whatever for negotiation. The assembly's deliberations became more acrimonious than ever, until they settled once more on Cotta himself.

On April 30, Cotta was again attacked on the floor of the Diet for using his publications to undermine the assembly.[80] One speaker, Heinrich Bolly from Marbach, declared that Cotta had subjected the estates to such public humiliation as to make any agreement with the crown impossible.[81] He moved that the new voting rule (which had been pro-

77. *Für und Wider*'s sales are unknown. List's *Archiv*, which sold for the same price, had 250 subscribers (List to Cotta, 16 June 1817, in Friedrich List, *Schriften, Reden, Briefe*, ed. Erwin Beckerath et al. [Berlin, 1927–35], 8:111).

78. "*Stuttgart," *AZ*, 4 March 1817.

79. "Stuttgart," *AZ*, 28 March 1817.

80. "Deutschland," *AZ*, 4–12 May 1817, passim.

81. Bolly was unusual among Cotta's opponents in having attempted to meet the *AZ* on its ground, by means of a pamphlet entitled *Contra principia negantem non est disputandum* [Stuttgart, April 1817]; cf. "Stuttgart," *AZ*, 27 April, 13 May 1817.

visionally rejected a few days before) be summarily adopted, as a gesture of rebuke. After six hours of debate this motion passed overwhelmingly; among the members from the old lands, only Cotta and his staunch ally Griesinger voted no. At the end of the session a crowd gathered outside the hall to confront the two men. By chance both had left, and after a search of the building the group disintegrated. It gathered again that night, breaking all the windows in Griesinger's house; Wangenheim's residence was also attacked with stones and garbage. Cotta's punishment was, in the words of the *AZ*, "even more distinguished": when the mob arrived at his house, its leader stepped forward to hurl a flask of ink against the door—but the missile misfired and flew into the foyer of the house next door, to the chagrin of all concerned.[82]

The failure of the ink flask to find its mark brought a faintly comic end to a potentially nasty situation. Publicly, Cotta was unperturbed. He took his accustomed seat in the Diet the next day, and the *AZ* reported laconically on the "dark deed" perpetrated on his astonished neighbor.[83] Privately, Cotta considered the incident senseless, though he was glad to have been among the first to leave the hall on the day in question.[84] Indeed, it would seem senseless, were it not for the ink. A bottle of ink is a weapon chosen with care, and under the circumstances its meaning should have been plain: all the ink at Cotta's disposal was not going to shift the Diet or unite the public behind the crown.

Cotta was slow to concede. A week or so after the attack a third number of *Für und Wider* appeared, and another, which proved to be the last, followed in June. The *AZ* remained as attentive as ever. William, however, was now resolved to "put an end to this insanity."[85] He responded to the attack on his most important supporters by threatening to expel from the city any representative who rejected the principle of majority rule. The Diet therefore recanted its defiant vote—but by then the time for negotiation had passed. On May 26 the assembly received a revised draft of the king's constitution, with instructions to vote it up or down in its entirety. A week later they voted it down, whereupon the king, after promising to uphold the constitution so decisively rejected, ordered the Diet dissolved.

On the night following William's demand for a final vote, Wangenheim's home was again besieged by a mob, an attack that, as the *AZ* noted, was unjust: Wangenheim had had nothing to do with the king's ultimatum.[86] On the contrary, the dissolution that followed was a defeat

82. *AZ*, 8 May 1817; cf. Wangenheim to Cotta, [1 May 1817,] in Fehling and Schiller, *Briefe an Cotta* 2:70.

83. "*Stuttgart," *AZ*, 8 May 1817.

84. Cotta to Goethe, 26 May 1817, in Kuhn, *Goethe und Cotta* 2:44.

85. Ibid.; cf. Grube, *Stuttgarter Landtag*, pp. 499–500.

86. "Stuttgart," *AZ*, 4 June 1817.

for Wangenheim and, by extension, for Cotta too. Over the last few months, and particularly following the debacle at the end of April, Wangenheim's counsel had depreciated steadily as William became increasingly persuaded that there really was no dealing with the assembly.[87] The de facto constitutional monarchy that he installed in lieu of further negotiations was, moreover, a strictly mechanical structure, of a kind that Cotta's friend could not have supported. When the cabinet was reorganized in the fall, Wangenheim was allowed an honorable exile as Württemberg's delegate to the Federal Diet. The finance ministry, so often rumored to be Cotta's, went to Karl von Malchus, a former official of the Grand Duchy of Westphalia and an expert on French administrative techniques.[88]

Cotta's feelings at being passed over are not recorded, but they must have included some measure of relief to go with the disappointment. The last two years had taken their toll on his health and spirit. His colleagues, whom he had once found exemplary in their devotion to the public welfare, now stood exposed as petty and corrupt.[89] His efforts to mobilize public opinion had failed: neither the public nor his political opponents had reacted as they were supposed to. The will of the people had remained inchoate; for the moment, even a government-inspired mass movement was out of the question.

The reaction in the Diet had been even more disappointing: a prolonged cry of outrage that never coalesced into anything more articulate. To Cotta, it was the reticence of the opposition that had made the *AZ* and *Für und Wider* seem so one-sided. Twenty years before, Cotta had regarded *Unparteilichkeit* as a positive obligation, which he, as a political publisher, was honor-bound to satisfy; in the last few years, however, conditions had begun to change. There were now plenty of newspapers in Germany, and many opportunities for political give-and-take. The Cotta press still remained open to all. But the responsibility to express opposing views would increasingly fall on those who held them. If some of the *AZ*'s reports were polemical, as Stegmann admitted more than once, then the burden lay with the other side to reply. Those who did not trust the public enough to do so would have to pay the price of their diffidence.[90]

Cotta's critics did not see things this way. For them, as Cotta had once

87. Wintterlin, "Württembergische Verfassung," p. 68; Wangenheim to Cotta, [22 May 1817,] in Fehling and Schiller, *Briefe an Cotta* 2:71–72.

88. Friedrich Wintterlin, *Geschichte der Behördenorganisation in Württemberg* (Stuttgart, 1902–6), 1:8–19.

89. Cotta to Friedrich Staegemann, 27 Sept. 1817, in Rühl, *Briefe und Aktenstücke* 2:164.

90. Editorial footnote [by Stegmann] to "Zweites Schreiben eines Reisenden," *AZ*, 24 Feb. 1817 (Beilage).

complained, "everything inclined toward the personal"—but not in the trivial way Cotta imagined. There was no denying that the *AZ* was Cotta's personal responsibility. The issue was therefore not one of freedom, but of honor. The charge against him was simple: if the *AZ*'s characterization of the Diet was justified, then he should resign out of pride; if not, then out of shame.[91] To this complaint must be added more nebulous, but evidently widespread, doubts about the conception of public life implied by the institutional power of the Cotta press, which threatened to overshadow the web of personal relationships that still constituted the chief bond between the assembly and its constituents. Even Cotta's allies—men like Griesinger, the bureaucratic reformer, and Justinus Kerner, the populist insurgent (about whom more will be said), who were eager to use publicity for their own purposes—nevertheless refused to support Cotta on the one measure that would have guaranteed the press's economic vitality and political autonomy: copyright. Even to them, the rights of press and parliament remained difficult to reconcile.[92]

It is thus hardly surprising that no meeting of the minds occurred. The majority of the estates continued to regard publicity as an intrusion rather than as an extension of their public function. They felt they were being manipulated, and they remained unimpressed by Cotta's offers of space in which to defend themselves. They would not have been surprised to learn what Cotta himself was loath to admit: articles touching on Württemberg's problems were liable to be shown to William in advance and were subject to his veto.[93] The Cotta press, in short, was not quite as level a field as Cotta pretended.

In the fall of 1817, all parties to Württemberg's constitutional debate entered enforced retirement. The king's opponents returned to their homes, to worry about revolution and await an opportunity to renew the struggle.[94] Cotta once again contemplated a retreat to the world of letters; his "political life," he wrote Goethe, "had, thank God, come to a close."[95] He hoped to regain a sense of proportion by traveling to Italy, a land whose recuperative powers Goethe himself had made famous.

91. [Bolly,] *Contra principia negantem,* passim.

92. Widmann, *Der deutsche Buchhandel* 2 : 357; idem, "Christian August Vulpius' Rache an den Reutlinger Nachdruckern," *Zeitschrift für württembergische Landesgeschichte* 29 (1970): 167–77. The only real ally Cotta ever had on this question was the poet Ludwig Uhland, who entered the Diet in 1819.

93. Between January and August 1817 Cotta corresponded regularly with William's secretary, Vellnagel, about manuscripts destined for the *AZ.* Vellnagel's replies are in CA.

94. Justinus Kerner to Cotta, 30 Sept. 1817, in Fehling and Schiller, *Briefe an Cotta* 2 : 109.

95. Cotta to Goethe, 2 Sept. 1817, in Kuhn, *Goethe und Cotta* 2 : 46; cf. Cotta to Goethe, 28 Sept. 1817, ibid., pp. 48–49.

Prior to his departure, Cotta applied for and received official recognition of his family's "ancient nobility," which entitled him to call himself Cotta von Cottendorf.[96] Even this may have been something of a disappointment: there were those who thought Cotta hoped to be made a baron.[97] But the application was in any event a remarkable farewell from a man who had had such hard words for the nobility just a few months before—a sign, perhaps, that it really had been nothing personal.

TRIBÜNE

Cotta remained in Italy for over four months, during which time, he was pleased to report, it rained only five times.[98] He returned to Stuttgart in April 1818 to find the atmosphere much as he had left it: cloudy, and too calm.[99] In October, a festival organized by the Jena *Burschenschaft* had been held on the Wartburg in Weimar to commemorate the three hundredth anniversary of the Reformation and, simultaneously, the fifth anniversary of the Battle of Leipzig. The celebration had reached its climax on the night of the eighteenth, when a bonfire was made of paper inscribed with the names of reactionary or unpatriotic books, and military paraphernalia thought to symbolize the repressive, antinational, and spiritually deadening nature of the Vienna settlement. For Württemberg, the festival was significant in two respects. First, its symbolic violence prompted Austria to reemphasize its intention to master the constitutional movement in Germany.[100] At the same time, by dramatizing the shortcomings of the present regime so effectively, the *Wartburgfest* encouraged a new alignment among those opposed to the bureaucratic values of William's unilateral settlement.

In Württemberg, those who shared the *Burschenschaftler*'s idealization of German liberty and brotherhood constituted a kind of populist party called the *Volksfreunde*. As compared to their northern counterparts, the membership in this group was more diverse, and their program more concrete. The *Volksfreunde* included members of the *bürgerlich* opposition in the Diet and some outsiders, notably Friedrich List, Heinrich Kessler, and Justinus Kerner, who supported Wangenheim's compromise. Their aim was to halt the centralization of power in Württemberg

96. Cotta submitted in evidence an imperial patent granted to his ancestor Bonaventure Cotta in 1420. The new title was awarded on 20 Nov. 1817.

97. Robert Marquant, *Thiers et le baron Cotta: Etude sur la collaboration de Thiers à la Gazette d'Augsbourg* (Paris, 1959), p. 12n.

98. Cotta to Goethe, 18 April 1818, in Kuhn, *Goethe und Cotta* 2:54.

99. Kerner to Cotta, 15 Nov. 1817, in Fehling and Schiller, *Briefe an Cotta* 2:113–14.

100. Eberhard Büssem, *Die Karlsbader Beschlüsse von 1819: Die endgültige Stabilisierung der restaurativen Politik im Deutschen Bund nach dem Wiener Kongress von 1814–15* (Hildesheim, 1974), pp. 36–37.

by restoring authority to local government (which had declined under both Frederick and William) and by reaffirming the rights of the Diet.[101] To this end, in January 1818 they founded a journal, the *Volksfreund aus Schwaben, ein Vaterlandsblatt für Sitte, Recht, und Freiheit*, in which they urged the revival of the constitutional debate. These efforts gained an air of urgency with the growing prospect of federal intervention, an outcome that no one wanted. By the time Cotta returned from Italy, there was already reason to believe the political obituary he had delivered to Goethe would prove premature.

Cotta's relationship to this new constellation of forces was ambiguous. The *Wartburgfest* itself was not the sort of event with which he could sympathize; Friedrich Gentz, who provided the *AZ*'s coverage, pronounced the whole affair a harbinger of decay.[102] Neither, however, did William's program approach the "contractual" settlement for which Cotta had fought. In the fall Justinus Kerner had considered Cotta a likely publisher for the *Volksfreund aus Schwaben*, an opportunity Cotta passed up when he went to Italy.[103] There were also more personal values to consider. Cotta shared the desire of the *Volksfreunde* to find some way around the stupefying contest between the Old Law and the new bureaucracy, but not the cultural baggage that went with it; he particularly resented their anti-Semitic attacks on one of his friends, Salomo Michaelis, who was then editing a small, semiministerial journal called (somewhat misleadingly) the *Württembergische Volksfreund*.[104] At the same time, William, on whom Cotta's political prospects depended, was socially and personally attached to the "higher nobility" and, like his father, found the *AZ*'s rough treatment of them unseemly.[105]

Despite the absence of a sitting diet, the press law that Cotta had helped engineer at the start of William's reign insured that journalism would remain a fruitful arena for political activity. Even while resting in Italy, Cotta had begun to consider a new initiative in this area, in the form of a reorganization of the *Europäische Annalen*, which had been without an official editor since Ernst Posselt's death in 1804. In the intervening years part of the slack had been taken up by Friedrich Buchholz in Berlin, who had become the *Annalen*'s most important contributor.

---

101. Wintterlin, "Württembergische Verfassung," p. 75; Hölzle, *Württemberg im Zeitalter Napoleons*, pp. 226–37.

102. "Oesterreich," *AZ*, 3 Dec. 1817, 20–22 Jan. 1818.

103. Kerner to Cotta, 19 Sept. 1817, in Fehling and Schiller, *Briefe an Cotta* 2 : 108–9. Cotta had also declined to take over publication of List's *Archiv* (List to Cotta, 16 June 1817, in List, *Schriften, Reden, Briefe* 8 : 111).

104. Max Müller, "Salomo Michaelis: Schützling, Mitarbeiter, und Freund des Frhrn. v. Wangenheim," *Zeitschrift für württembergische Landesgeschichte*, n.s., 3 (1939): 158–211 passim.

105. Vellnagel to Cotta, 2 Feb. 1817, CA.

During the War of Liberation, however, he and Cotta had gone separate ways, partly over money, but mainly because Buchholz could no longer tolerate the "spirit of miscellany" that had become the *Annalen's* besetting vice.[106] If the *Annalen* were moved from Tübingen to Stuttgart, however, or even to Frankfurt where Wangenheim could take it in hand, it might acquire a useful focus.[107] An opportunity to pursue the matter further arrived unexpectedly in June, in the person of an able journalist from Weimar named Friedrich Lindner.

Lindner came to Stuttgart a fugitive from controversy. He was a physician by training who had been politicized by the French occupation, in the sense that, like Buchholz, he had come to view Napoleon as a progressive force in Germany. After the Battle of Leipzig the Austrians had imprisoned him briefly for collaborating with the French,[108] and since his release he had devoted himself exclusively to political writing. In the fall of 1817 he became editor of Friedrich Bertuch's radical *Oppositionsblatt*, in which capacity he came into possession of one of August von Kotzebue's confidential reports to the czar. Lindner passed this along to Heinrich Luden, who published it in the Jena *Volksfreund*, which was immediately suppressed. Lindner was expelled from Weimar in disgrace. Like Bendix Daevel, he made contact with Cotta by way of Varnhagen von Ense, who judged Lindner to be an intelligent man with strong convictions. This last quality was not a pure virtue: Varnhagen was not sure Lindner's advanced views could be made palatable to Wangenheim, who was, after all, still the king's spokesman.[109] Lindner and Cotta got along splendidly, however, and they soon agreed, on the basis of "mutual trust and advantage," that, in January 1819, Lindner would begin editing a monthly journal called the *Stern*, which would replace the *Annalen*.[110]

In the meantime, Lindner turned his attention to the upcoming congress at Aachen, which Cotta wanted him to cover for the *AZ*. Ostensibly the sole purpose of this congress was to end the military occupation of France. It was likely, however, that its agenda would prove broader than that: both Austria and Prussia were showing increasing interest in using the Federation to restrain the constitutional movement in Germany, and

106. Buchholz to Cotta, 13 Feb. 1814, CA; the following year Buchholz began a monthly *Journal für Deutschland, historisch-politischen Inhalts*, published by Haude & Spener in Berlin.

107. Varnhagen von Ense to Cotta, 16 April 1818, and Wangenheim to Cotta, 17 April 1818, CA.

108. Marquant, *Thiers et le baron Cotta*, p. 6n.

109. Varnhagen von Ense to Cotta, 16 April and 13 May 1818, CA; Varnhagen von Ense to Cotta, 9 May 1818, in Fehling and Schiller, *Briefe an Cotta* 2:19.

110. Contract dated 8 Aug. 1818, in Hertel, "Cotta," cols. 491–92; cf. Varnhagen von Ense to Cotta, 4 June 1818, CA.

Aachen would provide occasion for frank discussions without interference from the middle states, whose representatives were not invited.[111] Lindner was an odd choice to report on these proceedings, having so recently and conspicuously compromised one of the czar's advisors. Varnhagen believed that if Cotta really wanted usable copy, he should send Lindner to Paris instead.[112] But Cotta had made up his mind, even going so far as to arrange for Lindner to report confidentially to William, as a way of making up for the lack of an official Württemberg delegate. Cotta then sent him on his way, with a letter of introduction to Friedrich Gentz.[113]

It proved to be a very short trip. Gentz, whose relations with Cotta were generally amicable, found Cotta's support for such a notorious troublemaker barely credible.[114] But even if he had wanted to help, he could have done nothing, since Lindner had only been in Aachen a few hours before he was expelled at the insistence of the Russians. William, whose good judgment was also called into question by the affair, wondered politely whether Cotta had known the details of Lindner's past associations; but he was satisfied with Cotta's reply and raised no objections to Lindner's employment as editor of the *Stern*.[115]

Cotta, however, now had doubts of his own. Aachen had indeed brought new movement to German affairs, in the form of a sensational, crudely reactionary memorandum on the press and universities by the Russian state councillor, Alexander Stourdza. Cotta soon managed to acquire a (surprisingly rare) copy of this document, which he published in full.[116] But he cannot have been pleased by its contents, or by the satisfaction with which it was viewed in Vienna and Berlin.[117] In its wake Wangenheim was persuaded that, as far as the Federation was concerned, publicity had become "a weapon to be grasped only in the most extreme emergency."[118] At the end of November Cotta went to Frankfurt to talk things over, and despite continued encouragement from Varnhagen,[119] he let the *Stern* contract lapse.

For the next few months Cotta's plans remained unsettled. In the fall of 1818 Württemberg's political impasse had begun to come unstuck.

111. Büssem, *Karlsbader Beschlüsse*, pp. 70–100.
112. Varnhagen von Ense to Cotta, 23 June 1818, in Fehling and Schiller, *Briefe an Cotta* 2:20.
113. Lindner to Cotta, 18 Aug. 1818, ibid., p. 20*n*.
114. Gentz to Pilat, 5 Oct. 1818, in Gentz, *Briefe an Pilat* 1:346.
115. Vellnagel to Cotta, 17, 19 Oct., 11 Nov. 1818, CA.
116. The complete text appeared in the *Annalen* in January; substantial excerpts were first published in "*Vom Neckar*," *AZ*, 10, 11, 21 Dec. 1818.
117. Büssem, *Karlsbader Beschlüsse*, pp. 109–17.
118. Wangenheim to Cotta, 6 Nov. 1818, in Fehling and Schiller, *Briefe an Cotta* 2:77–80.
119. Varnhagen von Ense to Cotta, 1 Dec. 1818, CA.

Bavaria and Baden had by then enacted constitutions of their own; if Württemberg was to avoid having to submit to Austrian arbitration, it would have to do the same. Malchus, the author of William's policy of unilateral reform, was dismissed in September—whether as a sacrifice to the *Volksfreunde* or to the nobility is hard to say.[120] His successor as William's chief minister, Paul Maucler, immediately prepared for new negotiations with the estates. His pace was quickened by the results of the Aachen Congress, which showed that even Russia, on whom Württemberg had long relied for support, was coming to share Metternich's vision of the Federation as a bastion of the counterrevolution. By the middle of February Cotta was again being drawn into consultation with the crown.[121]

As compared to two years before, though, his most important ally was now some distance away. Wangenheim could do little from his post in Frankfurt. Early in March he provided Cotta with a detailed analysis of Württemberg's situation, presumably for use in discussions with the ministry;[122] but advice of this kind would be of little use once a new Diet had convened. As far as publicity went, however, Wangenheim's pessimism had subsided. He wanted to go forward with a "nonpartisan opposition journal" capable of combating "all extremism, whether from the rulers or the ruled, the intelligentsia or the estates."[123] This was by now a thoroughly familiar idea to Cotta, and it suffered from a familiar defect: Cotta was not prepared to give final authority over the journal's contents to Wangenheim and his collaborator, Johann Schmidt. In this case the difficulty centered less on trust than utility: Cotta wanted the new journal, a monthly tentatively entitled the *Lotse*, to appear in Stuttgart; Schmidt and Wangenheim were tied to Frankfurt, and they insisted on approving all contributions themselves.[124] Such a time-consuming approach would have seriously limited the *Lotse*'s usefulness in Württemberg, which by the spring of 1819 had become Cotta's main concern.

Lindner, meanwhile, had been at loose ends since the fiasco at Aachen. In March his reputation sustained another blow when his erstwhile enemy, Kotzebue, was murdered by a student in Mannheim, an incident that caused William to inquire whether Cotta and Lindner still stood in a "literary relationship."[125] They did, but neither of them found it very satisfactory. Cotta was paying Lindner a monthly retainer under the

120. Hölzle, *Württemberg im Zeitalter Napoleons*, pp. 259–60.

121. Varnhagen von Ense to Cotta, 3 Feb. 1819, CA; and Varnhagen von Ense to Cotta, 18 Feb. 1819, in Fehling and Schiller, *Briefe an Cotta* 2:22.

122. Wangenheim to Cotta, 11 March 1819, CA.

123. Wangenheim to Cotta, 14/19 March 1819, in Fehling and Schiller, *Briefe an Cotta* 2:80–85.

124. Schmidt and Wangenheim to Cotta, 16, 23 April 1819, CA.

125. Vellnagel to Cotta, 31 March 1819, CA.

Stern contract, and he was getting nothing in return except occasional, albeit incisive, reports on French politics for the *AZ*.[126] Lindner disliked being subordinate to Karl Stegmann, who, he suspected, considered his work "too liberal or Bonapartist."[127] He wanted to strike out on his own, by producing a newspaper devoted exclusively to the middle-sized German lands and dedicated to "the history of our constitutional development, and to the examination of all matters pertaining to representative government."[128] Cotta did not hesitate, and three weeks later, on July 1, 1819, the first issue appeared, entitled the *Tribüne, württembergische Zeitung für Verfassung und Volkerziehung zur Freiheit.*

From the outset the *Tribüne* suffered from recriminations and misunderstandings, which can be traced directly to the cross-purposes in which it originated. Lindner's proposal had coincided almost exactly with William's long-awaited call for a new Diet, which would convene on July 13. Cotta immediately approached the king about publishing the *Tribüne* in consultation with the ministry, which would be expected to indemnify Cotta against financial loss and appoint a "co-controller" to share responsibility for the paper's contents.[129] William agreed, somewhat surprisingly: the blessings of publicity had been little evident so far in his reign, and he had already decided, in the interests of tranquility, to move the new Diet from Stuttgart to Ludwigsburg. He nevertheless seems to have been persuaded that his government needed some counter to the *Volksfreunde*, whose cardinal principle, "the majesty of the people," would find no place in any conceivable compromise with the estates.[130] Lindner also agreed to Cotta's arrangements—again somewhat surprisingly, since they did not accord very well with either his desire for personal independence or his deepest political sympathies. The government expected Lindner's paper to rebut the irresponsible claims being made on behalf of the common people. Lindner had already chosen a title recalling the Roman official who protected the plebs against the magistracy; it is just another tribute to Cotta's skill as a negotiator that no one noticed this at the time.

In the middle of these preparations Cotta suffered a stunning disappointment: he failed to win reelection to the Diet, ironically enough because he was thought to sympathize too much with the *Volksfreunde*.[131] He eventually found another seat, as the appointed spokesman for the mediatized count of Bissingen-Nippenburg—in itself a sure sign that

126. Lindner to Cotta, [April 1819,] CA.

127. Lindner to Cotta, 21 May 1819, in Hertel, "Cotta," col. 450.

128. Lindner to Cotta, 8 June 1819, ibid.

129. Hertel, "Cotta," cols. 498–502; Vellnagel to Cotta, 24, 25 June 1819, CA.

130. Wintzingerode to Cotta, 19 July 1819, in Hertel, "Cotta," col. 503.

131. Hölzle, *Württemberg im Zeitalter Napoleons*, p. 265; cf. M. Müller, "Salomo Michaelis," p. 183. Only twenty-seven members of the 1815 Diet were reelected in 1819.

both sides were losing their taste for the struggle. But even so, it was a disheartening beginning to a parliamentary session that would fall far short of Cotta's expectations. The Diet of 1819 had been convened to ratify a settlement whose essentials had been agreed upon in advance. After two weeks of meandering discussion it adjourned, to allow further refinements to be worked out by a joint committee. Cotta played no part in these deliberations, and when the Diet broke up, he left town, as was his custom in summer, to take the waters in Baden.

His departure made no difference to anyone except Lindner, who found his own situation most discouraging. Legal pressure on the press was everywhere on the rise. His old associates in Weimar were being persecuted and dispersed; Lorenz Oken, a colleague from Lindner's days on the *Oppositionsblatt*, had even been harassed en route to Switzerland by the Württemberg police.[132] The *Neue Stuttgarter Zeitung*, an organ of the populist opposition, had been suppressed on the pretext of a complaint by Hesse-Darmstadt.[133] As far as the *Tribüne* was concerned, Lindner feared that "the king's servants do not know what they want" and that it would not be long before they turned on him too.[134]

This apprehension was well founded. Although the ministry's view of the *Tribüne* was by no means confused, neither was it the same as Lindner's or Cotta's. Wintzingerode, the foreign minister, had general charge of the press, and he considered the *Tribüne* a ministerial organ intended to "combat blow for blow . . . the perfidious and dangerous doctrines" of the *Volksfreund aus Schwaben*. This the *Tribüne* did not do. On the contrary, in the absence of newsworthy material about the Diet, Lindner had addressed himself to more general issues, including the proper scope of the franchise, the nature of representative government, and the interdependence of the crown and the people. Some of his views proved remarkably like those he was supposed to be denouncing.[135]

Neither Cotta nor Lindner found such breadth of sympathy inappropriate. They considered the *Tribüne* a private venture in which the government had chosen to cooperate, and they believed Wintzingerode had misunderstood the king's intentions. They may have been right, up to a point. When Cotta returned from Baden in August, William assured him that he was not displeased with the paper.[136] But however tolerant William may have been of the *Tribüne's* domestic influence, he cannot have been pleased to have his government linked to a newspaper that Friedrich Gentz considered "the most important democratic journal in

132. Lindner to Cotta, 23 July 1819, CA.
133. Kissling, "Württemberg und die Karlsbader Beschlüsse," p. 23.
134. Lindner to Cotta, 5 Aug. 1819, in Hertel, "Cotta," col. 524.
135. Wintzingerode to Cotta, 18, 19 July 1819, ibid., cols. 502–4.
136. Vellnagel to Cotta, 18 Aug. 1819, CA.

Germany" and "the true organ of the revolutionary party."[137] To Lindner, of course, this was praise; nor was he disturbed by the immediate suppression of the *Tribüne* in Prussia.[138] To those around him, however, such a reception was cause for alarm.

On August 17 the *Tribüne*'s co-controller, Baron von Trott, resigned. He had imagined his role would be a modest one: to consult informally with Lindner, whose final responsibility as the *Tribüne*'s editor of record could not be subdivided. Wintzingerode, however, had regarded the co-controller as a censor, for which there was no provision under existing law, and for which Trott had no inclination.[139] Cotta interpreted Trott's departure as a sign of official displeasure, and despite immediate assurances to the contrary, he took Lindner to task in terms the younger man found impossible to bear. Cotta, Lindner complained, had implied that he was unreliable and that the *Tribüne* had become an embarrassment. If that were so, then as far as Lindner was concerned there could be no question of continuing their partnership.[140]

This personal breach was quickly mended; both men knew Lindner's real grievance was with Wintzingerode. Still, the informal, collaborative relationship between the *Tribüne* and the crown that was causing Lindner such grief was the paper's most salutary characteristic, as far as Cotta was concerned.[141] Cotta's contrivance was proving much too delicate for someone with Lindner's temperament. Lindner, moreover, did not consider his editorial judgment all that insensitive; often he was unable even to guess what sort of material might give offense.[142] On this point he received tacit support from Karl Stegmann, whose discretion Cotta seldom questioned. Stegmann reprinted one of Lindner's essays, a satire on conspiracy theories, in the *AZ*, an episode that caused Cotta more trouble than anything Lindner had done on his own, since it aroused the ire of the Austrians.[143] In any case, even if Lindner's view was entirely correct, it is not clear that it would have mattered much. At the Carlsbad conference, whose deliberations formed the darkening background for

---

137. Gentz to Pilat, 15 Aug. 1819, in Gentz, *Briefe an Pilat* 1:406. At Aachen Gentz had found Lindner "very mediocre"; now he considered him one of the most dangerous writers in Germany (Gentz to Pilat, 18 July 1819, ibid., p. 385).

138. Lindner to Cotta, 23 July 1819, CA.

139. Baron von Trott to William, 17 Aug. 1819, in Hertel, "Cotta," cols. 504–5; cf. Wangenheim to Cotta, 25 April 1819, in Fehling and Schiller, *Briefe an Cotta* 2:86.

140. Lindner to Cotta, 19 Aug. 1819, in Hertel, "Cotta," cols. 524–25; cf. E. Fehr, "Leben und Schriften des Kurländers Friedrich Ludwig Lindner, mit besonderer Berücksichtigung des 'Manuscripts aus Süddeutschland,'" *Baltische Monatsschrift* 42 (1895): 563.

141. Cotta to Interior Minister von Otto, 18 Aug. 1819, in Hertel, "Cotta," cols. 506–7.

142. Lindner to Cotta, 1, 8 Aug. 1819, ibid., cols. 523–24.

143. Pilat to Cotta, 28 Aug. 1819, in Fehling and Schiller, *Briefe an Cotta* 2:54. Lindner's article, "Gaukelspiel eines Franzosen, eine allgemeine Verschwörung gegen das menschliche Geschlecht glaublich zu machen," appeared in the *Tribüne* on August 11 and in the *AZ* on August 22.

the *Tribüne's* brief existence, Cotta's new venture had already been held up as a prime example of the "demagogic, fact-falsifying press,"[144] a characterization that Wintzingerode, Württemberg's delegate, did not dispute. By the time that meeting broke up, however, the decision to end the paper had already been made—and in effect, Lindner had made it.

The last issue of the *Tribüne* appeared on September 30. It included a brief announcement of the paper's termination and two documents: a new constitution for Württemberg and an edict, unanimously adopted by the Federal Diet, imposing crushing new restrictions on the press and the universities. Apart from the irony of their juxtaposition, these decrees were not unrelated. Two days after the conclusion of the Carlsbad conference, the Württemberg Diet hastily reassembled, for what would surely be its last chance to come to terms with the crown. After four years of controversy, the one vote that counted was taken: Württemberg would have its own constitution, and not someone else's. The charter was not the one Cotta wanted. It was dominated by a spirit of bureaucratic reform, aiming at efficient administration rather than representative government. It included an upper house filled by appointment and some fossilized remains of the Old Law: a modest *Ständekasse*, an executive committee to administer it, and some concessions on taxation.[145] But it was undeniably a "contractual" document, to which the king swore allegiance and under which Cotta would function successfully for many years. If the people of Württemberg deserved better, as Wangenheim believed, this rather strained compromise at least offered some prospects for continued improvement.[146]

Further progress, however, would depend on how well Württemberg's hard-won settlement could withstand the pressures reflected in the second half of the *Tribüne's* final issue. As far as Cotta could see, "the thrones of Germany have no hope of victory except through constitutions. The smaller princes are not endangered by the German people, but by the schemes of the greater princes."[147] Carlsbad was precisely such a scheme, and the means to resist it were not great. The constitu-

144. Metternich to the Emperor Francis, 8, 10 Aug. 1819, in Büssem, *Karlsbader Beschlüsse*, p. 325; cf. Gentz to Pilat, 28 Aug. 1819, in Gentz, *Briefe an Pilat* 1 : 409.

145. Wintterlin, "Württembergische Verfassung," pp. 78–81.

146. Wangenheim to Cotta, 19 Sept. 1819, in Fehling and Schiller, *Briefe an Cotta* 2 : 87–89. Württemberg's constitutional settlement proved both flexible and durable, qualities that derived in part from William himself, who ruled until 1864. But it was not until the 1890s that the Diet acquired the constitutional parity with the crown envisioned by the reformers of Cotta's generation. See Rosemarie Menzinger, *Verfassungsrevision und Demokratisierungsprozeß im Königreich Württemberg* (Stuttgart, 1969); and Franz Mögle-Hofacker, *Zur Entwicklung des Parlamentarismus in Württemberg: Der 'Parlamentarismus der Krone' unter König Wilhelm I* (Stuttgart, 1981).

147. [Cotta to Varnhagen von Ense, 1819,] in Hölzle, "Cotta," p. 588.

tional monarchs of the south would of course defend their constitutions, if not as repositories of their subjects' rights then at least as seals on their own sovereignty. The alliance between the crown and the people had thus been proclaimed, if only on paper; and the quality of the paper had improved: vellum now, not just newsprint. But how well it could stand up against the realities of political power and social dependence was at best a matter of doubt.

One might therefore suppose that the *Tribüne* was simply bound to fail, its announced intention to "educate the people to freedom" being both premature and irrelevant to Württemberg's immediate problems. What is most striking in the paper's brief history, however, is not its unrealistically democratic aspirations, but the attempt to reconcile them to the interests of the state. In this respect the *Tribüne* bore in high relief the hallmark shared by all Cotta's political publications after 1815. In Württemberg, with William on the throne, Cotta believed that he had found the right setting for a newspaper that would combine the critical perspective of the opposition press with the authority and security of ministerial journalism. He was not far wrong. The *Tribüne* did not collapse because it had lost the confidence of the king: William never expressed the least dissatisfaction with either Lindner or his newspaper, and he paid Cotta the indemnity he promised without quibbling.[148] Lindner, though, was for the moment unable to live with the limitations that Cotta had learned to take for granted. He had never meant to become anyone's hired hand, and he remained determined to conduct himself, as he told Cotta, like an adult.[149]

When compared to the proud defiance of someone like Lindner, Cotta's cautious solicitude toward the powerful can seem unattractively timid. Yet timidity, as he demonstrated repeatedly throughout Württemberg's constitutional crisis, was not part of his nature. Nonetheless, he was a man who valued success and knew it well enough not to get it confused with even the most distinguished failure. In publishing, success meant honesty, consistency, longevity, and service—to the community and to the government in which, for better or worse, the community's interest was vested. Since the War of Liberation the devising of a strategy that would yield this sort of success had never been far from Cotta's mind. But the magic formula had proved elusive. Even Varnhagen, to whom audacity always seemed in order, was finally obliged to admit that boldness was not the key. On the contrary, recent experience suggested

148. The claim in Büssem, *Karlsbader Beschlüsse*, p. 431, that Württemberg "withdrew its support" for the *Tribüne* in the wake of the Carlsbad Conference is not supported by the evidence. On William's indemnification of Cotta (over Wintzingerode's objections), see Hertel, "Cotta," cols. 460–61, 508–12.

149. Lindner to Cotta, 1 Aug. 1819, in Hertel, "Cotta," cols. 253–54.

that, in politics, "triviality and incompetence could dare to arouse far greater displeasure than talent ever could."[150] There is no denying the talent of Cotta and his associates or the seriousness of their purpose. But given the determination of Germany's "greater princes" to master the press, it seems idle to wonder whether their efforts were too bold, or not bold enough.

150. Varnhagen von Ense to Cotta, 1 Dec. 1818, CA.

EIGHT

Reaction

As long as Germany remains locked in her fragmented state she will be at the
service of foreign interests. From the time when she trembled before the interdic-
tion of the pope, up to the recent Congress at Vienna, . . . history shows that
Germany has never really belonged to herself. Yet she does not want to be French,
or Austrian, or Prussian. She wants to be German. And she has the right to want
this. Austria and Prussia, on the other hand, have no right to exercise a guard-
ianship over us which we feel we have outgrown. . . . Real politics, however,
must still be based on real conditions; and they must be pursued in all honesty,
lest they lead into a labyrinth of error.

Friedrich Lindner, *Manuscript aus Süd-Deutschland*, 1820

On March 23, 1819, August von Kotzebue was stabbed to death in
Mannheim by Karl Sand, a theology student at the University of Jena.
At its outset, 1819 had promised to be a banner year for Germany. The
newly established assemblies in Baden and Bavaria would meet for the
first time. Prussia's constitutional commission was expected to conclude
its deliberations. Württemberg's troubles seemed on the way to resolution. In the months following Kotzebue's murder, however, these tokens
of future progress lost their value. At a stroke, Sand caused the specter
of revolution to materialize before the eyes of his countrymen. For years
Metternich had cultivated the fears of reactionary factions at the various
German courts. Now Sand provided the final heightening of tension, the
vital pretext that would allow Metternich to gain the victory that had
eluded him at Vienna: the transfer of effective authority in Germany
into his own hands.

The decrees formulated at the Carlsbad Conference in 1819 were the
most significant police action of Cotta's lifetime, and they brought a swift
end to the Era of Reform. Their ultimate meaning has been subject to
grim speculation ever since. Such questions are in the final analysis beyond the reach of the historian. There is no way to know for sure
whether, but for Carlsbad, Prussia's reformers might have succeeded in
enacting a constitution, or whether Austria might have shaken off its
backwardness and kept pace with progressive forces in the Federation,
or whether the German public might have more readily acquired the
habits and instincts of a democratic society. But it is hard to dispute
Friedrich Meinecke's identification of 1819 as one of the black years in
Germany's modern history, a setback of enduring significance.[1]

1. Friedrich Meinecke, *1848: Eine Säkularbetrachtung* (Berlin, 1948), p. 9.

The effect of the Carlsbad decrees on Cotta's fortunes was mixed. New initiatives of the kind he had lately been undertaking were, for the time being, out of the question; but the survival of the Cotta press, certainly of the *Allgemeine Zeitung*, was never seriously in doubt. Metternich's aspirations as the arbiter of public life were less ambitious than Napoleon's. Whereas Napoleon had tried to reorganize the press into a closely held instrument of state power—a distinctly modern project that finally proved beyond his means—the policy inaugurated at Carlsbad was just as distinctly backward-looking: the press was henceforth to resume its traditional role as the disseminator of a conventionally apolitical culture. Some strides were taken in this direction. The social and intellectual range of German journalism contracted appreciably in the 1820s, and the insurgent press that had been troubling Metternich's sleep since the War of Liberation was effectively crushed. But the governmental solidarity achieved at Carlsbad did not approach the level necessary to silence the *AZ*. On the contrary, if anyone in Germany can be said to have profited from the Carlsbad decrees, it was probably Cotta.

CARLSBAD AND THE END OF REFORM

Among the innumerable motives for murder, political conviction is one of the rarest, and nowhere more so than in Cotta's Germany. Before Kotzebue there had been Wallenstein, and before him only the dimly remembered Austrian king Albrecht I, done to death by his nephew in 1308. Perhaps because of the rarity of such events, the political character of Sand's deed was not immediately apparent. Early reports in the *Allgemeine Zeitung* described the attack in lurid detail but offered only disturbing hints as to its motivation: Sand had carried a death warrant in the name of the *Tugenbund*; and as he drove his knife into his own chest (while his victim lay dying) he had cried out, "Long live Teutonia."[2] Sand was, quite obviously, insane.

But he did not die, though his self-inflicted wound, the doctors said, should have been mortal. To those who expected moral degeneracy to take its toll on a man's physical being, Sand's vigor was surprising. He was, the *AZ* reported, an attractive fellow—literate, religious, of good parents, a volunteer in 1813—who spoke freely of his decision to kill Kotzebue as a Russian spy.[3] The editors could not condone murder; nor was there any decent way to report that almost everyone disliked Kotzebue for having sold himself to the czar, particularly his fellow writers, who despised his plays for their cynicism and triviality. Nonetheless,

2. "*Mannheim," *AZ*, 27–30 March 1819.
3. "*Aus dem Badischen," *AZ*, 31 March 1819, and "*Mannheim," *AZ*, 2–10 April 1819 [by a writer named Fahnenberg].

these sentiments were readily recalled after the *AZ* published a letter from Sand to his family, in which he characterized Kotzebue as "the mouthpiece of all that is wretched in our time," hiding behind an undeserved reputation as an artist.[4]

By the time Sand went to his death in May, sensible people had come to appreciate the idealism of his crime.[5] Cotta believed that Sand was a political innocent who had become the instrument of others,[6] a judgment not far from the truth, nor from the view of Friedrich Gentz, who was, however, persuaded that the "others" were more numerous than Cotta could have imagined. That so circumspect a newspaper as the *AZ* should have published Sand's apologia, even under the guise of documentary objectivity, only confirmed Gentz's feeling that this disturbed young man had given living form to the dark impulses lurking in the hearts of reformers everywhere.[7] Sand died a martyr in the eyes of the public. On the gallows the executioner asked for his forgiveness. His atavistic gesture elicited a most ambiguous response from a people unaccustomed to political violence, a response that could be answered only by further reform, or more ruthless repression.

Germany's princes did not hesitate to choose the latter course. After preliminary conversations with Hardenberg, Metternich called the representatives of the major states together at Carlsbad, where it was agreed that the Federation would assume responsibility for regulating academia and the press. Universities would be placed under the authority of commissioners, and students and teachers found to engage in "unauthorized" political activity could be excluded from study or academic employment for life. The "uniform press laws" clause of the Federal Act, the precious residue of Cotta's mission to Vienna, was now interpreted to require each state to impose censorship of a sort that would "exclude the possibility of complaint" on all works shorter than a fair-sized book (160 quarto pages). Periodicals would have to carry the name of the "responsible editor," who could be barred from working in Germany for five years if his journal was suppressed. A Central Investigative Commission was formed to ferret out dissidents and to issue "orders of execution" (backed, in principle, by military force) against any state that failed to carry out the decrees.

To some of those in attendance at Carlsbad, such remarkable exertions seemed out of place. Almost no one would have denied the role of the press in preparing the ground for Kotzebue's death, but as Nassau's

4. "*Mannheim," *AZ*, 16, 17 April 1819.

5. Büssem, *Karlsbader Beschlüsse*, pp. 130–41.

6. Cotta to Friedrich Staegemann, 27 April 1819, in Rühl, *Briefe und Aktenstücke* 1:353–54.

7. Gentz to Metternich, 23, 25 April 1819, in Wittichen and Salzer, vol. 3, part 1, pp. 407–8, 411–12.

Baron von Marschall observed, the Federation might nevertheless be overreacting, as one is inclined to do when "contending with a ghost."[8] It is unlikely that even Metternich believed journalists were a revolutionary threat. He had gone to Carlsbad with bigger fish to fry. For him the critical weakness of the Federal Act was not its half-hearted attitude toward the press but its uncertain relationship to the new assemblies whose creation had become the main object of the reform movement. The weakness of these parliamentary bodies was to him small comfort, since their present condition did not exclude further innovation. But he was quite unable to persuade his fellow ministers to accept his narrowly traditionalist interpretation of "ständische Verfassungen."[9]

As a target for repression, the press was Metternich's second choice but not necessarily a bad one. When the Carlsbad decrees were enacted, the press was the only institution in Germany—not excepting the new southern diets, whose membership was drawn mainly from the nobility and the bureaucracy—that claimed to speak for the German people as a whole. The claim may have been inflated or even false, but that it should have been made at all was troubling. There was every reason to believe that, if the spread of constitutional initiatives was to be checked, the press, despite its overwhelming weakness in relation to the state, had to be controlled while it was still isolated.

In the decade following the Carlsbad Conference political writing in Germany declined precipitously.[10] Within a year, that portion of the "oppositional" press that had sheltered in the small states of the north had ceased to exist. In the south, however, the full weight of the decrees was felt more slowly. Württemberg in particular was home to a different view of the Federation than the one that prevailed at Carlsbad, a conception that emphasized the interests of the constitutional lands of "the Third Germany," as opposed to those of Austria and Prussia. This point of view found forceful expression in an anonymous book by Friedrich Lindner, the *Manuscript aus Süd-Deutschland*, which created a sensation when it appeared in 1820 and was attributed to a wide range of political personalities in the south, including Karl von Wangenheim and King William himself.[11] Although Württemberg's government had made no formal objection to the decrees, its adherence was nonetheless accompanied by important, if unstated, reservations about their propriety.[12]

---

8. Marschall to Duke William of Nassau, 18 Aug. 1819, in Albert Henche, "Die Karlsbader Konferenzen nach den amtlichen Berichten und den vertraulichen Briefen des Frh. von Marschall an Herzog Wilhelm von Nassau," *Nassauische Annalen* 59 (1939): 94.

9. So argues Büssem in *Karlsbader Beschlüsse*, the most exhaustive study of the conference and its origins; cf. Wolfgang Mager, "Das Problem der Landständischen Verfassungen auf dem Wiener Kongress 1814/15," *Historische Zeitschrift* 217 (1974): 296–346.

10. Büssem, *Karlsbader Beschlüsse*, p. 432.

11. Fehr, "Leben und Schriften des Kurländers Lindner," pp. 671–4.

12. Kissling, "Württemberg und die Karlsbader Beschlüsse," pp. 18–26.

Serious political writing thus survived longer in Cotta's homeland than elsewhere. In the wake of the *Tribüne*, Cotta personally had lost his taste for anything delicate. When Ludwig Börne approached him about taking over publication of his Frankfurt monthly the *Wage*, Cotta replied that it seemed to him "not advisable."[13] But Cotta did arrange for the journal to appear under the imprint of his longtime associate Heinrich Laupp, to whom he had sold his Tübingen facilities a few years before. Cotta also tried to persuade Börne to assume the editorship of the *Europäische Annalen*, whose revival was once again on his mind.[14] Börne declined, recommending instead his friend Friedrich Murhard.[15]

Murhard's background reflected the same intellectual predispositions and Francophile sympathies shared by so many of Cotta's collaborators. Like Ernst Posselt, the last man to have his name on the cover of the *Annalen*, Murhard had been educated at Göttingen, where he had been taught to see the press as the quintessential instrument of political and cultural progress. Like Friedrich Lindner, he drew as much inspiration from the Confederation of the Rhine as from the War of Liberation. Murhard regarded Napoleon as, on balance, a force for good in Germany. From 1810 to 1813 he edited the official *Moniteur Westphalien*, in which he portrayed the new regime as the harbinger of legal equality, administrative rationality, and, eventually, representative government.[16] In 1817 he moved to Frankfurt, where his politics acquired an increasingly federalist cast, mainly under the influence of Wangenheim. By the time he made Cotta's acquaintance, Murhard was convinced that Germany's future depended on the solidarity of the middle states.

Under Murhard's leadership Posselt's old journal, now retitled the *Allgemeine politische Annalen*, again acquired a vision and a voice. In the first issue Murhard described his intentions in terms Posselt would have found familiar, emphasizing the importance of historical context and the need (still allegedly unmet in Germany) for a broad view of public affairs.[17] It soon became clear, however, that the new *Annalen* was intended to be something more: "an organ that would foster the development of German federalism and protect and defend the rights of the less powerful states against the preponderance of the two great powers."[18] It thus stands in the same line of development as Wangenheim's

13. Cotta to Börne, 2 Nov. 1819, Stadt- und Universitätsbibliothek, Frankfurt am Main, Börne-Nachlass, letter 111.

14. Cotta to Börne, 18 Oct. 1820, ibid., letter 114.

15. Börne to Cotta, 25 Oct., 3 Nov. 1820, in Börne, *Sämtliche Schriften* 5:658–61. Cf. Murhard to Cotta, 21 Nov. 1820, in Fehling and Schiller, *Briefe an Cotta* 2:149–53.

16. Wilhelm Wiedemann, "Friedrich Murhard (1778–1853) und der Altliberalismus," *Zeitschrift des Vereins für hessische Geschichte und Landeskunde* 55 (1926): 238.

17. Friedrich Murhard, "Vorwort," *Allgemeine politische Annalen* 1 (1821): 3–6.

18. Murhard to Cotta, 4 Feb. 1823, CA; an advertisement in the *AZ* also described the *Annalen* as the organ of "the constitutional states of Germany" (17 April 1822 [Beilage]).

aborted *Lotse*, which the new *Annalen* closely resembled, and the *Tribüne* as originally conceived by Lindner. It proved a substantial success. Circulation, which had fallen into the low hundreds before Murhard's arrival, quickly rose to over a thousand,[19] a considerable achievement for a southern journal denied entry into Austria.

For over three years the *Annalen* remained exempt from the prevailing dullness of political writing in Germany. It published articles by a number of writers whose work had been suppressed elsewhere: the economist Julius von Soden, who, along with Murhard's brother Karl, was an early advocate of customs reform; Ludwig Börne; Joseph Görres; Hans von Gagern; Johannes Weitzel, former editor of the radical *Rheinische Blätter*; and Lindner, whose misadventure with Kotzebue, combined with his imperfectly concealed authorship of the *Manuscript aus Süd-Deutschland*, made him the most aggravating political writer of the early 1820s.[20] The journal also included regular reviews of recent political literature, some of which was otherwise unavailable, having already been placed under the ban.

The *Annalen*'s view of the Third Germany was moderate. It accepted the Federation, including its two great powers, as the only realistic expression of German nationhood, and it took a critical view of schemes that smacked of south German separatism—a common, and not unjustified, criticism of Lindner's *Manuscript*. But the contributors to the *Annalen* all insisted that the Federation was a freestanding entity, existing primarily to protect its members' international interests, which were thought to consist in thoroughgoing neutrality, particularly toward the insurrections then under way in Spain, Italy, and Greece. Secondarily, it ought to promote Germany's economic development, which was seen as intrinsic to the competition among nations. The Federation's role in these areas, furthermore, was legitimized as an extension of the consti-

---

19. Wiedemann, "Murhard," p. 241.

20. Julius Soden, "Aphorismen über Handelsfreiheit," *Annalen* 7 (1822): 185–92; Karl Murhard, "Die Nahrungslösigkeit in Deutschland seit hergestelltem Frieden und die Mittel zu deren Abhülfe," *Annalen* 8 (1822): 210–42; Ludwig Börne, "Ueber Herrn von Villele und dessen politischen Stellung," *Annalen* 8 (1822): 124–42; idem, "Politische Kleinigkeiten," *Annalen* 9 (1823): 285–88; Joseph Görres, "Politische Ideen," *Annalen* 5 (1822): 108–10, 191–94, and 6 (1822): 90–96 (cf. the favorable review of his controversial *Deutschland und die Revolution, Annalen* 4 [1821]: 227–55); Hans von Gagern, "Politische Reflexionen," *Annalen* 10 (1823): 230–35; Johannes Weitzel, "Gedanken über politische Dinge," *Annalen* 5 (1822): 288–92; idem, "Napoleon und dessen Urtheil über mehrer der ausgezeichnetsten Männer seiner Zeit," *Annalen* 9 (1823): 280–84 and 10 (1823): 218–29; and Friedrich Lindner, "Kritische Untersuchungen über die Politik des englischen Ministeriums," *Annalen* 6 (1822): 97–163, 193–260; idem, "Die politische Reform und die neuen Interessen," *Annalen* 7 (1822): 301–29. Cf. Murhard's review of Lindner's pamphlet *Ueber die gegenwärtige Lage von Europa* ("Neues Manuscript aus Deutschland," *Annalen* 5 [1822]: 195–220), and Gentz's scathing attack on the same work in the *AZ* ("Vom Lech," 21 March 1822 [Beilage]).

tutional life of its members; its political authority was correspondingly limited, so that even emergency measures, like those taken at Carlsbad, remained subject to the discretion of the princes and their assemblies.

That such views could be advanced with something approaching frankness four years after the establishment of universal censorship in Germany was a reflection of the sympathy they enjoyed in Stuttgart and of their congruence with the policy that Wangenheim pursued on William's behalf in Frankfurt.[21] Having agreed at Carlsbad to impose a censorship for which Württemberg law made no provision, William's government proceeded to treat the decrees as it might have treated an imperial press edict fifty years before: as an important general instruction, but one that admitted of distinctions—between political and nonpolitical writing, and between domestic and foreign affairs. But the Carlsbad decrees did not in fact acknowledge such considerations, and William's retreat from them was marked by the demise of a number of publications that his government, left to itself, would have tolerated. Börne, having grown weary of the need for ever greater discretion, gave up the *Wage* toward the end of 1821. The *Volksfreund aus Schwaben* disappeared the following June; its successor, the Tübingen *Patriot*, survived less than a year. And in May 1823 the Federation, acting on its own authority, banned publication of the Stuttgart *Teutsche Beobachter*.[22]

In constitutional terms, the order of execution against the *Teutsche Beobachter*, the first to be issued under the Carlsbad decrees, was an act without precedent, a decisive defeat that would eventually force William to recall Wangenheim from Frankfurt and abandon his attempts to create a coalition of constitutional monarchies within the Federation.[23] Thereafter Murhard's days as an editor were clearly numbered, though his fall, when it came, had an almost accidental quality: he was arrested in January 1824 while on a personal errand in Hesse and charged with the unlawful publication of official documents—confidential reports of the Central Investigative Commission in Mainz.[24] He was released eight months later, on condition that he refrain from working as a journalist for five years. It was, he told Cotta, a piece of awful luck, which "at any

21. Curt Albrecht, *Die Triaspolitik des Frhrn. K. Aug. von Wangenheim* (Stuttgart, 1914).

22. Kissling, "Württemberg und die Karlsbader Beschlüsse," pp. 27–90; Eugen Schneider, "Die Zensur der Presse in Württemberg," in *Aus der württembergischen Geschichte: Vorträge und Abhandlungen* (Stuttgart, 1926), pp. 136–54. On the action against the *Teutsche Beobachter*, see Julius Collmann, *Quellen, Materialien, und Commentar des gemein deutschen Preßrechts* (Berlin, 1844), pp. 538–626.

23. Albrecht, *Triaspolitik*, pp. 143–65.

24. See "Geschichte und Verhandlungen der Mainzer Zentral-Untersuchungs-Kommission für die demagogischen Umtriebe in Deutschland," *Annalen* 8 (1822): 13–71; and especially "Unterdrückung des *Teutschen Beobachters* durch einen Bundestagsbeschluß vom 30sten Mai 1823," *Annalen* 10 (1823): 239–79. Cf. Karl Murhard to Cotta, 22 Jan. 1824, in Fehling and Schiller, *Briefe an Cotta* 2 : 167n.

rate had the virtue of exposing, in all its fearful nakedness, the pervasive abuse of police power . . . [once] virtually unheard of in Germany."[25]

While this was arguably true, luck hardly entered into it. By 1824 Württemberg's isolation within the Federation was complete—its resistance to the Carlsbad decrees had already become an important argument for their renewal, to which William was now forced to accede. In defending the press, William had only been defending his own sovereign rights. The *Annalen*, in turn, had advanced a view of the Federation that was supposed to draw allies to his side. But when the test came, the alliance failed to gel—none of the middle states opposed the federal action against Württemberg—after which there could be no question of continuing in the same vein. By the time the decrees were reaffirmed in July, Cotta had already replaced Murhard with the Bavarian state councillor, Joseph von Belli de Pino, an appointment that effectively placed the *Annalen* under the protection of the Bavarian ministry of foreign affairs.[26] The journal again became a vehicle for nondescript essays and translations from the foreign press.

The failure of the Third Germany to present a serious challenge to the forces embodied in the Carlsbad decrees seems so inevitable that it is easy to forget how uncertain the future of the Federation looked in the early 1820s and how much credence was attached to the ideas being advanced by Lindner, Wangenheim, and Murhard. As a constitutional alternative for Germany, their program suffered from a fatal circularity: its articulation in journals like the *Annalen* depended on the real existence of the institutions they were trying to create. Even so, their careful calculations of population, wealth, and social resources, which showed that the heterogeneous lands of the west and south might constitute a match for their larger neighbors, were not wrong. The Federation simply offered no means of giving these resources a political shape. As an economic proposition, however, these ideas would soon prove their value, by contributing to the emergence of a broad movement for commercial and customs reform, as a stand-in for the constitutional debate that had now unmistakably fallen into abeyance.

PERFIDIOUS NEUTRALITY

Like Württemberg, Bavaria greeted the enactment of the Carlsbad decrees with mixed feelings. The mixture, though, was somewhat different. The consolidation of the German lands under Napoleon had left Württemberg the largest of the small German states. Bavaria remained, in its own eyes, the smallest of the large states. As far as the Wittelsbachs

25. Murhard to Cotta, 8 Oct. 1824, ibid., pp. 167–69.

26. See the correspondence between Karl von Gravenreuth and the Foreign Ministry, 7, 12 March 1825, M Inn 25097/II.

were concerned, there had always been a "Third Germany," and its capital was Munich. Whereas Württemberg's government considered the defense of its autonomy impossible without the support of the other constitutional lands, Max Joseph's ministers were more confident of their internal position, and of their ability to withstand the disapproval of outsiders. Although they had their own reservations about the preemptive character of the Federation's action, their response was not tinged by any lingering reformism. Rather, Bavaria reacted to Carlsbad in a spirit of old-fashioned particularism. Having voted for the decrees without scruple, Max Joseph's government proceeded to publish only those parts they deemed appropriate.[27] In the years to come they would accommodate themselves to the Federation's actions in the same spirit of grudging cooperation they had displayed toward the French a few years before.[28]

In a legal sense, the regulation of the Bavarian press had changed little since the War of Liberation: it remained vaguely repressive in spirit and haphazard in practice. The French-inspired constitution of 1808 had made Bavaria among the most modern states in Germany, with strong guarantees of civil and fiscal equality for all citizens, religious toleration, significant provisions encouraging land reform and abolishing serfdom, a judiciary well insulated from administrative corruption, and a rationally organized ministerial bureaucracy—a triumph, in short, of clear-eyed, reform-minded absolutism.[29] When it came to the press, however, the reforming vision had remained blurred: the press was simply accorded whatever freedom the law allowed. A seemingly more forthright formulation was achieved in the revised constitution of 1818, which in its fourth section guaranteed "freedom of the press and book trade"; but the accompanying third appendix asserted that this clause was simply a restatement of the law of 1803, the egregious obscurity of which had contributed to the subsequent suppression of the *Allgemeine Zeitung* in France. A plea for clarification from Finance Minister Maximilian von Lerchenfeld, the most progressive voice in the cabinet, was rejected by his colleagues.[30] The issue was then taken up in the Diet,

27. The *AZ* published the decrees intact on 3–7 Oct. 1819. They were officially promulgated ten days later in the *Münchener politische Zeitung*, minus those provisions that pertained to the Federation's right to issue orders of execution against member states, a fact to which the *AZ* later drew attention ("*München," 21 Oct. 1819). The Bavarian government held only the Federal Act of 1815 to be absolutely binding, because its authority was acknowledged in the Bavarian constitution three years later; this condition was not thought to apply to subsequent federal decrees. On the Carlsbad decrees specifically, see Max von Lerchenfeld, *Die Bairische Verfassung und die Karlsbader Beschlüsse* (Nördlingen, 1883).

28. The evolution of Bavarian press policy after Carlsbad is described in detail in Manfred Treml, *Bayerns Pressepolitik zwischen Verfassungstreue und Bundespflicht, 1815–1837* (Berlin, 1977); on the developments discussed in this section, see pp. 74–110.

29. So characterized by Aretin, *Bayerns Weg zum souveränen Staat*, p. 138.

30. Theodor Bitterauf, "Zensur der politischen Zeitungen," p. 328.

where the leaders of the liberal opposition demanded that firm instructions be given to the censors, an unusual spectacle, to say the least. With the enactment of the Carlsbad decrees, however, the firm instructions seemed to have arrived, the only remaining question being the manner in which they would be applied.

As far as the application of censorship went, official thinking had become more sophisticated. Censorship in Bavaria was always intended to protect certain ideas or institutions from public criticism. The list of topics deemed in need of protection might grow long or short, and its contents might be elaborated with greater or lesser specificity—length and specificity being roughly synonymous with hard times for the press. During the years of the French alliance the list of protected topics grew long, in part because of the presence of the *AZ*. Even then, the structure of the censor's job did not change: he was a gatekeeper with a list, sometimes illegible, often out of date, that he used to vet whatever came before him. With the defeat of France, however, German public life had become so clamorous as to confuse even the most diligent sentinels. For Montgelas, the issue had been cast in sharp relief by the *AZ*'s coverage of the Vienna Congress. Clearly it was no longer enough to declare certain topics out of bounds. It also seemed essential to eliminate "whatever tended to make newspapers into a battlefield of opinion, as was the case recently, for example, with the articles for and against Prussia and Saxony."[31]

Here was a standard as fatal to Cotta's aspirations as the centralization of censorship proposed by the French ten years earlier. Cotta's dealings with the Bavarian authorities always hinged on the defense of two principles. First, censorship of the *AZ* should be in the hands of senior local officials, to avoid the political hypersensitivity that would come from too much direct involvement with the ministry. Second, whatever offense might be taken could be compensated for by balanced coverage, so that offense, if it could not be avoided, would at least be evenly distributed. The first of these questions had dominated Cotta's relations with Munich in the Napoleonic period. The second would dominate the early 1820s. If Montgelas's view were to prevail, it would do far more than limit the range of the *AZ*'s reporting; it would undermine the very rationale for its existence, which was precisely to provide a battlefield on which the conflict of ideas could be played out.

The last two years of Montgelas's tenure were filled with bitter recrimination between Stegmann and the authorities, despite a sharp decline in foreign protests of the kind that had dogged the *AZ* in the past. A good deal of material was suppressed outright,[32] and the ministry sani-

31. Order of 12 March 1815, ibid., pp. 325–26.
32. Stegmann to Cotta, 12 April 1815, CA.

tized many other manuscripts.[33] Still, the censor continued to find his task confounding.[34] When Württemberg abolished censorship in 1817, however, it forced a change of heart in Bavaria too. Rather than see the *AZ* moved back to Stuttgart,[35] Max Joseph agreed that the newspaper should be allowed to "accept articles *pro et contra*, [to foster] a generally free and dignified discussion, . . . and also to accept analytic and polemical articles about German constitutional and religious affairs."[36] Thereafter the *AZ*'s troubles abated considerably.[37]

It was the express purpose of the Carlsbad decrees to eliminate just such indirect leverage, by insuring that a publisher's problems would follow him wherever he went. The burden to act, however, still rested with the states—and somehow this remained a problem. In the wake of Carlsbad, Bavaria was besieged by complaints from Vienna,[38] which persuaded Montgelas's successor, Alois von Rechberg, that he had to do more about Bavaria's "miserable newspapers." But what? Rechberg could only despair of Bavaria's local officials, men of "very limited experience" who, he wrote to Metternich, had been "corrupted by twenty years of false theories and literary license."[39] He also worried, with regard to the *AZ*, that a ban on opinion would damage the conservative cause the most, by making it impossible to publish material intended to thwart the "firebrands of revolution." Nothing Bavaria could do, finally, would matter much as long as Württemberg remained uncooperative. Better, then, for Austria to "strike and strike hard; a single example [will suffice] to communicate the true intentions of government, and drive these reptiles back into the darkness."[40]

Words of such precise ferocity are difficult to discount. But in fact there was never any question of allowing the *AZ* to be chosen as an ex-

33. Stegmann, "Protocoll," 6 Feb. 1816, and Gravenreuth to Montgelas, 9 April 1817, M Inn 25097/I.

34. Gravenreuth to the Foreign Ministry, 26 April 1817, and to Max Joseph, 10 Oct. 1817, ibid.

35. Cotta to the Foreign Ministry, 6 Sept. 1817, and Cotta to Gravenreuth, 4 Nov. 1817, M Inn 25097/I; Chevalier de St. Mars [French envoy in Munich] to Richelieu [French foreign minister], 25 Aug. 1817, in Anton Chroust, ed., *Gesandtschaftsberichte aus München, 1814–1848. Abteilung I: Die Berichte der französischen Gesandten*, Schriftenreihe zur bayerischen Landesgeschichte, vols. 18–19, 21, 24 (Munich, 1935–37), 1:33–34.

36. Decree of 14 Nov. 1817, in Bitterauf, "Zensur der politischen Zeitungen," pp. 327–28.

37. They did not disappear. Stegmann still found censorship delays trying, and it remained difficult to publish material critical of the Catholic church (Stegmann to Cotta, 4 Jan. 1819, CA).

38. Bitterauf, "Zensur der politischen Zeitungen," pp. 342–43.

39. Rechberg to Metternich, 15 Aug. 1820, in Anton Chroust, ed., *Gesandtschaftsberichte aus München, 1814–1848. Abteilung II: Die Berichte der österreichischen Gesandten*, Schriftenreihe zur bayerischen Landesgeschichte, vols. 33, 36–38 (Munich, 1938–43), 1:316–17.

40. Rechberg to Metternich, 9 Oct. 1820, ibid., pp. 321–23.

ample for the rest of Germany. However much Bavaria might have chafed from its presence, the government continued to have a strong stake in the newspaper's existence. Cotta's publication had brought Max Joseph's land a kind of prestige it enjoyed in no other field. The *AZ* provided an ideal platform for the government and its allies that even Rechberg was reluctant to give up; it had almost unfailingly presented Bavarian affairs in a satisfactory light; and it had become a tax-paying business of some importance.

All these considerations would become more pronounced in the post-Carlsbad era. Metternich, in laying waste to the opposition press, had also dispatched most of Cotta's competitors, thus ushering in an era of unprecedented growth for the *AZ*. In the aftermath of the war, the paper's circulation had gone up sharply, reaching thirty-one hundred at the height of Württemberg's constitutional crisis.[41] Thereafter it declined somewhat, owing to heightened competition for the public's attention.[42] Within a year of Carlsbad, however, sales increased by 50 percent, and by the end of the decade they would more than double.[43] At the time of Cotta's death in 1832, the *AZ*'s circulation stood securely above six thousand, and it was bringing in a clear profit of almost thirty-one thousand gulden per year. Its capital value was perhaps five times as great.[44]

The Carlsbad decrees thus set in motion two contradictory lines of development in the history of the *Allgemeine Zeitung*: a descending line of political reticence and an ascending line of increasing prestige and prosperity. In the beginning there is no question which was the stronger. The editorial copies that Stegmann sent on to Stuttgart in 1820–21 are full of marginal notations drawing Cotta's attention to the censors' interference. By the start of 1822, however, the two lines were already beginning to converge. After a letter from Friedrich Gentz had led to a ban on independent news from Austria,[45] Cotta went to Munich to talk things over with the king and his ministers, a visit that clearly went far beyond the usual mending of fences. Before the year was out Cotta had been admitted to the hereditary nobility of Bavaria, and he and his son Georg were made *Kammerherren*.[46] Cotta also strengthened his acquain-

---

41. Stegmann to Cotta, 10 May 1816, CA.

42. In 1817, 2,768 subscriptions were sold; in 1818, 2,684 (*Druckauftragsbuch*, CA).

43. The *Druckauftragsbuch* sets circulation at 3,800 for 1821 and at 4,007 for the first quarter of 1822 (cf. Stegmann to Cotta, 25 July 1822, CA). Subscriptions climbed above 6,000 early in 1831.

44. Circulation figure from *Druckauftragsbuch* (CA); financial data from Lohrer, *Cotta*, p. 88.

45. Stegmann to Cotta, 13 Dec. 1821, CA.

46. Otto Steuer, *Cotta in München, 1827–1831* (Munich, 1931), p. 14. Cotta became Baron Cotta von Cottendorf on September 4, 1822.

tance with Crown Prince Ludwig, who had long held Cotta in high es-
teem because of his literary associations and who hoped to attract part
of the Cotta Verlag to Munich.[47] None of these signs of personal regard
held any immediate benefits for the *AZ*: Stegmann still felt that it was
becoming impossible to honor the promise of "universality" implicit in
the *AZ*'s title.[48] But they did suggest that, in a crisis, Cotta would not be
without resources.

The crisis came the next summer, on the heels of the order of execution against Württemberg. Rechberg, hoping to take advantage of the
exemplary case for which he had pleaded, asked Metternich for another
"menacing gesture," aimed this time at the "perfidious and false neutrality" of the *AZ*, whose elusive practices seemed to him more dangerous than outright opposition.[49] Metternich obliged by sending a member
of the Vienna Book Commission, J. B. Rupprecht, to Stuttgart to im-
portune Cotta for allowing the *AZ* to become "a contemptible play-
ground for partisan mercenaries."[50] The two men then traveled together to Augsburg and Munich, where Cotta had to endure a bruising
interview with Rechberg. Rupprecht also provided the ministry with
what might have proven a crucial piece of advice: censors should insist
on receiving the original manuscripts of articles, not proofs or transcripts. This was a menacing gesture indeed, the first to go beyond moral
outrage and include a practical assault on the independence of the *AZ*'s
correspondents.

The order of execution against the *Teutsche Beobachter* ended what
chance there was of Cotta's moving the *AZ* to Stuttgart. It was still
possible, however, that he might give up a venture for which he was
losing his taste, a prospect made plausible by the fact that, in order to
carry on, he would have to incur major new expenses. By the middle of
1823 the *AZ*'s circulation was reaching the point where Cotta's manual
presses could no longer keep up. The alternative, he explained to Rechberg, was to purchase a steam press, which would allow him to maintain
the *AZ* at its present level and consolidate the production of another
dozen or so periodicals in Augsburg.[51] Other investments would flow

47. Ludwig to Cotta, 22 Feb. 1812, 5 June 1818, 4 Sept. 1822, CA; and Cotta to Ludwig, 15 Mar. 1822, Bayerisches Hauptstaatsarchiv, Abteilung III: Geheimes Hausarchiv,
Nachlass Ludwig I, I A 42/III.

48. Stegmann to Cotta, 26 June 1822, CA.

49. Rechberg to Metternich, 1 May 1823, in Chroust, *Berichte der österreichischen Gesandten* 1:500–501.

50. Rupprecht to Cotta, 22 July 1823, in Heyck, *Allgemeine Zeitung*, pp. 219–20.

51. Cotta's manual presses could produce forty-eight hundred copies per day as a theoretical maximum, which was by no means obtainable in practice (Stegmann to Cotta, 11
April 1822, CA). In July 1822 the *AZ*'s circulation was edging above forty-one hundred,
and logistical problems were becoming severe (Stegmann to Cotta, 25 July 1822, CA). The
steam-powered cylinder press that Cotta proposed to buy from Koenig & Bauer in Würz-

from this move, everything from a new building to house the press to a paper factory to keep it supplied. But machines of this kind were not cheap—the one Cotta had in mind cost sixty thousand gulden—and such a purchase could hardly be considered given the present atmosphere, "in which the publication of the *Allgemeine Zeitung* might well become impossible."

Cotta, moreover, had undertaken his own consultations with Vienna, and the instructions he had received were not the same as those proposed by Rupprecht, nor were they intended to "rob the *AZ* of its independence, impartiality, [or] its receptivity to all parties."[52] He soon returned to Munich for further discussions, at the end of which he informed Stegmann that the *AZ* could look forward to milder and more reasonable supervision.[53] Rupprecht's sound advice was not implemented; the steam press was purchased in due course, to the special satisfaction of Crown Prince Ludwig;[54] and Stegmann was pleased to report, early in 1824, that he was now allowed to publish even "oppositional" articles, provided they were balanced by comparable material from the other side.[55]

One thus arrives at a slightly cynical explanation for the *AZ*'s survival as an independent newspaper: Bavaria's political and pecuniary interest in Cotta—which would become even more pronounced following Ludwig's accession in 1825—finally outweighed its desire to please Austria. But one ought not to overlook the disingenuous note in Rechberg's original solicitation of "menace" from Vienna, which had come at a time when his own government was refusing to consider any revision of its press laws at the constitutional level, despite quite spontaneous encouragement from the same source.[56] Stegmann believed that the ministry's

---

burg could produce about eight hundred copies per hour. Such machines had been used in England for a decade, but Cotta's was only the second one purchased in Germany. On the technical characteristics of steam presses, see James Moran, *Printing Presses* (Berkeley and Los Angeles, 1973), pp. 107–41.

52. Cotta to Rechberg, 28 June 1823, M Inn 25097/I.

53. Cotta to Stegmann, 30 July 1823, in Heyck, *Allgemeine Zeitung*, p. 219; cf. Cotta to Rechberg, 10 Aug. 1823, M Inn 25097/I.

54. Cotta to Ludwig, 23 Sept. 1824, M Inn 25097/I.

55. Stegmann to Cotta, 20 Jan. 1824, CA; cf. Augsburg District Government to the Foreign Ministry, 18 Mar. 1824, and Gravenreuth to Rechberg, 29 Dec. 1823, M Inn 25097/I. All previous accounts of Rupprecht's mission are garbled except that of Treml (*Bayerns Pressepolitik*, pp. 103–4), which is based on Rupprecht's report to Metternich. But even Treml stops short of finding the real outcome of this incident, perhaps because, having construed press policy as a straightforward contest between freedom and repression, he fails to see that the *AZ*'s success improved Cotta's leverage, not the government's. He concludes that, after 1823, "the liberal spirit no longer found any loopholes through which to make itself visible [in the *AZ*]" (p. 105), a judgment that was not shared by the paper's readers, or by the authorities.

56. Bitterauf, "Zensur der politischen Zeitungen," pp. 349–50.

hearts were all with Metternich[57]—Rechberg, certainly, was an Ultra to the bone. But even Rechberg knew that Cotta's paper was not just an organ of the politically dispossessed; it was also an indispensable source of information and instruction for all sorts of people—scholars, businessmen, public officials—whose satisfaction with the status quo was not in doubt. And it cannot be sufficiently emphasized that Metternich understood this perfectly well. If Max Joseph's government had ever been called upon to justify its accommodation with Cotta, it need have looked no further than Austria, which might at any moment have excluded the *AZ* from its borders but never did.

In the hinterlands of the Habsburg empire the *AZ* had passed for some time as a champion of "unlimited popular sovereignty," whose effect on public opinion cried out for redress.[58] In Vienna, in contrast, it was accepted that, although one might take exception now and then, Cotta and Stegmann were possessed of sufficient "fear, and respect for humanity," to maintain a decent balance in their coverage.[59] Certainly the prospect of confronting the *AZ* in public was not appealing.[60] Given a general determination to act against the German press, however, the question of whether the *AZ* ought finally to be excluded from Austria had at least to be considered. Friedrich Gentz was reluctant to recommend any action unless it could be undertaken in concert with Prussia. Even then, the matter would be deserving of careful reflection.[61] Stegmann, moreover, was confident of the conclusion Gentz would reach. He found it most unlikely that Austria would take such a step against a newspaper that the Austrian public esteemed as an oracle and in which a single report could cause the value of Austrian currency to rise or fall on international exchanges.[62]

This judgment proved to be substantially correct. Over the course of the 1820s reports that the *AZ* was about to be banned in Austria became a routine part of Cotta's existence. Some had to be taken seriously; Stegmann's telling observation about the *AZ*'s financial influence was inspired by a demand from Gentz that that influence be wielded more carefully,[63] which it was. Others seem to have originated in efforts to assure provin-

57. Stegmann to Cotta, 11 Dec. 1823, CA.

58. Count von Bissingen [Governor of Tyrolia] to Police Minister Sedlnitzky, 24 Jan. 1819, in Giese, "Pressegesetzgebung," cols. 417–18.

59. Gentz to Pilat, 1 Aug. 1819, in Gentz, *Briefe an Pilat* 1 : 390–91.

60. The one occasion when such a feud threatened to break out brought a defiant reply from Stegmann (*AZ*, 31 Dec. 1815) and a quick apology from Gentz (Gentz to Cotta, 13 Jan. 1816, in Fehling and Schiller, *Briefe an Cotta* 2 : 42; cf. Gentz to Pilat, 2 Sept. 1816, in Gentz, *Briefe an Pilat* 1 : 390–91).

61. Gentz to Metternich, 31 May 1820, in Wittichen and Salzer, *Briefe*, vol. 3, pt. 2, pp. 1–2.

62. Stegmann to Cotta, 13 Dec. 1821, in Heyck, *Allgemeine Zeitung*, p. 253.

63. Gentz to Cotta, 4 Dec. 1821, in Fehling and Schiller, *Briefe an Cotta* 2 : 50–52.

cial governors that their concerns were being attended to.[64] But by and
large these persistent rumors were less a political program than a commercial venture, undertaken by Joseph Pilat to supplement his stipend
as a correspondent. Pilat's threats, Cotta would complain, were "as regular as the monsoons," coinciding with the semiannual renewal of the *AZ*'s
postal permit. Unlike the monsoons, however, these storms would always disperse once the appropriate payment had been made. In the long
run, what was most galling was not the expense but the "infrequent,
incomplete, and insignificant" correspondence that Cotta got in return.[65]
    The *AZ*'s relationship with Austria is thus best understood as one of
mutual dependence. Like the sword of Damocles, Metternich's campaign of intimidation is easily misinterpreted. It was a real sword, but it
wasn't really supposed to fall; if it had, the impact would have been felt
as keenly in Vienna as in Augsburg. By the end of the 1820s something
over 20 percent of the *AZ*'s circulation was in Austria;[66] and the loss
of that many subscribers would have been a blow to the paper's solvency—though not so severe as the one suffered in the worst years of
the Rheinbund, when sales were cut in half. From the Austrian side the
numbers looked equally impressive. Within the Empire as a whole the
AZ's circulation was exceeded only by that of the politically insignificant
Wiener Zeitung; by 1830 the *AZ* was outselling all other foreign newspapers and magazines combined.[67] If the *Allgemeine Zeitung* had been
presented to the Austrian authorities as a new venture, they might well

    64. Sedlnitzky to Otto von Hingenau [Governor of Upper Austria], 27 June 1824, in
Giese, "Pressegesetzgebung," cols. 420–21.
    65. Cotta to Bray, 24 Dec. 1828, in Heyck, *Allgemeine Zeitung*, pp. 253–57.
    66. According to the Vienna post office, the *AZ* had 1,223 Austrian subscribers during
the second half of 1830. The *AZ*'s total circulation at this time was around 6,000 (Giese,
"Pressegesetzgebung," cols. 446–47; and the *Druckauftragsbuch*, CA).
    The extent of the *AZ*'s sales in the Habsburg lands has been exaggerated: Kurt Koszyk
(*Deutsche Presse im 19. Jahrhundert* [Berlin, 1966], p. 62) puts it at "about half," as have
others before him. Although such levels might have been reached in the 1840s, when the
AZ was more firmly in the Austrian camp, during Johann Cotta's lifetime the *AZ*'s circulation was, as far as one can tell from imperfect evidence, disproportionately centered in the
middle-sized states of the Third Germany. In 1822, for instance, the *AZ* already had 300
subscribers in Frankfurt and its environs; and one of the important advantages of the
steam press was that it allowed better coordination with the westbound post (Stegmann to
Cotta, 6 May 1822, CA). That more of the *AZ*'s customers lived in Austria than in any
other state is certain (cf. Lindner to Cotta, 8 Jan. 1827, CA), but in no way is it surprising
demographically. If one adds the *AZ*'s 400 or so Prussian subscribers (Giese, "Pressegesetzgebung," col. 460) to the Austrian total above, it appears that, in 1830, the two German
powers accounted for about a third of the *AZ*'s sales, though they held about two-thirds of
the German-speaking population of Europe (B. R. Mitchell, *European Historical Statistics,
1750–1970* [New York, 1976], pp. 19–27, 57–76).
    67. Giese, "Pressegesetzgebung," cols. 443–54. Stamp taxes on the *AZ* amounted to
over twenty-five thousand gulden per year, just under half of all revenues from this
source, and five times the sum brought in by the *Oesterreichische Beobachter*.

have decided to exclude it from their territory, as they continued to exclude the Nuremberg *Correspondent* despite the judgment of Austria's ambassador in Munich that the *Correspondent* was no worse than the *AZ*.[68] But by 1820 the *AZ* was already a fixture of Austrian public life—it was in fact the chief prop to its existence—and tampering with it seemed to promise more trouble than leaving it alone. Even the suppression of individual issues was problematic.[69]

The internal importance of the *AZ* in Austria also tended to narrow the focus of the ministry's interest in the paper. As far as public opinion went, Bavaria had more to defend than Austria did. Anything that might indirectly strengthen the rudimentary opposition in the Bavarian Diet, or compromise the "monarchical principle" generally, was for Munich a subject of concern. Austria had no such worries. The government's attitude remained resolutely provincial, fixed on its own reputation with the *AZ*'s domestic audience. Gentz put the matter plainly to Cotta:

> For us to attempt to restrict the overall political course of the *AZ* would be a foolish undertaking. The paper is aimed above all at a public, the majority of whom need no instruction in the old ways and values. And if, despite the influence of this public feeling, [your newspaper] does not close itself off absolutely to articles written in the contrary sense, one can nevertheless demand nothing more from the editors. That some of the *AZ*'s political articles have a highly prejudicial effect on our public is certain. But if the *AZ* were excluded from the monarchy the same effect would still be felt through other organs, perhaps even more strongly.
>
> On the other hand, it is my conviction that the Austrian government is entitled to expect that one will not tread too closely to *itself* or to its *vital interests*. . . . Here, then, insofar as I have a voice in these matters, is my summary judgment: as regards European, Asian, African, and American politics, let the *AZ* print what it pleases. . . . But if it should proceed, even by ill-tempered insinuation, to mishandle the state system, the statesmen, or the state credit of Austria . . . then our honor—if not our interest—will force us to deny this newspaper entry to our lands.[70]

In practice, Austria's faith in the public was not as great as Gentz implied. Metternich found much to object to in the *AZ*'s coverage of France, particularly after 1824 when Cotta, perhaps emboldened by his success in facing down Rechberg, added the young opposition journalist Adolphe Thiers to his stable of correspondents in the French capital.[71] In

---

68. Ibid., cols. 515–20.

69. See the correspondence between Sedlnitzky and Hingenau, ibid., cols. 420–21, 424. In contrast to the *AZ*, dozens of issues of Cotta's apolitical *Morgenblatt* were suppressed during the 1820s, apparently for anticlericalism; after 1826 its distribution was severely restricted (ibid., cols. 501–2).

70. Gentz to Cotta, 4 Dec. 1821, in Fehling and Schiller, *Briefe an Cotta* 2:50–52.

71. Thiers's relationship with Cotta is thoroughly analyzed in Marquant, *Thiers et le baron Cotta*, which includes all of Thiers's reports to the *AZ* (roughly 150 between 1824 and

1828 the paper's handling of the Russo-Turkish War, which was perceived to favor Turkey, obliged Cotta to plead his case in Vienna personally;[72] and in the wake of the July Revolution Cotta was forced to place severe, and in the end crippling, restraints on the work of Thiers's even more annoying successor, Heinrich Heine.[73] Overall, however, Austrian pressure was not intended, and would not have sufficed, to deny Stegmann his cherished claim to "universality," which became more convincing with each passing year.

1831) as an appendix. On Cotta's other Parisian correspondents, see ibid., pp. 61–97; and Rutger Booß, *Ansichten der Revolution: Paris-Berichte deutscher Schriftsteller nach der Juli-Revolution 1830* (Cologne, 1977), pp. 83–96.

Cotta's association with Thiers had an important commercial dimension, since it originated in Cotta's desire to find a suitable front man for the purchase of a share in the French newspaper *Le Constitutionnel*, with which Thiers was associated. This transaction, which took place in March of 1824, proved highly profitable to both men. Thereafter an increasing share of the AZ's French correspondence was supplied by journalists associated with this somewhat left-of-center paper—balanced, characteristically, by the work of a prolific royalist, Baron Ferdinand d'Eckstein, editor of the conservative journal *Le Catholique*. Politically, however, the connection created by Cotta's stake in the *Constitutionnel* was strictly one-way. Cotta made no effort to influence the *Constitutionnel*'s political coloration (he owned but one of fifteen shares), or to provide inside information on German affairs of the kind he had once supplied Fouché. Cotta's letters to Thiers, some forty in all, almost invariably dry and businesslike, are in the Bibliothèque Thiers, T. MS. 561².

72. Cotta to Sedlnitzky, 16 June 1828, in Giese, "Pressegesetzgebung," cols. 496–98; Cotta to Bray, 24 Dec. 1828, in Heyck, *Allgemeine Zeitung*, pp. 253–57; cf. Georg Cotta to Johann Cotta, 30 Dec. 1828, CA.

73. It is a tribute to Metternich's reputation as a conspirator that he has been credited with both the genesis and the demise of Heine's correspondence from Paris, which was eventually republished as the *Französische Zustände*. The notion that Heine was an Austrian agent, first advanced by Margaret A. Clark (*Heine et la monarchie de juillet: Etude critique sur les Französische Zustände suivie d'une étude sur le Saint-Simonisme chez Heine* [Paris, 1927]) and repeated without serious demur by Marquant (*Thiers et le baron Cotta*, pp. 96–97), no longer commands much assent, since it was based on nothing more than the perception that his reports did not favor the postrevolutionary government and on the fact that they appeared in the AZ. The Austrian role in the series' end is more firmly established. In April 1832 Friedrich Gentz wrote to Cotta to express his by now familiar concern that the AZ should have opened itself to work of such "plebeian arrogance," to which he added the novel suggestion that Cotta had somehow taken up with an enemy of his own class, a reference to Heine's penchant for attacking not just "the clergy and the nobility," but "businessmen, bankers, men of property and affairs." That Cotta would have taken such a letter seriously is certain; but the prevailing impression that a word in his ear from Vienna was sufficient to cause him to fire the best man on his staff is false. Cotta responded to Gentz's letter by urging the same kind of stylistic circumspection on Heine (via a letter from Kolb) that he had earlier urged on Ludwig Börne, advice that Heine proved equally reluctant to follow (Heine to Cotta, 1 Jan. 1833, in Heine, *Säkularausgabe* 21:47; cf. Kolb to Heine, 15 Sept. 1832, ibid., 21:47), in part because he seems to have become a little bored with the whole project. The question is examined with care in Booß, *Ansichten der Revolution*, pp. 119–30, which includes the text of Gentz's letter and other relevant correspondence. See also Hans Hörling, *Heinrich Heine im Spiegel der politischen Presse Frankreichs von 1831–1841* (Frankfurt am Main, 1977), pp. 103–11.

In the year before the Carlsbad decrees, the *AZ* published articles from at least eighty private sources. Of these, twenty might count as regular contributors, whose articles appeared at least once a month. By 1830 the number of regular correspondents had grown to thirty-five, and their work appeared alongside reports from over one hundred other individuals—an estimate that does not include dozens of unattributed manuscripts passed on to the editors by Cotta. The paper had also grown in a physical sense, thanks to the use of "supplements," which had been introduced early in the *AZ*'s history to make room for long documents and advertising. Despite their nominally special status, these supplements had become a fixed part of every issue by the middle of the decade, so that by 1830 a year's run of the *AZ* was half again as large as it had been ten years before and even so-called extraordinary supplements were commonplace.

This steady expansion of the *AZ*'s coverage was accompanied by a corresponding growth in editorial staff. Since 1815 Stegmann's only professional assistant had been Joseph Widemann, at one time a member of Napoleon's entourage. His role was confined to excerpting and translating material from France and England, in part because, as Stegmann observed, "he tended to conduct himself as if he were the editor of the *Wiener Zeitung* under a Napoleonic government,"[74] a position he had in fact held for a while after 1809. Widemann was joined in 1824 by Albrecht Lebret, described by Austria's ambassador as "a well-known liberal of the Stuttgart type."[75] Politically, Lebret's views were close to Lindner's—his admiration for Napoleon having evolved into a broad sympathy for the Third Germany and the liberal opposition in France. But whether his presence contributed to the prominence these views received in the *AZ* is hard to judge, since his arrival coincided with the improved relations with the censors that followed Cotta's ultimatum to Rechberg.

Far more important was the arrival of Gustav Kolb. Kolb, like Lebret, was born in Stuttgart in 1798. He was thus only the second member of the *AZ*'s staff, and the first with real influence, whose views were not shaped by the cosmopolitanism of the old regime. Kolb had spent his early twenties as a member of the Tübingen *Burschenschaft*, an affiliation that led him to the fringes of the rebellion in Piedmont in 1821 and cost him the post in Württemberg's civil administration for which he was preparing at the university. In 1824 he and fifteen others were charged with conspiracy by the Central Investigative Commission in Mainz; Kolb was sentenced to four years in prison, more than any of his compatriots,

---

74. Stegmann to Cotta, 20 April 1815, CA.

75. Count Ferdinand von Trauttmansdorff to Metternich, 16 Oct. 1823, in Chroust, *Berichte der oesterreichischen Gesandten* 1 : 513.

because, as one of them recalled, "he stood up to everything, took everything on himself, and betrayed no one."[76] In the end he served two years
in Asperg Prison, facilities he shared for a while with Friedrich List, one
of the principal political influences on his life.

Kolb was released at the end of 1826. He was hired by Cotta on the
recommendation of a police official who had interrogated him, an indication that the strength of character Kolb's friends admired was also
evident to his detractors. Originally taken on as a translator, Kolb was
soon given overall responsibility for the AZ's coverage of Germany. Although this decision caused Stegmann some concern,[77] he also recognized that his new colleague (and eventual successor), thirty years his
junior, brought the AZ great energy and resourcefulness; when Kolb
came under fire from the authorities for his apparent sympathy for the
July Revolution, Stegmann defended him to their employer.[78] Like Stegmann, Kolb wrote little himself, but he nevertheless became a key member of the circle of younger men who gathered around Cotta during the
last years of his life.[79]

The political coloration of the newspaper these men produced on
Cotta's behalf was, by design and insistent proclamation, neutral. Yet the
neutrality was, as Rechberg so ineffectually complained, perfidious and
false. If one could somehow aggregate the AZ's coverage, balancing
those reports that favored the status quo against those that did not, one
would certainly discover that the weight lay on the side of passivity and
reaction. But people do not read newspapers in aggregate, and the impression one takes away is not formed by averaging the points of view
one encounters. Although Carlsbad muted the oppositional voices that
had grown up in Germany since the War of Liberation, it could not re-

76. Karl Hase, *Ideale und Irrthümer* (Leipzig, 1872); cited in Heyck, *Allgemeine Zeitung*,
p. 114.

77. Stegmann to Cotta, 11 May 1832, CA.

78. Ibid.

79. There is a considerable body of French historical scholarship on what Alan Spitzer
has called "the generation of 1820" (*The French Generation of 1820* [Princeton, 1987], see
esp. pp. 3–11)—that is, the cadre of young men born at the turn of the nineteenth century, who came of age in the first decades of the restoration. No comparable conception
exists on the German side, and none may be warranted: the generational cohesion Spitzer
describes derives not just from shared historical experiences, but from the centralized
educational and political apparatus of the French state and from the opportunities afforded by Paris as the undisputed center of French culture. It is nevertheless striking how
many men born between, say, the Peace of Basel and the Battle of Austerlitz, found their
way into Cotta's employ by the end of the 1820s. Among them (in addition to Kolb and
Lebret) are Heine (born in 1797), Karl Hermes (1800), Karl Mebold (1798), Wolfgang
Menzel (1798), Wilhelm Mönnich (1799), Friedrich Notter (1801), Paul Pfizer (1801),
Georg Puchta (1798), Wilhelm Schulz-Bodmer (1797), and Johann Wirth (1798). To these
may be added the Frenchman Thiers (1797) and Cotta's son Georg (1795), who assisted
his father in his later years. Most of these men are discussed in chapter 10 below.

store credibility to the official voices that remained. To suppose, for instance, that any number of pedestrian official bulletins could somehow "balance" the heart-felt philhellenism of Friedrich Thiersch's reports on the Greek revolution, or that the long excerpts from the *Journal des Débats* and the *Moniteur*, which formed the backbone of the *AZ*'s coverage of France, were any match for the work of Thiers, Lindner, or Heine, was simply an illusion.

By the time Cotta was called to Vienna to account for the *AZ*'s delinquencies during the Russo-Turkish War, he could no longer pretend that his paper had proven to be a true friend of the authorities. But, he argued, "there is no help for it if the greater talent and energy stand on the liberal side, so as to make a true middle way almost impossible. If this is so, I can only repeat that it is the fault of that wretched *fanaticism [Ultraismus]* that terrifies moderate, respectable people, and daily strengthens the liberal cause." The worst offender was Austria itself, the architect of the existing regime in Germany and the state toward which Cotta felt he had shown the greatest consideration. Apart from Pilat, whose articles usually amounted to little more than excerpts from the *Oesterreichische Beobachter*, Cotta's only regular correspondent in Vienna before 1830 was a dubious colporteur named Häberle, "a man at one moment in the hands of the police and at the next, as usual, one of their tools."[80]

The obligation to rise above the play of parties, in short, did not include the obligation to simulate their existence. Yet it was precisely in this respect that Cotta and his colleagues felt the weight of reaction most painfully. The virtues of *Unparteilichkeit*, after all, become less distinguished once the parties themselves have fallen silent. To the extent that the Carlsbad decrees were just another attempt to tighten censorship in Germany, Cotta was able to mitigate their effect with his usual skill. But Carlsbad also reached to the heart of the public's relationship to the state. By demonstrating that, as a matter of policy, Germany's rulers could simply redefine freedom of the press to mean systematic repression, the decrees threatened to expose the whole political culture of press and parliament to which the *AZ* had dedicated itself as a fraud. The decrees thus represented a calculated reversal of political values, an early application of the Orwellian principle that the sturdiest falsehoods are the exact opposite of the truth.

As sturdy as they were, though, they lacked the plausibility to prevail absolutely. Any application of force dissipates over time. It is thus unsurprising that the second half of the 1820s should have been palpably easier on the press than the first half. The Carlsbad decrees had made

80. Cotta to Bray, 24 Dec. 1828, in Heyck, *Allgemeine Zeitung*, pp. 253–57; cf. Cotta to Sedlnitzky, 16 June 1828, in Giese, "Pressegesetzgebung," cols. 496–98.

"politics" of the contentious variety that had invigorated the Cotta press since the Vienna Congress inconsequential. This was a development whose effects Cotta, for all his cunning, could not escape. But public life continued, flowing in narrower and more circuitous channels than before. The mediating role to which Cotta aspired thus remained available, in a somewhat different form, even in the darkest years of the postwar reaction.

NINE

Political Economy

Compared to the debates we've had over sugar, wine, and tobacco, the Treaty of Westphalia was child's play.

Friedrich von Luxburg to Joseph von Armansperg, May 30, 1829

The movement for economic reform that gave rise to the customs union of 1834 is among the most thoroughly studied aspects of German history between the War of Liberation and the Revolution of 1848.[1] The course of this movement falls into three phases. The first began in 1818 with the enactment of a new, relatively protectionist tariff in Prussia that abolished internal duties and established a unified customs frontier to protect manufacturers from foreign competition. This in turn inspired the second phase, a long series of negotiations that ultimately gave rise early in 1828 to two bilateral commercial treaties, one between Württemberg and Bavaria, the other between Prussia and Hesse-Darmstadt. The third phase began the following year with the reconciliation of these regional alliances and concluded with the establishment of a more comprehensive union in 1834, to which nearly all the Federation's members—with the important exception of Austria—would eventually adhere.

The relationship of these developments to the broader constitutional movement that met defeat in the wake of the Carlsbad decrees raised complex questions for contemporaries, questions that historians still have difficulty resolving. The fiscal crisis created by the wars with France

1. The documents published by Hermann Oncken and F.E.M. Saemisch, eds., *Vorgeschichte und Begründung des deutschen Zollvereins, 1815–1834*, 3 vols. (Berlin, 1934), are fundamental. Among secondary works, the second volume of Hermann von Petersdorff, *Friedrich von Motz: Eine Biographie* (Berlin, 1913); and Michael Doeberl, *Bayern und die wirtschaftliche Einigung Deutschlands* (Munich, 1915), are particularly worthwhile. There are two general studies in English: W. O. Henderson, *The Zollverein*, 2d ed. (Chicago, 1959); and Arnold Price, *The Evolution of the Zollverein* (Ann Arbor, 1949). Helmut Berding, "Die Entstehung des Deutschen Zollvereins als Problem historischer Forschung," in *Vom Staat des Ancien Regime zum modernen Parteienstaat: Festschrift für Theodor Schieder*, ed. Helmut Berding et al. (Munich and Vienna, 1978), pp. 225–37, provides an excellent review of the literature, and a reminder that a great deal remains to be learned on this subject.

had been an important spur to social and administrative reforms, which were in turn closely associated with the revival or modernization of representative institutions, on which the German states had traditionally relied to raise money.[2] If nothing else, the huge public debt left behind in 1815 insured that economic reform could not be dispensed with,[3] and efforts to bring it about remained largely (though not entirely) immune to the reactionary impulses that overwhelmed other aspects of the reformers' program. Customs reform, moreover, was a matter of widespread public comment and controversy right from the start;[4] its achievement thus had the appearance of being based on a broad, independently arrived at consensus. Nevertheless, when success came, it was achieved by purely diplomatic and bureaucratic means, which, far from advancing the cause of constitutional government, actually seemed to call the relevance of representative institutions into question.

This ambiguous connection between public opinion and official conduct is evident in Cotta's involvement with economic reform. As publisher of the *Allgemeine Zeitung* and as a member of the Württemberg Diet, Cotta played a role in educating public and official opinion in economic matters. When the moment for decisive action finally came, however, he was more than willing to lend himself to the clandestine diplomacy that finally made real progress possible. Throughout, he never ceased to insist on the political significance of tariff reform, even on those occasions when it might have been more expedient to cast the issue in narrowly fiscal terms. However narrow the bridge between public opinion and practical results may have been, in other words, it was at least wide enough for one man to cross.

NORTH AND SOUTH

The idea that the German-speaking lands of Europe constituted a single economic unit, defined by concrete interests as well as a common culture, first emerged as a political proposition during the Imperial Diet of 1521. Over the next three hundred years it was the consensus of expert

2. Herbert Obenaus, "Finanzkrise und Verfassungsgebung: Zu den sozialen Bedingungen des frühen deutschen Konstitutionalismus," in *Gesellschaft, Parlament, und Regierung: Zur Geschichte des Parlamentarismus in Deutschland*, ed. Gerhard A. Ritter (Düsseldorf, 1974), pp. 57–75; Hans-Peter Ullmann, "Überlegungen zur Entstehung des öffentlichen, verfassungsmäßigen Kredits in den Rheinbundstaaten (Bayern, Württemberg, und Baden)," *Geschichte und Gesellschaft* 6 (1980): *Napoleonische Herrschaft und Modernisierung*, ed. Helmut Berding, pp. 500–522.

3. Total public debt in Germany increased fivefold between 1780 and 1820, a period when economic activity overall was static or contracting. See Hans-Peter Ullmann, "Die öffentlichen Schulden in Bayern und Baden, 1780–1820," *Historische Zeitschrift* 242 (1986): 31–67.

4. This aspect of the subject is surveyed in Bernd Bab, "Die öffentliche Meinung und den Deutschen Zollverein zur Zeit seiner Entstehung," Ph.D. diss., Berlin, 1930.

opinion that this idea was wrong, a consensus expressed with perfect clarity by the eighteen-hundred-odd customs frontiers that crisscrossed Germany at the end of the eighteenth century. The wars that brought the century to a close were a formidable challenge to this state of affairs, and the forcible territorial consolidation that attended the dissolution of the Holy Roman Empire went a long way toward reducing the number of tariff lines to a more manageable size. The creation of the Confederation of the Rhine might have brought the process of rationalization to a point where it could have continued without external coercion; but the attempt by France to impose a common economic policy on the member states was too obviously a weapon of economic warfare to command real respect. Although the vision of the Third Germany as an economic unit would remain important as an idea, and even as a guide to action, in practice Napoleon succeeded only in elevating the regulation of trade in Germany to the status of a sovereign right, which the new states of the south and west were loath to compromise for any reason whatever.[5] Several attempts at the Congress of Vienna to draw positive lessons from these experiences were beaten back by a combination of Austrian disinterest and southern particularism. As in the matter of copyright, the question of "commerce and trade among the various federal states" was deferred to the Federal Diet, a disposition that would soon become tantamount to a joke.[6]

In the aftermath of the congress, however, Germany's difficulties proved worse than expected. Even under the best circumstances the postwar years would have required important adjustments as governments coped with their accumulated debts and demobilized soldiers were reabsorbed into an inelastic, largely agrarian economy. These problems were compounded by others of a more political character. Having suffered under the Continental system, the German states now suffered from its removal as English goods stockpiled during the war were brought forward at prices that native industry could not match. At the same time, England imposed a protective tariff on grain and other imported goods, a step that was mimicked by the other European powers. To this, finally, was added a gratuitous blow from nature herself, in

5. Eberhard Weis, "Napoleon und der Rheinbund," in *Deutschland und Italien im Zeitalter Napoleons*, ed. Armgard von Reden-Dohna (Wiesbaden, 1979), pp. 57–80; Helmut Berding, "Die Reform des Zollwesens in Deutschland unter dem Einfluß der napoleonischen Herrschaft," *Geschichte und Gesellschaft* 6 (1980): *Napoleonische Herrschaft und Modernisierung*, ed. Helmut Berding, pp. 523–37; and Roger Dufraisse, "Französische Zollpolitik, Kontinentalsperre, und Kontinentalsystem im Deutschland der napoleonischen Zeit," in *Deutschland zwischen Revolution und Restauration*, ed. Helmuth Berding and Hans-Peter Ullmann (Düsseldorf, 1981), pp. 328–52.

6. Ludwig Karl Aegidi, *Aus der Vorzeit des Zollvereins: Beitrag zur deutschen Geschichte* (Hamburg, 1865), p. 59.

the form of a volcanic eruption half a world away, which ruined the harvest of 1816 and laid bare the inability of German governments to cooperate with one another, even in the face of the most pressing public need.[7]

In considering the public and official response to these difficulties, and to the deeper economic deficiencies they revealed, it may be useful to recall that their solution, however obvious in retrospect, was not obvious at the time. The interests that divided the free-trading lands of the German west and north from the less developed, traditionally protectionist territories of the east were as substantive as "interests" can ever be, and the only relevant example offered by history was of little comfort: the abolition of internal tariffs and the creation of a common customs frontier in France had required the better part of a century and had finally been achieved only in the wake of revolution.[8] Economic reform thus became the one aspect of German public life in which relatively free discussion was indisputably useful to government, and the subject was accorded a high degree of tolerance by censors throughout the 1820s. It was thus entirely natural that the *Allgemeine Zeitung* should have become involved in this highly technical issue. After 1819 it was the only newspaper in Germany of national importance, hence a credible forum in which regional interests could be examined and compared; its official audience had always been uniquely extensive, an asset at a time when the crucial objective was to motivate and inform official opinion; and it had always been partial to the kind of erudite articles this question would inspire.

The relationship of the long and elaborate public debate on economic reform, which preoccupied the German press in the 1820s, to the official conduct that culminated in the customs union is difficult to assess. No government of the period would have admitted that any legislative act had been undertaken in response to public pressure. Those agreements that were reached were achieved in secret and unanticipated in the press. The public was thus most thoroughly acquainted with those proceedings that proved fruitless. Nonetheless, Germany's leaders were not indifferent to the controversy going on around them. Negotiations between the various states always included conversations detailing just how the resulting treaty should be publicized, and publication, when it came, was always accompanied by pointed reference to the sensitivity of Germany's princes to the needs of their subjects. Bavaria even went to the

7. The "hunger years" of 1816–17 were caused by the explosion of Mount Tambora in the Dutch East Indies, which produced climatic aberrations throughout the northern hemisphere (Henry Stommel and Elizabeth Stommel, *Volcano Weather: The Story of 1816, the Year Without a Summer* [Newport, R.I., 1983]).

8. See J. F. Bosher, *The Single Duty Project: A Study of the Movement for a French Customs Union in the 18th Century* (London, 1964).

trouble of conducting a kind of opinion poll, to gauge public feelings outside the capital.[9] At the very least, the journalistic debate constituted the essential background against which official decisions were made. In the *AZ*, where the provenance of articles was rarely spelled out, the whole distinction between "public" and "official" opinion can become difficult to maintain.

Summarizing the *AZ*'s treatment of any complex issue is always a thankless task,[10] made more so here because the newspaper's tolerance of diversity was matched by the proliferation of schemes for economic reform. Censorship, which can normally be relied on to simplify controversy, tended in this case to complicate it, by deflecting debate away from practical policy toward either a lower level of detail or a higher level of abstraction. Within this framework, however, the *AZ*'s columns were open to all: free traders and protectionists; regionalists and nationalists; spokesmen for industry, agriculture, and commerce. The only thing missing was a spirited defense of the status quo, but the only land in which such defenders could be found in any numbers was Austria, which had thrown away the opportunity to be heard on a regular basis when Friedrich Schlegel's correspondence from Frankfurt was allowed to lapse in 1818. The *AZ*'s reports from that vital commercial center were thereafter in different hands, and although Austria might complain about the results,[11] it never produced any sustained reply.

Some general patterns in the *AZ*'s coverage are nevertheless discernible, patterns that testify to the increasing sophistication with which economic questions were viewed. Following the Vienna Congress, Cotta's paper confined itself to detailing the hardships of the moment. The most consistent note was one of hostility toward England, whose competitive advantages were dissected and lamented in reports from the trade fairs at Leipzig and Frankfurt.[12] But the protectionist inferences that one would expect to be drawn from these conditions were overshadowed by the theoretical preference for free trade that prevailed among German officialdom and educated people generally. The Prussian tariff of 1818 was thus an unpleasant surprise to the *AZ*'s readers,

9. "Übersicht über die Berichte der bayerischen Kreisregierungen," [Oct. 1819,] in Oncken and Saemisch, *Vorgeschichte des Deutschen Zollvereins* 1 : 347–48.

10. In the present case it has nevertheless been undertaken twice: by Hans Friedrich Müller, "Die Berichterstattung der Allgemeinen Zeitung Augsburg über Fragen der deutschen Wirtschaft, 1815–1840," Ph.D. diss., Munich, 1936; and by Ingelora Vogt, "Die wirtschaftlichen Einigungsbestrebungen der deutschen Bundesstaaten während der Jahre 1828 bis 1834 im Spiegel der Augsburger Allgemeinen Zeitung," Ph.D. diss., Berlin, 1958.

11. Gentz to Cotta, 18 Oct. 1821, in Fehling and Schiller, *Briefe an Cotta* 2 : 49–50.

12. "Frankfurt," *AZ*, 27 Oct. 1816; "Leipzig," *AZ*, 1 Feb. 1815, 28 May 1818, 15 May 1820 [the last three by Karl Böttiger]. The *AZ* also published petitions that business groups sent to the Diet, e.g., "Leipzig," 5 May 1817, and "Deutschland," 20 July 1818 [the latter by Johann Benzenberg].

who had been led to believe that economic liberalism was on the rise in Berlin.[13] Although it was recognized that Prussia was merely doing what the Rheinbund had done ten years before,[14] Frederick William's government was still criticized for failing to await a "federal" solution.[15]

Exactly what such a solution would look like was unspecified. In some respects, the simple existence of the Federal Diet presented an obstacle to clarity in these matters, by holding out the possibility of reform as the result of pure reflection. In economic terms, however, the assembly in Frankfurt was only a marginal improvement over the old Imperial Diet: the unit of analysis remained the member states, and these were still too numerous to be reconciled at a single stroke. By 1820, though, all hope of a solution from this quarter had disappeared, the last glimmer being extinguished in May, when the Vienna Ministerial Conference found itself unable to act on matters of trade. The initiative therefore passed to the middle states, whose economies were less constrained than those of the Federation's smallest members but not so robust that they could adopt (or tolerate) the autarkic posture of Austria and Prussia. The *AZ*'s coverage would evolve accordingly; economic reform was increasingly seen to depend on the creation of new political combinations capable of setting parochial matters aside.

The politicization of the discussion is apparent, for instance, in the *AZ*'s surprisingly pessimistic coverage of the Darmstadt Conferences, a series of meetings extending over the years 1820–23 among representatives of the major states of the south and west. Their agenda had been shaped in good part by the League of German Merchants and Manufacturers, which had conducted a vigorous campaign in favor of free trade within the Federation and a common tariff against outsiders. The league's leading figure, Friedrich List, was on good terms with both Cotta and Karl von Wangenheim, who was in turn Württemberg's spokesman in Darmstadt and one of the organizers of the conferences. Despite these affinities, however, the *AZ* adopted a neutral stance toward the league, whose theoretical pronouncements could not conceal the narrow interests at its core.[16] The paper also took a distinctly jaun-

13. "Berlin," *AZ*, 7 May, 24 June, 2 Oct., 24 Nov. 1817, and 2 March 1818 [all by Friedrich Cölln].

14. "Von der Spree," *AZ*, 31 July 1818 [by Varnhagen von Ense].

15. "Berlin," *AZ*, 15 Oct. 1818; "Leipziger Messe," *AZ*, 11 Nov. 1818 [by Böttiger]; "Ueber Handelsfreiheit," *AZ*, 18 July 1820 [by "Hartmann vom Rheine"].

16. A number of articles originating with the league were accepted ("Von der Donau," *AZ*, 13 Jan. 1820; "Wien," *AZ*, 2 Feb., 10 April 1820), as well as a number attacks on it, for meddling in affairs of state ("Wien," *AZ*, 16 March, 4 June 1820), and for favoring the interests of merchants over industry ("Von der Elbe," *AZ*, 18 May 1820). One of the league's statements ("Deutschland," *AZ*, 21 May 1820 [Beilage]) was accompanied by payment of a twenty-five gulden fee, which has been taken as evidence that the *AZ*'s favor could be bought (Price, *Evolution of the Zollverein*, p. 174). Even if this were true, it is hard

diced view of the proceedings in Darmstadt, which became transfixed by such questions as whether manure should be considered a "foodstuff" or not.[17]

Some of these reports came from members of the league, who could not conceal their disappointment that their efforts were proving so barren.[18] Others came from Ludwig von Meseritz, a friend of Börne's whom Cotta hired to take over correspondence from the Diet in Frankfurt but who found the bourse a more compelling subject.[19] He was joined by Wilhelm Pietsch, a customs official in Mainz,[20] and Karl Böttiger, whose reports on the Leipzig trade fairs now focused mainly on the damage done to Saxony's economy by the tariff policies of its neighbors, particularly Prussia.[21] Many other voices besides these were heard in the *AZ*, ranging from those who would defend the right of sovereign states to act alone[22] to one unusual article rejecting tariff reform as a rich man's issue, remote from the needs of the people.[23] But to the extent that a newspaper's influence is defined by its regular contributors, it may be noted that in the *AZ* these writers came from the parts of Germany that suffered the most from the piecemeal policies of their neighbors and had the most to gain from comprehensive reform. Not until the end of 1826, for example, do significant reports from Berlin begin to appear.[24]

---

to imagine such favor could be had so cheaply. It seems at least as likely that the fee covered the expense of printing extra copies for separate distribution, as was done on other occasions (cf. Lindner to Cotta, 31 Aug. 1829, CA). The last word, at any rate, was given to List, who had grown impatient with his colleagues and used the *AZ* to reply both to the league's critics and to its more narrow-minded members ("Erklärung," 8 July 1820 [Beilage]; and "Antwort auf die Angriffe des Hrn. Hartmann vom Rheine," 24, 27 Oct. 1820 [Beilage]). Shortly thereafter he left the organization.

17. Adolf Suchel, *Hessen-Darmstadt und der Darmstädter Handelskongress von 1820–23* (Darmstadt, 1922), p. 44.

18. "Denkschrift," *AZ*, 28 March 1822, [by Friedrich Miller, a Bavarian merchant who represented the league in Darmstadt]; "Süddeutschland," *AZ*, 15 May 1822. Miller later contributed a remorseless postmortem, "Thatsächliche Darstellung der Handels- und Verkehrsverhältnisse Deutschlands im Jahr 1824," *AZ*, 30 June 1824 (Beilage).

19. "Vom Main," *AZ*, 9 Oct. 1821 (Beilage); "*Aus Süddeutschland," *AZ*, 23 April 1822; "**Rheinpreußen," *AZ*, 4 Feb. 1823. Most of Meseritz's later work was identified by the datelines "**Frankfurt" or "**Darmstadt." Cf. Börne to Cotta, 15 Dec. 1820, in Fehling and Schiller, *Briefe an Cotta* 2 : 37. The shift of Meseritz's focus from the Diet to the bourse was encouraged by Bavaria's censors, who became reluctant to accept summaries of the Diet's proceedings and insisted on fully contextualized transcripts, which were hardly warranted (Heyck, *Allgemeine Zeitung*, p. 237).

20. "*Mainz," beginning in the spring of 1824.

21. "Leipziger Messe," *AZ*, 6 June 1823 (Beilage), 19 June 1824 (Beilage), 4 Nov. 1826 (Beilage).

22. "**Berlin," *AZ*, 5 July 1825; "Vom Oberrhein," *AZ*, 19 Aug. 1826.

23. "*Darmstadt," *AZ*, 1, 2 Dec. 1826 (Beilage) [the latter by Theodor Hartleben, from Mannheim].

24. These began appearing in the fall under the rubrics "**Berlin," [by Eduard Gans] and "†Berlin" [by a writer named Schomberg].

Both the regional treaties of 1828 and the union between them the following year were hailed less for their own sake than as steps toward a national settlement.[25]

By the end of the twenties, as Britain's ambassador to Berlin would complain, the *AZ* spoke "the language of a very powerful commercial party" more forcefully than any other newspaper in Germany.[26] Exactly how far that voice carried would ordinarily have been uncertain. The essence of reform, as Paul Pfizer argued in a book published by Cotta in 1831, was not the reconciliation of liberals and conservatives or even, as was then commonly supposed, of north and south; it was, rather, a question of "theory and practice."[27] All the press could do was expose the issue—and this the *AZ* had done. The solution to the problem, however, depended on individuals in a position to act. It was thus a matter of real distress to Britain's representative, whose government had a lot to lose from Germany's economic consolidation, that those individuals should have included the *AZ*'s proprietor.

THEORY AND PRACTICE

Britain's ambassador took it for granted that the views most often expressed in the *AZ* were Cotta's own[28]—an unreliable assumption in some cases, but not in this one. Cotta had been close to Wangenheim and Lindner for too long to remain unaffected by their ideal of solidarity among the "constitutional" German states. His friendship with his fellow Württemberger Friedrich List is at least equally significant. Although Cotta's correspondence with List does not address economic questions, it does bespeak a high degree of personal intimacy. In 1820, List, a critic

25. "*Darmstadt," *AZ*, 18 April 1828 [by Karl Buchner, a former leader of the Heidelberg *Burschenschaft*]; "*Aus Süddeutschland," *AZ*, 17–18 April 1828 (Beilage) [by Meseritz]; "Betrachtungen über den Handelsverein zwischen Preußen, Bayern, Württemberg und Hessen-Darmstadt," *AZ*, 19–22 Sept. 1829 (Beilage) [by Lindner].

26. Lord Seymour to Lord Aberdeen [British foreign secretary], 29 Sept. 1829, in Oncken and Saemisch, *Vorgeschichte des Deutschen Zollvereins* 3:578–79.

27. Paul Pfizer, "Vorwort," *Briefwechsel zweier Deutschen* (Stuttgart, 1831), p. 3. This book, based on a real correspondence between Pfizer, a Tübingen *Gerichtsassessor*, and Friedrich Notter, an editor of Cotta's *Ausland* in Munich (see chapter 10), was widely misunderstood as a plea for the acceptance of Prussian hegemony in Germany. It was intended, however, as a plea for a more realistic and less dogmatic attitude in German affairs, which included (but was not limited to) a realistic appreciation of Prussian military and economic power. This fact was made clearer in the substantially revised second edition, which Cotta also published (Stuttgart, 1832). Cf. the collated edition, edited by Georg Künzel (Berlin, 1911).

28. Seymour to Aberdeen, 29 Sept. 1829, in Oncken and Saemisch, *Vorgeschichte des Deutschen Zollvereins* 3:578–79. Lord Seymour was particularly alarmed by the call for a customs union comprising (at least) the states of the Third Germany in an essay by Lindner, "Betrachtungen," *AZ*, 19–22 Sept. 1829 (Beilage), which Seymour regarded as a summary statement of the paper's point of view.

of Württemberg's bureaucracy since his days as a publicist for the *Volks-freunde*, won election to the Württemberg Diet. Shortly thereafter he prepared a comprehensive address attacking the administrative structure established under William's constitution, the delivery of which led to his expulsion from the assembly and to criminal prosecution. Cotta was one of a handful of people who saw this speech in advance, and the only one, as List would recall, who did not abandon him during the persecution that followed.[29] Cotta did his best to patch things up between List and the king, eventually arranging for List to avoid imprisonment by emigrating to the United States.[30] List, for his part, felt that Cotta's economic acumen qualified him "to stand at the head of the finances of a great nation."[31] Whether Cotta accepted List's ideas in detail is unknown, and in the event irrelevant. The two men certainly shared a broad understanding of Germany's economic dilemma—broader, for instance, than Wangenheim's, which conceived a southern union as an end in itself.[32] It was this breadth of vision that allowed Cotta to look beyond his regional loyalties and to succeed in the difficult role that would fall to him.

Those regional loyalties were well developed. Cotta had become involved with Württemberg's economic policy during the postwar "hunger years," when he helped found a number of organizations to promote economic development.[33] As a legislator he devoted himself to budgetary matters, emerging as the dominant member of the Diet's finance committee, where he argued against the ministry's tendency to treat tariffs simply as an expedient for raising revenues.[34] Cotta acquired an additional stake in economic reform in 1824, when he helped establish a company to operate steamships on Lake Constance. It was the kind of

29. List to Georg von Cotta, 21 Feb. 1834, in List, *Schriften, Reden, Briefe* 8:408–9.
30. See their correspondence, ibid., 8:214–324, passim.
31. Ibid., vol. 3, pt. 2, p. 785.
32. [K. V. Riecke, ed.,] "Zur Vorgeschichte des Deutschen Zollvereins: Auszüge aus Briefen des Freiherrn K. A. v. Wangenheim," *Württembergische Vierteljahrshefte für Landesgeschichte* 2 (1879): 101–11.
33. The first of these was a relief organization called the Wohltätigkeitsverein, founded under the patronage of the queen early in 1817. It was soon joined by the Landwirtschaftliche Verein, which promoted agricultural development; Cotta was a member of its governing board and the driving force behind the establishment of a system of savings banks for farmers and working people. These banks (the Württembergische Landessparkasse, which still exist) provided the credit that would make land reform a reality in Württemberg, by allowing tenant farmers to buy their holdings. In 1819 a third *Verein* was added, devoted to trade and industry. See Paul Gehring, "Das Wirtschaftsleben in Württemberg unter König Wilhelm I (1816–1864)," *Zeitschrift für württembergische Landesgeschichte*, n.s., 9 (1949–50): 200–220.
34. "Uebersicht über die Verhandlungen der würtembergischen Ständeversammlung vom 24 Mai 1824 bis zum Schluß des Landtages am 9 Juli 1824," *AZ*, 13–14 Jan. 1825 (Beilage).

undertaking that could only sharpen one's appreciation of the pitfalls of interstate commerce, requiring as it did the active cooperation of three states and half a dozen municipalities.[35] The venture also strengthened Cotta's political position by making him, somewhat unusually, the king's business partner—William being a major investor in one of the ships, which bore his name.

As far as the public was concerned, the sight of ships without sails plying the waters between Baden and Bavaria verged on the miraculous. Compared to the problem of getting those governments to concert their commercial policies, however, it was almost a triviality. If the Darmstadt Conferences had accomplished anything, they had shown that the lands of the Third Germany were by no means united in their economic goals. Bavaria, looking to protect its nascent industries, had been uncompromising in the defense of higher tariffs than could be tolerated by Baden and the trading states along the Rhine. Württemberg, in contrast, remained committed to a cooperative policy—if one could be devised. This posture reflected both the structure of its economy (mid-way between those of Bavaria and the Rhine states in terms of the balance between trade and industry) and the political instincts of its leadership. While most of Württemberg's neighbors were contemplating various forms of protectionism, William's government was negotiating bilateral treaties with Switzerland and the Hohenzollern enclaves that Württemberg had engulfed in 1803. In 1825 it approached Bavaria about a similar arrangement.

This offer would certainly have been ignored but for the death of Max Joseph a few months later. His successor, Ludwig, shared his father's protectionist impulses and inaugurated his reign by raising Bavaria's import duties. But Ludwig had also resented the reactionary lassitude of the Bavarian court during the last years of his father's life, and he was sensitive to the public expectations that had fallen on him as a relatively young (thirty-nine-year-old), putatively dynamic king. He was thus prepared to consider William's proposal, which was renewed in December 1826 after a storm of protest over Ludwig's new tariff arose in the Württemberg Diet.[36] A preliminary agreement followed, giving rise, in January 1828, to a treaty abolishing most duties between the two states and establishing a common customs frontier based on the higher Bavarian tariff.

35. In the end the experiment would leave Cotta poorer by sixty thousand gulden, owing to crippling disagreements over docking fees and repair privileges. See his correspondence with the Bavarian ministry of the interior, in M Inn 44819, "Dampfschiffahrt, 1824–25"; and M Inn 43971, "Acta des Ministerial-Bureau des Innern—Die projectierten Unternehmungen des Freyherrn von Cotta in Bayern, 1826 u. 1827"; and Schäffle, *Cotta,* pp. 154–60.

36. Doeberl, *Wirtschaftliche Einigung,* pp. 25–27, 71–73.

Cotta's contribution to these developments is somewhat elusive. By the end of 1826 his leadership in financial matters (the only business of any practical importance transacted in the Württemberg Diet during these years) had won him election as vice-president of the Chamber of Deputies,[37] in which capacity he must have had a hand in organizing the Diet's demands for action. During the ensuing negotiation Cotta went to Munich three times as William's representative.[38] There is no reason to suppose he contributed anything of technical substance to the treaty. Cotta's economic expertise was impressive, but not unique; although Cotta was in Munich when the talks concluded, Württemberg's ambassador signed the final draft. In the eyes of the French ambassador, however, it was Cotta who had played the decisive part, largely because of his well-known ability to thrive in an atmosphere of political intrigue, fomented in this instance by "the cabinets of Austria and Baden, who clearly sense that this commercial alliance also implies a more intimate political alliance of the greatest importance for the future of central Germany." Cotta also possessed the confidence of both kings, which allowed them to communicate with each other about these matters outside formal diplomatic channels and in complete secrecy.[39] It was, in short, Cotta's mastery of the personal and political context that counted.

The bilateral treaty that Cotta helped conclude in the first weeks of 1828 was intended to be a step toward regional economic integration, to which neighboring states in the south could be expected to adhere. This vision was undone, however, by the conclusion, three weeks later, of a similar accord between Prussia and Hesse-Darmstadt. The principal spur to the creation of the southern union, after all, had been the need to gain leverage against Prussian protectionism. While the two unions might be hailed in the *AZ* as parallel steps toward national consolidation, only the most naïve observer could fail to recognize the potential rivalry inherent in them.

That the two systems had common interests as well was also clear. William, although reluctant to contemplate any extension of Prussian influence in his direction, took it for granted that sooner or later his government would have to follow Hesse-Darmstadt's example, and come to terms with Berlin.[40] From the Bavarian point of view, Prussia was a more desirable trading partner than Württemberg: it possessed far

37. "Stuttgart," *AZ*, 12 Dec. 1826.

38. Cotta went to Munich in late December 1826, and again in November and December 1827. See Trauttmansdorff to Metternich, 29 Dec. 1826, in Oncken and Saemisch, *Vorgeschichte des Deutschen Zollvereins* 1:525–27; Hölzle, "Der Deutsche Zollverein," p. 134; and Cotta to King William, 6 Jan. 1828, ibid., p. 138.

39. Count Rumigny [French ambassador to Bavaria] to Baron Ange de Damas [French foreign minister], 24 Dec. 1827, in Chroust, *Berichte der französischen Gesandten* 2:94–95.

40. Heinrich Ulmann, ed., *Denkwürdigkeiten aus dem Dienstleben des hessen-darmstädtischen Staatsministers Freiherrn du Thil, 1803–1848* (Stuttgart and Berlin, 1921), p. 300.

greater economic weight, and its Rhine provinces bordered the Bavarian Palatinate, whose economic isolation (the result of its geographic detachment from the rest of Bavaria) was the most annoying problem Ludwig's government faced. But an early overture calling attention to these facts had been rebuffed by Frederick William's government, in part because it sided with Baden in a long-simmering dispute over the former imperial county of Sponheim, which Baden had received from Napoleon in 1802.

In a geographic sense, Sponheim could not have been more irrelevant to the issue at hand. Its possession by Bavaria would have brought the disconnected pieces of the state no closer together, and its retention by Baden simply lengthened an already elongated border with France. But the Rheinpfalz was Ludwig's natal place, and his determination to recover this particular part of his patrimony, or to receive suitably impressive compensation for it, far exceeded the normal demands of policy.[41] Berlin's support of Baden's claim had now been compounded by Hesse's adoption of the Prussian tariff, since it was Hesse, in a physical sense, that separated Bavaria from the Pfalz. The result was a spate of rumors about a pending retaliatory deal between Bavaria and France.[42]

Although these rumors proved false, the extraneous friction that divided Munich from Berlin was real, and of a kind that had proven intractable through conventional channels. In September 1828, however, a different sort of channel was opened, when Cotta decided to attend a convention of natural scientists in the Prussian capital, apparently with the intention of recruiting new authors for his firm. On his return he presented Ludwig with a long report, affirming the goodwill of many of those in Frederick William's court, and particularly of the finance minister, Friedrich von Motz, whom Cotta judged eager to conclude a treaty similar to the one linking Bavaria and Württemberg.[43]

The question has since been raised whether, on this occasion, Cotta was acting mainly for Württemberg or for Bavaria.[44] Disputes of this

41. Michael Dirrigl, *Ludwig I: König von Bayern, 1825–1848* (Munich, 1980), pp. 1028–42.

42. Spiegel to Metternich, 3 March 1828, in Chroust, *Berichte der österreichischen Gesandten* 2 : 185–86; Rumigny to Pierre Fenon, count de La Ferronays [French foreign minister], 18 June, 1 Nov. 1828, in Chroust, *Berichte der französischen Gesandten* 2 : 128, 145–47. It is sometimes forgotten that France opposed tariff reform in Germany at least as vigorously as Austria did; Cotta felt it was essential for Bavaria to demonstrate its independence of both powers (Cotta to Ludwig [Memorandum], [Oct. 1828,] in Doeberl, *Wirtschaftliche Einigung*, p. 74). See Karl Hammer, *Die französische Diplomatie der Restauration und Deutschland, 1814–1830* (Stuttgart, 1963), pp. 170–204.

43. Cotta to Ludwig [Memorandum], [Oct. 1828,] in Doeberl, *Wirtschaftliche Einigung*, pp. 73–75.

44. Cf. Hölzle, "Der Deutsche Zollverein," pp. 135–37; and Doeberl, *Wirtschaftliche Einigung*, pp. 34–35. Motz, for what it's worth, seems to have regarded Cotta as a Württemberger (see Petersdorff, *Friedrich von Motz* 2 : 202–3).

kind are not as interesting as they used to be. Better to ask how far Cotta had been instructed by anyone at all. It is clear from Cotta's report that he went to Berlin with the understanding that anything he could do to smooth things over would be appreciated in both Munich and Stuttgart.[45] But he carried neither credentials nor a written brief, and although Ludwig's quick-witted minister of foreign affairs and finance, Joseph von Armansperg, immediately recognized the value of what Cotta had done, he was also fearful, as Friedrich Perthes had been on the eve of Cotta's trip to Vienna, that Cotta was prone to take matters into his own hands.[46] Certainly it would not have been out of character for Cotta simply to have followed his nose from the science congress to the state chancellery, relying on his old friend and client, Alexander von Humboldt, for the necessary introductions.[47]

Armansperg's reservations about Cotta's conduct were well founded. Cotta had discovered that Motz was open to a range of possibilities, from mutual tariff reductions to a comprehensive customs union. But such agreements were to Cotta (and Motz) simply means to an end. The ill feeling between Munich and Berlin, Cotta reported, stemmed not from trade, or even the Sponheim question (a purely legal matter to Motz), but from the perception that Bavaria was "entirely at one with Austria." The customs union with Württemberg was thus viewed with equanimity in Berlin, as a sign that Ludwig's government was prepared to pursue its own interests even if these conflicted with Austria's. It seemed to Cotta "inherent in the nature of things" that those interests should lead to closer ties with Prussia, in the same way that it was natural for Saxony to seek alliance with Austria.[48]

That such an appraisal went beyond what Ludwig was used to hearing from his ambassadors need hardly be said. But the precision and depth

45. Cotta had last spoken to Ludwig in May, at which time the king complained about the "hostile demeanor" of the Prussian cabinet (Hölzle, "Der Deutsche Zollverein," p. 135). Cotta's conversations with William were more frequent; before going to Berlin, Cotta prepared a memorandum for him on "the current relations of the great powers" (Vellnagel to Cotta, 3 Sept. 1828, CA), and Cotta reported to William in person following his return (Vellnagel to Cotta, 2 Oct. 1828, CA). Precisely because personal contact was so easy, almost nothing passed between them in writing during these years. Our knowledge of Cotta's role comes entirely from Bavarian documents, but the impression that he was Ludwig's personal agent is misleading.

46. Armansperg to Cotta, 22 Oct. 1828, in Doeberl, *Wirtschaftliche Einigung*, pp. 75–76; and Armansperg to Ludwig, 23 Jan. 1829, Bayerisches Hauptstaatsarchiv, Abteilung III: Geheimes Haus Archiv, "Nachlass Ludwig I," ARO 25. Cf. Ludwig's annotation to Armansperg's report of 28 Dec. 1828, in Oncken and Saemisch, *Vorgeschichte des Deutschen Zollvereins* 3:445.

47. Humboldt is identified in Cotta's report as a key member of Frederick William's entourage. He may have been for Cotta's purposes, but he had no part in the proceedings that followed. Cotta had been Humboldt's publisher since 1806.

48. Cotta to Ludwig [Memorandum], [Oct. 1828], in Doeberl, *Wirtschaftliche Einigung*, pp. 73–75.

of Cotta's conversations with Motz also contrasted too sharply with the recent run of pro forma diplomatic contacts in Berlin to be ignored. Cotta therefore returned to Prussia at Ludwig's request, this time with instructions to discuss a commercial treaty in detail. That Cotta did not possess the power actually to conclude such an agreement was a disappointment to his hosts. Nonetheless, Cotta and Motz were able to produce a well developed working paper, calling for the incorporation of the Palatinate into the existing Prussian union with Hesse-Darmstadt, the general adoption of the Prussian tariff (less protectionist than Bavaria's), and the abolition of duties on most raw and finished goods moving between East Prussia and Württemberg on the one hand, and Bavaria on the other.[49] Cotta presented this proposal to Ludwig along with a report of his personal impressions, which assured the king that Prussia, although culturally sophisticated, socially progressive, and militarily strong, had no political ambitions as such and represented no threat to the independence of its smaller partners.[50]

Ludwig, not surprisingly, found this appraisal difficult to believe. He also judged the proposed adherence of the Palatinate to the northern union to be incompatible with the dignity of the Bavarian state, and Cotta's subsequent attempts to restore this item to the agenda would become a source of strain.[51] Cotta spent most of the first half of 1829 in Berlin, now fully instructed and accredited to deal for Württemberg and Bavaria.[52] Even so, Armansperg took the precaution of ordering Bavaria's ambassador, Friedrich von Luxburg, to keep an eye on him.[53] Left to himself, Cotta would undoubtedly have sought a more comprehensive agreement than the one he finally achieved. He was eager, for instance, to see Baden brought into the new system, and he attempted in various ways to mediate the Sponheim question, with no success.[54] Cotta also believed

49. Punctation between Cotta and Motz, Dec. 1828, ibid., pp. 76–77.

50. Cotta to Armansperg, 14 Dec. 1828, ibid., pp. 78–84. Cotta's report included most of a letter from Frederick William's adjutant, Job von Witzleben, who went out of his way to impress Cotta with Prussia's commitment to intellectual freedom. That Cotta should have been received as a representative of "Weimar," as well as of Württemberg and Bavaria, was to be expected (cf. Oncken and Saemisch, *Vorgeschichte des Deutschen Zollvereins* 1:lxxiii). But Cotta personally was more impressed by Prussia's military schools, and by the political education afforded by the *Landwehr*, than by the state's support of elite culture.

51. Cf. Ludwig's marginal notations to Cotta's report, 20 Dec. 1828, and Armansperg to Ludwig, 21 Dec. 1828, in Doeberl, *Wirtschaftliche Einigung*, p. 438; and Ludwig to Armansperg, 5 Feb. 1829, in Oncken and Saemisch, *Vorgeschichte des Deutschen Zollvereins* 3:437–38, 456.

52. Instructions and revised punctation, 18 Jan. 1829, in Doeberl, *Wirtschaftliche Einigung*, pp. 85–95.

53. Armansperg to Friedrich von Luxburg, 6 Nov. 1828, Geheimes Haus Archiv ARO 25; and 7 Feb. 1829, in Doeberl, *Wirtschaftliche Einigung*, p. 41.

54. Cotta pursued this matter long after its insolubility should have been apparent. Cf. Cotta to Ludwig, 10 April 1829, Geheimes Haus Archiv, "Nachlass Ludwig I—Verschiedene Briefe," 90-1-II; and Doeberl, *Wirtschaftliche Einigung*, p. 43.

the Prussian tariff, generally lower than that of the southern union,[55] was more conducive to economic growth. Here, too, he had to conceal his impatience with his instructions, which obliged him to equivocate on a number of points he thought he had already disposed of in his earlier conversations with Motz.[56] As it was, the details were not always handled as Ludwig wished,[57] and the audience in which Cotta presented the king with the draft treaty proved most unpleasant, with Ludwig implying that the Bavarian Diet might reject the bargain Cotta had struck as unconstitutional.[58] In the end, though, the necessary revisions were easily made, and the bargain was not rejected.

The commercial treaty joining northern and southern Germany in the spring of 1829 was the decisive step toward the comprehensive customs union established five years later. Although much toil would yet be expended on this issue, one need only look at a map to see that, except for a few states on the margins of the Federation, no serious alternative to economic cohesion now remained. Cotta's contribution to this achievement was variously judged by the others involved. In substance, the treaty belonged to Motz and his Prussian colleagues, who were grateful for the open-mindedness that Cotta brought to the proceedings and for the vigor with which he argued for their ideas in Stuttgart and Munich.[59] It is only to be expected that those on the receiving end of these arguments should have felt differently; to them, the very fact of Cotta's involvement was a minor embarrassment. Although his activities in Berlin were concealed behind a pretense of "literary undertakings,"[60] his real purpose soon became plain to the diplomatic community and the public alike. Armansperg could only insist to his ministerial colleagues, who sometimes found out about Cotta's role from reading the newspapers, that Cotta played merely a supporting part of no political significance.[61]

But this was the opposite of the truth. Armansperg did not need Cotta to impress upon him the advantages of a treaty with Prussia. It was Cotta, however, who argued most persistently that those advantages were worth the political risks they entailed. In Cotta's eyes, these risks were not negligible. Prussia was not a constitutional state, an unsettling

55. Cotta to Armansperg, 31 Jan. 1829, in Oncken and Saemisch, *Vorgeschichte des Deutschen Zollvereins* 3:451.

56. Armansperg to Cotta, 16 Feb. 1829, ibid., p. 460.

57. See Ludwig's revised instructions, 16 April 1829, in Doeberl, *Wirtschaftliche Einigung*, pp. 102–3.

58. Ibid., p. 47.

59. Motz to Cotta, 6 Dec. 1828, in Oncken and Saemisch, *Vorgeschichte des Deutschen Zollvereins* 3:425–26.

60. So reported in the *Moniteur*, 21 Jan. 1829.

61. See the correspondence between Armansperg and Maximilian von Lerchenfeld, 12–14 Feb. 1829, in Max von Lerchenfeld, ed., *Aus den Papieren des k. b. Staatsminister Maximilian Freiherrn von Lerchenfeld* (Nördlingen, 1887), pp. 409–12.

fact whose long-term consequences he found difficult to judge;[62] but he nevertheless insisted on seeking the broadest possible basis of agreement, even at the cost of some damage to his reputation for prudence.

In matters of technical detail, Cotta found himself out of his depth in Berlin. But just for this reason, his attention to more fundamental political questions remained unflagging. His was, in Motz's view, the decisive contribution, without which everyone else's efforts would have fallen short.[63] Even more revealing, though hardly flattering in its intent, is the report of Cotta's fellow negotiator, Luxburg, who complained that

> without [Württemberg's ambassador] Blomberg and me, Baron von Cotta would have accomplished little or nothing in Berlin. . . . [If] the good Cotta had not stood in our way, we might, here and there, have achieved better terms. There are people who are very good at bringing a subject up for discussion, and for setting things in motion. But when it comes to following through, they are entirely impractical. I have in mind the old adage that a man can serve only *one* master. Whoever is the friend and servant of all cannot possibly protect special interests as well as his duty demands.[64]

It is impossible not to sympathize with Bavaria's ambassador, who found himself drawn into negotiations of the most Byzantine intricacy, to which Cotta was quite indifferent.[65] And it must have been painful to discover that "a rich, independent man like Cotta can gain access to great men more easily than their own servants can."[66] But no one familiar with the decade-long controversy that preceded Cotta's meetings with Motz can doubt that the one thing missing all those years had been a man capable of serving many masters. Nor can there have been many men better suited to such a role. Viewed in light of its results, Cotta's mission to Berlin would have made the career of any professional diplomat.[67]

It has never been easy to settle on the context in which the economic reforms of the 1820s should be viewed. Heinrich von Treitschke's monumental interpretation, with the guns of Königgrätz thundering metaphorically in the distance, established the *Zollverein* as a Prussian shrine, while hopelessly simplifying the processes that actually brought it about. More recently, the political dimension that once loomed so large has

---

62. Cotta to Varnhagen von Ense, 16 Sept. 1831, in Hölzle, "Der Deutsche Zollverein," p. 145; cf. the *AZ*'s treatment of Prussia's treaty with Hesse-Darmstadt, in "**München" [Lindner] and "*Darmstadt" [Buchner], both beginning 13 May 1828 (Beilage).

63. Motz to Ludwig, 30 May 1829, in Doeberl, *Wirtschaftliche Einigung*, p. 48.

64. Luxburg to Armansperg, 5 May 1829, ibid., p. 45.

65. Luxburg to Armansperg, 30 May 1829, in Oncken and Saemisch, *Vorgeschichte des Deutschen Zollvereins* 3:513n.

66. Luxburg to Armansperg, 29 May 1829, ibid.

67. Cotta was decorated by all the parties to the treaty of 1829, receiving knighthoods from Württemberg and Bavaria and the Order of the Red Eagle, Second Class, from Prussia. Among several posthumous lithographs based on the Leybold portrait of 1824 there is one showing Cotta wearing these medals (Grube, *Stuttgarter Landtag*, facing p. 509).

been subsumed within a more comprehensive understanding of the industrial revolution in Germany, an entirely defensible approach, but one almost as remote from contemporary perceptions as Treitschke's.[68] In terms of the complexity of the interests involved, and of the skill necessary to reconcile them, the founding of the customs union compares easily to the contemporary movement for parliamentary reform in Britain. But it is unlikely that anyone involved, and certainly not Cotta, would have been tempted to claim, as G. M. Young would do for the Whigs, that they had done "the right thing . . . in exactly the right way at exactly the right time."[69]

Cotta might rather have echoed John Bright's famous remark, that the Reform Bill of 1832 "was not a good Bill, but it was a great Bill when it passed."[70] The negotiations to which Cotta lent his hand were carried on in isolation from the constitutional structures that he had supposed would be the real levers of change in Germany. This development was unanticipated by many observers at the outset. Wilhelm von Humboldt had argued, before the Prussian tariff of 1818 was adopted, that action should be delayed until a representative assembly was in place; and Bavaria's obstructive posture at Darmstadt was dictated in part by Rechberg's conviction that "tariff lines are not merely economic and mercantile institutions, but political and police institutions as well."[71] Progress had become possible only after everyone concerned had set such assumptions aside.

At the popular level tariff reform retained a political resonance that is hard to believe, given the obscurity of the underlying issues. In 1830 songs were sung to free trade, and it was no accident that customs houses were a favorite target of revolutionary mobs. But the songs held that free trade would be won by a free press, and this was conspicuously not so. Such contribution as the press was able to make depended on its credibility in official circles, which would not have been improved by greater freedom. While the Prussian parliament on which Humboldt would have waited never materialized, moreover, those representative bodies that did exist elsewhere played no decisive part in these proceedings. Ludwig's chiding of Cotta about the constitutionality of what he had done was stinging precisely because both of them knew that oppo-

68. See, for instance, Gerhard Seybold, *Württembergs Industrie und Außenhandel vom Ende der Napoleonischen Kriege bis zum Deutschen Zollverein* (Stuttgart, 1974); and Wolfram Fischer, *Wirtschaft und Gesellschaft im Zeitalter der Industrialisierung* (Göttingen, 1972). Cf. the discussion in Berding, "Entstehung des deutschen Zollvereins," pp. 227–30, 237.

69. George M. Young, "Macaulay," in *Victorian Essays*, ed. W. D. Hancock (London, 1962), p. 41.

70. Speech at Birmingham, 29 Jan. 1864, in John Bright, *Public Addresses*, ed. James E. Thorold Rogers (London, 1879), p. 29.

71. Doeberl, *Wirtschaftliche Einigung*, p. 20.

sition, when it came, would come from Cotta's putative allies: parliamentary liberals in the southern diets who stood for progressive and responsive government but who would oppose this treaty, and those that would follow, on the grounds that it deepened the "statism" of German life.[72] When Cotta left Berlin at the end of May, however, he had reason to believe that such fears were at least exaggerated. Economic reform had brought movement and energy to public life, which had been on the verge of stagnation only a few years before. It had provided an outlet for political creativity among those who, despite their eagerness to serve the state, had been relegated to the margins of politics after Carlsbad.[73] And in Bavaria, flexibility and vigor in matters of trade were accompanied by clear signs of cultural and political vitality in other areas, in which Cotta was ideally placed to take part.

72. See the outstanding discussion by Hans-Werner Hahn, "Zwischen deutscher Handelsfreiheit und Sicherung landständischer Rechte: Der Liberalismus und die Gründung des Deutschen Zollvereins," in *Liberalismus in der Gesellschaft des deutschen Vormärz*, ed. Wolfgang Schieder, *Geschichte und Gesellschaft*, Sonderheft 9 (Göttingen, 1983), pp. 239–71. Baden, the exemplary case, has recently been thoroughly examined; see Hans Peter Müller, *Das Grossherzogtum Baden und die deutsche Zolleinigung* (Frankfurt, 1983).

73. On the Prussian side, see Lawrence J. Baack, *Christian Bernstorff and Prussia: Diplomacy and Reform Conservatism, 1818–1832* (New Brunswick, N.J., 1980), pp. 253–63.

TEN

The Edge of Opposition

We are still not in a position to speak publicly of what the people want, expect, and believe. . . . One must simply speak of the most daring principles—for instance, that the people are a part of the state, that freedom of the press is not absurd—as if they were generally accepted facts.

Johann Droysen to Ludwig Moser, May 28, 1831

When Ludwig ascended his father's throne in October 1825, Bavaria's capital enjoyed the services of 62 breweries, 94 butcher shops, and 173 taverns. It also supported 9 printers, 5 bookstores, 4 magazines devoted to popular amusements, and 1 newspaper, published by the government.[1] Much of the king's energy during the early years of his reign would be devoted to redressing the imbalance between body and soul reflected in these figures. Before the year was out, Ludwig had ordered the relocation of the University of Landshut to Munich, where it would become an important object of royal patronage. The Academies of Science and Fine Arts were reorganized, public education was subjected to far-reaching reform, and a number of Catholic cloisters and hospices, whose secularization had been integral to the monarchy's consolidation, were restored, architecturally and institutionally. Underwriting the whole program, as Ludwig imagined it, would be a great publishing house, which would serve the needs of these revitalized agencies and project their achievements throughout Europe.

It is indicative of how much had changed since Max Joseph's coronation in 1799 that his son should have taken it for granted that cultural aspirations like these must have political consequences. It is indicative of how much had changed since the Carlsbad Conference, furthermore, that these consequences should have presented no immediate obstacle to the king's ambitions. Ludwig had found the vitality of the Stuttgart press in the early twenties unintimidating, and following his father's death he took the only step necessary to stimulate a comparable efflores-

1. Adolf von Schaden, *Topographisch-statistisches Taschenbuch, oder Beschreibung der Haupt- und Residenzstadt München, ihre Merkwürdigkeiten und Umgebung* (Munich, 1825), pp. 248–63.

cence in his own capital, by dramatically curtailing censorship of writing on domestic politics—an assertion of local autonomy of precisely the same kind as Württemberg's King William had found impossible to sustain just two years earlier. Ludwig thus guaranteed that his government would have to defend itself in print, often against the same intellectuals, both liberals and conservatives, whom Ludwig's other reforms would attract to Munich.

He also committed himself to a serious attempt at drawing Cotta deeper into Bavarian affairs. Among German publishers, only Cotta possessed the resources Ludwig needed. Cotta was the publisher of much that Ludwig admired in German literature (including some of the king's own youthful verse),[2] as well as of the only newspaper that Ludwig bothered to read every day.[3] On Cotta's side there was no mistaking the rarity of what Ludwig was trying to do. Not since William's accession in 1816 had Cotta been given a chance to act in concert with a sympathetic government. That earlier opportunity had been cut short by outside forces, whose affects had now begun to diminish. Ludwig's initiatives seemed to Cotta an occasion for political renewal, in which the collaborative principles he had first explored in the plan for the *Bundeszeitung* and in the *Tribüne* might finally prove their worth.

But of course, Ludwig was no more alone in the world than William had been. His resilience in the face of criticism proved to be more limited than he had imagined, particularly after 1830, when Bavaria's domestic problems, manifest most painfully in the crown's puzzling difficulties with the Bavarian Diet, would be compounded by revolution abroad. The political crisis that broke over Europe in the summer of 1830 thus brought an end to Cotta's last attempt to forge an alliance between the press and the state. It also raised anew the question whether the principles of "impartiality" and "fealty" on which Cotta had always relied could stand the strain of Germany's ever more febrile public life.

MUNICH

When Cotta moved the *Allgemeine Zeitung* to Bavaria in 1803 he did so for pragmatic reasons. Although he would later have cause to applaud his own good judgment (it is hard to imagine the *AZ* surviving the Napoleonic period in Heidelberg), it would be almost twenty years before he would give any sign of desiring closer relations with Württemberg's eastern neighbor. Early in 1822, however, Cotta bought a large estate near Freising from the Bavarian government, a purchase similar to others he had made as investments over the years, but one to which a larger

2. Ludwig to Cotta, 5 July 1818, CA.
3. Heinz Gollwitzer, *Ludwig I von Bayern: Königtum im Vormärz* (Munich, 1986), p. 366.

significance attached, particularly following Cotta's ennoblement in September, when then Crown Prince Ludwig suggested that Cotta move his residence and business to Munich.[4] Cotta in turn seems to have wished to be made a member of the Bavarian Chamber of Peers, a position for which his new estate and title would have qualified him.[5] Nothing came of these early soundings, thanks to the murkiness of the political atmosphere during Max Joseph's last years. Once Ludwig became king, however, he was quick to renew his earlier invitation, which he now saw as part of a general plan to elevate his capital to the first rank of European cities.

In rejecting Ludwig's original proposal Cotta had implied that there were conditions under which he might have accepted it: assistance in the acquisition of an appropriate building for his firm; relief from import duties on paper, pending construction of a factory for its manufacture; and a steep postal discount on goods shipped to Leipzig. These were hard terms, and now they became harder; with Ludwig on the throne, Cotta raised his price, negotiating (not always successfully) for the right to publish the Diet's proceedings, the ministry's official newspaper, and most of the schoolbooks used in Bavaria.[6] He also brought less to the bargain than Ludwig had hoped: once the steam press was installed in Augsburg there could be no question of uprooting the *AZ*.[7] But Ludwig was still convinced that Munich's existing publishing houses could not support the dynamic academic and artistic culture he hoped to foster; and while Cotta was reluctant to move any of his major ventures to the Bavarian capital, he was prepared to expand in that direction, if the king's initiatives warranted it. It was therefore agreed that the Cotta Verlag would establish a branch office in Munich, one capable of providing a full range of services and of making an independent contribution to the city.

The new branch, called the "Literarisch-artistische Anstalt," opened in January 1827 in an abandoned priory leased from the state.[8] Its business, initially, was the making of maps—a substantial enterprise, since maps, among their many other uses, were integral to the economic planning that had lately become so important, and Cotta employed about seventy people in their manufacture. The Anstalt's facilities for lithography and copper engraving were also suited to fine art reproduction. But if Cotta's Munich branch was to justify its name, diversification would be necessary. As an immediate project, Ludwig favored a general

4. Ludwig to Cotta, 4 Sept. 1822, CA.

5. Steuer, *Cotta in München*, pp. 14–15.

6. Cotta to Armansperg, 25 June, 19 July, 1 Sept., 28 Oct. 1826, M Inn 43971; Armansperg to Cotta, 12 Nov. 1826, in Steuer, *Cotta in München*, p. 19.

7. Cotta to Ludwig, 7 Nov. 1822, in Steuer, *Cotta in München*, p. 16.

8. Ibid., p. 20.

cultural review like Friedrich Gentz's *Wiener Jahrbuch*.[9] Cotta had recently begun another journal of this kind in Stuttgart, the *Jahrbücher für wissenschaftliche Kritik*, but perhaps just for this reason he took a different approach in Munich, though still one in line with the king's intention. The *Jahrbücher* was the organ of a cohesive group of intellectuals in Berlin, mainly disciples of Hegel, whose shared approach to cultural criticism gave the journal its character. In Munich, the task was to attract scholars to the city in the first place.[10] For this purpose Cotta tried to cast a wider net, in the form of a journal called *Ausland: Eine Zeitschrift für Kunde des geistigen und sittlichen Lebens der Völker außerhalb Deutschlands*.

Ausland was, like the Anstalt's lithography plant, a substantial venture in its fashion. It appeared daily except Sunday in large quarto format and sold for sixteen gulden per year, about the same as the *AZ*. Cotta hired three energetic young editors to insure comprehensiveness: Karl Mebold, a historian, and Friedrich Notter, a physician, both friends of Gustav Kolb's from the Tübingen *Burschenschaft*; and Karl Hermes, a literary critic and, like the others, a student radical, whom Cotta knew as a contributor to the *Morgenblatt*. Even before the first number appeared, however, there were signs that *Ausland* risked being drawn into the *AZ*'s orbit. For one thing, rather than subscribing a second time to the array of foreign periodicals necessary for journals of this kind, Cotta decided to have most sent on from Augsburg after Stegmann's staff was through with them.[11] Unlike the *AZ*, moreover, *Ausland* could not draw on an established network of contributors. The *AZ*'s secondhand journals thus became altogether too important to *Ausland*'s existence, reducing it, in Julius Campe's derisive estimation, to a "factory" producing excerpts from the foreign press.[12] The amount of original material published in *Ausland* was never great—translators soon outnumbered editors two to one[13]—and remained too miscellaneous to establish an intellectual identity.

By ordinary standards, *Ausland* was an enduring success. It appeared in January of 1828 and soon had over a thousand subscribers, despite having been excluded from Austria—proof, no doubt, that its contents, although derivative, were not entirely innocuous.[14] But there was nothing about *Ausland* that would tie it to Munich. Among the concessions Cotta had sought from Ludwig, one that was not forthcoming was the

9. Armansperg to Cotta, 12 Nov. 1826, ibid., p. 19.

10. Cf. Heinrich Heine to Friedrich Merkel, 1 Dec. 1827, in Heine, *Säkularausgabe* 20:310–11.

11. Friedrich Lindner to Cotta, 8 Jan. 1827, CA.

12. Julius Campe to Heine, 24 June 1828, in Heine, *Säkularausgabe* 24:42.

13. Lindner to Cotta, 7 March 1828, CA.

14. Mebold to Cotta, 2 July 1830, CA; cf. Cotta to Sedlnitzky, 16 June 1828, in Giese, "Pressegesetzgebung," cols. 496–98.

right to print the state's schoolbooks. Cotta had therefore declined to equip his new branch office with printing presses, on the assumption that the necessary work could be subcontracted to the Bavarian Schulbuch-Verlag. In the case of *Ausland*, he reasoned, printing and editing might just as well be done in Augsburg—which they were after the first year. All three editors left out of boredom in 1830,[15] eventually to be succeeded (in 1834) by the naturalist Eduard Widenmann, who discerned an original and surprising focus for *Ausland*'s internationalism in the up and coming science of geography, to which it would make important contributions for half a century.[16] Munich remained the official place of publication until 1836, but only as a courtesy to the king.

It was apparent within a few months of its inception that *Ausland* would not go far toward satisfying Ludwig's hopes for Munich. Unlike the *Jahrbücher für wissenschaftliche Kritik*, *Ausland* had no intellectual center; unlike the *AZ*, it had no political edge. These deficiencies make its public success all the more striking. It was entirely possible for a vaguely informative, professionally produced journal, standing in a general way for knowledge and progress, to do well in Germany at the end of the 1820s. Indeed it was the expected course, and *Ausland* was not the first Cotta journal to follow it. The *Allgemeine politische Annalen* had been treading it faithfully since Friedrich Murhard's arrest in 1824. It was a path Cotta was prepared to follow as long as it led upward. In the case of the *Annalen*, however, movement had been steadily downward, a slide that Cotta decided to reverse, in March 1826, by installing Friedrich Lindner as editor and moving the editorial office to Munich.[17]

Physically, the *Annalen* would be even less attached to Munich than *Ausland*, since it continued to be published in Stuttgart. Intellectually, however, Württemberg's capital no longer brought the journal any advantages. By setting up in Munich, Lindner would at least be near some stimulating collaborators: Kolb in Augsburg (who acted as a regular consultant to the Anstalt), Friedrich Thiersch at the university, and the new editors of *Ausland*, still in the planning stage when Lindner arrived in May of 1827. Unlike *Ausland*, the new *Annalen* would be a vehicle primarily for original work, analytical rather than documentary, and, as far as possible, of local origin.[18] While *Ausland* was at least originally intended as a magnet, the *Annalen* would be a lens, focusing and projecting the intellectual and political life of the city, as it had during Murhard's tenure, when King William's ideal of a Third Germany dominated the official culture of Stuttgart. This goal was, of course, more easily

15. Cf. Hermes to Cotta, 18 March 1829, and Mebold to Cotta, 2 July 1830, CA; and Heyck, *Allgemeine Zeitung*, p. 151.
16. Steuer, *Cotta in München*, pp. 36–37.
17. Lindner to Cotta, 4 April 1826, and contract dated 27 May 1826, CA.
18. Lindner to Cotta, 14 Oct. 1826, 20 May, 8 June 1827, CA.

imagined than achieved. Many of those drawn to Ludwig's capital were attracted not by the new atmosphere of vigor and tolerance, but by the romantic Catholicism that was also part of the king's nature.[19] It was not clear that the secular, rational atmosphere of the Cotta press could provide the focus that was called for, and after contemplating his new surroundings for four months Lindner felt he had cause to doubt his future.[20] His spirits were lifted, however, after he learned that Cotta, more or less on impulse, had taken on Heinrich Heine as the *Annalen's* co-editor.

When Heine first approached Cotta, via a letter of recommendation from Varnhagen von Ense, he enjoyed a rising fame as an author of lyric poetry and cultural criticism, which, he hoped, would lead to some type of arrangement with the *Morgenblatt*.[21] His political reputation, to the extent that it existed at all, derived from his slightly bohemian habits and personal associations. Cotta's offer of a permanent, salaried position was in a way unsettling. To Heine, Cotta was temptation, manifest most simply as money: while Julius Campe, Heine's publisher in Hamburg, had just agreed to bring out his *Book of Songs* for nothing,[22] Cotta wanted to pay him two thousand gulden per year as an advance on his services, which did not appear very demanding.[23] Cotta also held out a kind of automatic standing that was hard to pass up: one way to invite comparison with Goethe and Schiller, after all, was to get published by their publisher.[24] Finally, there was social standing to consider, clearly a more difficult problem: could Heine picture himself as editor of a conventional political review loosely tied to the court of the king of Bavaria?

The answer at first was maybe. Heine arrived in Munich in November 1827, after accepting six months' worth of the yearlong contract Cotta had offered. His performance was correspondingly halfhearted: although his personal contributions, based on his recent experiences in England, were lively and plentiful,[25] the work of soliciting and editing other manuscripts remained with Lindner. Toward his colleagues at the Anstalt Heine felt only a distant regard; toward Cotta he had a warmer admiration, for the older man's generosity and "truly liberal"

19. This fundamental division of Bavarian political culture was already becoming evident ten years earlier. See Demel, *Bayerische Staatsabsolutismus*, pp. 153–54.

20. Lindner to Cotta, 22 Oct. 1827, CA.

21. Heine to Varnhagen von Ense, 1 May 1827, in Heine, *Säkularausgabe* 20:287; Varnhagen von Ense to Cotta, 11 May 1827, in Fehling and Schiller, *Briefe an Cotta* 2:29.

22. Heine to Merkel, 16 Nov. 1826, in Heine, *Säkularausgabe* 20:276.

23. Heine to Varnhagen von Ense, 28 Nov. 1827, ibid., p. 307.

24. Cf. Friedrich Hirth, *Heinrich Heine: Bausteine zu einer Biographie* (Mainz, 1950), pp. 44–45.

25. Most of Heine's essays were reissued by Campe in *Englische Fragmente* (Hamburg, 1831). Heine also contributed reviews of Walter Scott's *Life of Napoleon* (*Annalen* 26, no. 2 [1828]: 173–80) and Wolfgang Menzel's *Deutsche Literatur* (*Annalen* 27, no. 3 [1828]: 284–90).

attitudes.[26] In the beginning there was something seductive about membership in Cotta's "literary *Staatsrat*," [27] particularly since, with Cotta's help, it seemed as if it might be parlayed into an even more secure position as a professor at the university. The king, Heine hoped, would see that he had become "milder, better, and perhaps entirely different" than his earlier work would suggest, and Cotta was to encourage Ludwig to "judge the sword by its sharpness and not, let us say, by the good or evil use to which it has been put in the past."[28] But this remarkable petition, which Cotta delivered on Heine's behalf along with a set of his books, came to nothing. Nor is it clear what it could have come to. Heine soon grew tired of being one of "Cotta's musketeers,"[29] so why he should have wished to become one of Ludwig's is something of a mystery. Once it became apparent that he would not be offered an official position, Heine decided to give up on the Anstalt too, and when his contract expired he moved on to Italy, and thence to Paris, where he would renew his connection with Cotta as correspondent for the *Allgemeine Zeitung*.

Heine's ambivalent response to the opportunities and demands of his position on the *Annalen* can be explained, in part, with reference to his determinedly ironic character, an appealing subject that lies beyond our reach in this instance.[30] Even after due allowance is made for Heine's recurring impulses toward self-invention, however, his behavior still sheds some useful light on his situation. Heine conducted himself like someone who senses something valuable in his surroundings but is unsure how to get at it—a condition that can be said to have afflicted the entirety of Cotta's operation in Munich in its first two years. In some respects Heine's encounter with Cotta recalls Cotta's failed recruitment of Friedrich Schiller to edit the *AZ*: like Heine, Schiller was a politically sensitive artist whose politics were so deeply personalized as to make him unfit for the day-to-day work of journalism. In fact, though, Heine's reaction was more ambivalent even than that. On taking leave of Cotta,

26. Heine to Wolfgang Menzel, 12 Jan. 1828, in Heine, *Säkularausgabe* 20:314–16; cf. Heine to Varnhagen von Ense, 12 Feb. 1828, and to Menzel, 2 May 1828, ibid., pp. 324, 330–31.

27. Heine to Menzel, 12 Jan. 1828, ibid., p. 315.

28. Heine to Cotta, 18 June 1828, ibid., p. 334; cf. Eduard von Schenk to Ludwig, 28 July 1828, in Max Spindler, ed., *Briefwechsel zwischen Ludwig I von Bayern und Eduard von Schenk, 1823–1841* (Munich, 1930), p. 56.

29. Campe to Heine, 24 June 1828, in Heine, *Säkularausgabe* 24:41–43; the expression seems to have been Heine's. Earlier, Heine had written to Varnhagen that he could feel himself growing "very earnest, almost German," in Munich because of the beer (1 April 1828, ibid., 20:323); and to Moses Moser that "I live here, God knows, in very congenial circumstances, almost like a prince. I am one of Cotta's most expensive puppets" (14 April 1828, ibid., p. 328).

30. This episode has not been given much space by Heine's biographers, perhaps because it somehow seems unflattering to him; but see Jeffrey L. Sammons, *Heinrich Heine: A Modern Biography* (Princeton, N.J., 1979), pp. 137–38.

Heine urged him to broaden the *Annalen's* horizons so as to attract the "belletristic public," a change that could be signaled by a slightly changed title: *Neue Annalen: Eine Zeitschrift für Politik, Literatur, und Sittenkunde.*[31] To Gustav Kolb, however, Heine offered entirely different advice: to "sustain [the] journal in the liberal spirit, which has so few dedicated organs in Germany," because, "in a time of intellectual struggle, journals are our bastions." In addition to a new title, then, a new motto was needed as well: "There are no longer any nations in Europe, only parties."[32]

Heine's new motto, had it been adopted, would certainly have marked an epoch in the history of the Cotta press. As it is, it marks the moment when circumstances were beginning to undermine the organizational usefulness of Cotta's nonpartisan approach, which tended to make significance synonymous with breadth. Cotta's Anstalt had grown up against a background of political strife, stimulated in varying degrees by Ludwig's legal and academic reforms, by the resulting influx into Munich of writers from elsewhere in Germany, and by the unexpectedly acrimonious response accorded the king's seemingly progressive program by the Bavarian Diet of 1827–28. These developments could not be adequately addressed in portmanteau periodicals like *Ausland* and the *Annalen*. Heine's two letters were not formulated as a choice, but that is what they represented: to succeed, Cotta's efforts in Munich would have to be more comprehensive, or more engaged. Both approaches, to Heine, had merit; but they were becoming difficult to combine.

PRESS VERSUS PARLIAMENT

The appearance of something like political parties in Bavaria at the end of the 1820s was recognized as unusual at the time,[33] and despite much intervening study it continues to seem so, less because of a lack of historical precedents, the search for which is rarely illuminating in itself, than because it occurred against the wishes of everyone involved: it is nearly impossible to find anyone in Bavaria, or for that matter in Germany, who did not find factionalism pernicious.[34] In its political sub-

31. Heine to Cotta, 11 Nov. 1828, in Heine, *Säkularausgabe* 20:348.

32. Heine to Kolb, 11 Nov. 1828, ibid., pp. 350–51.

33. See Ranke's acute assessment, "Aus einem Schreiben von München, betreffend den bayrischen Landtag von 1831," *Historisch-politische Zeitschrift* 1 (1832): 94–102.

34. In addition to the more specialized works cited in the notes that follow, see Hubert Ostadal, *Die Kammer der Reichsräte in Bayern von 1819–1848: Ein Beitrag zur Geschichte des Frühparlamentarismus* (Munich, 1968); Ludwig Bergsträsser, *Studien zur Vorgeschichte der Zentrumspartei* (Tübingen, 1910); and Wilhelm Lempfrid, "Der Bayerische Landtag 1831 und die öffentliche Meinung," *Zeitschrift für bayerische Landesgeschichte* 24 (1961): 1–101, a refinement of his earlier work, *Die Anfänge des parteipolitischen Lebens und der politischen Presse in Bayern unter Ludwig I, 1825–31* (Strasbourg, 1912), which remains invaluable as a source of citations from the (now rare) local press.

stance the controversy surrounding Ludwig's legislative program has lost much of the interest it once commanded. But the political realignment it inspired remains significant as a benchmark in the development of German liberalism, a word that begins to acquire a specifically political meaning around this time,[35] and of the German press.

At stake was the proper degree of dependency that should exist among three institutions—the Diet, the monarchy, and the press—all of which claimed to represent the public interest. This question had been broached in all the "constitutional" German lands ten years before, and the echoes of that earlier effort, particularly of Cotta's experience in Württemberg in 1817–19, are clear in the events we are about to consider. Their resonance is amplified, moreover, by a climate of official toleration that rivaled anything seen in Germany before the middle of the century[36] and by the deliberately obstructive way Bavaria's constitution proposed to manage relations between the parliament and the press.[37]

By law, the proceedings of both houses of the Bavarian Diet were taken down word for word. Those of the Chamber of Deputies were published; except in 1819, those of the Peers were not, a decision some of its members regretted, since it implied that their ideas were not of public interest. These arrangements were not designed to link the Diet to the people; they simply established an accurate legislative history. Members retained the right to publish their own speeches, provided they did not name other delegates in them, a practice that during the Diet of 1819 gave rise to lively discussion in the press. After Carlsbad, however, this material was subject to the same censorship as other political writing. Nor was this situation relieved by Ludwig's early press edicts, which effectively eliminated censorship of nonpolitical publications and of independent journalism touching domestic politics but did not apply to Diet proceedings. The right to publicize the assembly's work remained, for all practical purposes, with the crown.[38]

35. James J. Sheehan, *German Liberalism in the Nineteenth Century* (Chicago, 1978), pp. 5, 11; cf. idem, "*Partei, Volk*, and *Staat*: Some Reflections on the Relationship Between Liberal Thought and Action in Vormärz," in *Sozialgeschichte Heute: Festschrift für Hans Rosenberg zum 70. Geburtstag*, ed. Hans-Ulrich Wehler (Göttingen, 1974), pp. 162–74.

36. "Das deutsche Zeitungswesen während der letzten einundzwanzig Jahre," *Germania* (1852): 513, claims that, despite the nominal persistence of censorship, the range of published opinion in Bavaria by 1830 was not exceeded by even the smallest journals that appeared in 1848 (cited in Koszyk, *Deutsche Presse*, p. 109).

37. The provisions for recording the Diet's proceedings are described in Georg Raubold, *Die Bayerische Landtagsberichterstattung vom Beginn des Verfassungslebens bis 1850* (Munich, 1931), pp. 7–43.

38. Ibid., p. 13. Ludwig's press reform is almost always represented as abolishing certain categories of censorship outright. It is more accurately understood as an administrative reorganization, expressed in two cabinet orders (22 Nov. and 9 Dec. 1825) that revoked the strict interpretive rules imposed between 1820 and 1824 and shifted respon-

This constitutional disjunction between the Diet and the press was aggravated by the assembly's procedures. All German diets had rules about where delegates might sit: in Bavaria positions were assigned by lot, in Württemberg and Baden in order of precedence based on status and seniority. In Bavaria, however, the order of seating was also the order in which members were allowed to speak. Organized discussion was thus impossible, and the published record correspondingly incomprehensible. This excessive formality only compounded the inconsequentiality imposed by the Diet's inability, under the constitution, to initiate legislation. Combined with the exacting censorship of the early 1820s it led to a falling off of public interest in the assembly's activities and to resentment among its members, directed in equal parts toward the ministry and the press.

The only newspaper to cover the Bavarian Diet conscientiously throughout the 1820s was the *Allgemeine Zeitung*. During the session of 1819, almost 20 percent of the *AZ*'s space was devoted to the assembly's affairs.[39] Cotta's chief correspondent, Ignaz von Rudhart, sympathized with the proposals for further reform put forward in the Chamber of Deputies; nevertheless, he found the Diet's proceedings slow and trivial,[40] and he was soon at odds both with the Chamber of Peers, which began its life by announcing its opposition to all change, and with the progressive leadership in the lower house, who believed in the rights of the press but even more in the dignity of the Diet. At the start of the session, Stegmann had prefaced the *AZ*'s coverage with an announcement that public men were liable to closer scrutiny than private individuals—fair warning, intended to forestall the kind of anger the *AZ* had lately stirred up in Württemberg.[41] But his efforts at appeasement failed, and by the close of the Diet Cotta's newspaper had again become an object of criticism on the floor of an assembly whose interests it generally favored.[42]

---

sibility from the foreign to the interior ministry—the second change being at least as important as the first, since it made the whole apparatus less sensitive to outside complaints. The effect of this change was freedom-fostering, but it did not deprive the state of legal authority over the press. See Joseph Bayrle, "Die rechtliche Situation der bayerischen Presse von 1818–1848," Juris. diss., Munich, 1948, pp. 49–50.

39. Raubold, *Landtagsberichterstattung*, p. 58.

40. [Ignaz von Rudhart,] "Bemerkungen eines Unparteiischen," *AZ*, 23 Feb. 1819. Rudhart, a councillor in the ministry of finance, was elected to the Diet in 1825, where he became a spokesman for the liberal opposition. His career is described in Ferdinand Koeppel, *Ignaz von Rudhart: Ein Staatsmann des Liberalismus* (Munich and Berlin, 1933).

41. Editorial insert, *AZ*, 27 Jan. 1819.

42. Cf. Franz von Hornthal's speech of 23 June 1819, in *Verhandlungen der zweiten Kammer der Ständeversammlung des Königreichs Bayern* (Munich, 1819–48), 14:536–38; and "**München," *AZ*, 25 July 1819, and "*München," *AZ*, 26 July 1819. The same objections had been raised less vehemently earlier ("*München," *AZ*, 2 March 1819). Hornthal was an important advocate of freedom of the press.

The *AZ's* relations with the Diet were further strained by the post-Carlsbad reaction. In 1825 the assembly was accorded less than half the space of six years before, and no attempt whatever was made to clarify or comment on its conduct.[43] This decline continued during the Diet of 1827–28, the first of Ludwig's reign and one that had been eagerly anticipated in the pamphlet press, newly relieved of censorship by the king. This relief did not extend to the Diet itself. Cotta, realizing that the conditions that had prevailed in 1819 would not be restored, arranged for the *AZ's* reports to be officially prepared in Munich, a change that would at least speed up their appearance.[44] The number of these reports, however, was not great—less than 6 percent of the *AZ's* contents.

Ludwig's first Diet thus convened against a wildly improbable public background, in which a great deal of latitude was accorded private journalists but in which scarcely any effort was made to acquaint these commentators with the substance of politics. The result was the sudden appearance of a form of publicity almost unknown in Germany: political satire, expounded most notoriously in a weekly called the *Reisende Teufel*, which attracted tremendous attention through a series of articles entitled "The Parliament of the Animals." Whether the legislators' constituents would have been less amused if they had been better informed is open to question, but that they were amused is certain: in the spring of 1828 the *Reisende Teufel* was reputed to have four thousand subscribers.[45]

The end of this strange interlude can be dated from some articles by Friedrich Lindner that appeared in the *AZ* starting at the end of March.[46] Since his unhappy experience with the *Tribüne* Lindner had developed a talent for the kind of critical, progovernment activism exemplified (however fitfully) by that journal and (more successfully) by Murhard's *Annalen*. In the present instance this activism took the form of a detailed review of the Diet's scant progress so far and a demand, in the name of "the nation," for action. Lindner's remarks aroused much resentment in the assembly. There was no doubt that his articles were produced with the ministry's approval, and their publication coincided ominously with an attempt on Ludwig's part to break conservative resistance in the upper house by appointing new peers. But Lindner's views still bear thinking about for their own sake; although they were taken to be an attack on the Diet, that was not their real import. Lindner favored many of the same things the opposition in the lower house favored, in-

---

43. Raubold, *Landtagsberichterstattung*, p. 61.

44. Ibid., p. 63. After Carlsbad the Diet's minutes became subject to censorship prior to publication in the *AZ*, which, according to one of Stegmann's marginal notations (*AZ*, 20 April 1825, CA), delayed their appearance by about two weeks.

45. Raubold, *Landtagsberichterstattung*, p. 70.

46. "**München," *AZ*, 28 March 1828.

cluding abolishing restrictions on where delegates could sit, on when and how often they could speak, and on how their conduct could be publicized.[47] He even suggested that the emergence of genuine political parties (as against "merely personal factions") would aid the public's understanding.[48] He did all this in behalf of the king's legislation, which remained stalled by the obtuseness of the assembly's rules and the defensiveness of its posture overall. But he also argued that the Diet should take into account the larger claims of public opinion to be informed.[49] If taken seriously, his arguments, far from undermining the assembly's prestige, would have enormously enhanced its political importance.

From Ludwig's point of view, the changes Lindner called for would allow the Diet to fulfill its consultative function more efficiently—a function it would have performed to his satisfaction had it simply passed the legislation he proposed. Yet at the same time, he had no wish to see the Diet's more troublesome "representative" function amplified by the press. But the legal hedges erected against the second function also lamed the first—no disadvantage in the eyes of the constitution's framers, who had assumed that the impetus for change would always come from the Chamber of Deputies, but a grave impediment to an activist king: out of over two dozen acts presented for the Diet's approval in 1827–28, only seven had passed.[50] Far from breaking the deadlock, Lindner's articles had stiffened the Diet's spine, uniting conservatives and reformers most effectively. At bottom this shared resentment reflected the distortion that years of determined reaction, followed by a few months of tentative liberalization, had introduced into the relationship of press to parliament. It was not the Diet's fault that it labored under gross constitutional restraints that made it seem ridiculous; and although the *AZ*'s call for action also implied an end to those restraints, it is not surprising that this implication was overlooked. Nor was it Cotta's fault that the *AZ* was subject to censorship. And it certainly seemed unfair that the relative freedom of expression that he had preserved for his newspaper should in this instance have made it a target for the censor's enemies.

The resentment that the *AZ* inspired was, however, also a reflection of its nature and position. The *AZ* was too imposing in its reputation and too elusive in its editorial practices to play the kind of role the king's ministers wanted it to play. Much of what Lindner had to say indirectly favored the Diet's cause. Much of the offense taken to his reports, however, was not political but personal—a category of grievance to which

47. "**München," *AZ*, 13 May 1828 (Beilage).
48. "**München," *AZ*, 28 March 1828.
49. "**München," *AZ*, 28 May, 1 June 1828.
50. Summarized in Max Spindler, ed., *Handbuch der bayerischen Geschichte* (Munich, 1974), 4:140–41; cf. Ostadal, *Die Kammer der Reichsräte*, pp. 92–95.

the *AZ* was no more sensitive now than it had ever been. Even friends of the press found that they did not like to have their ideas, motives, and favorite rhetorical flourishes discussed by an anonymous commentator in a newspaper read all over Europe. Nor were they persuaded that nonpartisanship, even if sincere, could ever substitute for freedom.[51]

With the close of the Diet in August, such questions became moot. But the general problem of how to manage the press remained urgent. The early years of Ludwig's reign had seen the proliferation of short-lived, locally circulated newspapers, whose number far outstripped any reasonable estimate of public demand. The low quality of these publications was a matter of concern among serious journalists of all political persuasions, since such papers seemed to bring the whole enterprise of political publicity into disrepute. The Diet's convening, however, had encouraged the emergence of more sophisticated opposition papers, like the Nuremberg *Freie Presse*, which had humiliated the ministry by printing some of the Diet's proceedings without permission and getting away with it.[52] It was clear, moreover, that the *AZ* did not provide the means for the government to meet this new challenge. Nonpartisanship is no substitute for freedom, and it is no substitute for partisanship either: Lindner's articles would have been resented less if their support for the regime had not been obscured by the rhetoric of impartiality that suffused almost everything Cotta published. If the government was to have a public voice, it would have to be unambiguously its own.

The *AZ*'s failure to create sympathy for the government only compounded the king's disappointment with Cotta's Anstalt, whose potential was hardly being realized by projects like *Ausland* and the new *Annalen*. Lindner urged Cotta to come to Munich himself to provide leadership.[53] But Cotta declined to do this, and in March Ludwig in turn declined to include Cotta among the new, progovernment peers he was appointing to the upper house. Although the king knew that politically "Cotta would be with me in everything," he was not willing to suffer the storm that such a step would provoke, at least until he was convinced of Cotta's commitment to Munich.[54] As it was, the king's critics were already distressed that a "foreign" publisher had installed a "nest of Jacobins" in

51. The *AZ* acquitted itself very poorly on these issues. Lindner refused to identify himself unless it could be shown that he had violated the law; and Stegmann went so far as to publish an article by Lindner bearing the dateline "†München" (3 June 1828 [Beilage]) chiding the "** correspondent" (i.e., Lindner himself) for being too impartial. The *AZ* also published articles by Lindner's real critics, of course (e.g., "†München," 18 May 1828 [Beilage]).

52. Lempfrid, *Anfänge*, pp. 100–103.

53. Lindner to Cotta, 18 Feb. 1828, CA.

54. Recounted in Joseph von Hormayr to Cotta, 20 March 1828, in Fehling and Schiller, *Briefe an Cotta* 2 : 235.

the capital, including one troublesome Jew.[55] Yet Ludwig had little to show for having permitted this outrage; following Heine's withdrawal, the *Annalen*, which had taken no part in defending the crown, went into suspense for eighteen months, finally to reemerge, still in Stuttgart, under the editorship of the Badenese historian Karl von Rotteck, who sustained the journal's liberal spirit, as Heine had hoped, but not its connection to Bavaria.

Nothing that had happened ruled out a more politically productive collaboration. On the contrary, Cotta's personal relations with the key personalities in Munich were excellent, and in the course of the customs negotiations that were about to begin they would become positively intimate. A number of Ludwig's advisors—notably Joseph von Hormayr, who had general charge of cultural affairs at the foreign ministry—had long felt that, in addition to combating the "parochialism of intellectual life," it was essential to "use Cotta's institute in a way calculated to serve the higher purposes of the state."[56] Almost from the beginning of Ludwig's reign there had been vague talk about producing a ministerial journal, which became somewhat less vague during the worst weeks of the Diet. Nothing had come of these deliberations, however, apparently because Ludwig's advisors had understood the problem to be, as Hormayr put it, simply a matter of getting Cotta "to bake bread from the king's flour."[57]

Cotta was prepared to provide this sort of service, but not on the basis of discounted rent and transit concessions, however generous. He demanded a higher level of cooperation and a more equitable sharing of risks. With the cabinet reorganization that followed the Diet's close, however, these difficulties were overcome. Eduard von Schenk, Ludwig's main advisor on educational and church matters and a longtime literary associate as well, was named minister of the interior. He immediately offered Cotta the full support of his office, together with a financial indemnity in the event their joint venture proved unprofitable.[58] With this offer, plans for another attempt at a journal of general culture were set

55. Hormayr to Elizabeth von Cotta [Cotta's second wife], 20 Feb. 1828, ibid., p. 231; Johannes Friedrich, *Ignaz von Döllinger: Sein Leben auf Grund seines schriftlichen Nachlassen* (Munich, 1899–1901), 1:207–8; cf. Heine to Moses Moser, 14 April 1828, in Heine, *Säkularausgabe* 20:328–29.

56. Hormayr to Schenk, 21 Oct. 1827, Bayerische Staatsbibliothek, Schenkiana II 7; cf. Hormayr to Cotta, 20 Jan. 1828, in Fehling and Schiller, *Briefe an Cotta* 2:220–21.

57. Hormayr to Schenk, 21 Oct. 1827, Schenkiana II 7. Cotta discussed this project with Ludwig as early as January 1828, but he was offended by the treatment he received from the ministry and municipal officials. See Cotta to Armansperg, 27 Jan. 1828, and the subsequent correspondence between Armansperg and the Government of the Isarkreis, M Inn 25105.

58. Cotta to Alfred von Schönberg-Hartenstein [the Austrian ambassador to Munich], 1 May 1831, CA.

aside, and arrangements were made with great dispatch for a ministerial newspaper called *Inland: Ein Tagblatt für das öffentliche Leben in Deutschland, mit vorzüglicher Rücksicht auf Bayern.*[59]

INLAND

Inland appeared on January 1, 1829, a half-sheet daily printed in quarto by the Schulbuch-Verlag. A subscription cost twelve gulden per year, and in the first few months just under four hundred were sold, of which sixty-one went to government offices.[60] Physically, *Inland* resembled *Ausland*, to which it was also linked by the logic of its title. Politically, it occupied the position staked out by Lindner in his articles for the *AZ*: an organ of reformism and action generally, confronting opposition from what a contemporary Frenchman would have called the "left" and the "right." The metaphoric spectrum of interests suggested by these terms can be applied in a German context only with great caution. Ideological or factional identities were weak, and they were compromised by cultural, confessional, and regional loyalties that make it difficult to predict how an individual will view any particular issue. That *Inland* should finally have been put together by Schenk, a Catholic conservative (but also a man of letters), rather than by his predecessor, Armansperg, a former leader of the liberal opposition in the assembly (and for just that reason suspicious of the press), is indicative of how unpredictable personal attitudes could be. But neither is the image of left and right meaningless. It reflects a degree of political organization toward which many in Bavaria were striving (the terms derive from the customs of the French National Assembly, whose members could sit where they pleased); and it corresponds to the ministry's feeling of being beset from all sides, by opponents who were themselves irreconcilable.

In its leading personalities, *Inland* reflected the same "Jacobinical" tendencies as the Anstalt's other ventures. The editor, Wilhelm Mönnich, was another former *Burschenschaftler* who had made his living in the early 1820s by writing about literature for the *Morgenblatt*. He was supported by a number of established contributors to *Ausland* and the *AZ*—Lindner, Thiersch, Kolb, Rudhart, Hermes, and J. J. Lautenbacher, who had won high praise from Heine for his contributions to the *Annalen*.[61] To these men was added the rather difficult figure of Hor-

59. Preparations are discussed in Schenk to Ludwig, 23 Nov., 1 Dec., and 4 Dec. [two letters] 1829, M Inn 25105; Hormayr to Schenk, 17 Dec. 1831, Schenkiana II 7.

60. Schulbuch-Verlag to Interior Ministry, 30 May 1831, M Inn 45313. Although *Inland* called itself a "Tagblatt," it actually appeared less often because of the editor's habit of producing double numbers bearing two dates.

61. Heine to Kolb, 11 Nov. 1828, in Heine, *Säkularausgabe* 20:350. Schenk to Ludwig, 23 Nov. 1828, M Inn 25105, includes a list of thirty-five individuals, mainly officials and professors at the university, who might be expected to contribute to *Inland*.

mayr, an Austrian who had entered Bavarian service at the start of 1828. Hormayr had played a leading role in the Tyrolian uprising of 1809, and he believed in the power of public opinion. On arrival in Munich he had lobbied vigorously for a ministerial newspaper, arguing that the Anstalt's efforts up to then were "half measures" and bound to fail.[62] He thought *Inland* had been his idea all along, and he did not like the "demagogic young men" that Cotta had been hiring in recent years "by waiting around the prison door."[63] Hormayr's decisive political characteristic was rabid anticlericalism. Personally, he was an intriguer of the first water. Cotta, who had known Hormayr for years, did not trust him;[64] Ludwig did, and took his advice on press matters very seriously.

Left to themselves these men would have positioned *Inland* somewhere near the political center in Bavaria, to the extent that this middle ground could be located at all.[65] Over the course of its life *Inland* would reject the claims of the Catholic church to official influence—to control public education, civil marriages, and so on—but not the general importance of religious values in public life. It would likewise reject the most emphatic demands of the nascent left—for a dramatic broadening of the franchise and for parliamentary control of the army.[66] Its values were those of the constitution, understood not in the French sense, as a charter of abstract rights, but in the English sense, as the living structure of government.[67] It denounced partisanship as a matter of principle, and took it as part of its mission to restore civility to public life. But it also recognized that differences of opinion were part of a vigorous polity, and it invited "independent" contributions from all comers.[68] It did all these things, however, as the acknowledged organ of the king's ministers, and from the very beginning its public reception was dominated by questions about its status: about how far its conciliatory mission could be reconciled with its official role, and about how far supporting the constitution and supporting the government were really the same thing.

The issue was never freedom of the press: the only journal of domestic politics subject to regular censorship was *Inland* itself, which appeared under the supervision of a councillor in Schenk's ministry. Op-

62. Hormayr to Schenk, 11 June 1828, Schenkiana II 7.
63. Hormayr to Schenk, 17 Dec. 1831, ibid.
64. Cotta published Hormayr's *Kritisch-diplomatische Beiträge zur Geschichte Tirols im Mittelalter* in 1806. Hormayr was eager to trade on this acquaintance, but Cotta kept him at arm's length. Cf. Hormayr to Schenk, 22 April 1826, 30 April 1828, Schenkiana II 7; and Cotta to Schönberg-Hartenstein, 1 May 1831, CA.
65. Cf. "Die Parteyen in Bayern," *Inland*, 9 Nov. 1830.
66. *Inland*'s contents are summarized in more detail by Steuer, *Cotta in München*, pp. 37–81.
67. "Ueber einige Grundsätze der bayerischen Staatsregierung," *Inland*, 21–22 Jan. 1829.
68. "Was wir wollen," *Inland*, 1–2 Jan. 1829.

position journals were free of official interference, and with the belated publication of the Diet's proceedings at the end of 1828 the last important restraint on their contents fell away. Still, there were some who expressed concern about the propriety of a venture that seemed to have government employees working for the profit of a private individual, a charge *Inland* dismissed by pointing to foreign precedents like the *London Times* and the *Moniteur*.[69]

A more sophisticated view was taken by the *Bayerische Volksblatt*, which appeared a few weeks after *Inland* and quickly emerged as the leading liberal organ in Bavaria. Unlike older journals like the *Freie Presse*, which was almost entirely the work of its editor, Victor Coremans, the *Volksblatt* was the product of a large group of scholars, officials, and parliamentarians centered on the University of Würzburg. This fact gave the *Volksblatt* unusual depth and diversity, and strengthened the growing impression that journals could be vehicles for political organization. The *Volksblatt* hailed *Inland's* appearance as the logical prerequisite to the emergence of "constitutional" opposition, which could define itself only in relation to the government. In contrast to the *AZ*, *Inland* created the kind of unambiguous situation that ought to have obtained in the Diet itself—the ministry on one side, its critics on the other, and all debate open to the public. The *Volksblatt* thus looked askance on *Inland's* claim to impartiality, which threatened to introduce subtlety and evasion where clarity was wanted. It proved most critical of those articles that expressed the greatest independence from official policy.[70]

Inland, for its part, rejected as a contradiction in terms the *Volksblatt's* idea that it represented a "ministerial party." But it accepted the principle of "constitutional opposition," provided the opposition press did not give rise to "party activity, through which independence can be lost even more quickly than through agreement with the government."[71] In all this *Inland* professed to rise above controversy, an irritating habit that flew in the face of reality and contradicted its official role. Equally irritating was the condescending tone *Inland* could adopt toward its rivals, a tactic that often had the effect of prolonging controversy for which no substantive basis existed. For the most part, however, *Inland* shared the same vision of the press as the *Volksblatt* and the *Freie Presse*: a constitutionally protected institution with an obligation to promote progressive

69. "Kleiner Krieg einiger bayer'schen Blätter gegen Das Inland," 26–27 Jan., 19 Feb. 1829 [by Lindner; cf. Rechnung des Doctor Lindner, 30 April 1829, CA].

70. On the *Volksblatt*, see the biography of its founder by Heinrich Borngässer, "Gottfried Eisenmann: Ein Kämpfer für die deutsche Einheit und Vertreter des bayerischen Machtgedankens," Ph.D. diss., Frankfurt, 1931; and Lempfrid, *Anfänge*, passim.

71. "Ueber die Opposition, mit Hinblick auf Bayern," *Inland*, 28–29 Jan. 1829; "Neue Zeitschrift in Bayern," *Inland*, 25 March 1829 [by Lindner; cf. Rechnung des Doctor Lindner, 30 April 1829, CA].

(as opposed to merely efficient) government. Early on, Cotta's paper announced its intention to live in peace with its critics on the left,[72] and, sniping aside, it succeeded.

Not so with critics on the right. To an even greater extent than the nascent liberals in the Diet, the Catholic intellectuals attracted to Munich after Ludwig's coronation in 1825 had reason to be disappointed by the gap between the king's early promise and his actual performance. This gap was believed to reside in Ludwig's personality, in which religious piety and a deep attachment to the church competed with an equally strong loyalty to the principles of secular, bureaucratic government that had been ascendent in Germany since the turn of the century. These matters were explored most pointedly in the journal *Eos*, the organ of a group of conservative scholars at the university under the editorship of Joseph Görres, whose conversion to Catholicism and reaction in the early 1820s had left his powers as a journalist unimpaired.[73]

The issues dividing this group from the men at Cotta's Anstalt went to the heart of the state's existence, which the *Eos* group held to derive not from any kind of compact between ruler and ruled, but from a compact between God and his servant, the king. Where *Inland* stood for tolerance and diversity, which it believed were conducive to public order, *Eos* stood for order as such and despised the compromises of representative government as a mask for anarchy. The rivalry between the journals was tinged with contempt, since, apart from Friedrich Thiersch, none of *Inland*'s staff possessed the academic distinction of those at *Eos*. It was also tinged with envy. Görres and his professorial colleagues had come to Munich at the king's invitation, and they had expected that his confidence, so unaccountably bestowed on *Inland*, would fall to them. Like the liberal opposition, which feared the influence of the nebulous and conspiratorial "congregation," *Eos* believed Ludwig had fallen prey to sinister forces, whose agents had persuaded him to place his government's public presence in the hands of "a gang of wandering vagabonds, mercenary publicists, and shysters."[74] The conflict between *Eos* and *Inland* was thus only incidentally a contest for public influence. The real audience was the king himself.

The casus belli was a matter of purely symbolic importance: a calculated attack by Hormayr on the reputations of two recently deceased

72. "Ueber die Opposition, mit Hinblick auf Bayern," *Inland*, 28–29 Jan. 1829. By the middle of 1830 the Anstalt's director viewed the *Volksblatt* as a commercial competitor rather than a political rival and believed that, should the *Volksblatt* fail for financial reasons (as seemed possible at the time), *Inland* would inherit most of its customers (Sonntag to Cotta, 20 May 1830, CA).

73. For a detailed discussion, see Hans Kapfinger, *Der Eoskreis, 1828 bis 1832: Ein Beytrag zur Vorgeschichte des politischen Katholizismus in Deutschland* (Munich, 1928).

74. Ibid., pp. 115–16.

Catholic writers, Friedrich Schlegel and Adam Müller.[75] Görres in reply assailed *Inland* for betraying the government and for showing itself "entirely devoid of any sense of honor, any shred of decency, or any piety in the presence of the dead."[76] The controversy thereafter proceeded in a vein of increasingly personal vituperation, being slowed only briefly by the prospect of a libel action by Lindner against Görres.[77] At the end of March Hormayr claimed victory in a letter to Ludwig, on the grounds that the congregation had now shown itself contemptuous of the king's judgment and grasping in its ambition.[78] The claim was premature but in the end true enough. By summer Ludwig had let it be known that he was displeased with the fanaticism displayed by *Eos*, and in the fall the paper announced that its entire editorial board had resigned[79]—the result, as Karl Hermes would later remark, of "a bolt from heaven."[80]

A victory, then, but of a very damaging kind. Although *Eos* had failed to persuade the king that it was his true champion, the journal had called forth such an intemperate response as to raise questions about *Inland's* character. The *Volksblatt* at first supported the Anstalt unstintingly against the common enemy, only to express its disappointment later on that *Inland* had lost sight of its ministerial role.[81] This judgment was confirmed in the most striking fashion by the sudden appearance of deliberate gaps in *Inland's* copy, exposing the hand of the censor to public scrutiny and calling forth astonishment from the independent press, which had never seen such a thing in a ministerial newspaper.[82] Neither, it is safe to say, had Cotta. Having launched *Inland* in some haste, he had neglected its development, being completely absorbed by the customs negotiations then under way in Berlin. He now began a series of attempts to adjust the paper's political posture, to bring it more in line with the expectations of the ministry[83] and with the traditions of the Cotta press.

75. "Dresden," *Inland*, 10 Feb. 1829.

76. "Das Recht der Toten," *Eos*, 18 Feb. 1829; cf. Mönnich, "Das Recht des Lebenden," *Inland*, 29 Feb. 1829.

77. Cf. Görres, "Frecheit und kein Ende," *Eos*, 4–6 March 1829, and Lindner, "Erklärung," *Inland*, 17 Mar. 1829.

78. Hormayr to Ludwig, 19 March 1829, Bayerisches Hauptstaatsarchiv, Abteilung III: Geheimes Hausarchiv, "Briefe des Frhr. von Hormayr, 1825–30," II-A-23.

79. *Eos*, 23 Oct. 1829; cf. Kapfinger, *Eoskreis*, pp. 88–91.

80. "Uebersicht der periodischen Literatur in Bayern," *Inland*, 19 Aug. 1830.

81. For instance "Das *Inland* befehdet von der *Eos*," 7, 14 March 1829; cf. Lempfrid, *Anfänge*, pp. 117–21.

82. The issue of 6 Oct. 1829 appeared with a blank column on page one; blank lines were also inserted in an article on Oct. 11. On the public reaction, see *Bayerisches Volksblatt*, 17 Oct. 1829; and "Ueber einen in den Blätter für literarische Unterhaltung erschienen Aufsatz: 'Aus und über Bayern,'" *Inland*, 9–11 Dec. 1829.

83. No formal complaint seems to have reached Cotta. Nonetheless *Inland* had become an embarrassment to provincial officials. See Augsburg District Government to Ludwig, 13 Jan. 1830, M Inn 25105.

For much of what had happened, Cotta blamed Hormayr. Relations between them, never warm, became secretly bitter.[84] But Ludwig forbade a public breach, and Hormayr remained among *Inland*'s leading contributors, although Cotta refused to allow him any further editorial influence.[85] Mönnich, who as editor-in-chief had failed to consult effectively with the government, was replaced by an outsider named Georg Puchta, a Catholic (unlike almost everyone at the Anstalt) and a professor of law at the university, who had been put forward by Schenk and endorsed by Cotta's oldest friend in Munich, Friedrich Schelling.[86] Cotta also brought in another outsider, Friedrich Sonntag, to manage the Anstalt as a whole, a position that entailed regular meetings with *Inland*'s editors.[87]

In all this, Cotta was only doing what he had done under similar circumstances in the past—when he dispatched Friedrich Hartmann to assist Bendix Daevel in Hamburg, for instance, or when he brought Friedrich Schlegel into the *Bundeszeitung* project, or even when he tried to recruit Posselt and Schiller to edit the *Neueste Weltkunde*. By broadening the mix of personalities on the *Inland* staff and rearranging responsibilities among them, he looked to restore balance to the paper's contents. But apart from the successful partnership of Kolb and Stegmann on the *AZ*, this sort of thing had never worked very well, and it did not work now. The mix of ideological and confessional rivalries in Munich was beyond Cotta's experience, and he misjudged its volatility. Puchta in particular proved a disastrous choice, lacking any instinct for collegiality.[88] Politically, he was a kind of Trojan horse, with unexpectedly close ties to Görres and his circle.[89] In the first issue over which he had charge Puchta announced that the public impression of *Inland*'s ministerial status had been a mistake, trumped up by the liberal opposition for its own purposes.[90] This declaration inspired even greater astonishment than the blank copy of three months before, and in February Puchta, too, was dismissed.[91]

He was succeeded by Lautenbacher, whose interests ran to drama and literature as well as politics. Lautenbacher's main objective was to in-

84. Hormayr to Schenk, 9 Oct. 1829, Schenkiana II 7.

85. Cf. Hormayr to Ludwig, 24 Oct. 1829, Geheimes Hausarchiv II-A-23; J. J. Lautenbacher to Cotta, 25 March 1830, CA.

86. Georg Puchta to Cotta, 10 Nov. 1829, CA.

87. Friedrich Sonntag to Cotta, 29, 30 Dec. 1829, CA. Little is known about Sonntag. He hailed from Pforzheim in Baden and seems to have been a businessman (perhaps a book dealer) rather than a journalist.

88. Lautenbacher to Cotta, 12, 19, 24 Nov. 1829, CA.

89. Philipp von Schmitz-Grollenburg [Württemberg ambassador in Munich] to Cotta, 10 Feb. 1830, in Fehling and Schiller, *Briefe an Cotta* 2:245–46.

90. "Zum neuen Jahre 1830," *Inland*, 1–2 Jan. 1830.

91. Puchta to Cotta, 7 Feb. 1830, CA; cf. *Bayerisches Volksblatt*, 9 Jan. 1830, enclosed with Puchta to Cotta, 13 Jan. 1830, CA.

crease *Inland*'s circulation, which had not improved since its first appearance and which he took as a rejection of its combative style. Lautenbacher devoted more of the paper's space to theater criticism and book
reviews and to news from elsewhere in Germany. He also built bridges
to the clerical right and found room for half a dozen articles by the
former editors of *Eos*.[92] He arranged office space for himself at the interior ministry,[93] and thereafter *Inland*'s treatment of domestic events
acquired a more documentary cast. These developments displeased
some of the Anstalt's staff, notably Karl Hermes, who criticized *Inland* in
its own pages for becoming too concerned with trivialities.[94] Even more
confounding, however, was Lautenbacher's failure to satisfy the king.

The chief reason for the extraordinary absorption of *Inland* and its
rivals in questions about their own ideological identities had been an
acute shortage of real events about which to write—a shortage also evident in the insistent attention the press paid to the proceedings of the
last Diet.[95] By the winter of 1830, however, the end of this dry spell could
be foreseen. In the summer new elections would be held, followed by
another Diet. By almost any definition, the main task of a ministerial
newspaper should have been to prepare public opinion to receive the
government's program. *Inland*, under Lautenbacher as under Mönnich,
had shown itself ill adapted to this purpose, having drifted off into
vaguely cultural concerns at just the moment when a sharp political focus was called for. Ludwig therefore ordered Schenk to establish yet
another journal, one more popular in its orientation and better able to
come to grips with the liberal opposition.[96]

It was only thanks to Lautenbacher's alertness that this project found
its way to the Anstalt. It had originally been earmarked for another publisher, F. G. Franckh, whose interests Hormayr had taken to promoting
as a way of getting back at Cotta.[97] Lautenbacher regarded such a development as a potential disaster; *Inland*'s credibility could scarcely weather
anything as singular as the appearance of a rival ministerial newspaper.
He believed that the project showed all the signs of another effort at
subversion by the professoriat at the university; and he insisted that,
since *Inland* and the new journal shared the same nominal objectives,
they should at least appear side by side.[98] Schenk, whose confidence in
Cotta personally remained unshaken, was agreeable, and at the end of

92. Steuer, *Cotta in München*, p. 57.

93. Cotta to Schönberg-Hartenstein, 1 May 1831, CA.

94. Hermes, "Uebersicht der periodischen Literatur in Bayern" [in seven parts], *In-
land*, 19 Aug.–11 Nov. 1830. This series, highly critical of the Bavarian press, appeared with
Cotta's explicit approval, and over Lautenbacher's objections (Sonntag to Cotta, 20–26
July, 5 Aug. 1830, CA).

95. Lempfrid, *Anfänge*, p. 117.

96. Schenk to Ludwig, 31 March 1830, in Spindler, *Briefwechsel*, pp. 130–31 and 412n.

97. Steuer, *Cotta in München*, pp. 61–65.

98. Lautenbacher to Cotta, 23–30 March, 11 April 1830, CA.

April *Inland* announced an irregular supplement called the *Thron- und Volksfreund*.[99]

In retrospect the only remarkable thing about the *Volksfreund* was its title, which, harking back to the War of Liberation, called forth derision from *Eos* (now down but not out) and admiration from the *Volksblatt*, where its appearance, like *Inland*'s earlier, was hailed as a sign that the government trusted the people.[100] In a technical sense the *Volksfreund* was the most "popular" political journal Cotta ever published: it sold for three gulden per year (free to *Inland*'s subscribers) and was intended to reach the widest possible domestic audience.[101] But its contents were entirely in the hands of the ministry, and like all such publications it was plagued by a dearth of usable copy.[102] In all, seven or eight numbers seem to have appeared, the last in September, none of them in any way controversial.[103] But the *Volksfreund*'s passing was nevertheless a matter of grave concern, coming as it did in the wake of news of revolution in France.

In Bavaria, the most immediate effect of the July Revolution was to heighten the already well developed tension between the crown and the opposition press. Although the *Volksblatt* had initially felt confident that the government's loyalty to the constitution would render Bavaria immune to civil disturbance,[104] as the details of the revolution became known and its capacity to spread to some of the smaller German lands was demonstrated, a new light was cast on events that otherwise seemed rather remote.[105] The role of journalists in orchestrating the rising in Paris was particularly disturbing from Ludwig's point of view, and it convinced him that his tolerance of domestic controversy had been dangerously in error.[106] His fears can only have been confirmed by the remarkable complacency of *Inland* itself, which announced that, of the "three great powers" that controlled public life—money, the military, and public opinion—public opinion had now emerged as the strongest.[107] But Ludwig felt himself a prisoner of his earlier policy and concluded that any dramatic act of repression toward the press would call calamity down on him too.[108]

99. "Ankündigung," *Inland*, 29 April 1830.

100. Lempfrid, *Anfänge*, pp. 118–19.

101. It did not do so, however. In addition to *Inland*'s four hundred or so subscribers, the *Thron- und Volksfreund* attracted only seventeen customers of its own (Sonntag to Cotta, 9 July 1830, CA).

102. Schenk to Ludwig, 1 May 1830, in Spindler, *Briefwechsel*, p. 134.

103. Only the fifth number survives, in the Bayerische Staatsbibliothek.

104. *Bayerisches Volksblatt*, 14 Aug. 1830.

105. Ibid., 30 Oct., 20 Nov. 1830.

106. Ludwig to Lerchenfeld, 27 Sept. 1830, in Lerchenfeld, *Papieren*, pp. 423–24.

107. "Drey große Mächte," *Inland*, 28 Sept. 1830; cf. "Ueber Publizität," *Inland*, 25 Sept. 1830, and "Die Parteyen in Bayern," *Inland*, 9 Nov. 1830.

108. Ludwig to Lerchenfeld, 27 Sept. 1830, in Lerchenfeld, *Papieren*, pp. 423–24.

A number of steps were nevertheless taken to prepare for decisive action. The election of the new Diet was postponed until the end of the year, and special restrictions were placed on reporting about the royal family and the crown's ministers. News from France was closely censored, as existing law allowed. In November the editors of three popular periodicals were expelled from Bavaria, less because they were identified with the constitutional opposition than because, in the manner of the *Reisende Teufel*, they had cast aspersions on the processes of government generally.[109] That the *Volksfreund* should have been let fall under such circumstances was certainly a reflection of distrust toward the popular audience that this new journal was supposed to serve. But the ministry was still not prepared to concede full sway over public opinion to its opponents or to give up on *Inland*. Lautenbacher, who had avoided confrontation with the left, exchanged the editorship of *Inland* for that of *Ausland*. Karl Hermes also resigned, attacking *Inland* for falling into the hands of reactionaries.[110]

Although this last charge was untrue, the ministry was unquestionably determined to give *Inland* a more conventionally progovernment cast, especially in relation to the Diet.[111] It was therefore decided to "recall to the public's mind" *Inland*'s original purpose, which was "to inform [its readers] about every important event and every influential development in all areas of public life, and particularly about the activities of public officials and the peoples' representatives."[112] A year that had begun with a notice denying *Inland*'s ministerial status thus ended with an announcement affirming its devotion to the crown. The first notice had proven to be untrue. So, too, would the second.

DRAWING THE LINE

The Diet that opened on February 20, 1831, gathered in an atmosphere of greater apprehension and rancor than had any of its predecessors.[113] Europe, in Metternich's famous phrase, had caught cold, and the symptoms were as evident in Bavaria as elsewhere. Except for a few isolated incidents, including a student demonstration in December that forced the closing of the university in Munich, the July Revolution had not yet spawned any sympathetic disturbances in Bavaria; but it had reawakened enthusiasm for constitutional change, as opposed to the piecemeal

109. Lempfrid, *Anfänge*, pp. 161–65.

110. Ibid., pp. 214–15.

111. Schenk to Cotta, 10 Oct. 1830, CA.

112. "Ankündigung," *Inland*, 22 Dec. 1830; cf. Schenk to the Finance Ministry, 30 Dec. 1830, M Inn 25105.

113. Wilhelmine Gölz, "Der bayerische Landtag 1831: Ein Wendepunkt in der Regierung Ludwigs I," Ph.D. diss., Munich, 1926, is the only comprehensive study.

legislative program Ludwig had presented four years before, and the spectacle of more serious disorders elsewhere implicitly strengthened the assembly's position. Throughout the fall *Inland* insisted that political parties did not exist in Bavaria and that the universality of public opinion made nonsense of the very idea of organized opposition. It also attacked the *Volksblatt* and the *Freie Presse* for seeking to influence the election, a charge that was of course immediately thrown back in its face. But *Inland* also insisted that a public testing of candidates was essential if the government was to win the people's trust, and like its opponents on the left, it offered itself (to no avail) as a forum for debate among those seeking office.

There is no evidence that the controversy among Bavaria's increasingly agitated newspapers affected the election in any decisive way, since the vote was conducted under rules intended to make such influence impossible. Nevertheless, the results certainly revealed a desire for movement among the electorate: out of 124 members in the Chamber of Deputies, only 36 incumbents were returned, and none from the Rheinpfalz, where political excitement was running especially high.[114] Nor was there any question that this Diet would transact its business before the public eye, since the crown had finally conceded it the right to publicize its proceedings.[115] *Inland*, newly mindful of its ministerial responsibilities, reorganized itself as an afternoon newspaper to win a few extra hours' advantage for the government.[116] It began the year by acknowledging the right of "honorable" opposition,[117] and then proceeded to two series of articles on the constitutional rights of German kings and parliaments.[118] All these benevolent portents were thrown away, however, by the announcement, shortly before the Diet's opening, that five prominent opposition members would be denied their seats and that all periodicals touching on domestic politics would again be subject to censorship.[119]

It is beyond our purpose to consider the full significance of this decision on the history of Ludwig's regime. The reimposition of censorship has long been recognized as having marked the end of one phase of his

114. Lempfrid, "Der Bayerische Landtag 1831," p. 5; see Karl H. Wegert, "Ideologie und Aktion: Liberale Bewegung und Volkstradition in der Pfalz, 1830–1834," in *Liberalismus in der Gesellschaft des deutschen Vormärz*, ed. Wolfgang Schieder, *Geschichte und Gesellschaft*, Sonderheft 9 (Göttingen, 1983), pp. 167–87.

115. Raubold, *Landtagsberichterstattung*, pp. 13–14.

116. "Ankündigung," *Inland*, 22 Dec. 1830.

117. "Ueber den Zweck des Inlandes, nach den Forderungen der jüngsten Zeit," *Inland*, 1–2 Jan. 1831.

118. "Das Recht des Königs in deutschen constitutionellen Staaten," *Inland*, 8–10 Jan. 1831.

119. Press Order of 28 Jan. 1831, in Spindler, *Handbuch der bayerischen Geschichte* 4:153*n.*

rule, variously characterized as "liberal" or "pseudo-liberal,"[120] and as having begun another, whose reactionary, defensive aspect is unmistakable and which would end with Ludwig's abdication in March 1848. The immediate effect of the decision was to unify the Diet against the crown and to revive its determination to challenge the king's control of the press by holding the state's finances hostage. At the same time, Ludwig deprived himself of whatever leverage public opinion might have afforded. On the one hand, censorship dislocated the opposition press but did not silence it, thanks to another of the endless imprecisions that beset Bavarian press laws. Brochures and pamphlets, even those published seriatim, remained free under the new law and quickly became the dominant form of independent journalism.[121] On the other hand, a credible ministerial press was now out of the question. There was no sympathy whatever at the Anstalt for the king's action. Through all its vicissitudes, *Inland* had held fast to the notion that a free press was the very foundation of constitutional government, and it had always defined itself as a participant in the formation of public opinion, not as a regulator of it. Although at first the paper sought to discourage the Diet from using its fiscal powers to pressure the king,[122] Lautenbacher's successor, Wilhelm Schulz-Bodmer, believed there was no choice but for *Inland* to detach itself from the ministry.

This Cotta refused to do. From the start he had approached his ventures in Munich with a distinct reserve that reflected his understanding of where the initiative lay: with the king. This stance had been a disappointment to Ludwig, who had hoped for a display of entrepreneurial zeal and political energy on Cotta's part that never occurred. On the contrary, Cotta had acted simply as a royal contractor. This deferential attitude, however, now paid a modest dividend to the crown: Cotta had long since ceased to regard censorship as a matter of principle, and it was certainly not the sort of issue that would lead him to abandon a government that had invested such confidence in him; he therefore acceded to Schenk's proposal that a new editor be hired, one who would undertake to cover the Diet in a spirit that suited the king. Schenk recommended a young lawyer named Johann Wirth, who had earlier expressed an interest in publishing a *Landtagszeitung*.[123] Prior to going to work for *Inland*, Wirth had no particular reputation as a radical; but he hailed from Bayreuth, which had become part of Bavaria only in 1803,

120. Cf. Treml, "Vom Scheinliberalismus zur Reaktion," in *Bayerns Pressepolitik*, pp. 112–66; and Spindler, "Die liberale Period," in *Handbuch der bayerischen Geschichte* 4:105–57.

121. Lempfrid, *Anfänge*, pp. 207–26.

122. "Verfassungswidrigen Aufruf an die Stände," *Inland*, 25 Feb. 1831.

123. Recounted in Cotta to Schönberg-Hartenstein, 1 May 1831, CA; cf. Schenk to Cotta, 29 Jan., 2 Feb. 1831, CA.

and like most of the inhabitants of Ludwig's "new" territories his loyalty was to the constitution, not the dynasty. Whether Schenk realized that his own censors had squelched Wirth's earlier publication is not clear.[124] But it is entirely of a piece with the rest of *Inland's* peculiar history, and with Cotta's feelings in the matter, that if anyone was to lead *Inland* into opposition, it might as well be the ministry's hand-picked man.

On March 10 *Inland* announced for the fourth time in just over two years that it had changed its course and that its principal objective now would be "to freely support the constitutional government and administration through the defense of moderate constitutional principles." It would also put forward "well-considered and practical proposals for the improvement of the domestic situation."[125] This was obviously not what Schenk had in mind, and two weeks later Ludwig wrote to Cotta personally, expressing his indignation that *Inland* should have "assumed the role of an opposition newspaper" while "circulating as an organ of the ministry." Although Ludwig remained convinced of Cotta's loyalty and believed him to be ignorant of the situation, he now demanded decisive action, including Wirth's dismissal.[126] Cotta—who was not at all ignorant of the situation[127]—responded with a detailed review of *Inland's* tortuous history, together with a signed letter of dismissal for Wirth, which the king could use at his pleasure. But Cotta also warned that Wirth's departure would create a scandal, and would in any case not keep the young lawyer out of print for long. He believed that a similar scandal would attend the closing of *Inland* as well, which Cotta was nonetheless willing to do if so instructed. His recommendation, however, was that the censorship of *Inland* simply be tightened to avoid further misunderstandings.[128]

This letter transformed the issue of *Inland's* management from a sticky political problem into a question of honor—the kind of dispute in which Cotta's gift for compromise always failed him. Schenk responded on Ludwig's behalf that the censor's only job was to insure that the contents of a periodical, ministerial or otherwise, did not violate the law, whereas a publication's "tone" was the publisher's responsibility. He demanded that Cotta insert an announcement in *Inland* stating that it no longer represented the government and that its recent drift had occurred as the result of Cotta's absence.[129] Cotta rejected any such conces-

124. Cf. Sonntag to Cotta, 5 April 1831, CA.

125. "An das Publikum," *Inland*, 10 March 1831.

126. Ludwig to Cotta, 25 March 1831, CA; cf. Ludwig to Schenk, 29 March 1831, M Inn 45313.

127. Cf. Johann Wirth to Cotta, 3 March 1831, CA.

128. Cotta to Ludwig, 28 March 1831, M Inn 45313, and draft, CA; cf. Cotta to Schenk [draft], 28 March 1831, CA (apparently not sent).

129. Schenk to Cotta, 4 April 1831; and cf. Schenk to Ludwig, 31 March 1831, M Inn 45313.

sion.[130] Thus *Inland's* fate was sealed. On April 5 an entire issue was suppressed for the first time, prompting a protest from Wirth and an explanation from the censor that, while the material in question was not illegal, it was inappropriate to a ministerial newspaper.[131] Wirth then inserted an advertisement in the *AZ* offering subscribers a free, uncensored pamphlet as a substitute for the missing issue,[132] whereupon the ministry forbade the pamphlet's distribution by the Anstalt.[133] Ten days later *Inland* was placed under the authority of the regular district censors, and official announcements were printed in the *AZ* and the *Münchener politische Zeitung* declaring its ministerial status at an end.[134] Wirth, for his part, denied that *Inland* was an opposition newspaper and reaffirmed its commitment to the constitution—"but only to that, and not to an unconstitutional ministry."[135] This hard attitude, it should be said, was actually encouraged by Bavaria's foreign minister and Schenk's chief rival in the government, Armansperg, who wanted *Inland* to maintain its strong constitutionalist line as a way of distancing Bavaria from the eastern powers in the event of war with France—another illustration, if any were needed at this stage, of how treacherous ministerial journalism could be.[136] But Armansperg's support within the councils of government made no difference. Ludwig could decide for himself who his opponents were, and *Inland* was now numbered among them.[137]

Inland's slide into opposition occurred against a background of general confrontation between the regime and the Diet, whose position *Inland* now supported unreservedly. In the short term the Diet had the best

---

130. Cotta to Schenk, 10, 14 April 1831, M Inn 45313.

131. Wirth to Ludwig, 5 April 1831, and Protocol by Ministerial Councillor von Abel, 5 April 1831, M Inn 45313.

132. *AZ*, 10 April 1831 (außerordentliche Beilage).

133. Sonntag to Schenk, 6 April 1831, M Inn 45313; Schenk to Cotta, 8 April 1831, CA.

134. Schenk to the President of the Isarkreis, 15 April 1831, and to the editors of the *Allgemeine Zeitung* and the *Münchener politische Zeitung*, 15 April 1831, M Inn 45313. Cf. *AZ*, 17 April 1831.

135. "An das Publikum," *Inland*, 17 April 1831.

136. Cf. Sonntag to Cotta, 8 April 1831, CA. The internal conflict within the ministry may account for some references in Schenk's correspondence to his fears about the impression *Inland* was making on other governments. Prussia did take exception to *Inland* on one occasion (Armansperg to Schenk, 19 May 1831, M Inn 25105), and Cotta thought it prudent to provide a detailed account of *Inland's* history, emphasizing its official character, to Austria's ambassador, Schönberg-Hartenstein (1 May 1831, CA). But outside pressure played no part in *Inland's* eventual demise. On Armansperg's rather devious policies, which eventually led to his dismissal, see Robert D. Billinger, "The War Scare of 1831 and Prussian–South German Plans for the End of Austrian Dominance in Germany," *Central European History* 9 (1976): 203–19.

137. *Inland* was handled roughly by local officials, who suppressed ten issues in two months and bowdlerized many others. The suppressed issues were all distributed as pamphlets from Wirth's home.

of the struggle. Schenk, cast in the role of "the Bavarian Polignac" for his role in the restoration of censorship, was forced to resign at the end of May. A few weeks later the censorship decree was revoked, an act that *Inland* celebrated by printing an issue bordered in blue and white, the colors of the Wittelsbach dynasty.[138] Although these developments could not mend the rift between *Inland* and the king, they would certainly have allowed Cotta's newspaper to continue as an organ of the parliamentary opposition, a role in which it commanded more public interest than it ever had as an organ of the crown.[139] Cotta, however, no longer wished to proceed. Early in June he sought an audience with Ludwig, a last attempt, if not to save *Inland*, then at least to make amends personally for its failure. This request was rebuffed,[140] and on June 18 the Anstalt announced that *Inland* would cease publication at the end of the month.[141] It left behind a residue of ill feeling that never passed; Cotta spent the next seven months fruitlessly trying to collect the indemnity he had been promised in the event *Inland* failed to turn a profit—a promise that Ludwig refused to honor because *Inland* had betrayed his government.[142]

Inland also left behind a successor, called the *Deutsche Tribüne*, which its editor, Wirth, envisioned as continuing the "emancipation" of the press from the state already evident in *Inland*'s history.[143] The *Deutsche Tribüne* was in many ways a natural child of the Cotta press, springing directly from *Inland* in its final stages and consciously harking back to the earlier journal edited by Lindner, who allowed some of his essays from the old *Tribüne* to be reprinted in the new one. Wirth's paper was also financed by the manager of the Anstalt, Sonntag, who reported to Cotta regularly on the paper's progress. But Cotta kept his distance, and refused to allow his name to be brought into the venture.[144]

This distancing was more than mere prudence. The line between reformism and opposition was one of which Cotta had been aware all his

---

138. "Es lebe der König," *Inland*, 13 June 1831.

139. A correspondent from Bamberg reported on April 24 that *Inland*, not widely read there in the past, was now being fought over in the cafés.

140. Ludwig to Cotta, 14 May 1831, CA; cf. Schenk to Ludwig, 30 May, 7 June 1831, in Spindler, *Briefwechsel*, pp. 193–95.

141. "Anzeige," *Inland*, 18 June 1831.

142. Ludwig to Cotta, 28 Oct. 1831, and Cotta to Ludwig, 1, 21 Nov. 1831, CA; Cotta to Ludwig, 29 Feb. 1832, and Isarkreis to Interior Ministry, 6 March 1832, M Inn 45313. Schenk had promised Cotta that the government would make up the difference between *Inland*'s income and the value of seven hundred subscriptions. Over three years this short-fall came to 8,376 gulden (Literarisch-Artistische Anstalt to the Interior Ministry, 30 May 1831, M Inn 45313).

143. "An das deutsche Publikum," *Inland*, 19 June 1831 (Beilage). On the *Deutsche Tribüne*, see Koszyk, *Deutsche Presse*, pp. 67–75.

144. Cotta to Sonntag [draft], 29 June 1831, and Sonntag to Cotta, 16 July 1831, CA.

life, and he was not going to cross it now. The Cotta press had not been created to seek emancipation from the state, but partnership with it. That such a thing as constitutional opposition existed was clear; *Inland* had hailed its virtues even during those periods when the paper was most attentive to its ministerial role. But what made opposition "constitutional" was its meliorative aspect—its willingness to share the state's objectives, to acknowledge its primacy, and to be comprehended, in the end, by its formal institutions. The Bavarian Diet was supposed to be one such comprehending institution. The press was another, in which the universality of the state's interests was supposed to be mirrored by the universality of public opinion, a force that *Inland* always declared to be beyond partisan strife. In both press and parliament opposition was to be tolerated, even honored, insofar as it helped the state grasp the comprehensiveness of its interests. But that only the state's interests could be comprehensive was taken for granted, as was the partiality of those who opposed it. It was precisely in this sense that the Cotta press had always been "impartial"; and it was for precisely this reason that even "constitutional" opposition remained, for Cotta, an unattractive diminishment of the press's natural, integrative role.

Cotta's instinctive sense that the pursuit of the press's rights for their own sake would prove, if not pernicious, then at least futile, would soon be confirmed by events. The abrogation of the January press edict had by no means restored the constructive (if slightly overwrought) political atmosphere that existed before the edict's enactment. The assembly, after securing Schenk's resignation and the repeal of censorship, was invited by Schenk's successor to ratify a new press statute that would have codified the permissive standards established administratively in 1825. This bill was defeated by combined conservative and liberal opposition, as was virtually all other legislation submitted by the ministry. The Diet of 1831 ended in deadlock. The unprecedented assertion of the principle of ministerial accountability in the matter of Schenk's resignation, hailed by *Inland* as the triumph of responsible opposition,[145] thus proved barren of results, since it did not address the fundamental defect of the Diet's position: its lack of legislative initiative. The Diet was in no position to follow up its victory, nor was the press in any position to defend itself in the absence of an ally with firm constitutional standing.

The public itself was not yet such an ally, although, as in the War of Liberation, the generally high level of political excitement and the temporarily indecisive, defensive posture of Germany's governments suggested that it might be. The so-called Deutsche Press- und Vaterlandsverein, founded shortly after the close of the Diet by Wirth and another Bavarian journalist, Philipp Siebenpfeiffer, was an attempt to give that

145. "Sieg der bayrischen Opposition," *Inland*, 18 May 1831.

alliance an institutional form and a national dimension, and it enjoyed sufficient success to hold out hope for the future: the Verein itself attracted five thousand dues-paying members from all over Germany, and the three-day *Volksfest* held under its auspices at Hambach in May 1832 was impressive testimony to the breadth of popular support for a free press.[146] The present, however, still belonged to the princes. Ludwig personally would have preferred all along to reimpose censorship under a federal mandate; he acted alone only when it became clear that the Federation could not act quickly enough to solve his domestic problems.[147] That it would act, though, could be foreseen—Wirth himself predicted that the *Tribüne* would be suppressed, an event that he imagined would lead to civil violence.[148] But nothing of the kind occurred, and in the summer of 1832 the Federation, acting with the unanimity that it customarily displayed when the control of public opinion was at stake, reaffirmed the spirit of Carlsbad in every particular and brought the brief flourishing of opposition journalism, in Bavaria and elsewhere, to an end.[149]

146. The Press- und Vaterlandsverein, whose official name was "Der Deutsche Vaterlandsverein zur Unterstützung der freien Presse," has attracted surprisingly little attention, though the *Hambachfest* itself has been thoroughly studied, particularly in its social dimensions; see Cornelia Foerster, "Sozialstruktur und Organisationsformen des Deutschen Preß- und Vaterlandsvereins von 1832/33," in *Liberalismus in der Gesellschaft des deutschen Vormärz*, ed. Wolfgang Schieder, *Geschichte und Gesellschaft*, Sonderheft 9 (Göttingen, 1983), pp. 148–66.

147. Ludwig to Lerchenfeld, 27 Sept. 1830, in Lerchenfeld, *Papieren*, pp. 423–24; cf. the full discussion in Treml, *Bayerns Pressepolitik*, pp. 197–227.

148. "Der Kampf des Deutschen Bundes mit der Deutschen Tribüne," *Deutsche Tribüne*, 15 Feb. 1832.

149. The Federal Diet's deliberations are described, with copious excerpts from the official proceedings, in Ludwig Bentfeldt, *Der Deutsche Bund als nationales Band, 1815–1866* (Göttingen, 1985), pp. 159–84.

Conclusion: The Cotta Press in 1830

Cotta affects me deeply. He seems caught in a painful conflict between his devotion to the crown, his advocacy of a false liberalism, and his financial interests. The courtier, the businessman, and the idealistic statesman struggle within him. Compound characters of this sort are seldom reliable.

Eduard von Schenk to Ludwig I, June 7, 1831

REFORMISM AND OPPOSITION

Cotta's refusal to follow *Inland* into opposition was of a piece with the entirety of his career, which was characterized throughout by loyalty to the state as the sole source of legitimate political authority and as the chief engine of social progress. His feelings in this matter had all the warmth that normally derives from a lifetime of political experience, exacerbated in this case by the alarm with which he viewed the German response to the July Revolution. In principle, the values of those who organized the *Hambachfest* were scarcely distinguishable from those of the Cotta press in its infancy: the advancement of reason and justice in public life and "the moral improvement of the nation through education and Enlightenment."[1] But such sentiments acquire a new meaning when addressed to a heterogeneous crowd of perhaps twenty thousand people, united in the conviction that these things could be achieved, not by force, and not all at once, but soon. "Force breeds force," Philipp Siebenpfeiffer would declare, "and sin breeds sin; only spiritual regeneration is worthy of the nineteenth century."[2] Ernst Posselt could not have said it better. By the spring of 1832, however, there was no denying that the nineteenth century, the Century of Words, was well along.

As a young man Cotta had drawn inspiration from an earlier, more dangerous revolution in France. Even now he spared the Bourbons no sympathy. The prospect that the coup d'état of July might be but the opening act of a much larger drama, however, was another matter. In congratulating his protégé Thiers on the "great things" he had achieved,

1. J.G.A. Wirth, "Die Rechte des deutschen Volkes. Vertheidigungsrede vor dem Schwurgericht zu Landau," and P. J. Siebenpfeiffer, "Das Juste-Milieu oder die richtige Mitte," *Deutschland: Zeitschrift für allgemeine Politik und deutsches Bürgertum* 2 (1832); both cited in Wegert, "Ideologie und Aktion," pp. 171–72.

2. Ibid., p. 172.

Cotta was careful to indicate that congratulations were due mainly because, in helping to install the duc d'Orléans so expeditiously on the throne of his cousin, Thiers "had spared France an upheaval that could spread throughout all Europe."[3]

This remark soon began to look like wishful thinking. By the summer of 1831 there had been significant revolts in half a dozen German states, in Italy and Belgium, and, even more seriously, in Poland, where popular unrest had led to a Russian invasion and partial mobilization in Prussia and Austria. In Paris there was much talk in official circles about reclaiming the Rhine frontier. Increasingly it seemed to Cotta that a constructive sense of the traditions and limitations of German society, which in the 1790s had contributed to the resiliency with which the challenge of the great revolution had been met, were being lost. The press in particular had forsaken its integrative role and had begun to assert its own interests to the point where it threatened the stability of society and the peace of Europe. How far, in such circumstances, did the rights of the press extend? This was not an academic question. It was put to Cotta quite directly by Metternich apropos of the *Allgemeine Zeitung*,[4] which had done more than its share to insure that the prerevolutionary opposition in France had gotten a fair hearing in Germany and that the new regime now received its due.[5]

Although Cotta offered no immediate reply, the issue was nevertheless a serious one, to which he addressed himself in a series of articles published in the fall.[6] To Cotta the French revolt, however justified it

3. Cotta to Thiers, 16 Sept. 1830, Bibliothèque Thiers, T. MS. 561[2].

4. Metternich to Cotta, 13 July 1831, Haus, Hof, und Staatsarchiv, Vienna, Staatskanzlei: Wissenschaft und Kunst, Karton 13 (Zeitungen).

5. In the wake of the July Days, Cotta had seen the contributions from a number of his regular Parisian correspondents fall off somewhat as the authors suddenly found themselves in line for government jobs. For a while he had hoped that Thiers would continue to send reports despite his new responsibilities (Cotta to Thiers, 16 Sept. 1830, Bibliothèque Thiers, T. MS. 561[2]); he also appealed to the French ambassador in Munich to find him a correspondent in the capital acceptable to the new government (Count Rumigny to Louis Molé [French foreign minister], 4 Nov. 1830, in Chroust, *Berichte der französischen Gesandten* 2:307), a proposal the ambassador strongly endorsed on the grounds that the AZ was "the only newspaper read by all the princes of Germany" and that its proprietor was "entirely on our side" (Rumigny to Horace Sébastiani [French foreign minister], 3 Dec. 1830, ibid., p. 318n). The request was nevertheless ignored, and in the fall of 1831 Cotta took advantage of a visit to Paris by Gustav Kolb to solicit correspondence from Heinrich Heine, whose "Französische Zustände" subsequently went so far as to criticize the new regime's tendency to forget its true origins in "the idea of popular sovereignty" and to make unseemly common cause with "absolutist princes" (AZ, 28 Dec. 1831). In addition, Stegmann kept AZ readers supplied with regular reports excerpted from the French press, which were not noticeably affected by the tightening of Bavarian censorship.

6. Between November 1831 and March 1832, the AZ published five essays on the rights of the press written by Cotta himself. This attribution is based on internal references identifying them all as the work of a single author, and on the survival of a manuscript for one

may have been, still demonstrated the dangers, rather than the benefits, of a press unrestrained by law:

> What fruit, after all, has unlimited freedom of the press borne in France? Has it won for this land and its people more practical insight, morality, piety, a greater sense of duty or civic virtue? Have these journalists advanced the nation's unity, tranquility, or welfare? Improved the realm's finances? Advanced the cause of law and public order? Strengthened the government in its various powers and protected it from inimical elements and factious parties? Or has it not, directly or indirectly, done precisely the opposite?[7]

The choice for Germany was thus the same as it had been since Cotta's youth: revolution or reform, of the kind that had already yielded important advances in matters of trade, agriculture, and administration but that could not survive the corrosive influence of journalism uninhibited by any sense of social responsibility and appealing most directly to those classes whose political education was least advanced.[8]

Cotta found the opposition press to display two reprehensible qualities: narrowness of vision and excessive self-interest, both of which were inimical to the "true republicanism" he always admired. These defects revealed themselves most disastrously in a dogmatic particularism. "Even if all the complaints of the opposition press [about the persistence of poverty and injustice in Germany] are true," Cotta wondered, "is it *national*, is it *patriotic*, in a time of pressing danger, and under the threat of powerful enemies, . . . to sow mistrust between the rulers and the ruled, to spread unrest and disorder?"[9] This tendency Cotta considered sheer egotism, of the kind that had caused the early promise of Ludwig's reign to be thrown away in a sterile dispute over the press's corporate interests; it was magnified, moreover, by the liberality with which most of the German lands had lately treated political journalism. Given a choice between the spirit of Carlsbad and the spirit of faction, Cotta did not hesitate to choose the former.[10]

That he should have done so must seem deeply strange. But in fact,

---

of them (2–3 Dec. 1831) in Cotta's hand (CA). The articles, which appeared in *außerordentliche Beilage*, are "Auch ein Wort über Preßfreiheit," 5 Nov. 1831; "Ueber den Geist der deutschen Opposition und ihrer Organe," 11–12 Nov. 1831; "Ueber öffentliche Meynung und ihre Wortführer," 2–3 Dec. 1831; "Ueber die Verbindlichkeit der Bundestagsbeschlüsse von 1819 für die einzelnen Bundesstaaten," 26 Dec. 1831; and "Die deutsche Opposition," 22 March 1832.

    7. "Auch ein Wort über Preßfreiheit," *AZ*, 5 Nov. 1831.

    8. "Ueber den Geist der deutschen Opposition und ihrer Organe," *AZ*, 11–12 Nov. 1831.

    9. Ibid.; cf. "Ueber öffentliche Meynung und ihre Wortführer," *AZ*, 2–3 Dec. 1831.

    10. "Ueber die Verbindlichkeit der Bundestagsbeschlüsse von 1819 für die einzelnen Bundesstaaten," *AZ*, 26 Dec. 1831.

although Cotta's ideas now appeared tinged with bitterness and fear, their underlying logic had changed little since his journey to Vienna as the paladin of a free press. Cotta exempted from criticism those parliamentary institutions whose oppositional nature was constitutionally agreed upon and whose free access to public opinion was therefore just. And he still looked forward to the enactment of the "uniform press law" called for in the Federal Act, which would replace censorship with a system of civil penalties, which in turn would tend to limit the social, more than the intellectual, range of political journalism.[11] Failing that, though, Cotta was still prepared to accept the censor as a serviceable expression of the public interest, an affirmation by the state of the same nonpartisan values he believed journalists should embrace as a matter of principle.

That the Federation should finally have struck out at the Cotta press itself, suppressing Karl von Rotteck's *Annalen* in the same sweeping gesture that brought an end to Wirth's *Tribüne*,[12] must have seemed to Cotta a misjudgment. But in good conscience he could not have found the attack unjust. Among the publishers and journalists of the Reform Era, none was more sensitive than Cotta to the merits of the nonpartisan tradition, which he defended long after events had begun to expose its limitations. He also understood as well as anyone the democratizing and factionalizing character of the modern political press. But the reconciliation that he was able to achieve between these conflicting principles was never completely convincing—certainly not to his critics, and probably not to himself. He suffered all the frustrations one would expect to befall someone who devoted himself to the political education of a society where neither democracy nor faction, nor even public controversy, had any acknowledged role.

It would be hard to overestimate the consequences of the nonpartisan tradition for the German press, which continued to seek partnership with the state long after most journalists and publishers in western Europe and America had embraced the lessons of the revolutionary era and found security and significance under the protection of one political party or another. By holding fast to traditional values, the publishers and journalists of Cotta's generation helped to insure that the claims of public opinion to a share in the nation's political life would be cast in reformist rather than revolutionary terms. It was, under the circumstances, a considerable achievement, for which the journalistic community expected some suitable reward. None was forthcoming. No alternative to the adversarial role its members rejected ever materialized.

---

11. Ibid.
12. F. Schneider, *Pressefreiheit und politische Öffentlichkeit*, pp. 262–63; cf. Karl von Rotteck to Cotta, 20 Aug. 1832, CA.

Public opinion remained in thrall to the state, substantially indifferent not just to the call to revolution but to the whole concept of legitimate opposition—that is, opposition that goes beyond incidental criticism of personalities and policies and proclaims its own constitutional standing.

Reform helped to foster an instrumental conception of the state as the guardian of the public welfare. It did not inspire any acknowledgment of the fiduciary nature of government, nor any recognition that the legitimacy of political authority might be enhanced by sharing it. To Germany's reformers and the princes they served, preserving the solidarity of the ruling elite was necessary to preserve the power and autonomy of the German lands. Party spirit, which threatened that solidarity, was the harbinger of revolution, and revolution was the enemy not merely of the status quo but of reform itself. This was a conclusion from which most journalists of Cotta's day did not dissent. Neither, however, did they expect that one of its implications would be to relegate the press to the margins of political power. Ludwig Börne was not alone in complaining that, while he faced a life of self-imposed exile, his fellow journalist Thiers was entering the highest levels of his country's government.[13]

By the end of Cotta's life the divergence of the German press from the path taken by its western counterparts was already becoming clear. The July Revolution, the English Reform Bill of 1832, and (if the example is not too remote) even the election of Andrew Jackson in 1828 as president of the United States were all, among other things, clear demonstrations that the press in those countries had come of age as a political force. Nowhere had this development occurred unaided, a fact that ought not to be overlooked. A public cause, whether liberty or any other, can be proclaimed by individuals, but only institutions can secure it. One of the most striking features of the German press in Cotta's lifetime is its relative isolation from those parliamentary institutions that proved such sturdy allies of the press in other lands—an alliance that Cotta regarded as natural and self-evident, and which he repeatedly tried, with no success, to forge.

In its absence, however, he was still willing to proceed, seeking his allies where he could find them. Reform, after all, was a task in which, to echo Talleyrand's advice to diplomats, success depended on the absence of zeal. Although Cotta was in some ways an uncompromising character, it is hard to think of a moment, in a public life of some forty years, when he was not prepared to be patient. In this respect he was perfectly suited to his age, and to a calling in which decisive victories were bound to be rare. To survive, after all, meant to fight another day. It also meant that the ground for which he fought would change very

13. Ludwig Börne, "Briefe aus Paris," 3 Nov. 1830, in *Sämtliche Schriften* 3:56–57.

little over time. Between the revolutions of 1789 and 1830 the general
circumstances of the German press changed enormously; but the underlying continuities—in the relationship of the press to political authority
and in the values that journalists sought to promote in public life—are
equally impressive, and the analytic challenge they pose is equally
great.[14] For Cotta the tension between the meliorative work of reform
and the need for journalists to free themselves from the tutelage of the
state was a problem to be faced over and over again. No one who consid-
ers his career as a whole can fail to be struck by the similarity between
the difficulties he faced at the beginning and those he faced at the end,
or by the intellectual and political consistency of his attempts to overcome them.

In the final analysis the most appropriate perspective from which to
judge Cotta's rejection of opposition is probably the one afforded by his
own newspaper, a political instrument whose significance far exceeded
its creator's grasp and in whose pages his was but one among many competing voices. By 1830 most of those who shared the political space Cotta
provided in the *AZ* did not share his anxiety about the consequences of
freedom and were prepared to trust the press as a guarantor of the
public interest. But even this is not really the point. By virtue of its nonpartisan principles, the *Allgemeine Zeitung*, like the rest of the Cotta press,
stands at some distance from the liberal journalism that would mature
in Germany after the middle of the century, a distance that is not reduced by the marginal predominance of liberal opinion in its pages. Nor
is it bridged by vaguely anachronistic notions like "preliberalism." The
AZ was not a surreptitious or half-hearted organ of liberalism, but a self-
conscious demonstration of it. In insisting on the virtues of impartiality,
it revealed the virtues of engagement as well. Its tolerance of controversy
and contention allowed it to display within its pages the spectacle, unprecedented in Germany, of a diverse and intellectually sophisticated
people thinking seriously about politics. The adoption of these same serious and contentious habits by ever broader elements of German society, and their application to the realm of political struggle, was a spectacle of another kind, from which Cotta in his old age personally drew
back. But that he helped bring it about can hardly be doubted.

14. The continuity of German political culture between the Seven Years' War and the
Revolution of 1848 has lately come in for increasing attention. The recent literature is
discussed in Rudolf Vierhaus, "Aufklärung und Reformzeit: Kontinuitäten und Neuansätze in der deutschen Politik des späten 18. und beginnenden 19. Jahrhunderts," in *Reformen im rheinbündischen Deutschland*, ed. Eberhard Weis (Munich, 1984), pp. 287–301. It
probably goes too far to suggest, as Vierhaus does, that the Old Regime really ends in
Germany in 1848, a point of view that undervalues the transformation of the "Third Germany" after 1800; but the history of the Cotta press certainly supports the impression that
in Germany the Old Regime was a long time ending, the more so because the Cotta press
itself was so clearly a product of the revolutionary era.

CULTURE AND DEMOCRACY

Cotta died in Stuttgart on December 29, 1832, a victim of the cholera that had carried off Goethe in March. His health, never robust, had been declining for years, his trips to Berlin in the depths of a Prussian winter having taken an especially heavy toll. But his death, when it came, was unexpected. Even had it been foreseen, it is unlikely that Cotta would have done anything to prepare his posthumous reputation: a man who cannot be bothered to keep copies of his own letters is not liable to write his memoirs. In the event, posterity has been kind, albeit in a way that has taken some of the edge off Cotta's character and career. Almost from the hour of his death Cotta has been granted a place in the circle of light that surrounds the legacy of Goethe and Schiller. Although the place is well deserved, it is at least a little incongruous that Cotta's claim to it should have been strengthened by his qualities as a striver, a self-made man in an age when self-made men inspired condescension rather than envy. The extreme diversity of Cotta's ventures, which attests to these social circumstances and to a restless, free-floating ambition, has since been understood to complement the ideals of emotional freedom and artistic universality so prominent in the literature of his day. More than a century after his death, Cotta's heterogeneous achievements were still being compared, in all seriousness, to the palace of Versailles.[15]

In his lifetime Cotta was widely judged susceptible to the sin of pride, a charge seemingly confirmed by the defensiveness it could awaken in him. In its political dimensions it was capable of inspiring reflection as well. Early on, Cotta recognized a certain incongruity in his feelings about public life, and about the divergence of his cultural and political aspirations. To Friedrich Schiller, with whom he developed a warm friendship, he wrote openly of the satisfaction he felt when men like Goethe, and Schiller himself, treated him as an equal. "Nothing," he confided, "hurts me more than to establish a relationship with an out-standing individual and then see it fail, or continue only partially. As much as I am otherwise a democrat, I cannot deny an aristocratic tendency in my outlook as a publisher. Yet I can only say in my own defense that it is not financial interest alone that makes me this way."[16]

The tension between culture and democracy, which Cotta detected in his own personality, has been noted more than once by students of the age in which he lived. The tendency to formulate the "German question" in terms of a recurring dynamic of political failure and cultural success accordingly remains strong. Cotta's career bears unmistakably on this

15. Joseph Eberle, "Johann Friedrich Cotta," *Sonderdruck aus der Stuttgarter Zeitung*, 1952, CA.

16. Cotta to Schiller, 26 Dec. 1798. This letter, listed as missing in Vollmer, *Briefwechsel*, p. 331n, may be found among Cotta's letters to Goethe in the Goethe-Schiller Archiv, Weimar, no. 95; typescript CA.

interpretive tradition, though perhaps more obliquely than it appears at first glance. The frustrations of Cotta's political career were largely absent from his experience in the world of letters, which, unlike politics, yielded its rewards more nearly in proportion to the effort it demanded. His inability to integrate his cultural and political concerns, symbolized so conspicuously by his early failure to interest Schiller in his newspaper, was always a disappointment. But this shortcoming can hardly be considered decisive in the history of the Cotta press, whose successes and failures, however they may be judged, all occurred in the context of a most determined pursuit of intellectual distinction. On the contrary, many would hold that Cotta's political achievement might have been greater if his devotion to the aristocratic ideals of excellence and objectivity had not led him to slight other, less distinguished but preeminently democratic values—like simplicity and clarity of conviction—which later generations would value more.

It is at any rate for this reason that Cotta's sterling personal reputation should have come to stand in such marked contrast to the more ambiguous reception accorded the *Allgemeine Zeitung* in later years. The *AZ* would receive its full share of recognition as one of the great newspapers of the nineteenth century. By 1840 the diplomatic community would routinely identify it as the most influential public organ in Europe,[17] a position that no one would have thought attainable by a German newspaper even twenty years before. Nevertheless, it is easy to find intelligent observers who considered that influence pernicious, and always for the same reason: Cotta's newspaper had no conscience. Alois von Rechberg's early indictment of the *AZ*'s "perfidious neutrality" would thus echo down its history in exactly the opposite form: that the *AZ*, far from being a clandestine force for change, was in fact a pillar of the status quo, which feigned liberality only to insure its own continuance.

During Johann Cotta's last years, the rising generation of journalists already had their doubts whether the *Allgemeine Zeitung*'s pervasive influence had not been achieved, as Karl von Rotteck suspected, through "a certain inconsequentiality."[18] Ten years later Karl Marx would complain, even more pointedly, that the *AZ* had become a newspaper in which "freedom is on the one hand too young, on the other too old, but never the order of the day."[19] Nor was this sort of grievance confined to men of the left. Heinrich von Treitschke, who cannot be said to have shared much with Rotteck or Marx (or Rechberg, for that matter), put the case more plainly than any of them. The *Allgemeine Zeitung*, he judged, was "so chameleonlike" that "it could not fail to exercise a profoundly disastrous influence upon the political culture of the nation, which, in its

17. Chroust, *Berichte der französischen Gesandten* 4:192, 215, 223.

18. Rotteck to Cotta, 6 Jan. 1830, in Fehling and Schiller, *Briefe an Cotta* 2:286n.

19. *Rheinische Zeitung*, 3 Jan. 1843; in *Karl Marx–Friedrich Engels Gesamtausgabe* (East Berlin, 1975–), 1:294.

nebulous embitterment and obscure yearning, above all needed relent-
lessly straightforward instruction. It nourished in its readers that erudite
political impotence by which the cultured Germans were tragically distinguished from neighboring nations."[20]

This charge, whatever its merits, deserves to be laid at the feet of the
AZ's founder, for whom political detachment was no vice. Neither, however, was it supposed to be the all-encompassing virtue it eventually became. Cotta took it for granted that a newspaper's readers had con-
sciences of their own, which had to be respected; he certainly never
intended to discourage their use. Treitschke's objections to the contrary,
the *Allgemeine Zeitung* honored "straightforward instruction" more than
any newspaper of its time, and it did so for no other reason than to
establish an intellectual basis for political action, of the kind in which
Cotta himself was always deeply engaged. Cotta's life thus provides an
important clue to his political intentions as a publisher, albeit one that
was lost on subsequent generations, who held his aristocratic outlook to
be the center, rather than the surface, of his character.

As a political publisher Cotta would find no immediate successor. It
would be fifty years before men like Rudolf Mosse and Leopold Ullstein
would again achieve the same grasp of the political landscape that Cotta
enjoyed at the end of his life. Cotta's son Georg was his heir, but not his
equal in intellect or ambition. Georg's political legacy, moreover, was not
an empire, as his father doubtless had hoped, but a monument. The
Cotta press died with Johann Cotta. Out of a lifetime of effort, only the
Allgemeine Zeitung remained—his finest achievement, but one that was
almost inevitably misunderstood in isolation from its lesser cousins. In a
political sense the *AZ* was always mortgaged to the hilt while its founder
was alive, as a way of obtaining the personal credit necessary to undertake the more speculative, politically vulnerable journals that sprang up
around it whenever circumstances permitted. Georg preferred to treat
the *AZ* as though it were destined to remain a solitary symbol of excellence, and it did. Its reputation for sophistication came to overshadow
the more elusive heritage of reformism and independence that his father had nurtured with such uncommon dexterity. By the middle of the
century Cotta's newspaper had drifted into firm sympathy with Austria,
the only European state in which political detachment was an end in
itself. In the years to come its founder's ideal of public enlightenment
would become an ever-receding vision; the nation's unending political
education would become a substitute for a democratic public life; and
Unparteilichkeit, on which personal culture and public authority were
equally dependent, would become just another form of service to the
state.

20. Treitschke, *History of Germany* 4 : 109.

Bibliography

The bibliography contains only those manuscripts, books, and articles that are cited in the text. The list of "Other Periodicals" (i.e., those published by someone other than Cotta) includes only journals mentioned more than once in the text and notes.

PRIMARY SOURCES

Manuscripts

Bayerisches Hauptstaatsarchiv, Munich.
    Abteilung I: Geheimes Staatsarchiv, Archiv des Innenministeriums.
        M Inn 25097/I: "Verhandlungen über die *Allgemeine Zeitung*."
        M Inn 25097/II: "Acten die *Allgemeinen Politischen Annalen* betreffend."
        M Inn 25105: "Geheim. Raths-Acten—Die Zeitschrift *Das Inland*, 1828–32."
        M Inn 45313: "Acten des Ministerial-Bureau des Innern—Die Zeitschrift *Das Inland* dessen Redaction durch den Dr. Schulz usw. und die Censur derselben, 1831–32."
        M Inn 43971: "Acta des Ministerial-Bureau des Innern—Die projectierten Unternehmungen des Freyherrn von Cotta in Bayern, 1826 u. 1827."
        M Inn 44819: "Dampfschiffahrt, 1824–25."
    Abteilung III: Geheimes Haus Archiv.
        ARO 25: "Nachlass Ludwig I."
        90-1-II: "Nachlass Ludwig I—Verschiedene Briefe."
        I-A-42(III): "Nachlass Ludwig I."
        II-A-23: "Briefe des Frhrn. von Hormayr, 1825–30."
Bayerische Staatsbibliothek, Munich.
    Schenkiana II 7.
Bibliothèque Thiers, Paris.
    T. MS. 561².
Deutsches Literaturarchiv, Marbach am Neckar, Cotta Archiv.

Haus, Hof, und Staatsarchiv, Vienna.
Staatskanzlei: Wissenschaft und Kunst, Karton 13 (Zeitungen).
Stadt- und Universitätsbibliothek, Frankfurt am Main.
Börne-Nachlass.

Cotta Periodicals

Allgemeine Zeitung. Stuttgart, 1798–1803; Ulm, 1803–10; Augsburg, 1810–.
Ausland. Munich, 1828–.
Deutscher Beobachter. Hamburg, briefly Bremen, 1813–19 (by Cotta 1815–17).
  Title variant: *Hanseatische Zeitung von Staats- und gelehrten Sachen* (1813–14).
Europäische Annalen. Tübingen, 1795–1820; Stuttgart, 1821–28, 1830–32. Title
  variants: *Allgemeine politische Annalen* (1821–27); *Neue allgemeine politische An-
  nalen* (1827–30); *Allgemeine politische Annalen, neueste Folge* (1830–32).
Für und Wider. Stuttgart, 1817.
Horen. Tübingen, 1795–97.
Inland. Munich, 1829–31.
Jahrbücher für wissenschaftliche Kritik. Stuttgart, 1827–33 (then by Duncker &
  Humblot in Berlin, 1833–46).
Landtag im Herzogthum Wirtemberg. Tübingen (copublished by Metzler in Stutt-
  gart), 1797–99.
Morgenblatt für gebildete Stände. Stuttgart, 1807–.
Neueste Weltkunde. Tübingen, 1798.
Staats-Archiv. Brunswick, 1800–1807 (originally published by Vierweg, 1796–
  1800).
Thron- und Volksfreund. Munich, 1830.
Tribüne. Stuttgart, 1819.

Other Periodicals

Allemannia (Munich, 1814–24); *Allgemeine preussische Staatszeitung* (Berlin,
  1819–); *Bamberger Zeitung* (Bamberg, 1795, 1802, 1803–9); *Bayerisches Volksblatt* (Würzburg, 1829–32); *Berliner Abendblätter* (Berlin, 1810–11); *Bundeslade* (Frankfurt, 1816); *Constitutionnel* (Paris, 1815–); *Correspondent* (Hamburg, 1710–); *Correspondent* (Nuremberg, 1804–); *Deutsche Tribüne* (Munich,
  then Zweibrücken, 1831; Homburg, 1832); *Eos* (Munich, 1825–32); *Frankfurter Journal* (Frankfurt, 1783–1810, 1814–); *Frankfurter Oberpostamtszeitung*
  (Frankfurt, 1615–); *Freie Presse* (Nuremberg, 1827–30; Munich, 1830–31);
  Jahrbücher der Literatur (Vienna, 1818–); *Journal des Débats* (Paris, 1789–); *Minerva* (Hamburg, 1792–); *Moniteur Universel* (Paris, 1789–); *Münchner politische Zeitung* (Munich, 1807–); *Nemesis* (Weimar, 1814–18); *Neuer Rheinischer
  Merkur* (Offenbach, 1816–19); *Neue Stuttgarter Zeitung* (Stuttgart, 1817–19);
  Oesterreichischer Beobachter (Vienna, 1809–); *Oppositionsblatt* (Weimar, 1817–
  20); *Politisches Journal* (Hamburg, 1781–); *Preussischer Correspondent* (Berlin, 1813–14); *Reisender Teufel* (Munich, 1828); *Rheinischer Merkur* (Coblenz,
  1814–16); *Schwäbischer Merkur* (Stuttgart, 1785–); *Stats-Anzeigen* (Göttingen, 1782–93); *Teutscher Beobachter* (Stuttgart, 1822–23); *Teutscher Merkur*

(Weimar, 1773–1810); *Volksfreund aus Schwaben* (Stuttgart, 1817–19); *Wage* (Frankfurt, 1818–19, then Tübingen, 1819); *Wiener Zeitung* (Vienna, 1781–); *Württembergischer Volksfreund* (Stuttgart, 1817); *Württembergisches Archiv* (Heidelberg, 1816–17).

Other Published Sources

"Actenstücke und Briefe zur Geschichte der Deputation der deutschen Buchhändler beim Wiener Congresse, im Jahre 1814." *Börsenblatt für den deutschen Buchhandel* 4, nos. 50–54, 57, 58 (23 June–21 July 1837): cols. 1097–1308.

Arndt, Ernst Moritz. *Briefe*. Edited by Albrecht Dühr. 4 vols. Darmstadt: Wissenschaftliche Buchgesellschaft, 1972.

Assing, Ludmilla, ed. *Briefwechsel zwischen Varnhagen von Ense und Oelsner, nebst Briefen von Rahel*. 3 vols. Stuttgart: A. Körner, 1865.

Baxa, Jakob, ed. *Adam Müller's Lebenszeugnisse*. 2 vols. Munich: Paderborn; Vienna: Ferdinand Schöningh, 1966.

Bertuch, Carl. *Tagebuch vom Wiener Kongress*. Edited by Hermann von Egloffstein. Berlin: Paetel, 1916.

Blackstone, William. *Commentaries on the Laws of England*. 4 vols. Oxford: Clarendon Press, 1765–69.

Börne, Ludwig. *Sämtliche Schriften*. Edited by Inge Rippmann and Peter Rippmann. 5 vols. Düsseldorf and Darmstadt: Metzler, 1964–68.

[Bolly, Heinrich.] *Contra principia negantem non est disputandum*. [Stuttgart, April 1817].

Bright, John. *Public Addresses*. Edited by James E. Thorold Rogers. London: Macmillan, 1879.

Buchner, Karl, ed. *Aus den Papieren der Wiedmannschen Buchhandlung*. Berlin: Wiedmannsche Buchhandlung, 1871.

Chroust, Anton, ed. *Gesandtschaftsberichte aus München, 1814–1848. Abteilung I: Die Berichte der französischen Gesandten*. Schriftenreihe zur bayerischen Landesgeschichte, vols. 18–19, 21, 24. Published by the Kommission für bayerische Landesgeschichte, Bayerische Akademie der Wissenschaften. Munich: C. H. Beck, 1935–37.

———. *Gesandtschaftsberichte aus München, 1814–1848. Abteilung II: Die Berichte der österreichischen Gesandten*. Schriftenreihe zur bayerischen Landesgeschichte, vols. 33, 36–38. Published by the Kommission für bayerische Landesgeschichte, Bayerische Akademie der Wissenschaften. Munich: C. H. Beck, 1938–43.

Collmann, Julius. *Quellen, Materialien, und Commentar des gemein deutschen Preßrechts*. Berlin: Wilhelm Besser, 1844.

Czygan, Paul, ed. *Zur Geschichte des Tagesliteratur während der Freiheitskriege*. 2 vols. Leipzig: Duncker & Humblot, 1909–11.

Die Debatten über den Bücher-Nachdruck, welche in der Württembergischen Kammer der Abgeordneten stattfanden. Stuttgart: Metzler, 1822.

Dorow, [Wilhelm,] ed. *Briefe des Königl. Preus. Legationsraths Karl E. Oelsner an den wirkl. Geheimen Rath Fr. Aug. von Staegemann aus den Jahren 1815–1827*. Leipzig: B. G. Teubner, 1843.

Düntzer, Heinrich, and Ferdinand Gottfried von Herder, eds. *Von und an Herder: Ungedruckte Briefe aus Herders Nachlass.* 3 vols. Leipzig: Dyk, 1861–62.

Fehling, Maria, and Herbert Schiller, eds. *Briefe an Cotta.* 3 vols. Stuttgart and Berlin: J. G. Cotta, 1925–34.

Forster, Georg. *Sämtliche Schriften.* Edited by G. G. Gervinus. 9 vols. Leipzig: F. A. Brockhaus, 1843.

————. *Werke: Sämtliche Schriften, Tagebücher, Briefe.* East Berlin: Akademie-Verlag, 1968–.

Fournier, August, ed. *Die Geheimpolizei auf dem Wiener Kongress: Eine Auswahl aus ihren Papieren.* Vienna: G. Freytag, 1913.

Fuhrmans, Horst, and Liselotte Lohrer, eds. *Schelling und Cotta: Briefwechsel, 1803–1849.* Stuttgart: Ernst Klett, 1965.

Geiger, Ludwig, ed. "Buchhändlerbriefe von 1786 bis 1816." *Archiv für Geschichte des deutschen Buchhandels* 8 (1883): 311–27.

Gentz, Friedrich von. *Briefe von Friedrich von Gentz an Pilat: Ein Beitrag zur Geschichte Deutschlands im XIX. Jahrhundert.* Edited by Karl Mendelssohn-Bartholdy. 2 vols. Leipzig: F.C.W. Vogel, 1868.

————. *Schriften von Friedrich von Gentz.* Edited by Gustav Schlesier. 5 vols. Mannheim: Heinrich Hoff, 1838–40.

Gerhardt, Luise, ed. *Schriftsteller und Buchhändler vor hundert Jahren: Karl August Böttiger und Georg Joachim Göschen im Briefwechsel.* Leipzig: H. Haessel, 1911.

Gilchrist, J., and W. J. Murray, eds. *The Press in the French Revolution.* New York: St. Martin's Press, 1971.

Göschen, Georg Joachim. *Meine Gedanken über den Buchhandel und über dessen Mängel. . . .* Leipzig: G. J. Göschen, 1802.

Goethe, Johann Wolfgang von. *Goethes Werke.* Weimar: Hermann Böhlau, 1887–1912.

Gradmann, Johann Jacob. *Das gelehrte Schwaben, oder Lexicon der jetzt lebenden schwäbischen Schriftsteller.* Ravensburg, 1802; reprint Hildesheim: Gerstenberg, 1979.

Grävell, M.K.F.W. *Drei Briefe über Preßfreiheit und Volksgeist.* Berlin: F. Maurer, 1815.

Hegel, Georg Wilhelm Friedrich. "Beurteilung der Verhandlungen in der Versammlung der Landstände des Königreichs Württemberg im Jahre 1815 und 1816." *Heidelbergische Jahrbücher der Literatur,* nos. 66–68, 73–77 (1817). Reprinted in *Werke,* edited by Eva Moldenhauer and Karl Markus Michel, 4: 462–597. Frankfurt am Main: Suhrkamp, 1970–79.

————. "Daß die Magistrate . . ." [Essay fragment, April–July 1797]. In *Sämtliche Werke.* Vol. 7: *Schriften zur Politik und Rechtsphilosophie,* edited by G. Lasson, 150–54. Leipzig: F. Meiner, 1913.

Heine, Heinrich. *Heinrich Heine Säkularausgabe.* East Berlin: Akademie-Verlag; Paris: Editions du CNRS [Centre National de la Recherche Scientifique], 1970–.

Hoven, Friedrich Wilhelm von. *Biographie des Doctor Friedrich Wilhelm von Hoven . . . von ihm selbst geschrieben.* Edited by Dr. Merkel. Nuremberg: J. L. Schrag, 1840.

Huber, Ludwig. *Sämtliche Werke seit dem Jahre 1802, nebst seiner Biographie.* [Edited by Theresa Huber.] Tübingen: J. G. Cotta, 1806.

Kleist, Heinrich von. *Sämtliche Werke und Briefe.* [Edited by Helmut Sembdner.] 2d rev. ed. 2 vols. Munich: Hanser, 1961.

Klessmann, Eckart, ed. *Deutschland unter Napoleon.* Düsseldorf: Rauch, 1965.

Klopstock, Friedrich Gottlieb. *Die deutsche Gelehrtenrepublik.* Hamburg: J.J.C. Bode, 1774.

Klüber, Johann Ludwig, ed. *Acten des Wiener Congresses in den Jahren 1814–1815.* 9 vols. Erlangen: J. J. Palm and E. Enke, 1815–35.

Körner, Josef, ed. *Krisenjahre der Frühromantik: Briefe aus dem Schlegelkreis.* 3 vols. Brünn: R. M. Rohrer, 1936–58.

Kuhn, Dorothea, ed. *Goethe und Cotta: Briefwechsel, 1797–1832.* 3 vols. in 4. Stuttgart: J. G. Cotta, 1979–83.

Lang, Wilhelm. "Analekten zur Biographie des Grafen Reinhard." *Württembergische Vierteljahrshefte für Landesgeschichte,* n.s., 17 (1908): 17–100.

Legerlotz, G., ed. "Aus den Hartknoch'schen Geschäftspapieren." *Archiv für Geschichte des deutschen Buchhandels* 8 (1883): 328–29.

Lerchenfeld, Max von, ed. *Aus den Papieren des k. b. Staatsminister Maximilian Freiherrn von Lerchenfeld.* Nördlingen: C. H. Beck, 1887.

Lindner, Friedrich [anon]. *Manuscript aus Süd-Deutschland.* Edited by George Erichson. London [i.e., Stuttgart]: James Griphi [actual publisher unknown], 1820.

List, Friedrich. *Schriften, Reden, Briefe.* Edited by Erwin Beckerath, Karl Goeser, Friedrich Lenz, William Notz, Edgar Salin, and Artur Sommer. 10 vols. in 12. Berlin: Reimar Hobbing, 1927–35.

Löffler, Franz Adam. *Ueber die Gesetzgebung der Presse.* Leipzig, 1837.

Marx, Karl, and Friedrich Engels. *Karl Marx–Friedrich Engels Gesamtausgabe.* East Berlin: Dietz, 1975–.

Metternich, Prince Klemens von. *Aus Metternich's nachgelassenen Papieren.* Edited by Alfons von Klinkowström and Prince Richard Metternich-Winneburg. 8 vols. Vienna: W. Braumüller, 1880–84.

Meyer, Philipp Guido von, ed. *Corpus Juris Confoederationis Germanica.* 2 vols. in 1. Frankfurt am Main: F. Boselli, 1822.

Oncken, Hermann, and F.E.M. Saemisch, eds. *Vorgeschichte und Begründung des Deutschen Zollvereins, 1815–1834.* 3 vols. Berlin: Reimar Hobbing, 1934.

Paulus, Heinrich Eberhard Gottlob. Review of *Idee der Staatsverfassung,* by Karl von Wangenheim. *Heidelberger Jahrbücher der Literatur* 10 (1817): 145–83.

Pfizer, Paul. *Briefwechsel zweier Deutschen.* Stuttgart: Cotta, 1831; 2d rev. ed., Stuttgart: Cotta, 1832. Collated edition, edited by Georg Künzel, Berlin: B. Behrs, 1911.

Protokolle der Deutschen Bundesversammlung. 19 vols. in 18. Frankfurt am Main: Andreäische Buchhandlung, 1817–28.

Pütter, Johann Stephan. *Der Büchernachdruck nach ächten Grundsätzen des Rechts geprüft.* Göttingen: Vandenhoeck, 1774.

Ranke, Leopold von. "Aus einem Schreiben von München, betreffend den bayrischen Landtag von 1831." *Historisch-politische Zeitschrift* 1 (1832): 94–102.

Reich, Philipp Erasmus. *Der Bücher-Verlag in allen Absichten genauer bestimmt.* Leipzig: Wiedmanns Erben & Reich, 1773.

———. *Zufällige Gedanken eines Buchhändlers über Herrn Klopstocks Anzeige einer gelehrten Republik.* Leipzig: Wiedmanns Erben & Reich, 1774.

Reyscher, August Ludwig, ed. *Vollständige, historisch und kritisch bearbeitete Sammlung der württembergischen Gesetze.* 29 vols. Stuttgart: J. G. Cotta, 1826–51.

Richter, Jean Paul Friedrich. "Sieben letzte oder Nachworte gegen den Nachdruck." *Morgenblatt für gebildete Stände,* 17–22 April 1815.

[Riecke, K. V., ed.] "Zur Vorgeschichte des Deutschen Zollvereins: Auszüge aus Briefen des Freiherrn K. A. v. Wangenheim." *Württembergische Vierteljahrshefte für Landesgeschichte* 2 (1879): 101–11.

Rühl, Franz, ed. *Briefe und Aktenstücke zur Geschichte Preussens unter Friedrich Wilhelm III, vorzugsweise aus dem Nachlass von F. A. von Stägemann.* 3 vols. Leipzig: Duncker & Humblot, 1899–1902.

Schaden, Adolf von. *Topographisch-statistisches Taschenbuch, oder Beschreibung der Haupt- und Residenzstadt München, ihre Merkwürdigkeiten und Umgebung.* Munich: J. Lindenauer, 1825.

Scheel, Heinrich, ed. *Jakobinische Flugschriften aus dem deutschen Süden Ende des 18. Jahrhunderts.* East Berlin: Akademie-Verlag, 1965.

Schiller, Friedrich von, and Christian Gottfried Körner. *Briefwechsel zwischen Schiller und Körner von 1784 bis zum Tode Schillers.* [Edited by Ludwig Geiger.] 4 vols. Stuttgart: J. G. Cotta, 1895.

Schubart, Christian Friedrich Daniel. *Briefe.* Munich: C. H. Beck, 1984.

Schwarzkopf, Joachim von. *Über Zeitungen: Ein Beytrag zur Staatswissenschaft.* Frankfurt am Main: Varrentrapp & Wenner, 1795.

Spaun, Franz von. *Politisches Testament: Ein Beitrag zur Geschichte der Preßfreiheit im allgemeinen und in besonderer Hinsicht auf Bayern.* Edited by Dr. Eisenmann. Erlangen: J. J. Palm and E. Enke, 1831.

Spindler, Max, ed. *Briefwechsel zwischen Ludwig I von Bayern und Eduard von Schenk, 1823–1841.* Munich: Parcus, 1930.

Stein, Karl vom. *Freiherr vom Stein: Briefe und amtliche Schriften.* 10 vols. in 11. Edited by Walter Hubatsch, Erich Botzenhart, P. G. Thielen, M. Botzenhart, and A. H. von Wallthor. Stuttgart: W. Kohlhammer, 1957–74.

Thugut, Johann Amadeus von. *Vertrauliche Briefe des Freiherrn von Thugut: Beiträge zur Beurteilung der politischen Verhältnisse Europas in den Jahren 1792–1801.* Edited by Alfred von Vivenot. 2 vols. Vienna: W. Brandmüller, 1872.

Trattner, Johann Thomas von. *Der gerechtfertigte Nachdrucker.* Leipzig [i.e., Vienna]: Weidmanns Erben & Reich [actual publisher unknown], 1774.

Ulmann, Heinrich, ed. *Denkwürdigkeiten aus dem Dienstleben des hessen-darmstädtischen Staatsministers Freiherrn du Thil, 1803–1848.* Stuttgart and Berlin: Deutsche-Verlags Anstalt, 1921.

Verhandlungen in der Versammlung der Landstände des Königreichs Württemberg. 45 parts. Edited by Dr. Schott and Procurator Feuerlein. Heidelberg: Mohr & Weise, 1815–19.

"Verhandlungen in der Versammlung der Landstände des Königreichs Würtemberg." *Edinburgh Review* 29, no. 58 (February 1818): 337–63.

Verhandlungen der zweiten Kammer der Ständeversammlung des Königreichs Bayern. Munich: Königliche Hof- und Universitäts-Buchdruckerei, 1819–48.

Vollmer, Wilhelm, ed. *Briefwechsel zwischen Schiller und Cotta.* Stuttgart: J. G. Cotta, 1876.

Vreede, George Willem, ed. *La Souabe après la paix de Bâle: Recueil de documents diplomatiques et parlementaires. . . .* Utrecht: J. L. Beijers, 1879.

Wangenheim, Karl von. *Die Idee der Staatsverfassung in ihrer Anwendung auf Württembergs alte Landesverfassung und den Entwürf zu deren Erneuerung.* Frankfurt am Main: B. Körner, 1815.

Widmann, Hans, ed. *Der deutsche Buchhandel in Urkunden und Quellen.* 2 vols. Hamburg: Ernst Hauswedell, 1965.

Wittichen, F. C., and Ernst Salzer, eds. *Briefe von und an Friedrich von Gentz.* 3 vols. in 4. Munich and Berlin: R. Oldenbourg, 1909–13.

SECONDARY SOURCES

Aegidi, Ludwig Karl. *Aus der Vorzeit des Zollvereins: Beitrag zur deutschen Geschichte.* Hamburg: Noyes & Geisler, 1865.

Albrecht, Curt. *Die Triaspolitik des Frhrn. K. Aug. von Wangenheim.* Stuttgart: W. Kohlhammer, 1914.

Aretin, Karl Otmar von. *Bayerns Weg zum souveränen Staat: Landstände und konstitutionelle Monarchie, 1714–1818.* Munich: C. H. Beck, 1976.

Baack, Lawrence J. *Christian Bernstorff and Prussia: Diplomacy and Reform Conservatism, 1818–1832.* New Brunswick, N.J.: Rutgers University Press, 1980.

Baasch, Ernst. *Geschichte des hamburgischen Zeitungswesens von den Anfängen bis 1914.* Hamburg: Friedrichsen, de Gruyter, 1930.

Bab, Bernd. "Die öffentliche Meinung und den Deutschen Zollverein zur Zeit seiner Entstehung." Ph.D. diss., Berlin, 1930.

Bahrs, Kurt. *Friedrich Buchholz: Ein preussischer Publizist, 1768–1843.* Berlin: Matthiesen, 1907.

Baker, Keith Michael. "Politics and Public Opinion Under the Old Regime: Some Reflections." In *Press and Politics in Pre-revolutionary France,* edited by Jack R. Censer and Jeremy D. Popkin, 204–46. Berkeley and Los Angeles: University of California Press, 1987.

Bayrle, Joseph. "Die rechtliche Situation der bayerischen Presse von 1818–1848." Juris. diss., Munich, 1948.

Beer, Adolf. *Die Finanzen Oesterreichs im XIX. Jahrhundert.* Prague: F. Tempsky, 1877.

Bentfeldt, Ludwig. *Der Deutsche Bund als nationales Band, 1815–1866.* Göttingen: Musterschmidt, 1985.

Berding, Helmut. "Die Entstehung des Deutschen Zollvereins als Problem historischer Forschung." In *Vom Staat des Ancien régime zum modernen Parteienstaat: Festschrift für Theodor Schieder,* edited by Helmut Berding, Kurt Düwell, Lothar Gall, Wolfgang Mommsen, and Hans-Ulrich Wehler, 225–37. Munich and Vienna: R. Oldenbourg, 1978.

———. "Die Reform des Zollwesens in Deutschland unter dem Einfluß der napoleonischen Herrschaft." In *Geschichte und Gesellschaft* 6 (1980): *Napoleonische Herrschaft und Modernisierung,* edited by Helmut Berding, 523–37.

Berding, Helmut, and Hans-Peter Ullmann, eds. *Deutschland zwischen Revolution und Restauration.* Düsseldorf: Droste, 1981.

Bergmann, Heinz. "Der *Deutsche Beobachter* und die deutsche Verfassungsbewegung am Beginn der Befreiungskriege bis zum Ausgang des Wiener Kongresses." Ph.D. diss., Cologne, 1940.

Bergsträsser, Ludwig. *Studien zur Vorgeschichte der Zentrumspartei.* Tübingen: J.C.B. Mohr, 1910.

Bettmann, Otto. "Die Entstehung buchhändlerischer Berufsideale im Deutschland des XVIII. Jahrhundert." Ph.D. diss., Leipzig, 1927.

Billinger, Robert D. "The War Scare of 1831 and Prussian–South German Plans for the End of Austrian Dominance in Germany." *Central European History* 9 (1976): 203–19.

Bitterauf, Theodor. *Geschichte des Rheinbundes.* Vol. 1: *Die Gründung des Rheinbundes und der Untergang des alten Reiches.* Munich: C. H. Beck, 1905.

———. "Die Zensur der politischen Zeitungen in Bayern, 1799–1825." In *Riezler-Festschrift*, edited by Karl Alexander von Müller, 305–51. Gotha: F. A. Perthes, 1913.

———. "Zur Geschichte der öffentlichen Meinung im Königreich Bayern im Jahre 1813 bis zur Abschluss des Vertrages von Ried." *Archiv für Kulturgeschichte* 11 (1914): 31–69.

Blanning, T.C.W. *The French Revolution in Germany: Occupation and Resistance in the Rhineland, 1792–1802.* Oxford: Oxford University Press, 1983.

———. "German Jacobins and the French Revolution." *Historical Journal* 23 (1980): 985-1002.

———. *Reform and Revolution in Mainz, 1743–1797.* Cambridge: Cambridge University Press, 1974.

Bleyer, Jakob. *Friedrich Schlegel am Bundestage in Frankfurt.* Munich and Leipzig: Duncker & Humblot, 1913.

Boehn, Max von. *Biedermeier: Deutschland von 1815–1847.* Berlin: B. Cassirer, 1932.

Booß, Rutger. *Ansichten der Revolution: Paris-Berichte deutscher Schriftsteller nach der Juli-Revolution 1830.* Cologne: Pahl-Rugenstein, 1977.

Borck, Heinz-Günther. *Der schwäbische Reichskreis im Zeitalter der französischen Revolutionskriege (1792–1806).* Stuttgart: W. Kohlhammer, 1970.

Borngässer, Heinrich. "Gottfried Eisenmann: Ein Kämpfer für die deutsche Einheit und Vertreter des bayerischen Machtgedankens." Ph.D. diss., Frankfurt am Main, 1931.

Bosher, J. F. *The Single Duty Project: A Study of the Movement for a French Customs Union in the 18th Century.* London: Athlone Press, 1964.

Brandt, Hartwig. *Landständische Repräsentation im deutschen Vormärz: Politisches Denken im Einflußfeld des monarchischen Prinzips.* Neuwied am Rhein and Berlin: Hermann Luchterhand, 1968.

Breitenbruch, Bernd. "Der Karlsruher Buchhändler Christian Gottlieb Schmieder und der Nachdruck in Südwestdeutschland im letzten Viertel des 18. Jahrhunderts." *Archiv für Geschichte des Buchwesens* 9 (1968): cols. 643–732.

Brockhaus, Heinrich Eduard. *Friedrich Arnold Brockhaus.* 3 vols. Leipzig: F. A. Brockhaus, 1872–81.

———. "Metternichs Plan einer staatlichen Organisation des deutschen Buchhandels." *Archiv für Geschichte des deutschen Buchhandels* 1 (1878): 91–119.

Bruford, W. H. *Culture and Society in Classical Weimar, 1775–1806.* New York: Cambridge University Press, 1962.

Büsch, Otto, and Walter Grab, eds. *Die demokratische Bewegung in Mitteleuropa im ausgehenden 18. und frühen 19. Jahrhundert: Ein Tagungsbericht.* Berlin: Colloquium Verlag, 1980.

Büssem, Eberhard. *Die Karlsbader Beschlüsse von 1819: Die endgültige Stabilisierung der restaurativen Politik im Deutschen Bund nach dem Wiener Kongress von 1814–15.* Hildesheim: H. A. Gerstenberg, 1974.

Censer, Jack, and Jeremy Popkin. "Historians and the Press." In *Press and Politics in Pre-revolutionary France*, edited by Jack R. Censer and Jeremy D. Popkin, 1–23. Berkeley and Los Angeles: University of California Press, 1987.

Chartier, Roger, and Daniel Roche. "Les pratiques urbaines de l'imprimé, XVIIe-XVIIIe siècles." In *Histoire de l'édition française*, edited by Henri-Jean Martin and Roger Chartier, 2:402–29. Paris: Promodis, 1982–.

Clark, Margaret A. *Heine et la monarchie de juillet: Etude critique sur les Französische Zustände suivie d'une étude sur le Saint-Simonisme chez Heine.* Paris: Rieder, 1927.

Consentius, Ernst. "Die Berliner Zeitungen während der Französischen Revolution." *Preussische Jahrbücher* 117 (1904): 449–88.

———. "Friedrich der Grosse und die Zeitungs-Zensur." *Preussische Jahrbücher* 115 (1904): 220–49.

Cotta, Regina von. *Werden, Sein, und Vergehen des Verleger-Geschlechts: Cotta.* Zurich: Juris Druck, 1969.

Czygan, Paul. "Über die französische Zensur während der Okkupation von Berlin und ihren Leiter, den Prediger Hauchecorne, in den Jahren 1806 bis 1808." *Forschungen zur brandenburgischen und preußischen Geschichte* 21 (1908): 99–137.

Dann, Otto. "Die Lesegesellschaften des 18. Jahrhunderts und der gesellschaftliche Aufbruch des deutschen Bürgertums." In *Buch und Leser*, edited by Herbert Göpfert, 160–93. Hamburg: Ernst Hauswedel, 1977.

Darmstadt, Rolf. *Der Deutsche Bund in der zeitgenössischen Publizistik.* Frankfurt am Main: Peter Lang, 1971.

Darnton, Robert. *The Business of Enlightenment: A Publishing History of the "Encyclopédie," 1775–1800.* Cambridge, Mass.: Harvard University Press, 1979.

———. *The Literary Underground of the Old Regime.* Cambridge, Mass.: Harvard University Press, 1982.

Deinet, Klaus. *Konrad Engelbert Oelsner und die Französische Revolution.* Munich and Vienna: R. Oldenbourg, 1981.

Demel, Walter. *Der bayerische Staatsabsolutismus 1806/08–1817: Staats- und gesellschaftspolitische Motivationen und Hintergründe der Reformära in der ersten Phase des Königreichs Bayern.* Munich: C. H. Beck, 1983.

Dirrigl, Michael. *Ludwig I: König von Bayern, 1825–1848.* Munich: Hugendubel, 1980.

Doeberl, Michael. *Bayern und die wirtschaftliche Einigung Deutschlands.* Munich: Verlag der Königlich Bayerischen Akademie der Wissenschaften, 1915.

———. *Entwicklungsgeschichte Bayerns.* Edited by Max Spindler. 3d ed. Munich: R. Oldenbourg, 1928–31.

Droz, Jacques. *L'Allemagne et la Révolution Française.* Paris: Presses Universitaires de France, 1949.

Dufraisse, Roger. "Französische Zollpolitik, Kontinentalsperre, und Kontinentalsystem im Deutschland der napoleonischen Zeit." In *Deutschland zwischen Revolution und Restauration*, edited by Helmuth Berding and Hans-Peter Ullmann, 328–52. Düsseldorf: Droste, 1981.

Dunan, Marcel. *Napoléon et l'Allemagne: Le Système continental et les débuts du royaume de Bavière, 1806–1810.* Paris: Plon, 1942.

Eichler, Herbert. "Zur Vorgeschichte des *Oesterreichischen Beobachters*." *Jahrbuch der Grillparzer-Gesellschaft* 28 (1926): 170–81.

Eisenhardt, Ulrich, *Die kaiserliche Aufsicht über Buchdruck, Buchhandel, und Presse im Heiligen Römischen Reich Deutscher Nation (1496–1806): Ein Beitrag zur Geschichte der Bücher- und Pressezensur.* Karlsruhe: C. F. Müller, 1970.

Engelsing, Rolf. *Analphabetentum und Lektüre: Zur Sozialgeschichte des Lesens in Deutschland zwischen feudaler und industrieller Gesellschaft.* Stuttgart: J. B. Metzler, 1973.

———. *Der Bürger als Leser: Lesergeschichte in Deutschland, 1500–1800.* Stuttgart: J. B. Metzler, 1974.

———. "Die Perioden der Lesergeschichte in der Neuzeit: Das statistische Ausmaß und die soziokulturelle Bedeutung der Lektüre." *Archiv für Geschichte des Buchwesens* 10 (1970): cols. 945–1002.

———. "Zeitung und Zeitschrift in Nordwestdeutschland, 1800–1850: Leser und Journalisten." *Archiv für Geschichte des Buchwesens* 5 (1964): cols. 849–956.

Erning, Günter. *Das Lesen und die Lesewut: Beiträge zu Fragen der Lesergeschichte, dargestellt am Beispiel der schwäbischen Provinz.* Bad Heilbrunn: Julius Klinkhardt, 1974.

Faber, Karl-Georg. *Die Rheinlande zwischen Restauration und Revolution: Probleme der rheinischen Geschichte von 1814 bis 1848 im Spiegel der zeitgenössischen Publizistik.* Wiesbaden: Franz Steiner, 1966.

Fehr, E. "Leben und Schriften des Kurländers Friedrich Ludwig Lindner, mit besonderer Berücksichtigung des 'Manuscripts aus Süddeutschland.'" *Baltische Monatsschrift* 42 (1895): 531–82, 671–99, 756–88.

Fehrenbach, Elisabeth. "Deutschland und die Französische Revolution." In *200 Jahre Amerikanische Revolution und moderne Revolutionsforschung*, edited by Hans-Ulrich Wehler, 238–42. *Geschichte und Gesellschaft*, Sonderheft 2. Göttingen: Vandenhoeck & Ruprecht, 1976.

Fischer, Walter. "Die Abwanderung des Buchhandels von der Frankfurter Messe nach Leipzig." Ph.D. diss., Leipzig, 1934.

Fischer, Wolfram. *Wirtschaft und Gesellschaft im Zeitalter der Industrialisierung.* Göttingen: Vandenhoeck & Ruprecht, 1972.

Flad, Ruth. *Der Begriff der öffentlichen Meinung bei Stein, Arndt, und Humboldt.* Berlin and Leipzig: Walter de Gruyter, 1929.

Foerster, Cornelia. "Sozialstruktur und Organisationsformen des Deutschen Preß- und Vaterlandsvereins von 1832/33." In *Liberalismus in der Gesellschaft des deutschen Vormärz*, edited by Wolfgang Schieder, 148–66. *Geschichte und Gesellschaft*, Sonderheft 9. Göttingen: Vandenhoeck & Ruprecht, 1983.

Fournier, August. *Historische Studien und Skizzen.* Prague: F. Tempsky, 1885; 2d ser. Vienna: W. Braumüller, 1908.

Friedrich, Johannes. *Ignaz von Döllinger: Sein Leben auf Grund seines schriftlichen Nachlassen.* 3 vols. Munich: C. H. Beck, 1899–1901.

Frobe, Heinz. "Die Privilegierung der Ausgabe 'letzter Hand' Goethes sämtlicher Werke." *Archiv für Geschichte des Buchwesens* 2 (1960): cols. 186–229.

Fuchs, Karlheinz. *Bürgerliches Räsonement und Staatsräson: Zensur als Instrument des Despotismus, dargestellt am Beispiel des rheinbündischen Württemberg (1806–1813).* Göppingen: Alfred Kümmerle, 1975.

Fürst, Friederike. *August Ludwig Schlözer: Ein deutscher Aufklärer im 18. Jahrhundert.* Heidelberg: C. Winter, 1928.

Gagliardo, John G. *Reich and Nation: The Holy Roman Empire as Idea and Reality, 1763–1806.* Bloomington: Indiana University Press, 1980.

Garber, Jörn. "Geschichtsphilosophie und Revolution: Spätaufklärerische Geschichtstheorien im Einflussfeld der Französischen Revolution." In *Deutschland und die Französische Revolution,* edited by Jürgen Voss, 168–93. *Beiheft* to *Francia* 12 (1983).

Gehring, Paul. "Das Wirtschaftsleben in Württemberg unter König Wilhelm I (1816–1864)." *Zeitschrift für württembergische Landesgeschichte,* n.s., 9 (1949–50): 196–257.

Gerth, Hans H. *Bürgerliche Intelligenz um 1800: Zur Soziologie des deutschen Frühliberalismus.* Göttingen: Vandenhoeck & Ruprecht, 1976.

Giese, Ursula. "Johann Thomas Edler von Trattner: Seine Bedeutung als Buchdrucker, Buchhändler, und Herausgeber." *Archiv für Geschichte des Buchwesens* 3 (1961): cols. 1013–1454.

———. "Studie zur Geschichte der Pressegesetzgebung, der Zensur, und des Zeitungswesens im frühen Vormärz." *Archiv für Geschichte des Buchwesens* 6 (1966): cols. 341–564.

Gieseke, Ludwig. *Die geschichtliche Entwicklung des deutschen Urheberrechts.* Göttingen: Otto Schwartz, 1957.

Glossy, Karl. "Ein Kapitel aus der Zeitungsgeschichte Alt-Österreichs." *Jahrbuch der Grillparzer-Gesellschaft* 33 (1935): 134–43.

Gölz, Wilhelmine. "Der bayerische Landtag 1831: Ein Wendepunkt in der Regierung Ludwigs I." Ph.D. diss., Munich, 1926.

Gollwitzer, Heinz. *Ludwig I von Bayern: Königtum im Vormärz.* Munich: Süddeutscher Verlag, 1986.

Griffity, Eugene J. "Political Writing and Enlightened Monarchy in Württemberg During the Reign of Duke Carl Eugen, 1744–93." Ph.D. diss., University of Illinois, 1979.

Gross, Else R., ed. *Karl Friedrich Reinhard, 1761–1837: Ein Leben für Frankreich und Deutschland. Gedenkschrift zum 200. Geburtstag.* Stuttgart: K. Wittwer, 1961.

Groth, Otto. *Die Geschichte der deutschen Zeitungswissenschaft: Probleme und Methoden.* Munich: Konrad Weinmayer, 1948.

———. *Die Zeitung: Ein System der Zeitungskunde (Journalistik).* 4 vols. Mannheim: J. Bensheimer, 1928–30.

Grube, Walter. *Der Stuttgarter Landtag, 1457–1957: Von den Landständen zum demokratischen Parlament.* Stuttgart: E. Klett, 1957.

Guggenbühl, Gottfried. *Geschichte der schweizerischen Eidgenossenschaft.* 2 vols. Erlenbach and Zurich: E. Rentsch, 1947–48.

Guyot, Raymond. *Le Directoire et la paix de l'Europe: Des Traités de Bâle à la deuxième coalition (1795–1799).* Paris: F. Alcan, 1911.

Haas, Arthur. *Metternich: Reorganization and Nationality, 1813–1818.* Wiesbaden: Steiner, 1963.

Haase, Carl. "Obrigkeit und öffentliche Meinung in Kurhannover, 1789–1803." *Niedersächsisches Jahrbuch für Landesgeschichte* 39 (1967): 192–294.

Habermas, Jürgen. *Strukturwandel der Öffentlichkeit: Untersuchungen zu einer Kategorie der bürgerlichen Gesellschaft.* Neuwied am Rhein and Berlin: Hermann Luchterhand, 1962.

Hahn, Hans-Werner. "Zwischen deutscher Handelsfreiheit und Sicherung landständischer Rechte: Der Liberalismus und die Gründung des Deutschen

Zollvereins." In *Liberalismus in der Gesellschaft des deutschen Vormärz*, edited by Wolfgang Schieder, 239–71. *Geschichte und Gesellschaft*, Sonderheft 9. Göttingen: Vandenhoeck & Ruprecht, 1983.

Hammer, Karl. "Deutsche Revolutionsreisende in Paris." In *Deutschland und die Französische Revolution*, edited by Jürgen Voss, 26–42. Beiheft to *Francia* 12 (1983).

———. *Die französische Diplomatie der Restauration und Deutschland, 1814–1830.* Stuttgart: Anton Hiersemann, 1963.

Harris, H. S. *Hegel's Development: Toward the Sunlight, 1770–1801.* London: Oxford University Press, 1972.

Henche, Albert. "Die Karslbader Konferenzen nach den amtlichen Berichten und den vertraulichen Briefen des Frh. von Marschall an Herzog Wilhelm von Nassau." *Nassauische Annalen* 59 (1939).

Henderson, W. O. *The Zollverein.* 2d ed. Chicago: Quadrangle Books, 1959.

Hertel, Karin. "Der Politiker Johann Friedrich Cotta: Publizistische verlegerische Unternehmungen, 1815–1819." *Archiv für Geschichte des Buchwesens* 19 (1978): cols. 365–562.

Hertz, Deborah. "The Varnhagen Collection Is in Kraków." *American Archivist* 44 (1981): 223–28.

Hertz, Frederick. *The Development of the German Public Mind: A Social History of German Political Sentiments, Aspirations, and Ideas.* 2 vols. Vol. 3 [posthumous]: *The German Public Mind in the Nineteenth Century*, edited by Frank Eyck. London: Allen & Unwin, 1957–75.

Hess, Christel. *Presse und Publizistik in der Kurpfalz in der zweiten Hälfte des 18. Jahrhunderts.* Frankfurt am Main: Peter Lang, 1987.

Heyck, Eduard. *Die Allgemeine Zeitung, 1798–1898: Beiträge zur Geschichte der deutschen Presse.* Munich: Verlag der *Allgemeine Zeitung*, 1898.

Heyd, Wilhelm, et al., eds. *Bibliographie der württembergischen Geschichte.* 9 vols. in 11. Stuttgart: W. Kohlhammer, 1895–1965.

Heyderhoff, Julius. *Johann Friedrich Benzenberg: Der erste rheinische Liberale.* Düsseldorf: Düsseldorfer Geschichts-Verein, 1909.

Hintze, Otto. "The Preconditions of Representative Government in the Context of World History." In *The Historical Essays of Otto Hintze*, edited by Felix Gilbert, 305–53. New York: Oxford University Press, 1975.

Hirth, Friedrich. *Heinrich Heine: Bausteine zu einer Biographie.* Mainz: Florian Kupferberg, 1950.

Hölscher, Lucian. "Öffentlichkeit." In *Geschichtliche Grundbegriffe: Historisches Lexikon zur politisch-sozialen Sprache in Deutschland*, edited by Otto Brunner, Werner Conze, and Reinhard Koselleck, 4:413–67. Stuttgart: Klett-Cotta, 1972–.

Hölzle, Erwin. *Das alte Recht und die Revolution: Eine politische Geschichte Württembergs in der Revolutionszeit, 1789–1805.* Munich and Berlin: R. Oldenbourg, 1931.

———. "Cotta, der Verleger und die Politik." *Historische Vierteljahrsschrift* 29 (1934): 576–96.

———. "Der Deutsche Zollverein: Nationalpolitisches aus seiner Vorgeschichte." *Württembergische Jahrbücher für Statistik und Landeskunde* 33 (1932–33): 131–45.

———. *Württemberg im Zeitalter Napoleons und der deutschen Erhebung.* Stuttgart and Berlin: W. Kohlhammer, 1937.

Hörling, Hans. *Heinrich Heine im Spiegel der politischen Presse Frankreichs von 1831–1841.* Frankfurt am Main: Peter Lang, 1977.

Hohendahl, Peter Uwe. "Kritische Theorie, Öffentlichkeit, und Kultur: Anmerkungen zu Jürgen Habermas und seinen Kritikern." *Basis: Jahrbuch für deutsche Gegenwartsliteratur* 8 (1978): 60–91.

Hokkanen, Kari. *Krieg und Frieden in der politischen Tagesliteratur Deutschlands zwischen Baseler und Lunéviller Frieden (1795–1801).* Studia Historica Jyväskyläensia, no. 11. Jyväskylä, Fin.: Kirjapaino, 1975.

Ibbeken, Rudolf. *Preußen, 1807–1813: Staat und Volk als Idee und in der Wirklichkeit.* Cologne and Berlin: Grote, 1970.

Iggers, George. *The German Conception of History.* Middletown, Conn.: Wesleyan University Press, 1968.

Ilse, Leopold Friedrich. *Geschichte der Deutschen Bundesversammlung, insbesondere ihres Verhaltens zu den deutschen National-Interessen.* 3 vols. Marburg: N. G. Elwert, 1861–62.

Isey, Oswald. "Untersuchungen zur Lebensgeschichte des Frhrn. Karl August von Wangenheim." Ph.D. diss., Freiburg, 1954.

Jentsch, Irene. "Zur Geschichte des Zeitungslesens in Deutschland am Ende des 18. Jahrhunderts, mit besonderer Berücksichtigung der gesellschaftlichen Formen des Zeitungslesens." Ph.D. diss., Leipzig, 1937.

Jentzsch, Rudolf. *Der deutsch-lateinische Büchermarkt nach den Leipziger Ostermeß-Katalogen von 1740, 1770, und 1800 in seiner Gliederung und Wandlung.* Leipzig: R. Voigtländer, 1912.

Jordan, Sabine Dorothea. *Ludwig Ferdinand Huber (1764–1804): His Life and Works.* Stuttgart: Akademischer Verlag Hans-Dieter Heinz, 1978.

Kapfinger, Hans. *Der Eoskreis, 1828 bis 1832: Ein Beytrag zur Vorgeschichte des politischen Katholizismus in Deutschland.* Munich: F. A. Pfeiffer, 1928.

Kapp, Friedrich. "Die preussische Pressgesetzgebung unter Friedrich Wilhelm III (1815–1840)." *Archiv für Geschichte des deutschen Buchhandels* 6 (1881): 185–249.

Kapp, Friedrich, and Johann Goldfriedrich. *Geschichte des deutschen Buchhandels.* 4 vols. Leipzig: Verlag des Börsenvereins der Deutschen Buchhändler, 1886–1913.

Kiesel, Helmuth, and Paul Münch. *Gesellschaft und Literatur im 18. Jahrhundert: Voraussetzungen und Entstehung des literarischen Markts in Deutschland.* Munich: C. H. Beck, 1977.

Kirchhoff, Albrecht. "Ursprung und erste Lebensäußerungen der 'Leipziger' Buchhandlungs-Deputirten." *Archiv für Geschichte des deutschen Buchhandels* 16 (1893): 326–53.

Kirchner, Joachim. *Das deutsche Zeitschriftenwesen: Seine Geschichte und seine Probleme.* 2d rev. ed. 2 vols. Wiesbaden: Otto Harrassowitz, 1958–62.

———. *Die Grundlagen des deutschen Zeitschriftenwesens.* 2 vols. Leipzig: Karl W. Hiersemann, 1928–31.

Kissling, Walter. "Württemberg und die Karlsbader Beschlüsse gegen die Presse: Ein Beitrag zur württembergischen Pressezensur–Pressegesetzgebung." Ph.D. diss., Munich, 1956.

Kleinpaul, Johannes. *Die Fuggerzeitungen, 1568–1605.* Leipzig, 1921; reprint Walluf bei Wiesbaden: M. Sandig, 1972.

————. *Das Nachrichtenwesen der deutschen Fürsten im 16. und 17. Jahrhundert: Ein Beitrag zur Geschichte der geschriebenen Zeitungen.* Leipzig: A. Klein, 1930.

Klüpfel, Karl. "Die Friedensunterhandlungen Württembergs mit der Französischen Republik, 1796–1802." *Historische Zeitschrift* 46 (1881): 385–429.

Koeppel, Ferdinand. *Ignaz von Rudhart: Ein Staatsmann des Liberalismus.* Munich and Berlin: R. Oldenbourg, 1933.

Körber, Esther-Beate. *Görres und die Revolution: Wandlungen ihres Begriffs und ihrer Wertung in seinem politischen Weltbild, 1793 bis 1819.* Husum: Matthiesen, 1986.

Koppitz, Hans-Joachim. "Zur Bibliographie der deutschen Buchproduktion des 18. Jahrhunderts." *Zeitschrift für Bibliothekwesen und Bibliographie* 9 (1962): 18–30.

Koszyk, Kurt. *Deutsche Presse im 19. Jahrhundert.* Berlin: Colloquium Verlag, 1966.

————. *Vorläufer der Massenpresse: Oekonomie und Publizistik zwischen Reformation und Französischer Revolution.* Munich: Wilhelm Goldmann, 1972.

Kraehe, Enno E. *Metternich's German Policy.* 2 vols. Princeton, N.J.: Princeton University Press, 1963–83.

Krauss, Rudolf. "Zur Geschichte des Nachdrucks und Schutzes der Schillerschen Werke." *Württembergische Vierteljahrshefte für Landesgeschichte*, n.s., 13 (1904): 187–201.

Kuhn, Dorothea. "Schiller und Goethe in ihrer Beziehung zu Johann Friedrich Cotta." In *Unser Commercium: Goethes und Schillers Literaturpolitik*, edited by Wilfried Barner, Eberhard Lammert, and Norbert Oellers, 169–85. Stuttgart: J. G. Cotta, 1984.

Kuranda, Peter. "Konrad Engelbert Oelsner." In *Schlesische Lebensbilder*, 4:218–29. Breslau: W. G. Korn, 1931.

Lang, Wilhelm. *Graf Reinhard: Ein deutsch-französisches Lebensbild, 1761–1837.* Bamberg: C. C. Buchner, 1896.

————. "Die Jugendjahre des Grafen Reinhard." *Württembergische Vierteljahrshefte für Landesgeschichte*, n.s., 2 (1893): 53–101.

————. "K. Fr. Reinhard im auswärtigen Ministerium zu Paris." *Preussische Jahrbücher* 56 (1885): 362–88.

Lempfrid, Wilhelm. *Die Anfänge des parteipolitischen Lebens und der politischen Presse in Bayern unter Ludwig I, 1825–31.* Strasbourg: Herder, 1912.

————. "Der Bayerische Landtag 1831 und die öffentliche Meinung." *Zeitschrift für bayerische Landesgeschichte* 24 (1961): 1–101.

Lerchenfeld, Max von. *Die Bairische Verfassung und die Karlsbader Beschlüsse.* Nördlingen: C. H. Beck, 1883.

Lettow Vorbeck, Max von. *Zur Geschichte des Preussischen Correspondenten von 1813 und 1814.* Berlin, 1911; reprint Vaduz, Liecht.: Kraus, 1965.

List, Albrecht. *Der Kampf um's gute alte Recht (1815–1819), nach seiner ideen- und parteigeschichtlichen Seiten.* Tübingen: Mohr, 1913.

Lohrer, Liselotte. *Cotta: Geschichte eines Verlags, 1659–1959.* Stuttgart: J. G. Cotta, 1959.

Macartney, C. A. *The Habsburg Empire, 1790–1918.* New York: Macmillan, 1969.

Mager, Wolfgang. "Das Problem der Landständischen Verfassungen auf dem Wiener Kongress 1814/15." *Historische Zeitschrift* 217 (1974): 296–346.

Marquant, Robert. *Thiers et le baron Cotta: Etude sur la collaboration de Thiers à la Gazette d'Augsbourg.* Paris: Presses Universitaires de France, 1959.

Marx, Roland. "Strasbourg, centre de la propagande révolutionnaire vers l'Allemagne." In *Deutschland und die französische Revolution,* edited by Jürgen Voss, 16–25. *Beiheft* to *Francia* 12 (1983).

Meier, Ernst. *Zeitungsstadt Nürnberg.* Berlin: Duncker & Humblot, 1963.

Meinecke, Friedrich. *1848: Eine Säkularbetrachtung.* Berlin: L. Blanvalet, 1948.

Menzinger, Rosemarie. *Verfassungsrevision und Demokratisierungsprozeß im Königreich Württemberg.* Stuttgart: W. Kohlhammer, 1969.

Meyer, F. Herm. "Der deutsche Buchhandel gegen Ende des 18. und zu Anfang des 19. Jahrhunderts." *Archiv für Geschichte des deutschen Buchhandels* 7 (1882): 199–249.

Meyer, H. F. "Zeitungspreise in Deutschland im 19. Jahrhundert und ihre gesellschaftliche Bedeutung." Ph.D. diss., Münster, 1967.

Misch, Carl. *Varnhagen von Ense in Beruf und Politik.* Gotha: F. A. Perthes, 1925.

Mitchell, B. R. *European Historical Statistics, 1750–1970.* New York: Columbia University Press, 1976.

Mögle-Hofacker, Franz. *Zur Entwicklung des Parlamentarismus in Württemberg: Der 'Parlamentarismus der Krone' unter König Wilhelm I.* Stuttgart: W. Kohlhammer, 1981.

Mojasevic, Miljan. "Die Augsburger *Allgemeine Zeitung* in der fürstlich-serbischen Kanzlei, 1821–1834." *Archiv für Kulturgeschichte* 47 (1965): 338–50.

Moran, James. *Printing Presses.* Berkeley and Los Angeles: University of California Press, 1973.

Mortier, Roland. "Une Revue germanisante sous l'Empire: Les *Archives littéraires de l'Europe* (1804–08)." *Revue de la littérature comparée* 25 (1951): 43–64.

Müller, Hans Friedrich. "Die Berichterstattung der Allgemeinen Zeitung Augsburg über Fragen der deutschen Wirtschaft, 1815–1840." Ph.D. diss., Munich, 1936.

Müller, Hans Peter. *Das Grossherzogtum Baden und die deutsche Zolleinigung.* Frankfurt am Main: Peter Lang, 1983.

Müller, Max. "Salomo Michaelis: Schützling, Mitarbeiter, und Freund des Frhrn. v. Wangenheim." *Zeitschrift für württembergische Landesgeschichte,* n.s., 3 (1939): 158–211.

Nipperdey, Thomas. *Deutsche Geschichte, 1800–1866: Bürgerwelt und starker Staat.* Munich: C. H. Beck, 1980.

Obenaus, Herbert. "Finanzkrise und Verfassungsgebung: Zu den sozialen Bedingungen des frühen deutschen Konstitutionalismus." In *Gesellschaft, Parlament, und Regierung: Zur Geschichte des Parlamentarismus in Deutschland,* edited by Gerhard A. Ritter, 57–75. Düsseldorf: Droste, 1974.

O'Boyle, Lenore. "The Image of the Journalist in France, Germany, and England, 1815–1848." *Comparative Studies in Society and History* 10 (1967–68): 290–317.

Opel, Julius Otto. "Die Anfänge der deutschen Zeitungspresse, 1609–1650." *Archiv für Geschichte des deutschen Buchhandels* 3 (1879): 1–268.

Ostadal, Hubert. *Die Kammer der Reichsräte in Bayern von 1819–1848: Ein Beitrag zur Geschichte des Frühparlamentarismus.* Munich: Wölfle, 1968.

Ozouf, Mona. "L'Opinion publique." In *The French Revolution and the Creation of Modern Political Culture*. Vol. 1: *The Political Culture of the Old Regime*, edited by Keith Michael Baker, 419–34. Oxford: Pergamon Press, 1987.

Paret, Peter. *Clausewitz and the State*. New York: Oxford University Press, 1976.

Perthes, Clemens Theodor. *Friedrich Perthes Leben*. 3d ed. 3 vols. Gotha: F. A. Perthes, 1855.

Pertz, Georg Heinrich. *Das Leben des Ministers Freiherrn vom Stein*. 6 vols. Berlin: G. Reimer, 1854.

Petersdorff, Hermann von. *Friedrich von Motz: Eine Biographie*. 2 vols. Berlin: Reimar Hobbing, 1913.

Pfister, Christoph. *Die Publizistik Karl Ludwig von Hallers in der Frühzeit, 1791– 1815*. Bern: Herbert Land, 1975.

Popkin, Jeremy. "Buchhandel und Presse im napoleonischen Deutschland." *Archiv für Geschichte des Buchwesens* 26 (1986): 285–96.

———. "The Prerevolutionary Origins of Political Journalism." In *The French Revolution and the Creation of Modern Political Culture*. Vol. 1: *The Political Culture of the Old Regime*, edited by Keith Michael Baker, 203–23. Oxford: Pergamon Press, 1987.

———. *The Right-Wing Press in France, 1792–1800*. Chapel Hill: University of North Carolina Press, 1980.

Press, Volker. "Von den Bauernrevolten des 16. zur konstitutionellen Verfassung des 19. Jahrhunderts: Die Untertanenkonflikte in Hohenzollern-Hechingen." In *Politische Ordnungen und soziale Kräfte im alten Reich*, edited by Hermann Weber, 85–112. Wiesbaden: Franz Steiner, 1980.

Price, Arnold. *The Evolution of the Zollverein*. Ann Arbor: University of Michigan Press, 1949.

Prignitz, Christoph. *Vaterlandsliebe und Freiheit: Deutscher Patriotismus von 1750 bis 1850*. Wiesbaden: Steiner, 1981.

Prys, Joseph. "Das württembergische Nachdruckprivileg für Goethe." *Württembergische Vierteljahrshefte für Landesgeschichte*, n.s., 39 (1933): 136–60.

Quint, Wolfgang. *Souveränitätsbegriff und Souveränitätspolitik in Bayern: Von der Mitte des 17. bis zur ersten Hälfte des 19. Jahrhunderts*. Berlin: Duncker & Humblot, 1971.

Raabe, Paul. *Bücherlust und Lesefreuden: Beiträge zur Geschichte des Buchwesens im 18. und frühen 19. Jahrhundert*. Stuttgart: J. B. Metzler, 1984.

Ranke, Leopold von. *Hardenberg und die Geschichte des preussischen Staates von 1793–1813*. 2d ed. 3 vols. Leipzig: Duncker & Humblot, 1879–81.

Raubold, Georg. *Die Bayerische Landtagsberichterstattung vom Beginn des Verfassungslebens bis 1850*. Munich: Institut für Zeitungsforschung, 1931.

Reill, Peter Hans. *The German Enlightenment and the Rise of Historicism*. Berkeley and Los Angeles: University of California Press, 1975.

Reinöhl, Walther. *Uhland als Politiker*. Tübingen: H. Laupp, 1911.

Rheinwald, Ernst. "Christian Jakob Zahn, 1765–1830." In *Schwäbische Lebensbilder*, 2: 522–36. Stuttgart: W. Kohlhammer, 1941.

———. "Johann Friedrich Cotta in seiner Tübinger Verlagsanfängen." *Tübinger Blätter* 44 (1957): 7–9.

Richter, Gregor. "Der Staat und die Presse in Württemberg bis zur Mitte des 19. Jahrhunderts." *Zeitschrift für württembergische Landesgeschichte*, n.s., 25 (1966): 394–425.

Ritter, Gerhard. *Stein: Eine politische Biographie.* 2 vols. Stuttgart and Berlin: Deutsche Verlags-Anstalt, 1931.

Rosenzweig, Franz. *Hegel und der Staat.* 2 vols. Munich and Berlin: R. Oldenbourg, 1920.

Salomon, Ludwig. *Geschichte des deutschen Zeitungswesens von den ersten Anfängen bis zur Wiederaufrichtung des Deutschen Reiches.* 3 vols. Oldenburg and Leipzig, 1906–7; reprint Aalen: Scientia Verlag, 1973.

Sammons, Jeffrey L. *Heinrich Heine: A Modern Biography.* Princeton, N.J.: Princeton University Press, 1979.

Salzbrunn, Ingeborg. "Studien zum deutschen historischen Zeitschriftenwesen von der Göttinger Aufklärung bis zur Herausgabe der 'Historischen Zeitschrift' (1859)." Ph.D. diss., Münster, 1968.

Sauer, Paul. *Revolution und Volksbewaffnung: Die württembergischen Bürgerwehren im 19. Jahrhundert, vor allem während der Revolution von 1848/49.* Ulm: Süddeutsche Verlag, 1976.

Sautter, Guido. "Friedrich Cotta, General-Postdirektor der Französischen Republik in Deutschland, 1796." *Historisches Jahrbuch der Görres-Gesellschaft* 37 (1916): 98–121.

Schäffle, Albert. *Cotta.* Berlin: Ernst Hofmann, 1895.

Scheel, Heinrich. *Süddeutsche Jakobiner: Klassenkämpfe und republikanische Bestrebungen im deutschen Süden Ende des 18. Jahrhunderts.* East Berlin: Akademie-Verlag, 1962.

Schenda, Rolf. *Volk ohne Buch: Studien zur Sozialgeschichte der populären Lesestoffe, 1770–1910.* Frankfurt am Main: Vittorio Klostermann, 1970.

Schiller, Herbert. "Johann Friedrich Cotta." In *Schwäbische Lebensbilder,* 3:72–124. Stuttgart: W. Kohlhammer, 1942.

Schmidt, Wilhelm Adolf. *Geschichte der deutschen Verfassungsfrage während der Befreiungskriege und des Wiener Kongresses 1812 bis 1815.* Edited by Alfred Stern. Stuttgart: G. J. Göschen, 1890.

Schneider, Eugen. *Aus der württembergischen Geschichte: Vorträge und Abhandlungen.* Stuttgart: W. Kohlhammer, 1926.

Schneider, Franz. "Presse, Pressefreiheit, Zensur." In *Geschichtliche Grundbegriffe: Historisches Lexikon zur politisch-sozialen Sprache in Deutschland,* edited by Otto Brunner, Werner Conze, and Reinhard Koselleck, 4:899–927. Stuttgart: Klett-Cotta, 1972–.

———. *Pressefreiheit und politische Öffentlichkeit: Studien zur politischen Geschichte Deutschlands bis 1848.* Neuwied am Rhein and Berlin: Hermann Luchterhand, 1966.

Schröder, Felix von. *Die Verlegung der Büchermesse von Frankfurt a. M. nach Leipzig.* Leipzig: Jäh & Schunke, 1904.

Schulz, Günter. *Schillers Horen: Politik und Erziehung.* Heidelberg: Quelle & Meyer, 1960.

Schürmann, August. *Die Rechtsverhältnisse der Autoren und Verleger sachlich-historisch.* Halle: Weisenhaus, 1889.

Seeley, John Robert. *Life and Times of Stein.* 3 vols. Cambridge: Cambridge University Press, 1878.

Seybold, Gerhard. *Württembergs Industrie und Außenhandel vom Ende der Napoleonischen Kriege bis zum Deutschen Zollverein.* Stuttgart: W. Kohlhammer, 1974.

Sheehan, James J. *German Liberalism in the Nineteenth Century.* Chicago: University of Chicago Press, 1978.

——. *"Partei, Volk,* and *Staat*: Some Reflections on the Relationship Between Liberal Thought and Action in Vormärz." In *Sozialgeschichte Heute: Festschrift für Hans Rosenberg zum 70. Geburtstag,* edited by Hans-Ulrich Wehler, 162–74. Göttingen: Vandenhoek & Ruprecht, 1974.

——. "What Is German History? Reflections on the Role of the Nation in German History and Historiography." *Journal of Modern History* 53 (1981): 1–23.

Siebeck, Werner. "Der Tübinger Buchhandel um 1800." *Tübinger Blätter* 19 (1927–28): 4–15.

Simon, Walter. *The Failure of the Prussian Reform Movement, 1807–1819.* Ithaca, N.Y.: Cornell University Press, 1955.

Sondermann, Ernst Friedrich. *Karl August Böttiger: Literarischer Journalist der Goethezeit in Weimar.* Bonn: Bouvier Verlag Herbert Grundmann, 1983.

Spindler, Max, ed. *Handbuch der bayerischen Geschichte.* 4 vols. Munich: C. H. Beck, 1974.

Spitzer, Alan B. *The French Generation of 1820.* Princeton, N.J.: Princeton University Press, 1987.

Sporhan-Krempel, Lore. "Die Papierrechnungen von Johann Fr. Cotta, 1788–1806." *Archiv für Geschichte des Buchwesens* 5 (1964): cols. 1369–1471.

Srbik, Heinrich Ritter von. *Metternich: Der Staatsmann und der Mensch.* 3 vols. Munich: F. Bruckmann, 1925–54.

Stern, Ludwig. *Die Varnhagen von Ensesche Sammlung in der Königlichen Bibliothek zu Berlin.* Berlin: Behrend, 1911.

Steuer, Otto. *Cotta in München, 1827–1831.* Munich: Institut für Zeitungsforschung, 1931.

Stommel, Henry, and Elizabeth Stommel. *Volcano Weather: The Story of 1816, the Year Without a Summer.* Newport, R.I.: Seven Seas Press, 1983.

Storz, Gerhard. *Karl Eugen: Der Fürst und das "alte gute Recht."* Stuttgart: Klett-Cotta, 1981.

Ströhmfeld, Gustav. "Johann Friedrich Cotta: Der Volksfreund." *Balinger Tagblatt,* no. 304 (28 December 1932).

Suchel, Adolf. *Hessen-Darmstadt und der Darmstädter Handelskongress von 1820–23.* Darmstadt: Hessischer Staatsverlag, 1922.

Tiainen, Jorma. *Napoleon und das napoleonische Frankreich in der öffentliche Diskussion des "Dritten Deutschland," 1797–1806.* Studia Historica Jyväskyläensia, no. 8. Jyväskylä, Fin.: Kirjapaino, 1971.

Treitschke, Heinrich von. *Deutsche Geschichte im neunzehnten Jahrhundert.* 5 vols. Leipzig: G. Hirzel, 1879–94. Published in English as *History of Germany in the Nineteenth Century.* Translated by Eden Paul and Cedar Paul. 7 vols. New York: McBride, Nast, 1915–19.

——. "Karl August von Wangenheim." In *Historische und politische Aufsätze,* 1: 197–268. 7th ed. Leipzig: Hirzel, 1911.

Treml, Manfred. *Bayerns Pressepolitik zwischen Verfassungstreue und Bundespflicht, 1815–1837.* Berlin: Duncker & Humblot, 1977.

Tschirch, Otto. *Geschichte der öffentlichen Meinung in Preussen vom Baseler Frieden bis zum Zusammenbruch des Staates (1795–1806).* 2 vols. Weimar: Hermann Böhlaus, 1933–34.

————. "Joseph Görres, der Rheinische Merkur, und der preußische Staat." *Preussische Jahrbücher* 157 (1914): 225–47.

Uhland, Robert. *Geschichte der Hohen Karlsschule in Stuttgart.* Stuttgart: W. Kohlhammer, 1953.

Ullmann, Hans-Peter. "Die öffentlichen Schulden in Bayern und Baden, 1780–1820." *Historische Zeitschrift* 242 (1986): 31–67.

————. "Überlegungen zur Entstehung des öffentlichen, verfassungsmäßigen Kredits in den Rheinbundstaaten (Bayern, Württemberg, und Baden)." In *Geschichte und Gesellschaft* 6 (1980): *Napoleonische Herrschaft und Modernisierung,* edited by Helmut Berding, 500–522.

Ungern-Sternberg, Wolfgang von. "Schriftsteller und literarischer Markt." In *Hansers Sozialgeschichte der deutschen Literatur vom 16. Jahrhundert bis zur Gegenwart.* Vol. 3: *Deutsche Aufklärung bis zur Französischen Revolution, 1680–1789,* edited by Rolf Grimminger, 133–85. Munich and Vienna: Carl Hanser, 1980.

Vann, James Allen. *The Making of a State: Württemberg, 1593–1793.* Ithaca, N.Y.: Cornell University Press, 1984.

Vierhaus, Rudolf. "Aufklärung und Reformzeit: Kontinuitäten und Neuansätze in der deutschen Politik des späten 18. und beginnenden 19. Jahrhunderts." In *Reformen im rheinbündischen Deutschland,* edited by Eberhard Weis, 287–301. Munich: R. Oldenbourg, 1984.

Vierneisel, Emil. "Ernst Ludwig Posselt, 1763–1804." *Zeitschrift für die Geschichte des Oberrheins,* n.s., 49 (1936): 243–71; 51 (1938): 89–126; 52 (1939): 444–99.

Vogt, Ingelora. "Die wirtschaftlichen Einigungsbestrebungen der deutschen Bundesstaaten während der Jahre 1828 bis 1834 im Spiegel der Augsburger Allgemeinen Zeitung." Ph.D. diss., Berlin, 1958.

Walker, Mack. *German Home Towns: Community, State, and General Estate, 1648–1871.* Ithaca, N.Y.: Cornell University Press, 1971.

————. *Johann Jakob Moser and the Holy Roman Empire of the German Nation.* Chapel Hill: North Carolina University Press, 1981.

Ward, Albert. *Book Production, Fiction, and the German Reading Public, 1740–1800.* London: Oxford University Press, 1974.

Wegert, Karl H. "Ideologie und Aktion: Liberale Bewegung und Volkstradition in der Pfalz, 1830–1834." In *Liberalismus in der Gesellschaft des deutschen Vormärz,* edited by Wolfgang Schieder, 167–87. *Geschichte und Gesellschaft,* Sonderheft 9. Göttingen: Vandenhoeck & Ruprecht, 1983.

Weis, Eberhard. "Kontinuität und Diskontinuität zwischen den Ständen des 18. Jahrhunderts und den frühkonstitutionellen Parlamenten von 1818/1819 in Bayern und Württemberg." In *Festschrift für Andreas Kraus zum 60. Geburtstag,* edited by Pankraz Fried and Walter Ziegler, 337–55. Kallmünz: Michael Lassleben, 1982.

————. "Napoleon und der Rheinbund." In *Deutschland und Italien im Zeitalter Napoleons,* edited by Armgard von Reden-Dohna, 57–80. Wiesbaden: Steiner, 1979.

————, ed. *Reformen im rheinbündischen Deutschland.* Munich: R. Oldenbourg, 1984.

Welke, Martin. "Gemeinsame Lektüre und frühe Formen von Gruppenbildung im 17. und 18. Jahrhundert: Zeitungslesen in Deutschland." In *Lesegesellschaften und bürgerliche Emanzipation: Ein europäischer Vergleich*, edited by Otto Dann, 29–53. Munich: C. H. Beck, 1981.

——. "Die Legende vom 'unpolitischen Deutschen': Zeitungslesen im 18. Jahrhundert als Spiegel des politischen Interesses." *Jahrbuch der Wittheit zu Bremen* 25 (1981): 160–83.

——. "Zeitung und Öffentlichkeit im 18. Jahrhundert: Betrachtungen zur Reichweite und Funktion der periodischen deutschen Tagespublizistik." In *Presse und Geschichte: Beiträge zur historischen Kommunikationsforschung*, edited by Elger Blühm, 71–99. Munich: Verlag Dokumentation, 1977.

Wendland, Wilhelm. *Versuche einer allgemeinen Volksbewaffnung in Süddeutschland während der Jahre 1791 bis 1794*. Berlin: E. Ebering, 1901.

Widmann, Hans. "Christian August Vulpius' Rache an den Reutlinger Nachdruckern." *Zeitschrift für württembergische Landesgeschichte* 29 (1970): 157–88.

——. *Geschichte des Buchhandels vom Altertum bis zur Gegenwart*. 2d rev. ed. Wiesbaden: Otto Harrassowitz, 1975.

——. "'Die Krisis des deutschen Buchhandels': Bemerkungen zu einer Apologie für den Büchernachdruck aus dem Jahre 1815." *Gutenberg-Jahrbuch* (1968): 257–61.

——. *Tübingen als Verlagsstadt*. Tübingen: Mohr, 1971.

Wiedemann, Wilhelm. "Friedrich Murhard (1778–1853) und der Altliberalismus." *Zeitschrift des Vereins für hessische Geschichte und Landeskunde* 55 (1926): 229–76.

Wintterlin, Friedrich. *Geschichte der Behördenorganisation in Württemberg*. 3 vols. in 2. Stuttgart: W. Kohlhammer, 1902–6.

——. "Die württembergische Verfassung, 1815–1819." *Württembergische Jahrbücher für Statistik und Landeskunde* 104 (1912): 47–83.

Wolff, Karl. *Die deutsche Publizistik in der Zeit der Freiheitskämpfe und des Wiener Kongresses, 1813–1815*. Plauen: Günther Wolff, 1934.

Wolzogen, Karoline von. *Schillers Leben: Verfasst aus Erinnerungen der Familie, seinen eigenen Briefen, und den Nachrichten seines Freundes Körner*. 2d ed. Stuttgart: J. G. Cotta, 1851.

Young, George M. *Victorian Essays*. Edited by W. D. Hancock. London: Oxford University Press, 1962.

Zelger, Renate. "Der historisch-politischer Briefwechsel und die Staatsanzeigen August Ludwig von Schlözer als Zeitschrift und Zeitbild." Ph.D. diss., Munich, 1953.

Zollmann, Günther. "Adelsrechte und Staatsorganisation im Königreich Württemberg 1806 bis 1817." Ph.D. diss., Tübingen, 1971.

Zorn, Wolfgang. "Reichs- und Freiheitsgedanken in der Publizistik des ausgehenden 18. Jahrhunderts (1763–1792): Ein Beitrag zur Vorgeschichte der deutschen Nationalbewegung." In *Darstellung und Quellen zur Geschichte der deutschen Einheitsbewegung im neunzehnten und zwanzigsten Jahrhundert*, edited by Paul Wentzcke, 11–66. Heidelberg: Carl Winter, 1959.

Index

Compositor:	G & S Typesetters, Inc.
Text:	10/12 Baskerville
Display:	Baskerville
Printer:	Braun-Brumfield, Inc.
Binder:	Braun-Brumfield, Inc.